Springer Texts in Business and Economics

More information about this series at http://www.springer.com/series/10099

Debra Z. Basil • Gonzalo Diaz-Meneses •
Michael D. Basil
Editors

Social Marketing in Action

Cases from Around the World

EXTRAS ONLINE

 Springer

Editors
Debra Z. Basil
Dhillon School of Business
University of Lethbridge
Lethbridge, AB, Canada

Gonzalo Diaz-Meneses
Faculty of Economy, Business and Tourism
University of Las Palmas de Gran Canaria
Las Palmas de Gran Canaria, Spain

Michael D. Basil
Dhillon School of Business
University of Lethbridge
Lethbridge, AB, Canada

Additional material to this book can be downloaded from http://extras.springer.com.

ISSN 2192-4333   ISSN 2192-4341   (electronic)
Springer Texts in Business and Economics
ISBN 978-3-030-13019-0   ISBN 978-3-030-13020-6   (eBook)
https://doi.org/10.1007/978-3-030-13020-6

Library of Congress Control Number: 2019931520

This Springer imprint is published by the registered company Springer Nature Switzerland AG.
The registered company address is: Gewerbestrasse 11, 6330 Cham, Switzerland

*We dedicate this book to our wonderful
children Lisa and David. We appreciate
Lisa's artistic contribution to the book, and
David's never ending patience through the
summer of 2018 as we were constantly
"working on the book".*
—Debra Z. Basil and Michael D. Basil

*I dedicate this book to my wife, Magdy, and
my children Malena, Mónica and Gonzalo,
who accompanied me during my stay in
Lethbridge. We met warm people with
generosity and many other values, our friends
from the Lethbridge Public Library,
Lethbridge College, Meadow Primary
School, Lethbridge School District 51, and
Dhillon Business School of the University of
Lethbridge, in beautiful Alberta, Canada.*
—Gonzalo Diaz-Meneses

Preface

This book was written for those interested in creating social change for the greater good. In this book, we provide a wide selection of social marketing cases from which we can learn and teach. The book is intended for both academic and practitioner use. Part I of this book offers a brief yet comprehensive review of social marketing. This provides the reader with the background in social change and marketing necessary to read and analyze the subsequent cases. Parts II, III, IV, and V of this book offer a total of 24 social marketing cases, from a variety of countries, addressing many different issues.

For classroom use, this book is written to serve as a stand-alone tool, with Part I providing a concise introduction to social marketing principles and theory. Chapter appendices provide links to further readings on social marketing principles for those wishing to delve deeper. If still further detail on social marketing principles and theory are desired, this book can easily be paired with another social marketing textbook as well. We have aimed the book to be accessible to undergraduate students but also offer sufficient material to challenge students at the graduate level. Advanced students should be encouraged to further explore the references and links provided, to critique the case approaches, and to offer alternative strategies for the cases provided. A separate teaching guide collection is available for the book as well. This collection contains answers to the discussion questions in the cases, as well as suggested activities for inside and outside of the classroom. Additionally, the teaching guides for many cases offer suggestions for further reading and other helpful resources.

For practitioner use, Part I offers a refresher on basic social marketing principles. In addition, a variety of references are offered, allowing for further personal study. Parts II through V offer detailed information about a wide variety of actual social marketing programs. You can compare and contrast these cases with your own situation, hopefully gaining insights that will be helpful in your own social marketing efforts.

Lethbridge, Canada   Debra Z. Basil
Las Palmas de Gran Canaria, Spain   Gonzalo Diaz-Meneses
Lethbridge, Canada   Michael D. Basil

Acknowledgements

Many people helped us bring this book to fruition. First and foremost, we wish to thank our wonderful slate of authors. Our contributing authors obviously provided the bulk of the material for this book. In addition to providing the content, they were diligent, timely, and conscientious, helping to make this effort run smoothly.

The initial impetus for this book was a Public Outreach Grant from the Social Sciences and Humanities Research Council of Canada (SSHRC). This funding helped those of us in the Centre for Socially Responsible Marketing at the University of Lethbridge to offer a community practitioner workshop that occurred in conjunction with our SMART (Social Marketing Advances in Research and Theory) conference in Vancouver in 2012. Specifically, we wish to acknowledge our colleagues Tanya Drollinger, Walter Wymer, and Sameer Deshpande, who all played important roles in the SMART conference.

We also thank our many former Master of Science students who provided support in various ways including spurring us to think more deeply about social marketing. In particular, former Master of Science students Katherine Lafreniere, Janelle Marietta-Vasquez, and Pamela Gonzalez were very helpful in the creation of this book, and their efforts are greatly appreciated. In addition, we thank Aerin Caley, our copy editor, for her positive attitude and patience throughout this process.

The University of Lethbridge (U of L) provided financial support in two ways. The first was by funding one of our co-editors, Gonzalo Diaz-Meneses, to serve as a Burns Research Chair, which greatly facilitated our collaboration on this project. The second form of U of L funding was offered by the Office of the Vice President (Research) Strategic Opportunities Fund to provide copyediting assistance. We are grateful for this support.

We would also like to thank Springer publishers for their faith in this project.

This effort was partially supported by the European Union's Horizon 2020 research and innovation program under grant agreement No. 727474 entitled improving digital health literacy in Europe.

This research was supported by the Social Sciences and Humanities Research Council of Canada.

 Social Sciences and Humanities Research Council of Canada   Conseil de recherches en sciences humaines du Canada   Canada

About This Book

This book is presented in two parts. Part I offers background information on the practice of social marketing. Specifically, Chap. 1 offers a big picture view of social marketing. Chapter 2 offers a step-by-step strategy for creating a social marketing program. Chapter 3 discusses the role of research and evaluation in social marketing. Chapter 4 reviews commonly used theories in social marketing and in the presented cases. Finally, Chap. 5 provides a brief historical perspective on social marketing. Each of the five chapters in Part I includes an appendix with helpful online links providing further information on the key topics within the chapter. These links are open source for easy access. The chapters are intentionally relatively short; the appendices offer further detailed information for those wishing to attain greater depth and additional perspectives.

Parts II through V of this book include a total of 24 social marketing cases. The cases are all presented in a consistent format to facilitate comparison between cases. Cases were sourced from around the world, and they address a wide variety of topics.

Case Structure

- Background
- SWOT
- Objectives
- Target audience
- Barriers and benefits
- Competition
- Positioning
- Research
- The 4 P's
- Evaluation
- Discussion

The cases are placed within the categories of social welfare (Part II), health (Part III), environment (Part IV), and education (Part V) within the book. There are, however, many other ways that they could be categorized, depending on your interests. The following tables offer some alternative schemes for grouping the cases including geographic location (Table 1) and theoretical frameworks (Table 2). Additionally, the final table indicates specific cases we think do a particularly good job of demonstrating particular program components (Table 3).

Table 1 Cases by topic areas and geographic locations

Chapter number	Broad topic area				Geographic location					Specific topics with multiple cases	
	Social welfare	Health	Environment	Education	North America	Europe/UK	India	Australia	Other locations	Hand washing	Litter
6	X							X			
7	X					X					
8	X							X			
9	X					X					
10	X								X		
11	X					X					
12	X				X						
13		X					X			X	
14		X				X					
15		X					X				
16		X				X					
17		X					X			X	
18		X					X				
19		X							X	X	
20			X		X						
21			X							X	
22			X		X						X
23			X		X						X
24			X		X						X

(continued)

Table 1 (continued)

Chapter number	Broad topic area				Geographic location					Specific topics with multiple cases	
	Social welfare	Health	Environment	Education	North America	Europe/UK	India	Australia	Other locations	Hand washing	Litter
25			X					X			
26				X		X					X
27				X		X					
28				X			X				
29				X		X					

Table 2 Cases by theories applied

Chapter number	Theories applied					
	Exchange theory	Diffusion of innovations	Self-efficacy	Theory of planned behavior	Trans-theoretical model	Community readiness
6				X		
7						X
8	X					
9	X	X				
10						
11	X			X		
12	X					
13						
14	X		X			
15					X	
16						
17	X	X		X		
18						
19	X		X			
20			X			
21						
22						
23		X			X	
24						
25						

(continued)

Table 2 (continued)

Chapter number	Theories applied					
	Exchange theory	Diffusion of innovations	Self-efficacy	Theory of planned behavior	Trans-theoretical model	Community readiness
26						X
27						X
28						
29						X

Table 3 Exemplars for specific case components

Chapter number	Exemplars of specific case components											
	Understanding the environment	SWOT	Segmenting and targeting	Formative research	Barriers and benefits	Objectives	Product	Price	Place	Promotion	Public/Private partnership	Evaluation
6	X	X			X					X		
7												
8												
9												
10	X											
11								X				
12											X	
13											X	
14				X								
15								X	X			
16												
17										X	X	
18												
19					X		X			X		X
20			X									
21			X									
22			X									
23									X			
24						X						X
25						X						X

(continued)

Table 3 (continued)

Chapter number	Exemplars of specific case components											
	Understanding the environment	SWOT	Segmenting and targeting	Formative research	Barriers and benefits	Objectives	Product	Price	Place	Promotion	Public/Private partnership	Evaluation
26		X										
27				X			X					
28				X			X				X	
29							X					

We hope that you find the book useful. We welcome any comments or suggestions. Please contact Debra Basil at debra.basil@uleth.ca if you have suggestions for future versions of this book.

Contents

Part I
Understanding Social Marketing

The Big Picture in Social Marketing

1

Debra Z. Basil

Chapter Overview
This chapter introduces social marketing as a tool to influence individual behavior and societal structure for the benefit of the individual and society, ethically using commercial marketing and other tools. Social marketing is needed because societies value personal freedom, and personal freedom often leads to negative externalities. The chapter stressed the importance of understanding the broader context within which individuals operate and addressing the barriers they face. Social marketing was differentiated from education and law by the use of incentives and barrier removal to encourage voluntary behavior change. Social marketing can occur at a macro-level, focusing on broader societal structures, or at a micro-level, focusing on individuals. When social marketing occurs at the macro-level, it examines the entire system and uses all available tools, including education and law when feasible. Social marketing can be focused downstream, upstream, or both. Downstream social marketing refers to efforts focusing on those whose behavior we wish to directly influence. Upstream social marketing refers to efforts focused on those who can influence the system within which the behavior occurs, such as policy makers, in order to encourage or discourage the behavior. Micro-social marketing focuses on individual behavior change. It may be used to influence the behavior of individuals directly (downstream), or it may be used to influence upstream policy makers and others whose decisions could influence the social environment. Finally, with social marketing it is important to understand strengths, weaknesses, opportunities, and threats relative to the program, as well as the behaviors that compete with your goals.

D. Z. Basil (✉)
Dhillon School of Business, University of Lethbridge, Lethbridge, Canada
e-mail: debra.basil@uleth.ca

© Springer Nature Switzerland AG 2019
D. Z. Basil et al. (eds.), *Social Marketing in Action*,
Springer Texts in Business and Economics,
https://doi.org/10.1007/978-3-030-13020-6_1

3

In the next chapter, we outline the specific steps involved with creating a social marketing program. Chapter 2 also addresses ethical issues in social marketing. Chapter 3 introduces research used in social marketing, Chap. 4 reviews key theories, and Chap. 5 provides a brief history of social marketing.

Introduction

Worldwide, over a billion tons of food is wasted each year. At the same time, 815 million people in the world go hungry. In Italy, Banco Alimentare, an Italian food bank, seeks to address these two major social issues at once—hunger and food waste. Banco Alimentare is working at several levels to bring about change. They work with restaurateurs and food retailers to bring unused food to a food bank for those in need. They also work with policy makers to advocate for policies to encourage food recovery. Their full story is told in Chap. 7. This is social marketing in action.

In this chapter, we provide a definition of social marketing, and discuss the context within which social marketing occurs. We start with a "bird's eye view" of the field, considering the broader societal influences that impact individual behavior. We discuss the distinctions between macro- and micro-social marketing, and the importance of considering the entire system when developing a social marketing program instead of focusing exclusively on the individual. To help understand the importance of the environment, we introduce marketing's SWOT model and the concept of competition. Finally, the appendix at the end of the chapter offers links to additional online resources so that you can study key topics in greater detail.

Influencing and changing behavior are the goals of commercial marketing. Social marketing applies these principles to behavior that benefits the individual, their community, or the environment. This may mean adopting a new, beneficial behavior such as exercising, or it may mean abandoning a current, undesirable behavior such as smoking. However, at times the social marketing effort may actually be focused on keeping people from starting an undesirable behavior. In these cases, social marketing is seeking to *influence* behavior rather than to actually change it (Andreasen, 1994). For example, social marketing may be used to discourage teens from starting to smoke. In addition to these individual-level behavior influence efforts, social marketing efforts are increasingly being applied at the community or larger societal level, to change structures and practices that are detrimental to individual and societal well-being. In commercial marketing, for example, fast-food companies try to cater to consumer demand by opening more locations to be more convenient while also competing on price. Similarly, social marketing can involve efforts to increase the availability of items that benefit social welfare—condoms for example—and lower their price to encourage use.

The principles of social marketing can be applied to a wide array of topics, both micro and macro. It involves applying principles from commercial marketing and related fields in order to influence behavior. Increasingly, these efforts are being applied to change societal structures as well as individual behaviors. Any time you would like to influence people's behavior, social marketing is a potential strategy to achieve it. The Banco Alimentare (Chap. 7) described above encourages people in the food services industry to donate their food to those in need, but other social marketing efforts seek behavior change in different areas. Social marketing involves offering benefits and removing barriers, so people voluntarily choose to perform a behavior that is better for them and/or their community and natural environment. Chapter 16, for example, describes the UK's Make Every Contact Count campaign. That campaign encourages a wide range of government workers to engage in health discussions with the general population, at every point of contact. Chapter 23 discusses how the community of Akureyri, Iceland used social marketing in their efforts to become carbon neutral. Examples of other social marketing efforts include efforts to encourage people to wash their hands to prevent disease transfer (Chaps. 13, 17, and 19), to eat smaller portion sizes (Chap. 14), or to pay their taxes (Chap. 11), among others. The cases in part 2 of this book offer insight into a wide variety of social marketing efforts and provide context for the foundational material presented in part 1.

Defining Social Marketing

Marketing principles were being applied to the health sector as early as the 1960s, though the practice was not yet widely recognized by academics. For example, in 1967 the Nirodh project in India was the first known nation-wide condom project to use social marketing practices in an attempt to increase the use of condoms and other family planning activities (Lefebvre, 2011; Walsh, Rudd, Moeykens, & Moloney, 1993). The introduction of social marketing as an academic field of study is attributed to Kotler and Zaltman (1971), who offered the first formal social marketing definition:

> Social marketing is the design, implementation, and control of programs calculated to influence the acceptability of social ideas and involving considerations of product planning, pricing, communication, distribution, and marketing research. (Kotler & Zaltman, 1971)

The use of social marketing has continued to grow both in practice and as a field of study in universities. With this, academic debates emerged over the appropriate boundaries for the field. Additionally, academics claimed that practitioners were not always applying the principles of social marketing appropriately, sometimes resulting in ineffective programs that wasted money, failed to provide the desired outcomes, and were hurting the reputation of the field (Andreasen, 1994). To address these concerns, academic scholar Alan Andreasen proposed what was to become a very popular definition of social marketing:

> Social marketing is the adaptation of commercial marketing technologies to programs designed to influence the voluntary behavior of target audiences to improve their personal welfare and that of the society of which they are a part. (Andreasen, 1994, p. 110)

This definition focuses our attention on influencing behavior, rather than other outcomes such as attitude change or increased knowledge. It also highlights the voluntary nature of the behaviors which social marketing addresses. Social marketing does not force people to behave in a certain way—laws do that. It also does not merely share knowledge and information—that is the realm of education. Instead, social marketing motivates behavior change by effectively applying the principles of commercial marketing (Rothschild, 1999). As with Kotler and Zaltman's (1971) definition, Andreasen's (1994) definition suggests that social marketing is anchored firmly to the tools of commercial marketing, and in using these tools for social good. This definition of social marketing provided valuable grounding for the field in the earlier stages. As the field continued to grow, new debates emerged, and again social marketing scholars felt a need to offer a refined definition of social marketing. This time, rather than one or two respected authors offering a definition, three of the world's leading social marketing organizations worked together to develop a new, research-based definition.

Specifically, the International Social Marketing Association, European Social Marketing Association, and Australian Association of Social Marketing proposed the following definition in 2013. The definition was developed by surveying members of these prominent social marketing organizations, and including in the definition the components cited as most important for successful social marketing efforts. The top two priorities for social marketing suggested by that research were (1) set and measure behavioral objectives and (2) use[s] audience insight and research (Morgan, 2012–2018), which are both included in the definition.

Definition of Social Marketing

Social marketing seeks to develop and integrate marketing concepts with other approaches to influence behaviors that benefit individuals and communities for the greater social good. Social marketing practice is guided by ethical principles. It seeks to integrate research, best practice, theory, audience and partnership insight, to inform the delivery of competition sensitive and segmented social programs that are effective, efficient, equitable, and sustainable. (Morgan, 2012–2018)

This definition offers several important advancements over previous definitions of social marketing. First, we see explicit reference to the use of "other approaches" beyond traditional commercial marketing tools. Researchers within the field of social marketing have recognized that many fields offer useful tools to influence behavior, and the best social marketing practice involves using the most effective tools, regardless of their field of origin. Another important advancement with this definition is the inclusion of specific program components, such as theory and research that were identified by social marketers as vital to implementing a successful program. Finally, explicit reference is made to the ethical use of social marketing. There are many ways in which social marketing can raise ethical dilemmas; these are discussed in Chap. 2. Since social marketers are focused on efforts to benefit individuals and society, an explicit commitment to ethics is consistent with the goals of the field.

This is the definition of social marketing adopted within this textbook; however, we strongly support the notion of "using what works" for your current situation. If another definition of social marketing better suits your needs, then by all means use it. We also encourage you to examine, critique, and debate this and other definitions of social marketing. In doing so, you can gain a clearer understanding of what is and is not central to the effective practice of social marketing.

Social Marketing Versus Education Versus Law

Social marketing, education, and law each provide a means of influencing behavior change. Each is appropriate in certain circumstances. A seminal social marketing article by Rothschild (1999), entitled "Carrots, Sticks, and Promises: A Conceptual Framework for the Management of Public Health and Social Issues Behaviors", offers a helpful guide to understanding when the use of each is appropriate. Here, we summarize those findings and encourage you to read the article for yourself, as it is quite insightful.

We have just defined social marketing above. Education focuses on providing information and more general knowledge, often with the goal of influencing voluntary behavior change as well. Modern educational efforts certainly can be advanced and sophisticated, but the goal is not generally to attain a specific, focused behavior change. Also, education does not usually offer incentives, remove barriers, or facilitate the behavior change in any way as social marketing does. Law also seeks to change behavior. Like social marketing, law uses additional tools beyond merely educating in order to motivate behavior change. However, these legal efforts tend to be coercive and punitive, and therefore this approach is different from the voluntary approach of social marketing (Rothschild, 1999).

Each of these three tools (social marketing, education, and law) is useful in the right situation. When to use each depends largely on the individual's motivation to change behavior, opportunity to change behavior, and ability to change behavior (MacInnis, Moorman, & Jaworski, 1991; Rothschild, 1999). If individuals are motivated to change, have the opportunity to perform the desired behavior, and the ability, then educating them on the need to do so may be sufficient. Education may be easier to execute than social marketing or law and more familiar in fields such as "health education," so use education if it is sufficient to get the behavior you are seeking. If individuals have the opportunity and ability to perform the behavior, but are very resistant (lack the motivation), and you cannot identify sufficient incentives to voluntarily motivate them, implementing a law may be the only option. This tends to be a difficult route to implement so it is generally a last resort. If an individual has the motivation and ability, but lacks opportunity, social marketing can help to create this opportunity and should be the strategy chosen. If you consider all the possible scenarios of motivation, opportunity, and ability combinations, there are many situations where more than one strategy is viable. Social marketing is often the most reasonable choice in these cases, as it can be more compelling than simply providing education, and does not require the legal effort of implementing or changing laws (see Rothschild, 1999, p. 31 for an explanation of each specific condition). Additionally, some situations are so complex that a combination of all three is needed to attain the desired goal. In macro-social marketing, described below, all three are often used in tandem to address the most difficult societal problems.

Externalities, Free Will, and Self-interest

The impetus for social marketing programs often stems from a desire to reduce what economists call "negative externalities." Externalities are the side effects that can occur from people's behavior (or lack of behavior). Rothschild (1999) defines externalities as:

> freely chosen behaviors that result in social costs for which other members of the society must pay either directly or indirectly. (Rothschild, 1999, p. 24)

Although not explicitly stated, Rothschild is referring to *negative* externalities in this definition. Externalities can be either positive or negative. Most of these side effects are unintended (Mundt, 1993). They can occur for the person performing the behavior (e.g., for a smoker, lung cancer would be a negative externality), or they may occur for others who are unintentionally impacted by their behavior (e.g., negative smoking externalities for others include second-hand smoke and increased burden on the healthcare system). As an example of a positive externality, imagine a company that instates a program that provides incentives to its employees to bicycle to work; this program is intended to improve employee health. Although not intended, a positive externality of this program could be to reduce traffic congestion near the company office.

In most societies today free will is valued, although this varies to greater or lesser degrees. Generally, citizens are allowed to perform a wide variety of behaviors if they so choose. In most cases, people will behave according to their own self-interest (Rothschild, 1999) and there are many political theorists such as Adam Smith who believe that acting in one's one self-interest results in the overall greatest good. However, this is not always the case. The right to act freely and the tendency to put one's own interests first can lead to a wide array of negative externalities. This creates a tension between the rights of some individuals to behave as they choose, and the rights of other individuals to be free of negative externalities thrust upon them. Additionally, within society, there are many shared resources or public goods. These include all things seen as public property or things to which we all feel we have a right, things like our public spaces, streets, and parks. They also include broader public goods, like fresh air and a clean water supply. If some people overuse or misuse a public good, it can have a damaging effect on others, creating a negative externality. Often, the focus of social marketing programs is to find ways to reduce these negative externalities without removing citizens' rights to choose their behaviors.

In order to influence voluntary behaviors, marketers first must understand the elements that determine people's current behaviors. Effective social marketing requires us to understand the social, environmental, structural, and economic forces that influence individuals' behavior in order to fully understand it. Various perspectives exist regarding behavior and free will. In this book, we view behavior as partly dictated by free will and individual choice, but also partly dictated by one's environment and how the particular individual responds to their particular environment. Therefore, if you want to be effective at influencing people's behavior, it is essential to first understand the social and environmental factors that influence that behavior.

The "social" aspect of social marketing is that we want to influence individual behaviors that will benefit individuals and society. To do this effectively, we often need to focus on ways to insure that the cards are not stacked against the individual. Consider if you encouraged a group of friends to participate in a game in which there is no realistic way they could win. Most likely, they would choose not to play. The same is true with social marketing. If the situation is structured so that success is unlikely, the individual would most likely choose not to participate (Fig. 1.1).

Structural Barriers to Behavior Change

For many of the behaviors being advocated by social marketers, structural barriers can stand in the way of individual behavior change. Consider, for example, efforts to encourage healthier eating habits. To be successful, individuals must first have affordable and convenient access to healthy foods. Many lower-income people may live in a "food desert," where the nearby stores are small convenience stores which do not sell fresh fruits and vegetables. Similarly, buying a salad at a fast-food restaurant is generally quite a bit more expensive than buying less healthy options. Often too, restaurant foods assumed to be healthy, such as salads, are actually laden with calories, fat, and sodium. All of these structural barriers make it more difficult for motivated individuals to eat a healthy diet. A good social marketing program, in

Fig. 1.1 Forces influencing individual behavior. *Artistic credit* Lisa Basil

addition to focusing on individual change, would also try to identify and eliminate or reduce these barriers.

> Before initiating change, it is important to create infrastructure to enable change. That is, by considering the behavioral ecological environment in which behaviors occur and managing the environment in addition to the individuals. Changing attitudes to motivate people to behave is pointless if people have no opportunity or ability to undertake the desired behaviors. (Brennan & Parker, 2014, online)

This quotation aptly summarizes growing sentiment toward social marketing. Social marketers should think broadly, using traditional tools from commercial marketing as well as other strategies that may fall outside of marketing. Social marketers should examine societal, environmental, economic, and infrastructure influences, and attempt to remove any barriers these pose before advocating behavior change. Wymer (2011) embraces this philosophy and proposes a four-step model for addressing public health initiatives. In his model, he suggests first addressing any lack of basic sustenance needed to survive, then removing harmful elements from the environment. Only after these basic essentials have been addressed does it make sense to proceed. The third step would be to assure the individual has sufficient knowledge about the healthy behavior, and then the final step is to increase the individual's motivation to perform the behavior. All too often, social marketing programs attempt to start at steps three or four, which greatly reduces program success.

Macro Versus Micro and Upstream Versus Downstream Approaches to Social Marketing

Social marketing often focuses on influencing behavior at the micro, individual level, based on principles from psychology and sociology. This can lead to a narrow perspective that fails to address the root of the problem. Effective social marketing requires that we take a macro-approach by taking a broader perspective, looking at the big picture, and considering all factors that influence the behavior we are trying to influence. This approach draws more from the fields of economics, anthropology, as well as sociology. Additionally, social marketing can focus downstream, on those whose behavior we wish to influence, or it can focus upstream, on policies and decision makers who have the power to facilitate the desired behavior change (Gordon, 2013). When the program focuses on individual behavior change, whether it is the downstream behavior we directly wish to influence or the upstream behavior of individual policy makers and influencers, we are practicing at the micro-level. When we consider all of the forces that influence the behavior we wish to change, including structural, economic, social, and policy forces, we are practicing macro-social marketing (Kennedy, 2016). In this section, we examine these principles (Fig. 1.2).

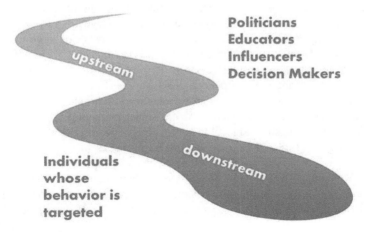

Fig. 1.2 Upstream versus downstream focus. *Artistic credit* Debra Z. Basil, Unbox Science and Pixabay

For a variety of reasons, traditional approaches to social marketing tended to focus primarily on simply applying commercial marketing principles to individual behavior change. More recently, however, many social marketers have adopted the perspective that we should use a wider variety of tools if they will help us attain the desired goal (e.g., Wymer, 2011). Social marketers are recognizing that, in order to attain many desired goals, the change needed may be at the community or societal level, rather than at the individual level. For example, consider a community that has a roadway intersection with a particularly high rate of accidents and fatalities. Various social marketing programs could be implemented to encourage people to change their driving behavior, including placing signs that say "drive safely." However, a more effective strategy might be to structurally change the intersection itself—such as adding a traffic signal.

Often the most effective way to encourage behavior change is to focus "upstream" of the problem, to remove the barriers to positive behaviors, rather than simply addressing outcomes. The notion of upstream social marketing stems from a story about people drowning in a stream that is credited to Irving Zola (French, 2014). The story has been told in many different ways—here is our abridged version. Imagine that you come upon a rushing stream, and see many people drowning. A downstream social marketing effort would look for ways to help those who are drowning now. A midstream effort would go a bit farther up the stream, to where people are getting into the water, and teach them to swim. An upstream social effort would go even farther up the stream to influence government officials to build a dam in order to regulate water flow, so those who choose to get into the stream will not drown.

Upstream social marketing focuses on identifying the causes of the problem, by influencing policies, structures, and decision makers that can help to alleviate the problem "upstream" of where the behavior actually occurs. The food bank described in the opening scenario, Banco Alimentare (Chap. 7), offers a good example of taking an upstream approach. They seek to influence government policy to reduce food waste. Generally, upstream efforts focus on adding incentives and removing barriers that impact the downstream behavior we wish to address.

There are many problems in this world that unfortunately are too large and complex to address with one tool. They require the use of everything we can possibly throw at them. These are "wicked problems," such as the obesity epidemic in developed countries, climate change, or indigenous disadvantage (Kennedy & Parsons, 2012). So many interdependent factors are working together with problems such as these that the entire system must be considered. Macro-social marketing applies social marketing principles at the societal level to address the issue, often in a government-led effort (Domegan, 2008). "Macro-social marketing seeks to use social marketing techniques in a holistic way to effect systemic change, as opposed to individual level change" (Kennedy, 2016, p. 344). For example, where micro-level social marketing may address the "wicked problem" of nicotine addiction by developing a program to help individuals overcome their smoking habit, macro-level social marketing may involve government efforts to reduce the commercial effectiveness of cigarette marketing, perhaps through limitations on how and where cigarettes can be promoted and displayed. Macro-social marketing uses a *systems* approach, removing barriers, and adding benefits throughout the entire system to encourage the desired behavior.

For effective social marketing, the entire system within which the problem resides must be considered. We must recognize all the forces working upon individuals, and the way these forces work within society. This systems' perspective should consider the forces that have enabled the problem to grow, the precipitating circumstances that contribute to the problem, and the general societal motivation to address the issue (Duhame, Mctavish, & Ross, 1985; Kennedy & Parsons, 2012). With a view to the entire system, macro-social marketing not only uses traditional social marketing tools, but can also engage education and law to address the issue, and any other tool available. Often the most effective solution for a large problem is to provide new infrastructure that will allow individuals to more easily change their behavior. Macro-social marketing can do this. Macro-social marketing generally involves both the use of social marketing tools and policy change (Hoek & Jones, 2011; Kennedy & Parsons, 2012). For example, rather than engaging in social marketing programs to encourage citizens to boil their water to avoid disease, installing a water purification system would address the issue more efficiently. While this may appear to come at greater financial cost, examining the entire system may reveal that it would save costs in other areas such as health care or lost worker productivity. Examining the issue at a systems perspective provides a clearer view of the overall cost of the problem and the proposed solutions.

Planning a Social Marketing Program

Understanding the macro environment is an important initial step in developing a social marketing program. To do this, you need a clear view of your purpose, and a thorough understanding of the entire system within which your behavior influencing efforts are positioned. In the remainder of this chapter, we discuss two key steps to understanding your macro-system—conducting a situation analysis and identifying your competition. Both of these steps focus on being aware of the bigger picture within which your problem resides. In Chap. 2, we introduce the remaining steps in creating a social marketing program.

Situation Analysis

A critical step in any social marketing effort is to clearly identify your purpose. What is it you are seeking to accomplish? What problem must be addressed? What behavior or behaviors are you trying to influence? This is the big-picture statement regarding your reason for creating this program. For example, in Chap. 11, the program purpose is to reduce tax evasion, and in Chap. 12, the program purpose is to reduce clothing waste, which is done by reducing the frequency of clothing repurchase.

Once you have a clear purpose, you should conduct background research to better understand the overall situation, including any structural barriers that may impact your efforts. This involves thoroughly examining your landscape. You need a clear picture of the scope of the issue, its sources, factors that contribute to it and exacerbate it, and factors that reduce it. You need to understand how it is viewed in society, who it affects directly, who it affects indirectly, and how. In short, you want to gather as much information as you possibly can about the issue. Information is your strongest weapon.

A variety of resources exist to help you gather background information. Many federal governments have free statistical data online. For example, Statistics Canada offers a wealth of information and reports that are useful for Canadian social marketers (www.statcan.gc.ca). In the USA, the Centers for Disease Control and Prevention offer many reports and statistics relevant to the health arena (www.cdc.gov). Additionally, many non-profit organizations post free articles and reports online that can be very helpful. The Points of Light Foundation offers information and articles to help with volunteer management, which is often an important part of a social marketing effort (www.pointsoflight.org). Case studies about social marketing programs related to your focal issue can provide valuable background and guidance. A simple Internet search will often reveal a wealth of resources. To dig more deeply into existing academic literature and case studies, search Google Scholar, which is a repository of a vast number of academic articles (www.scholar.google.com). Even for-profit companies that work in the social benefit space may offer valuable online resources. Globescan (www.globescan.com) and Euromonitor International (www.euromonitor.co) both offer free reports and webinars that can be helpful. In order to identify structural barriers, it is often necessary to conduct formative research regarding your topic. A common mistake made by social marketers is to mistakenly assume an understanding of the situation, but such assumptions are often wrong. It is important to speak directly with those whose behavior you wish to influence, to see the situation from their perspective. More information on research is provided in Chap. 3.

SWOT (Strengths, Weaknesses, Opportunities, and Threats)

A SWOT analysis is a useful tool adopted from commercial marketing that you can apply to better understand your landscape. SWOT stands for strengths, weaknesses, opportunities, and threats. The origin of SWOT is contested (Helms & Nixon,

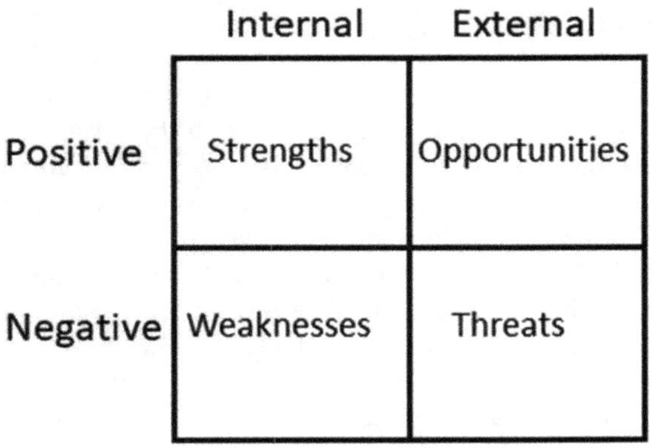

Fig. 1.3 SWOT framework

	Internal	**External**
Positive	Strengths	Opportunities
Negative	Weaknesses	Threats

2010) with credit often being given to researchers at Stanford and/or Harvard in the early 1960s. The idea behind SWOT is to examine the positive and negative influences you face both within your own organization (strengths and weaknesses) and outside of your organization (opportunities and threats). Strengths and weaknesses are internal to the organization; they represent your own assets and liabilities. Think broadly, considering all characteristics of your organization, and the people and resources of your organization, that might affect your social marketing effort. For example, is your organization slow to approve new programs? This could be a weakness for your program. Do you have a strong existing volunteer base who are eager to help, as with the Coulee Clean-up litter removal effort in Chap. 24? This is a strength.

SWOT involves considering external factors as well, in the form of opportunities and threats. What opportunities external to your organization might help your efforts? For example, if the city has just passed a law increasing the number of riders necessary for a car to legally use the carpool lane, this may represent an opportunity for a social marketing program seeking to increase bicycle ridership. What threats to your program exist? Threats come in many forms—any factor external to your organization that will make it more difficult for your program to succeed, is a threat. For example, if your purpose is to reduce all forms of smoking, and your state or province has just approved the legalization of marijuana for recreational purposes, this is a threat to your program.

It is important to think deeply and broadly when considering your SWOT. Is the influencing factor positive or negative? Is it controlled within your organization, or is it external to your organization? These pieces of information are essential in order to properly categorize influencing factors. See Fig. 1.3 for a SWOT framework.

Competition

With social marketing, it is important to understand strengths, weaknesses, opportunities, and threats relative to the program, as well as the behaviors that compete with your goals. All successful commercial marketers know the importance of understanding the competition. Social marketing is no different. You need to understand the behaviors that are competing with your efforts. Lee and Kotler (2011) position competition as what the target would prefer to do, including habits people have formed that might keep them from doing what you advocate, as well the individuals, organizations, and programs that will lead them away from your efforts (Lee & Kotler, 2011). Other theorists define competition more broadly, seeing competition as "competing ideas" (Peattie & Peattie, 2003, p. 376), and these may come from commercial competition, social discouragement (such as social norms), general apathy (such as an involuntary disinclination) or other forms of influence, such as addiction (Peattie & Peattie, 2003). Free choice, apathy, and inertia serve as strong competitors to most social marketing programs (Rothschild, 1999), as these factors deter the target audience from the desired behavior.

Competition can exist at various levels of abstraction (generic, entity, product, and brand; Andreasen, 2006; Noble & Basil, 2011). In some cases, something can be seen as a competitor at one level, but as complementary at another. Chapter 17's social marketing program promotes hand washing with Lifebuoy soap to reduce childhood mortality. At a generic level, any behavior that keeps the individual from washing is competition; therefore, apathy serves as a key competitor. At the entity level, any form of hand cleaning other than washing is competition, so wiping hands on one's clothing or rubbing with sand would be competing behaviors. At the product level, any form of hand cleansing other than soap would be a competitor; thus, the use of hand sanitizer could be seen as competition at this level. Finally, the narrowest form of competition is the brand level, where use of any soap brand other than Lifebuoy brand soap could be seen as competition. Though social marketers would undoubtedly be pleased with any form of hand cleansing that sufficiently kills germs, it is helpful to consider the various levels of competition (generic, entity, product, and brand) in order to thoroughly understand the many things that can detract from your effort.

Increasingly, organizations that might normally be seen as competitors are working together for common goals, a practice labeled co-opetition (Noble & Basil, 2011). Turning a competitor into a complementor or collaborator is an excellent way to reduce competition. For example, when addressing drunk driving, a social marketer might consider working *with* alcohol companies to offer programs such as free soft drinks for designated drivers.

Appendix: Additional Resources for the Big Picture in Social Marketing

Debra Z. Basil

This appendix provides open source links for the major topics discussed in this chapter. These links will allow you to explore the chapter topics in greater detail. Given the fleeting nature of the Internet, some links may no longer be working, so we have provided three resources per topic.

1. Competition

   - This short article from ORAU (Oak Ridge Associated Universities) discusses competition in a social marketing setting, and the importance of understanding your competition at each stage of the program planning process. https://www. orau.gov/cdcynergy/soc2web/content/phase02/phase02_step01_deeper_com petition.htm

   - This short article from the NSMC (National Social Marketing Centre) provides guidance in conducting a competitive analysis for your social marketing program. http://www.thensmc.com/content/conduct-competition-analysis-1

   - This article from Community Tool Box discusses competition in the context of benefits and costs or barriers. https://ctb.ku.edu/en/table-of-contents/ sustain/social-marketing/promote-behavior-change/main

2. Externalities

   - This article from the International Monetary Fund explains the nature of externalities. http://www.imf.org/external/pubs/ft/fandd/basics/external.htm
   - This article from Economics Help explains negative externalities from an economics perspective. https://www.economicshelp.org/micro-economic-essays/marketfailure/negative-externality/
   - This article from Tutor 2 U also takes an economics perspective in explaining externalities. https://www.tutor2u.net/economics/reference/neg ative-externalities

3. Macro- Versus Micro-Social Marketing

   - This short commentary by Craig Lefebvre discusses the micro–macro levels and the dilemma of operating at both levels. http://socialmarketing.blogs. com/r_craiig_lefebvres_social/2012/09/the-micro-macro-problem-in-social-marketing.html
   - This longer article by Ann-Marie Kennedy defines macro-social marketing and places it in the context of an overall systems approach. https://aut.

researchgateway.ac.nz/bitstream/handle/10292/9121/2%20Macro-Social%
20Marketing.pdf?sequence=10&isAllowed=y
- This slide show by the UBSUP social marketing team fully describes macro-
and micro-approaches in a sanitary toilet use program. http://www.water
fund.go.ke/safisan/downloads/0701010205_UBSUP's%20Social%20Market
ing%20Approach.pdf

4. Situation Analysis

- This article from Health Compass provides an excellent guide to developing
a situation analysis for social marketing efforts. It is clear and detailed,
providing a step-by-step strategy. https://www.thehealthcompass.org/how-
to-guides/how-conduct-situation-analysis
- This article from Public Health Ontario offers six detailed steps to creating a
situation analysis for a social marketing program. https://www.
publichealthontario.ca/en/eRepository/FocusOn-Situational_Assessment_
2015.pdf
- This article discusses the importance of justifying your social marketing
plan. It offers a sample justification section, which shows information one
might also include in a situation analysis. https://ebrary.net/8732/business_
finance/use_social_marketing

5. SWOT (Strengths, Weaknesses, Opportunities, and Threats)

- This article from Community Tool Box offers basic guidance on creating a
SWOT analysis for community organizations and social marketing programs.   https://ctb.ku.edu/en/table-of-contents/assessment/assessing-comm
unity-needs-and-resources/swot-analysis/main
- This article from NSMC (National Social Marketing Centre) discusses the
importance of examining internal and external factors, and provides a link to
a WORD document template for creating a SWOT analysis. http://www.
socialmarketing-toolbox.com/content/review-internal-and-external-factors-0
- This article from Business News Daily offers background information on
SWOT from a commercial marketing perspective; however, the concepts are
applicable to social marketing as well. It also provides useful categories to
consider for each factor in your SWOT. https://www.businessnewsdaily.
com/4245-swot-analysis.html

6. Upstream Versus Downstream Social Marketing

- An article from the Centre of Excellence for Public Sector Marketing discussing the difference between upstream and downstream social marketing.
https://cepsm.ca/blog/importance-of-upstream-social-marketing/

- This short article by Jeff French defines the terms upstream, downstream, and midstream.   https://www.linkedin.com/pulse/20140819142011-50216498-up-stream-mid-stream-and-down-stream-social-marketing-defining-the-term/
- This is a longer, journal-type article by Gary Noble that discusses upstream versus downstream, proposes the need for both to working together, and supports this proposal with two program examples from Australia. https://ro.uow.edu.au/cgi/viewcontent.cgi?referer=https://www.google.ca/&httpsredir=1&article=2336&context=commpapers.

7. Social Marketing Centers and Organizations: This is a non-exhaustive listing of some of the major social marketing centers internationally.

- The Australian Association of Social Marketing:

"The Australian Association of Social Marketing is an independent, volunteer based organization. It is the peak body representing social marketers in Australia and aims to provide support for social marketers throughout the country and act as a central resource for those engaged in, or interested in, social marketing practice and research." https://www.aasm.org.au/

- Bristol Social Marketing Centre:

"Contributing to the improvement of health, the environment, and overall quality of life via world class behavior change and social marketing research." https://www.ecojam.org/organisation/bristol-social-marketing-centre

- The Institute for Consumer and Social Well-being (formerly the Centre for Socially Responsible Marketing), University of Lethbridge:

"The Institute for Consumer and Social Well-being is a Dhillon School of Business research team with the objective to foster research, to teach and to generate involvement in three related areas: Social Marketing…Social Responsibility and Sustainability…Not-for-Profit Marketing." https://www.uleth.ca/dhillon/about-the-school/research/centre-socially-responsible-marketing

- European Social Marketing Association:

"By creating a community where people practicing and researching social marketing in Europe can connect with other colleagues to share experiences, knowledge, findings, methods, and practices ESMA endeavors to contribute to the development, evidence base, and promotion of the social marketing discipline in Europe. ESMA aims: To establish a community of Social Marketers in Europe. To enhance and facilitate knowledge and experience exchange in the different fields of

social and behavior change. To promote the use of social marketing as an approach
to social change in Europe." http://www.europeansocialmarketing.org/2016/05/12/
the-role-of-strategic-social-marketing-in-public-policy/

- International Social Marketing Association:

"iSMA's Mission is to:
   Advance social marketing practice, research, and teaching through collaborative
networks of professionals, supporters, and enthusiasts. Educate the public, organizations, professionals, and governments about the value of social marketing to
facilitate behavioral change and social progress.
   Develop, document, and market international standards and best practices in social
marketing theory, research, and practice. Encourage and enable wider use of social
marketing in addressing complex social issues. Foster and support the development of
local, national, and regional social marketing associations." https://www.
i-socialmarketing.org/index.php?option=com_content&view=article&id=32:mission&
catid=20:about&Itemid=111#.W4Qd585KjIV

- The National Social Marketing Centre:

"The NSMC is the centre of excellence for social marketing and behavior change
based in the UK. Our mission is to maximize the effectiveness of behavior change
programmes across the globe. We do this by working directly with clients and by
promoting and sharing best practice." http://www.thensmc.com/

References

Andreasen, A. R. (1994). Social marketing: Its definition and domain. *Journal of Public Policy & Marketing, 13*(1), 108–114.
Andreasen, A. R. (Ed.). (2006). *Social marketing in the 21st century.* Thousand Oaks, CA: Sage.
Brennan, L., & Parker, L. (2014). Beyond behavior change: Social marketing and social change. *Journal of Social Marketing, 4*(3). https://doi.org/10.1108/JSOCM-08-2014-0052.
Domegan, C. T. (2008). Social marketing: Implications for contemporary marketing practices classification scheme. *Journal of Business & Industrial Marketing, 23*(2), 135–141.
Duhame, C., McTavish, R., & Ross, C. (1985). Social marketing: An approach to third world development. *Journal of Macromarketing, 5*(Spring), 3–13.
French, J. (2014). *Up-stream, mid-stream, and down-stream social marketing. Defining the term.* Retrieved August 12, 2018 from https://www.linkedin.com/pulse/20140819142011-50216498-up-stream-mid-stream-and-down-stream-social-marketing-defining-the-term/.
Gordon, R. (2013). Unlocking the potential of upstream social marketing. *European Journal of Marketing, 47*(9), 1525–1547.
Helms, M. M., & Nixon, J. (2010). Exploring SWOT analysis—Where are we now? A review of academic research from the last decade. *Journal of Strategy and Management, 3*(3), 215–251.
Hoek, J., & Jones, S. C. (2011). Regulation, public health and social marketing: A behavior change trinity. *Journal of Social Marketing, 1*(1), 32–44.
Kennedy, A. M. (2016). Macro-social marketing. *Journal of Macromarketing, 36*(3), 354–365.

Kennedy, A. M., & Parsons, A. (2012). Macro-social marketing and systems engineering: A systems approach. *Journal of Social Marketing, 2*(1), 37–51.

Kotler, P., & Zaltman, G. (1971). Social marketing: An approach to planned social change. *The Journal of Marketing, 35*(3), 3–12.

Lee, N. R., & Kotler, P. (2011). *Social marketing: Influencing behaviors for good*. Los Angeles: Sage.

Lefebvre, R. C. (2011). An integrative model for social marketing. *Journal of Social Marketing, 1* (1), 54–72.

MacInnis, D. J., Moorman, C., & Jaworski, B. J. (1991). Enhancing and measuring consumers' motivation, opportunity, and ability to process brand information from ads. *The Journal of Marketing, 55*(4), 32–53.

Morgan, W. (2012–2018). The iSMA, ESMA and AASM1 consensus definition of social marketing. *International Social Marketing Association*. Retrieved July 15, 2018 from http://www.i-socialmarketing.org/social-marketing-definition#.W0uxodVKjIX.

Mundt, J. (1993). Externalities: Uncalculated outcomes of exchange. *Journal of Macromarketing, 13*(2), 46–53.

Noble, G., & Basil, D. Z. (2011). Competition and positioning. In G. Hastings, K. Angus, & C. A. Bryant (Eds.), *The Sage handbook of social marketing* (Vol. 9, pp. 136–151). London: Sage.

Peattie, S., & Peattie, K. (2003). Ready to fly solo? Social marketing's dependence on commercial marketing theory. *Marketing Theory, 3*, 365–385.

Rothschild, M. L. (1999). Carrots, sticks, and promises: A conceptual framework for the management of public health and social issue behaviors. *The Journal of Marketing, 63*(4), 24–37.

Walsh, D. C., Rudd, R. E., Moeykens, B. A., & Moloney, T. W. (1993). Social marketing for public health. *Health Affairs, 12*(2), 104–119.

Wymer, W. (2011). Developing more effective social marketing strategies. *Journal of Social Marketing, 1*(1), 17–31.

The Fundamentals of Social Marketing

2

Debra Z. Basil

Chapter Overview
This chapter introduces the key principles of planning a social marketing program. Social marketing is the application of commercial marketing and other principles to influence behavior for the good of the individual and society. In order to develop a social marketing program to influence behavior for good, it is important to set clear objectives regarding what you want your target audience to do, know, and believe. To reach these objectives, set specific, measurable, relevant, and time sensitive goals. You should then segment the potential audience into prospective groups, and target the most promising group or groups. When selecting a target, consider who has the greatest need for change, will be receptive to change, is reachable, of sufficient group size, fits with your organization, and will be cost effective to reach. Once you have selected your target audience, position your program in a way that will appeal to your target, considering the benefits this behavior could offer them, and the barriers they face. When developing your program, clearly define your product. Know the price of it for your target audience, particularly considering the non-monetary costs, and try to minimize this price. Consider the placement of your product offering, including all aspects of how the target audience will attain it as well as any augmenting components, and make these placements as convenient as possible for your target. Then develop the promotion for your program, realizing that promotion is not the most important element and is not always achieved through advertisement pieces. Always consider the ethical implications of your program, and give voice to the target audience when developing the program. Include research at all stages of your program to enhance your chances of program success.

D. Z. Basil (✉)
Dhillon School of Business, University of Lethbridge, Lethbridge, Canada
e-mail: debra.basil@uleth.ca

© Springer Nature Switzerland AG 2019
D. Z. Basil et al. (eds.), *Social Marketing in Action*,
Springer Texts in Business and Economics,
https://doi.org/10.1007/978-3-030-13020-6_2

Valuable further guidance in social marketing can be found online. See this chapter's appendix for a listing of further resources.

Introduction

Every April, in the hills overlooking the river valley of Lethbridge, Canada, you can see groups of people dotting the hillsides, each carrying a large garbage bag. They are participating in the Coulee Clean-up, an annual social marketing program to clean litter from the river valley. Participants take the opportunity to enjoy nature and each other's company while cleaning the nature preserve. This program has been very successful, with participation increasing each year. This success comes from careful planning, perceptive implementation, and regular evaluation. In this chapter, we cover the steps necessary for developing a successful social marketing program.

In Chap. 1, we discussed the big picture surrounding social marketing. We explained the importance of examining the macro-environment and using all tools available to influence behavior for good. This includes considering all of the social, structural, and environmental influences that affect individual behavior. We discussed the important first steps of fully analyzing your situation and identifying competing behaviors when designing a social marketing program. In this chapter, we outline the basic principles of creating a social marketing program. Most of these are explained in terms of downstream individual-level behavior change, and the examples given in this chapter tend to focus on how to encourage an individual to perform (or give up) a certain behavior. As discussed in Chap. 1, social marketing can also be applied upstream to influence decision makers who develop the social and environmental policies and structures that contribute to individual behavior. For example, social marketing could be used to influence local government lawmakers to make decisions which will promote healthier communities, such as creating bicycle paths. Downstream, a social marketing program could be created to encourage people to choose to ride their bikes more frequently. Ideally, these would both be addressed, as well as examining other structural, economic, social, and policy factors that influence people's bicycling behavior, in a macro-social marketing effort, for the most effective outcome. An appendix at the end of the chapter offers online links for further study of the topics in this chapter.

Program Objectives

A wide variety of factors can lead to the development of a social marketing program. In the area of health, these are often epidemiological, such as concern about increased rates of diabetes or heart disease within the population. Similarly, environmental changes could motivate program development, such as increases in pollution levels or fire devastation. Often funding organizations will establish priorities, and offer funding for program proposals that address their priorities. Whatever the motivation, your first step is to look at the overall problem, then consider which aspect you could realistically address. From there you determine a feasible objective for your program. For example, if your organization is concerned about the increased threat of fire, before beginning a social marketing program you would consider the potential sources of fire, such as lightning, cigarettes, and campfires. You then would select program objectives that are feasible. You cannot reduce the incidence of lightning, so you would instead elect to specifically address one or more of the human-made risks, such as campfire safety.

All social marketing programs should have clear, measurable objectives. For example, Chap. 25 presents a dog training program for koala safety. The authors set out specific objectives for their program, specifying 1000 Dog Fest attendees within 12 months, and at least a 10% improvement in dog behavior, on average. Setting out clear objectives allows you to plan your program more effectively, because you know what you are striving for. If you don't know your goal, you will never know whether you have reached it. Setting objectives can be one of the most difficult parts of planning a social marketing program, because setting goals and objectives necessarily means accepting that you cannot do everything.

Each social marketing program should have a clear *behavioral objective*. This is the behavior you are seeking to encourage (or discourage). For example, consider the Coulee Clean-up program in Chap. 24, which we described at the opening of this chapter. The program had a behavioral objective to get volunteers to clean up the riverbed area. In addition to behavioral objectives, social marketing programs often have *knowledge* and *belief objectives* as well (Lee & Kotler, 2011). A knowledge objective specifies information we want our target audience to have. These are facts about the topic. For example, in the Coulee Clean-up program, a knowledge objective was set that every volunteer understands the fragility of the coulee landscape, and the danger of walking on it after a rain. A belief objective addresses what we want our audience to believe and to feel about the issue. These are more subjective views on the issue. Using the same example, the Coulee Clean-up had a belief objective of influencing perception so individuals believed environmental protection to be a social norm.

Social Marketing Objectives

Behavioral Objectives: What they do
Knowledge Objectives: What they know
Belief Objectives: How they feel/what they believe

Objectives should be considered at the individual level as well as at higher social levels. For example, in Chap. 6, which seeks to increase citizens' safe behavior around rail crossings, getting people to sign an online pledge of rail safety was an individual level objective, and the community level behavioral objective was to gain 12,000 online pledges of rail safety.

From here, it is important to set specific goals regarding your objectives. How much of a change will signify success? Goals should be *SMART*, that is *specific, measurable, achievable, relevant, and time sensitive* (Lee & Kotler, 2011, p. 165). It is difficult to know if you have attained a goal that is too vague (not specific) or one where you have no way of actually measuring your success. Similarly, if you select an unrealistic goal (not achievable), or one that is not important (not relevant) you will simply be wasting resources. Finally, if your goal lacks a specific time frame by which it will be achieved, you will not know when to make your final assessment. So, for example, the Coulee Clean-up in Chap. 24 has a behavioral objective of getting people to participate in their annual clean-up effort. The specific behavioral goal is for 550 participants per year to volunteer with the program, which fits the requirements for a SMART goal.

Setting SMART Goals
Social marketing *goals* specify the way in which you will reach your objective. Goals must be:

- Specific
- Measurable
- Achievable
- Relevant
- Time Sensitive

One of the difficulties in objective setting is that it is hard to know what objectives and goals are realistic. In Chap. 1, we discussed how to assess your situation, in order to determine where you are now. Chapter 3's discussion of research will help with this. Formative (preliminary) research can provide you with an initial, concrete measure of your situation, in order to determine what goals might be reasonable. Then later in your social marketing program, outcome research will allow you to evaluate your program's success, by measuring how far you have come toward meeting your goals. Past research and existing research theory can also provide valuable grounding, to help you better understand the background of your situation based on what others have found previously, without having to reinvent the wheel. Commonly used theories in social marketing are reviewed in Chap. 4, with a historical perspective offered in Chap. 5.

Segmenting, Targeting, and Positioning (STP)

Harvard Professor Michael Porter, renowned for his theories on business strategy, astutely noted that "Strategy 101 is about choices. You can't be all things to all people" (Michael Porter, as cited in Hammonds, 2001). That is the primary notion behind segmenting, targeting, and positioning. These three are essential components of commercial marketing, and they are so inextricably intertwined that together they have come to be known as STP. Segmenting, targeting, and positioning are principles from commercial marketing that are welcomed in social marketing with very little debate. The general idea behind STP is that people have different needs, and respond to different motivators; therefore, you should choose who you wish to reach, and do that well, rather than trying to reach everyone with the same approach.

Segmenting

The first step in STP is to *segment* the audience. Segmenting means that you examine the full population you could potentially reach with your behavior influence efforts, and then you determine the most logical or appropriate way to break this population up into smaller groups. Importantly, you want to create groups that are meaningful. The groups should be those who you would be able to influence, with enough of them to allow your program to have a measurable impact, but small enough that you can effectively reach those people with your available resources. The people within a group should be similar enough that the same strategy would appeal to them. If different people in your selected target require a different approach, then you probably do not have a single segment and you will need to reassess your segmentation effort. And finally, you have to be able to reach the group. If you have no way to effectively reach a particular group, then it cannot be a viable target.

Behavioral segmentation is the gold standard. If there is some way to identify and reach people based on their current behavior, your task is relatively straightforward. For example, if your program can reach sexually active men who are not monogamous, further understanding this group, finding ways to influence their behavior, or providing them with free or low-cost condoms could be a very efficient strategy. Sometimes there is a means to reach such a behavioral segment who would respond well to the same program strategy. Behavioral segmentation allows us to consider how people live their lives. For example, a 20-year-old male and a 50-year-old female who both run 10 km per day may have more in common than two 20-year-old males with very different activity levels. These behavioral segments might include church attendance, whether they eat meat, or current recycling habits. However, reaching people who only fit into a particular behavioral segment is often difficult. Alternatively, lifestyle segmentation can help identify life-stage or life-style choices that may be relevant for your program. For example, reaching new mothers might provide a group of people who would be particularly receptive to a children's nutrition effort. Although *demographics* can sometimes be a useful method of segmentation, this is only if the behavior you are interested in varies based on demographics, or if you can create a more effective program by adjusting for demographics (demographics includes age, sex, employment status, income, ethnicity, etc.). *Geographic segmentation* can also be helpful. This can include targeting certain geographic areas, such as certain neighborhoods, cities, or countries. Geographic segmentation can also focus on where people are physically located relative to something your program addresses, for example, distance from an emergency room, or distance from a grocery store that sells fresh produce. Finally, *psychographic* segmentation addresses various psychological variables and how these influence elements relevant to your program. For example, people differ in terms of their risk-taking attitudes, and this can be important for some social marketing programs (see Chap. 6, which discusses risk-taking and thrill-seeking attitudes and their relevance to a social marketing rail safety program).

You may also wish to combine several factors when segmenting. You can consider a variety of ways to segment your audience, keeping in mind that the method(s) you select need to produce groups that are an appropriate size, that will respond well to the same strategy and that you can effectively reach. For example, if you were to develop a mountain bike safety program you might choose a behavioral segmentation (by bicycling status), a demographic segmentation (segment by sex and age), and a psychographic segmentation (segment by risk-taking orientation). Remember that segmenting means cutting the larger population into groups. You have not yet chosen a focal group or groups at this point; you have just created groups based on variable(s) that are relevant to your intended program.

Targeting

After you segment your population, you then select the group or groups that will be the focus for your program. This is your *target audience*. You will design your program to appeal to your target audience. Although you may wish you could reach everyone, trying to do so generally wastes resources and results in a very ineffective program. It is usually better to target a specific group or groups for whom the issue is relevant, who may be receptive to your efforts, and "speak" to them in a way that suits their needs and preferences. For example, a train safety program may be better targeted toward 20-year-old males and would likely look different than one targeted toward 60-year-old women. Although segmenting and targeting are intertwined, it is important to remember that they are separate steps—segmenting involves understanding the different types of people and targeting means selecting from among them. Be sure you consider a wide variety of possible ways to segment the population before selecting a target audience—your first inclination may not be the best choice.

Several factors should be considered when selecting a target. Lee and Kotler (2011) identify four key issues for selecting a target audience: who needs the program most, who will actually be receptive to the program, who you can realistically reach, and who your organization is best suited to work with. Along with these issues, you must consider your budget, the size of the target group, and the timing of the intended program. Each factor must be assessed in light of the others to determine the most promising target audience(s).

Target Selection Criteria

- Need for change
- Receptive to change
- Reachable
- Good fit
- Affordable
- Appropriate size

Commercial marketers are increasingly moving toward customization in marketing. Advances in technology offer commercial marketers the ability to customize a product to the desires of an individual customer, effectively creating a target audience consisting of one person. As technology continues to advance, social marketers too can customize their efforts to more specifically suit the individual. For example, this can be done with electronic applications that are customized for the individual, such as exercise and dieting apps.

Positioning

Once you have selected a target audience, you need to determine the positioning of your program. Positioning is how your program will be viewed in the eyes of your target audience. Positioning is what makes your effort unique based on how your program will be perceived from your target audience's point of view (Ries & Trout, 2001). This is important because the same program can often be positioned in many different ways. For example, a free after-school sports program for children could be positioned to parents as a safer alternative than leaving children home alone, as a healthier option than letting children watch television, or as a good way to help children make friends. You could use formative research (discussed further in Chap. 3) to determine whether parents (the target audience) are more concerned about their children's safety, health, or social connections to determine how to position your program. As you may have guessed from this example, you should consider the primary benefits your target audience may be seeking and the barriers they may face when determining program positioning. These are discussed in the next section.

Exchange, Benefits and Barriers

The concept of *exchange* is a central tenant of the field of marketing (Alderson, 1957; Kotler, 1972; see Chap. 4). In its most simplified form, exchange theory involves each party offering the other something they value and a trade occurring where each feels they are better off than they were before. The notion of exchange as the foundation of marketing assumes that people are largely motivated by self-interest (Rothschild, 1999). Exchange theory is just as applicable to social marketing as it is to commercial marketing. The social marketer must offer something of value to the target audience in order to influence the desired behavior. To do this, a social marketer must identify what the target audience values. Specifically, in order to position your program in a way that appeals to your target audience, you should consider the benefits they can gain from the behavior you are addressing—this is what will motivate them to change their behavior. You should also consider the things they may have to give up and other barriers that are likely to keep them from doing what is advocated. Then you can proactively address each, to create an appealing offering that will lead to the desired behavior.

Benefits

It is important to try to identify all the benefits your target audience could gain from adopting the suggested behavior (or abandoning it, depending on the program). This will probably require some research with your target audience. Do not assume you can guess what they are thinking, and what will motivate them—instead, find out from them, through research (discussed further in Chap. 3). When considering benefits, identify *who* will receive the benefit, and the *time frame*. In terms of who receives the benefit, benefits may accrue for them personally, for their family and friends, their communities, or society in general. As rule of thumb, the more closely a benefit is directly beneficial to the individual him or herself, the more compelling it tends to be, however, general notions of humanitarianism and altruism can also be compelling.

It is also important to consider the time frame of the benefit. In social marketing, the benefits can often be delayed and vague, which can make it more difficult to encourage behavior change (Rothschild, 1999). The more immediate the benefit, the more appealing it is. As the benefit becomes more distant, it becomes less persuasive. A benefit to oneself that can be experienced immediately is more appealing than a benefit to society in general that will happen at some general time in the future. For example, the immediate and personal benefit of saving $1 right now for bringing your own bags for grocery shopping may be more appealing than the distant and impersonal benefit of knowing you may have helped the planet sometime in the future. Whenever possible offer immediate, concrete, and personally relevant benefits to the target audience. Again, considering the Coulee Clean-up program in Chap. 24, a barbeque event with prizes is offered at the end of the clean-up period as a benefit for all participants and whomever they wish to bring along. Saving the environment for general community benefit is good, but attending a free party with friends and/or family offers a more immediate, concrete benefit.

Barriers

Good social marketing efforts require that you identify and understand the barriers your target will face. Barriers can be real or perceived (Lee & Kotler, 2011). Keep in mind that perceived barriers are actually quite real to the perceiver. Barriers can also be internal to the individual, or external (McKenzie-Mohr, 2011). *Internal barriers* relate to factors within the target audience themselves, such as a lack of skill, knowledge, and confidence. *External barriers* relate to their environment, such as a lack of community infrastructure, resources, and supportive social norms. As with benefits, you should conduct research with the target audience in order to correctly identify barriers. As an example, Rothschild and colleagues (2006) wanted to reduce drunk driving in rural Wisconsin, but, after talking with young men in the target audience, found that not being able to get drunk at the bar was a huge barrier; as a result, their "Road Crew" program bought used limousines and provided rides to and from the bar to allow drinking to continue but at minimal risk. The benefit that they were later able to communicate was Road Crew allowed them to get drunk without having to worry about how they would get home or the risks associated with drunk driving. Minimizing or removing barriers, both real and perceived, is critical to achieving success.

The Four (or Seven) P's of Social Marketing

Social marketing applies commercial marketing (and other) tools to influence behavior in order to gain individual and societal benefit. The core structure for this is the classic "four P's" of marketing. In commercial marketing, *product, price, place, and promotion* have long been seen as the key components for any marketing plan. This four P's structure dates back to McCarthy (1964). Although the structure certainly has its limitations, it provides a useful framework for considering many social marketing issues. All of the cases in part 2 of this book apply a four P's approach in order to lend an ordered structure to the creation and assessment of social marketing programs.

Product

In social marketing, the *product* is the behavior that you are trying to encourage (or discourage). So, for example, your product could be riding one's bicycle to work rather than driving a car. The notion of product in social marketing has been discussed, debated, and elaborated upon. Here, we see it as a useful frame upon which to place our program objectives. This is what you want your target audience to (not) do. Kotler, Armstrong, Saunders, and Wong (1999) added two additional levels to the definition of product, labeling the benefits the target audience receives from behavior change as the *core product*, the behavior change itself as the *actual product*, and any services or tangible objects the program offers to help the target reach behavior change as the *augmented product*. Some find this to be a useful way to further refine the notion of social marketing product.

Since social marketers do not create the behavior, but instead rely on the individual for this, scholars have questioned the applicability of the term *product* in a social marketing setting. Peattie and Peattie (2011) proposed that social proposition might be a good substitute. The social proposition is the value the individual and/or society gain from the behavior change. This value could include a wide variety of things, including things like money saved from quitting smoking, or cleaner air from reducing one's driving. Subsequent cases in this book tend to use the term *product* in their frameworks, but you may find it useful to also consider what the *social proposition* is within each case.

Price

Price is what it will cost your target audience to adopt (or abandon) the behavior. Generally, the greatest cost to the target is not money. There may be social costs to changing a behavior (e.g., "my friends will think I'm not cool if I don't smoke"). There may be time costs (e.g., preparing healthy meals at home takes more time than buying fast food at a restaurant). There may be hedonic costs (e.g., it feels better to lay on the couch and watch television than it does to exercise). There may be psychological costs (e.g., I am afraid to get an HIV test—I wouldn't know how to react if it comes back positive). And of course, there may be financial costs (e.g., using only the prescribed amount of water when mixing baby formula is too expensive). It is important to identify all of the costs your target audience perceives regarding the behavior, and to offset or minimize these costs as much as possible. For example, if they are concerned about the additional time it takes to prepare healthy food, a cooking guide could be offered providing quick and healthy recipes (this would be an augmented product).

Place

Place is where the behavior will be performed. It is also where the target audience will get any goods or services that facilitate their behavior change (the augmented products). Given the wide array of possible social marketing programs, place may mean a lot of different things in different situations. In some cases, place is actually where a service occurs, such as getting a vaccine at the doctor's office. Place may also be where the individual performs a behavior, such as making healthier food choices in the cafeteria.

Place encompasses the whole channel involved with the desired behavior change. This may involve the location where the target audience obtains the augmented product, as well as where they perform the actual behavior. They may pick up healthy recipes and purchase healthy food at the grocery store, but they would then take these things home to prepare them.

An essential goal for social marketers is to make the behavior change as easy as possible for the target audience. This means conveniently placing all support elements. If you are trying to increase bike ridership within your city, then carefully assess where citizens want to ride, and put bike paths in these places. The more convenient you make the behavior, the more likely it is people will adopt it.

Promotion

Promotion is how you will communicate and share meaning with your target audience in order to persuade them to adopt the desired behavior change. It is very important to remember that promotion is just one part of the social marketing program, and if the other components are done well, promotion may be one of the least important components. Unfortunately, social marketers sometimes place all of their emphasis on crafting a persuasive message, overlooking the importance of the other components. Even the most persuasive message cannot overcome high perceived cost of behavior adoption, or inconvenient placement. A social marketer must first reduce the perceived costs and increase the perceived convenience and benefits of the behavior as much as possible, before crafting a message. The message then simply needs to communicate the benefits of the new advocated behavior and how it overcomes the barriers.

When considering promotion, the social marketer must specify what will be said, by whom, in what way, and through what format or media. For example, a social marketer targeting teen smoking may want to communicate the message that smoking makes your breath stink, they may wish to do it in a humorous way, they may want to have a famous teen idol communicate the message, and they may wish to distribute the message through popular social media platforms.

Often social marketing does not involve advertising-style communications pieces. It may instead involve personal communication, such as having doctors mention to patients that they offer free HIV testing. In this case, the promotion is coming through word of mouth from one's doctor. It is important that you do not confuse promotion and communication with social marketing. These are components of social marketing, but on their own they do not constitute a social marketing program. Putting together an eye-catching billboard that tells people not to drive drunk, on its own, is not a social marketing program.

The Other Three P's

Commercial marketing scholars recognized that services require additional considerations, and expanded the four P's to seven P's to accommodate these considerations. Specifically, the notions of *People, Process, and Physical Evidence* were developed (Booms & Bitner, 1981). These concepts are often relevant to social marketing as well. *People* address who will be providing the service or executing the program. For example, if you plan to offer a needle exchange program to reduce the spread of disease among intravenous drug users, who will be handing out the needles? This can be extremely important, as the target audience may avoid the program if they are not comfortable with the people administering it. *The process* must also be considered. What exactly takes place, and what does it require of the target audience? Perhaps you want to offer free nicotine patches to help the target audience quit smoking. That is great, but what do they have to do to attain the patches? If they have to go to a specific government office to pick up a voucher, then take that voucher to a specific retailer to redeem it, they may find the process too cumbersome. Can you simplify the process for the target audience? Can you make it more appealing? Finally, *physical evidence* should be considered. This concept was introduced specifically for services in the commercial marketing realm, because the service itself is fleeting and often has no physical trace. Marketers found that they could more effectively position, and gain more value, when they included physical evidence to support their services. In a commercial setting, banks offer a service. Some of the few pieces of physical evidence offered to customers are the debit and credit cards customers use to access their accounts. If these appear to be flimsy or of low quality, customers may infer that they also receive inferior banking service. Similarly, with social marketing, there may be physical evidence to accompany any services received. This physical evidence may be the augmented product, such as nicotine patches to facilitate smoking cessation. It may also be other physical elements of the situation, such as the appearance of the waiting room for HIV testing. The goal should be to make all aspects of the desired behavior change as positive and pleasant as possible, and this may include adding or improving any physical evidence.

Concerns with the Four P's (or Seven P's) in Social Marketing

The four P's approach has received quite a bit of criticism for many reasons, including its lack of clarity and specificity (Van Waterschoot & Van den Bulte, 1992), nonetheless it has proven to be a handy tool for marketing scholars so its use endures. The four P's are frequently applied to social marketing, and here too their application has received criticism (see Peattie & Peattie, 2011), yet the functionality of the framework seems to offset the concerns for many social marketers. The cases in this book use a four P's (and sometimes seven P's) approach because we find the framework useful, though we acknowledge that it is also somewhat problematic.

We encourage you to carefully consider the benefits and drawbacks of the approach within each case, and to consider possible alternatives as well.

Community-Based Social Marketing

The field of psychology offers a wealth of insight regarding why people make the choices they do. These insights can be extremely valuable to social marketers. McKenzie-Mohr (2000) has proposed a social marketing framework to ensure that social marketers apply psychological theories to their efforts, to maximize their effectiveness. This framework, called community-based social marketing (CBSM), was originally focused on environmental issues, but the general principles can be applied to any social marketing effort. CBSM proposes that social marketing efforts should begin by identifying barriers to the desired behavior, similar to any social marketing approach. The difference, however, is the strong emphasis CBSM places on identifying underlying psychological theories that help us to understand and explain the behavior, and identifying effective means of overcoming the barriers. CBSM stresses the need to perform formative research (research to help you develop or form the program) in order to identify these barriers (research is discussed further in Chap. 3), and from here to develop the program. The next step is to pilot test the program, to be sure it will be effective before fully rolling it out. Changes should be made to the program, based on the results of the pilot study, and then the program is ready for implementation. The final step is to evaluate the program's success through outcome or evaluative research.

Performing formative research within the target community and conducting a pilot study of the program within the target community allow social marketers to develop a more effective program. In addition, these steps allow social marketers to develop inclusive programs, whereby they are truly listening to the needs and desires of those they are seeking to help. In this way, social marketing can be done "with" the target audience, rather than "to" the target audience.

Ethics

Social marketing is filled with ethical dilemmas. Many may already have occurred to you as you read this chapter. Others will come to you as you read actual cases later in this book. A social marketer should always be looking for and proactively responding to ethical concerns. Some may be relatively easy to address, but most will not. Some ethical concerns tug at the very fiber of social marketing. We do not believe that there are right (or wrong) answers here, but in this section we raise some of the questions that you should consider as you move forward with social marketing. Here, we identify some of what we feel are the largest and most compelling arguments, recognizing that there are many other very important ethical issues that we do not address.

Social Marketing as Manipulation

First and foremost is the practice of social marketing itself. Some see it as manipulative, and view manipulation as bad by definition. We believe there is an element of truth to this. In social marketing, we seek to influence behavior. It may be only a small step from influencing to manipulating. Social marketing supporters will argue at this point that it is "for their own good" or perhaps "for the greater good." The counterargument to this is that many historical efforts were performed for these reasons, and we now see the error of those efforts—forced sterilization, lobotomies, and forcing indigenous children into residential schools are a few examples of misguided efforts to benefit individuals and society.

When considering whether social marketing is manipulative, it is perhaps appropriate to consider the larger societal context. Many social marketing programs are developed to counter the effects of commercial marketing efforts. If you view social marketing as manipulative, then commercial marketing must certainly be manipulative. Is it appropriate to use manipulation to counter manipulation? Taking this a step further, consider commercial marketing efforts that go beyond manipulation into the realm of deception. Sadly, a number of large-scale lies come to mind. Volkswagen has intentionally installed devices to cheat government-mandated emissions (Blackwelder, Coleman, Colunga-Santoyo, Harrison, & Wozniak, 2016). The sugar industry funded questionable research to implicate fat intake as a culprit in heart disease, while covering up the negative effects of their own product (Kearns, Schmidt, & Glanz, 2016). Major financial institutions were pressuring their personnel to sell additional, unneeded products to customers, and many did so without customer knowledge or consent (Johnson, 2017) and in fact financial institutions around the world were implicated in various forms of deception (Luong, 2018). A social marketing program that discourages driving in the interest of the environment, one that discourages sugar intake, or one that promotes financial literacy may be an appropriate response. Nonetheless, social marketing should never be manipulative. Social marketing is intended to influence behavior through informed, voluntary, and ethical means. Social marketing can encourage and incentivize, but it must not cross into manipulation. Each and every social marketer is beholden to this principle and must assure their practices remain ethical.

Social Marketing as Hegemony

A second argument against social marketing relates to the question of who is deciding what for whom. Generally, a group with more power is deciding how a group with less power should behave. Often, the decision makers do not come from the target audience's social or ethnic group, sometimes not even from their country. This may suggest an inappropriate hegemony. Social marketing best practice suggests that program development always involve the target audience through research and consultation, to avoid or minimize these concerns. The community-based social marketing model (CBSM) described above offers a method for this. Consultative, formative research should be conducted to access the voices of the target audience. These voices should be honored when developing a social marketing program. In addition to avoiding an inappropriately paternalistic or hegemonic approach, this consultation will also result in a more effective program, one that is much more likely to gain acceptance from the target audience.

On the other hand, rather than being concerned with who is targeted for social marketing programs, there can be concern with who is not targeted. Social marketing uses effort and resources to improve the situation of individuals and communities. When one audience is targeted, it necessarily means that others are not. If the program effectively offers benefit, then the non-targeted groups are in effect being relatively disadvantaged. This is the troubling reality faced by any one responsible for distributing limited resources. Formative research is again a valuable tool to counter this concern. Research can suggest which groups are at greatest risk, and which are likely to attain the greatest benefit from the limited resources. These factors must be weighed when determining a target audience. This approach does not change the fact that some groups will receive the social marketing benefits while others will not, but it does add reason and rationale to the distribution of scarce resources.

Another ethical concern with social marketing involves uncertainty of the outcome. What if the effort fails? Perhaps the program will not be effective, and limited resources will have been wasted, when they could have been put to a better use. Even if the program is successful, how does one know that was the best use for the funds? All social marketing efforts should be planned and executed with the highest level of rigor, to guard against wasting precious and limited resources. Here again, research is important. Conducting research throughout the process can help to develop program design and assess effectiveness, allowing you to make informed changes if the program fails to perform as expected.

Concern with the Social Marketing Message
Sometimes it is the message itself that prompts concern. Social marketing efforts often communicate social norms. Social norms indicate to a target population what the "average" person does. This helps people to gauge and adjust their behavior (Cialdini, Kallgren, & Reno, 1991). For example, if teenagers learn that, despite tall tales being told, their peers are not actually having sex at high rates, then they will feel less pressure to have sex. Though effective for the group who had overestimated the norm, this effect can backfire for those who had underestimated the norm, and may lead them toward undesirable behaviors (Werch et al., 2000). For example, if a teen learns that they are well below the norm for drinking alcohol, they may choose to increase their alcohol intake. In this way, the use of social norms in social marketing can backfire. It is possible though to avoid this boomerang effect with proper execution (Schultz, Nolan, Cialdini, Goldstein, & Griskevicius, 2007).

Fear appeals have long been used in social marketing efforts. This appeal type often depicts a frightening and/or gory scene in order to discourage a behavior. Such messages can be upsetting and distressful. Research suggests that in order to be effective, fear appeals must contain several specific components—fear alone is not enough (Witte & Allen, 2000). Even when a fear appeal is well executed, it may be unnecessary. Research on HIV suggests that if individuals are already scared about a risk, there is little benefit in trying to scare them further with fear appeals (Muthusamy, Levine, & Weber, 2009). Fear appeals tend to be overused and they are often ineffective. Unless research demonstrates a clear and non-damaging benefit for the use of fear appeals, it may be best to avoid their use in social marketing.

Social Marketing Partnerships
Consumers increasingly expect companies to be socially responsible. This can take many forms, but one of these is to support a "good cause" (Cone/Ebiquity, 2015). To meet these expectations, companies are becoming involved in social marketing efforts in various ways; Patagonia's Worn Well campaign in Chap. 12 is a good example of this. Patagonia encourages consumers to keep their clothing longer, to reduce fashion waste going to the landfill or garbage dump. To facilitate, they offer mobile clothing repair services. In some cases, companies partner with non-profit organizations in order to engage with social marketing efforts. The airline Jet Blue, for example, facilitates customer donations to carbonfund.org to offset the carbon emissions created from their flights. Similarly, Aquafina is working with schools on a recycling program, and Sam's Club is taking back used coats to give to those in need (examples from Engage for Good's (ND) Halo Award winners, http://engageforgood.com). These are all examples of companies engaging in social marketing efforts. In programs such as these, the fit between the company and the cause can impact the effectiveness of the program. The preceding were all examples of negative fit. That is, the company actually causes the problem they are addressing in the program (Basil, Runte, & Liebetrau, 2018). Sometimes companies partner with causes in an effort to legitimize their negative behaviors. Should social marketers simply be happy for the support? Or should they refuse to partner with those who caused the problem in the first place? This is an ethical dilemma that most likely will depend on the situation and the social marketer, but it should be considered thoroughly and carefully.

Many other important ethical issues in social marketing exist but are not addressed here. For further study in this area, we encourage you to see Alan Andreasen's book, Ethics in Social Marketing (2001).

Appendix: Additional Resources for the Fundamentals of Social Marketing

Janelle Marietta-Vasquez
This appendix provides supplementary resources online to help better define social marketing and the components needed to conduct social marketing programs. This is a list of online resources to help you understand each step of the social marketing process. We note that online resources and links change rapidly, and therefore it is possible that some of the links provided may no longer be available.

1. Audience Segmentation

This Web page from the USA Centers for Disease Control and Prevention discusses the importance of identifying the population segments and audience. https://www.cdc.gov/healthcommunication/audience/index.html

The Health Compass Web site provides a how-to-guide on audience segmentation. https://www.thehealthcompass.org/how-to-guides/how-do-audience-segmentation

This video, taken from the World Social Marketing Conference in Washington in May 2017, discusses branding and segmentation in social marketing. Jeff Jordan, Founder of Rescue Social Change Group, provides specific examples of segmentation in youth and how to create targeted social marketing campaigns. https://www.youtube.com/watch?v=Z28al_fsW40

In the Marketing Review Final Report prepared for the National Institute for Health and Clinical Excellence created by the University of Stirling, they describe the process of how to segment and target your audience. On page 16, point 4, they describe three criteria for defining your segmented audience. https://www.nice.org.uk/guidance/ph6/evidence/behavior-change-review-6-social-marketing-pdf-369664530

2. Benefits and Barriers

In Chap. 7 of Lee and Kotler's Up and Out of Poverty: The Social Marketing Solution, they discuss benefits and barriers. On pages 168 and 171, they provide tables clearly identifying the types of barriers and benefits within a social marketing campaign. https://nscpolteksby.ac.id/ebook/files/Ebook/Business%20Administration/Up%20and%20Out%20of%20Poverty%20The%20Social%20Marketing%20Solution%20(2009)/9.%20Chapter%207%20-%20Understanding%20Barriers-Benefits%20and%20the%20Competition%20for%20Change.pdf

Fostering Sustainable Behavior: Community-based social marketing Web site, they have created a guide to identifying barriers and benefits. This guide shows how to conduct research in order to identify benefits and barriers perceived by the target audience. http://www.cbsm.com/pages/guide/step-2:-identifying-barriers-and-benefits/

This article by sustainable brands discusses the importance of perceived benefits and barriers from the perspective of the target audience. It provides examples of perceived value to provide more context to these terms. https://www.sustainablebrands.com/news_and_views/behavior_change/changing-behavior-through-social-marketing

The Division of Pollution Prevention and Environmental Assistance provides a sheet with specific examples of barriers within a recycling program. http://www.p2pays.org/socialmarketing/barriers.asp

3. Four Ps of Social Marketing

Product
In this PowerPoint, the Community Women's Health Education Centre of Tulane University, demonstrates how product is identified within a social marketing

campaign. It provides examples and shows how product differs in social marketing and commercial marketing campaigns. http://womenshealth.tulane.edu/uploads/ Social_Marketing_and_the_4_Ps_version_2-1389204479.pdf

In this online booklet *Social Marketing: Behavior Change Marketing in New Zealand*, presented at the Social Marketing Conference in Wellington in 2003, New Zealand social marketers Tracey Bridge of Senate Communication Counsel and Nick Farland of the Bridge provide a detailed three-step guide to social marketing. On page 14, they provide a clear example of a social marketing campaign targeting binge drinking, and demonstrate how product is used to support behavior change. http://www.nzaf.org.nz/assets/ee-uploads/files/20_socialmarketing.pdf

Price
This blog article, Incentives for Change in Public Health and Social Marketing Programs, discusses price in more detail, with two cases to demonstrate the use of charging nominal fees in public health social marketing initiatives: http://socialmarketing.blogs.com/r_craiig_lefebvres_social/price/

The Community Tool Box, Social Marketing and Sustainability of the Initiative discusses costs in Sect. 6. This section demonstrates an individual's decision process and how they weigh the costs and benefits of adopting a desired behavior. https://ctb.ku.edu/en/table-of-contents/sustain/social-marketing/promote-behavior-change/main

Place
"Right Place, Right Time" marketing approach is discussed in this exchange article. This article emphasizes the importance of strategic placement of messaging in any marketing campaign. These principles can be applied in social marketing to ensure desired behavior is adopted. https://exchange.cim.co.uk/editorial/the-rise-of-the-right-place-right-time-marketer/

In the online booklet *Social Marketing: Behavior Change Marketing in New Zealand* mentioned above, New Zealand social marketers Tracey Bridge and Nick Farland provide an example for the Retirement Commission program on page 15, showing how the "place" p was adjusted to better meet the needs of the target audience. http://www.nzaf.org.nz/assets/ee-uploads/files/20_socialmarketing.pdf

Promotion
In the Marketing Review Final Report to the National Institute for Health and Clinical Excellent (NICE), created by the University of Stirling, they provide detail on the use of promotion and promotional channels used by food marketers to reach children (page 36, 5.1). How can we use our knowledge of commercial promotion to strengthen counter social marketing campaigns? https://www.nice.org.uk/guidance/ph6/evidence/behavior-change-review-6-social-marketing-pdf-369664530

Richtopia provides eight examples of social marketing promotional material used within campaigns. These examples demonstrate eight distinctly different topics and how promotional materials can effectively get a message across to their target audience. https://richtopia.com/strategic-marketing/what-is-social-marketing-how-does-it-work

This list of campaign videos and print materials provided by Brogan and Partners offers 21 examples of social marketing campaign promotional materials. https://brogan.com/blog/21-creative-social-marketing-campaigns

4. Ethics in Social Marketing

This was a presentation at the Social Marketing Workshop for the National Social Marketing Centre entitled Inequalities and Ethical Considerations in Social Marketing. It clearly and simply identifies key issues in ethical social marketing. https://pdfs.semanticscholar.org/presentation/7f15/23b0099a88acaa9cf6809d8db344859596fe.pdf

This extensive report prepared by Lynne Eagle for the National Social Marketing Centre (NSMC) defines ethics, offers ethical frameworks, and identifies key areas in targeting where ethical dilemmas often occur. http://www.thensmc.com/sites/default/files/public-files/NSMC_social_marketing_ethics.pdf

This academic conference paper by Jones and Hall examines community complaints about social marketing efforts in Australia and New Zealand from an ethical perspective. https://ro.uow.edu.au/cgi/viewcontent.cgi?referer=https://www.google.ca/&httpsredir=1&article=1528&context=hbspapers

5. Objective Setting

The National Social Marketing Centre provides an article outlining the process in setting objectives for a social marketing campaign. http://www.thensmc.com/content/define-behavioral-goals-and-objectives-1

This short article from Dorie Clark at Duke University discusses the importance of having clear behavior, knowledge, and belief objectives. https://www.huffingtonpost.com/dorie-clark/social-marketing-goals_b_1011641.html

This short video from Hootsuite focuses on social media and commercial marketing, but the information is useful for social marketers as well. It discusses how to create goals and objectives, and the importance of identifying KPIs (key performance indicators). https://hootsuite.com/education/courses/social-marketing/strategy/objectives-kpis

6. Research, Monitoring, and Evaluation

This article from the Centre for Research and Education on Violence Against Women and Children, provides a step-by-step guide on the research, monitoring and evaluation of a social marketing campaign, specifically using Violence Against

Women as the case study. http://www.vawlearningnetwork.ca/research-monitoring-and-evaluating-vaw-social-marketing-campaigns

This article on testing, dissemination, and evaluation of a social marketing campaign, is taken from the article series, Principles of Social Marketing provided by FrogDog marketing firm in Houston, Texas. This article series covers various social marketing topics, with a guide on dissemination and evaluation techniques to implement in a campaign. https://frog-dog.com/social-marketing-testing-dissemination-and-evaluation/

7. Social Marketing as a Field of Study

This is a seminal academic article by Kotler and Zaltman (1971) which introduced the idea of social marketing. https://pdfs.semanticscholar.org/f2c7/1a435b2d3e54c6dbd179417570bed0b85893.pdf

The Web site Ninja Outreach created a simple comparison of Commercial Marketing to Social Marketing. The chart created simplifies the definition of product, objectives, and focus when conducting social marketing. This helps in understanding how to apply commercial marketing practices to social marketing and behavior change. https://ninjaoutreach.com/commercial-marketing-vs-social-marketing/

This video is an overview of marketing, and the various types of marketing including social marketing, presented by Dr. Philip Kotler, Professor at Northwestern University. https://www.youtube.com/watch?v=sR-qL7QdVZQ

8. Training and Tools for Social Marketing

The CDCynergy is an interactive training and decision-support tool specifically designed for staff and public health professionals to help plan communication programs within a health context. https://www.orau.gov/cdcynergy/soc2web/default.htm

Tools of Change are an interactive Web site which was supported by Health Canada and Natural Resources Canada to provide resources around the social marketing framework to support sustainable programs. http://www.toolsofchange.com/en/tools-of-change/

The Tools of Change workbook was developed in 1998 by Jay Kassirer as a resource for the National Round Table on the Environment and the Economy. http://www.cullbridge.com/Projects/TOOLSE.pdf

The National Social Marketing Center Web site provides step-by-step guides and resources to better understand each the decisions made in a social marketing campaign. http://www.thensmc.com/content/what-social-marketing-1

This one-page quick reference guide, developed by Nancy Lee and Philip Kotler, explains social marketing and the 10-step guide to planning. It provides easy to apply steps and definitions of key social marketing terms and theories. https://www.socialmarketingservice.com/site/assets/files/1010/socmkt_primer.pdf

This article developed for the CDC's Healthy Community Program, provides tips for implementing social marketing on a budget. https://www.cdc.gov/nccdphp/dch/programs/healthycommunitiesprogram/tools/pdf/social_marketing.pdf

The National Clearinghouse developed the Social Marketing Toolkit, specifically designed to build capacity of change agents within the school setting. It offers resources on developing a campaign. https://supportiveschooldiscipline.org/learn/reference-guides/social-marketing-toolkit

The Community Tool Box step-by-step guide to implementing a social marketing campaign. https://ctb.ku.edu/en/implement-social-marketing-effort

9. Overview of Social Marketing

This is a practice-oriented guide provided by the National Social Marketing Centre that gives a brief yet relatively comprehensive overview of one approach to the social marketing process:
http://www.thensmc.com/sites/default/files/Big_pocket_guide_2011.pdf

This article published in the Journal of Public Administration discusses and provides a guide for the development of a social marketing plan specific to health campaigns. This article provides an overview on the use of social marketing in the health field. https://www.researchgate.net/publication/290648934_Developing_Social_Marketing_Plan_for_Health_Promotion

This video is a presentation from the 2013 World Social Marketing Conference in Toronto. Jeff Jordan, founder of Rescue Social Change Group, explains the difference between commercial marketing and behavior change marketing. https://www.youtube.com/watch?v=EcPcrPFhqPA

References

Alderson, W. (1957). *Marketing behavior and executive action*. Homewood, IL: Richard D. Irwin, Inc.

Andreasen, A. R. (Ed.). (2001). *Ethics in social marketing*. Washington, DC: Georgetown University Press.

Basil, D. Z., Runte, M., & Liebetrau, J. (2018). Environmental cause marketing. In H. Borland, A. Lindgreen, J. Vanhamme, F. Maon, V. Ambrosini, & B. Palacios-Florencio (Eds.), *Business strategies for sustainability: A research anthology*. Abingdon: Routledge.

Blackwelder, B., Coleman, K., Colunga-Santoyo, S., Harrison, J. S., & Wozniak, D. (2016). *The Volkswagen scandal*. Case study. University of Richmond: Robins School of Business.

Booms, B. H., & Bitner, M. J. (1981). Marketing strategies and organizational structures for service firms. In J. H. Donnelly & W. R. George (Eds.), *Marketing of services* (pp. 47–51). Chicago: American Marketing Association.

Cialdini, R. B., Kallgren, C. A., & Reno, R. R. (1991). A focus theory of normative conduct: A theoretical refinement and re-evaluation. *Advances in Experimental Social Psychology, 24*, 201–234.

Cone/Ebiquity. (2015). 2015 Cone Communications/Ebiquity Global CSR Study. Boston, MA: Cone Communications LLC. Retrieved from http://www.conecomm.com/research-blog/2015-cone-communications-ebiquity-global-csr-study.

Engage for Good. (ND). *Halo awards*. http://engageforgood.com. Accessed July 19, 2017.

Hammonds, K. H. (2001). Michael Porter's big ideas. *Fast Company*. https://www.fastcompany.com/42485/michael-porters-big-ideas. Accessed August 14, 2018.

Johnson, E. (2017). "We are all doing it". Employees at Canada's big 5 banks speak out about pressure to dupe customers. *Radio Canada*. https://www.cbc.ca/news/business/banks-upselling-go-public-1.4023575. Accessed August 14, 2018.

Kearns, C. E., Schmidt, L. A., & Glanz, S. A. (2016). Sugar industry and coronary heart disease research: A historical analysis of internal industry documents. *Journal of the American Medical Association, 176*(11), 1680–1685.

Kotler, P. (1972). A generic concept of marketing. *The Journal of Marketing, 36*(2), 46–54.

Kotler, P., Armstrong, G., Saunders, J., & Wong, V. (1999). *Principles of marketing* (Second European Edition ed.). Upper Saddle River: Prentice Hall Inc.

Kotler, P., & Zaltman, G. (1971). Social marketing: an approach to planned social change. *Journal of marketing, 35*(3), 3–12.

Lee, N. R., & Kotler, P. (2011). *Social marketing: Influencing behaviors for good*. Los Angeles: Sage.

Luong, S. (2018). Five banking scandals in the world that shook customer faith. *Vietnam Investment Review*. http://www.vir.com.vn/five-banking-scandals-in-the-world-that-shook-customer-faith-56628.html. Accessed August 14, 2018.

McCarthy, E. J. (1964). *Basic marketing, a managerial approach*. Homewood, IL: Richard D. Irwin, Inc.

McKenzie-Mohr, D. (2000). Fostering sustainable behavior through community-based social marketing. *American Psychologist, 55*(5), 531.

McKenzie-Mohr, D. (2011). *Fostering sustainable behavior: An introduction to community-based social marketing*. Gabriola Island: New Society Publishers.

Muthusamy, N., Levine, T. R., & Weber, R. (2009). Scaring the already scared: Some problems with HIV/AIDS fear appeals in Namibia. *Journal of Communication, 59*(2), 317–344.

Peattie, K., & Peattie, S. (2011). The social marketing mix—A critical review. In *The Sage handbook of social marketing* (pp. 152–166).

Ries, A., & Trout, J. (2001). *Positioning. The battle for your mind*. New York: McGraw-Hill.

Rothschild, M. L. (1999). Carrots, sticks, and promises: A conceptual framework for the management of public health and social issue behaviors. *The Journal of Marketing, 63*(4), 24–37.

Rothschild, M. L., Mastin, B., & Miller, T. W. (2006). Reducing alcohol-impaired driving crashes through the use of social marketing. *Accident Analysis and Prevention, 38*(6), 1218–1230. https://doi.org/10.1016/j.aap.2006.05.010.

Schultz, P. W., Nolan, J. M., Cialdini, R. B., Goldstein, N. J., & Griskevicius, V. (2007). The constructive, destructive, and reconstructive power of social norms. *Psychological Science, 18*(5), 429–434.

Van Waterschoot, W., & Van den Bulte, C. (1992). The 4P classification of the marketing mix revisited. *The Journal of Marketing, 56*(4), 83–93.

Werch, C. E., Pappas, D. M., Carlson, J. M., DiClemente, C. C., Chally, P. S., & Sinder, J. A. (2000). Results of a social norm intervention to prevent binge drinking among first-year residential college students. *Journal of American College Health, 49*(2), 85–92.

Witte, K., & Allen, M. (2000). A meta-analysis of fear appeals: Implications for effective public health campaigns. *Health Education & Behavior, 27*(5), 591–615.

Research and Evaluation in Social Marketing

3

Michael D. Basil

Chapter Overview

The wide variety of ways of evaluating social marketing efforts can be intimidating to a new social marketer but empowering to those more familiar with the variety of methods. However, research is essential for a successful social marketing program. Each type of research has its own use, and you want to use that which is most appropriate for the questions you need to answer. Time and money are typically limited. One strategy is to think about what you'd most like to know at every stage of the process. First, use formative research before beginning the program to determine what we currently know (secondary research) and what we would most like to know about what people are doing, and why. Before engaging time, effort, and money, we should find out what people think about this possible approach. Second, process research is needed to determine how things are going during the program. It is better to evaluate the effort as it is going than to wait until the effort is over to realize a mistake. As the saying goes, "A stich in time saves nine." Finally, after the social market effort has concluded, outcome evaluation is conducted to determine what succeeded and what did not. This helps us to understand what should be repeated, what should be changed, and what should be eliminated next time. Social marketers should make use of any or several of the large variety of available research methods depending on what best suits their particular question. An apt quote from David Ogilvy, the advertiser who co-founded Ogilvy, a major international advertising agency, is "People who ignore research are as dangerous as generals who ignore...enemy signals." That is, research should be a servant who helps us learn and improve our social marketing efforts before we start, as we go along, and at the end of the effort.

M. D. Basil (✉)
Dhillon School of Business, University of Lethbridge, Lethbridge, Canada
e-mail: michael.basil@uleth.ca

© Springer Nature Switzerland AG 2019
D. Z. Basil et al. (eds.), *Social Marketing in Action*,
Springer Texts in Business and Economics,
https://doi.org/10.1007/978-3-030-13020-6_3

45

Introduction

Social marketing efforts do not only benefit from research, but research is essential to effective social marketing. This research can be done at several points in time. Before the program begins (or, as it is often labeled, intervention), you can find out what people are already doing, why they are doing, what they are doing, how they see the desired behavior, and whether they have any desire to change; during the intervention, you can ask how well your effort is working, and what they think about your social marketing intervention; afterward, you can discover how effective the intervention was, where it succeeded and where it didn't. You can also understand which of the social marketing tools were employed in a given intervention and compare that to how successful the effort was. That is, research is critical in finding out what people do and why, and this provides an understanding of what you should do, as well as what worked, what didn't, and why. This chapter will review the major categories and approaches to social marketing research. In the appendix following this chapter, online resource links are provided for further guidance in research and evaluation.

According to leading social marketing theorists, two distinguishing characteristics of social marketing are that we have a customer focus and that we provide something of value to people—an exchange (Grier & Bryant, 2005; Lefebvre & Flora, 1988; Rothschild, 1999). To accomplish these goals, it is important to understand your audience. Research tells us what the audience is like and what they want. Ideally, this means not just their initial knowledge and behavior, but also their habits, motivations, and barriers. Overall, social marketers should understand *what* people are doing, *why* they are doing it, what might *motivate* people to act differently, their *reactions* to social marketing strategy ideas, and ultimately, examine what people actually *do* after our efforts. This range of evaluation possibilities can be characterized as *formative*, *process*, and *evaluation* research. Additionally, after a program has been conducted, we can evaluate which social marketing strategies were actually employed, in order to aid future programs. This practice has become known as "benchmarking."

Useful Forms of Research

There are a wide variety of research methods that are and can be employed to evaluate social marketing efforts. As a brief explanation, these approaches "diagnostic" research is used to identify problems and causes, while "evaluation" research is used to investigate the effectiveness of an effort. "Primary" data are collected for a particular problem or client but when these same data are then used for other purposes they become "secondary" data. "Qualitative" research and data are based on words, usually through talking directly with people, while "quantitative" research and data are based on numbers, which could be from counting things that occur in the environment (such as the number of television commercials showing unhealthy foods), measuring things such as a person's weight, or through surveys which ask people to answer some structured questions and then counts the number of people who mark a particular response such as "yes" or "no" or "strongly agree."

Formative Research

Formative research is diagnostic and undertaken before the social marketing effort is developed. Too often social marketing programs, especially many health interventions focus on education with the assumption that people behave the way they do as a result of a lack of knowledge, or sometimes because they be lacking in skills or values. Sometimes this is the case, but often it is not. For example, several countries are now requiring that children sit in approved protective seating while in automobiles. Formative research might investigate: (1) whether parents are aware of these laws, (2) whether they currently own child seats, (3) whether they currently use the child seats they own, or (4) for those who do not own child seats, if they are motivated to purchase these seats. If the results of the research show that parents are not aware of the law but would be eager to take protective measures to protect their children, such as purchasing these seats, then an educational approach can be taken. Social marketing efforts can center on providing information about these laws and the safety improvements offered by these seats. If, however, parents are aware of these laws and believe the seats would protect their children, but feel the seats are too expensive, then finding ways to reduce the costs of these seats for these parents would be an ideal strategy. If parents are aware, willing, and find the price acceptable, but find the seats hard to use, then social marketing efforts should probably focus on redesigning the seats to make them easier to use. In these cases, formative research is important in learning how to attack the problem. If the social marketing effort assumes that the issue was a lack of knowledge, then the educational efforts could succeed in the first situation, but not in the other two. This is why formative research is fundamentally important to social marketers and social marketing efforts.

The topic of obesity offers a good example of the importance of formative research. Some health efforts assume that people do not know what a healthy weight is, the advantages of maintaining a healthy weight, or why people gain weight. In these cases, interventions often focus on educating people about these factors. Yet many efforts that started with formative research have found that people know what a healthy weight is and want to maintain a healthy weight, yet they find themselves overweight or gaining weight despite their knowledge and motivation. In these cases, interventions should focus on providing easier access to healthy foods that are tasty, low cost, and convenient. An excellent example of this can be seen in Celebrity Chef Jamie Oliver's television miniseries, "Ministry of Food." This popular TV show focused on teaching people how to prepare healthy low-cost foods and developed programs which encouraged people to spread those recipes to others. In other cases, local food banks and gardening programs have also helped those who are knowledgeable and eager but might lack money or skills. Finally, structural changes such as providing nutrition information on packaged foods and in restaurants can also enable those who are knowledgeable and eager to make better choices. In each of these cases, formative research can help social marketers understand what the target audience needs in order to eat a healthier diet.

Typical areas of formative research examine awareness and knowledge—what do people know about the issue; motivation—how motivated and eager they are to do something about it; and opportunity—if they feel they are able to do a particular behavior or the barriers they feel stand in their way. Although knowledge is often seen as an antecedent to behavior, in many instances, knowledge is not required to change behavior. Specifically, there are "low-involvement" models which propose that when people do not care very much about the issue, it is best not to overload then with information. Instead, "dissonance models" such as the behavior–knowledge–attitude (B-A-K) approach where the marketer tries to start with behavior change (such as using free samples or coupons) and expects attitudes to change as a result, leading to new knowledge, are better approaches. Which approach may work best may hinge on people's involvement with the issue (Ray et al., 1973).

Formative research can be done in a variety of ways, including using existing data (which is called "secondary" research), conducting face-to-face qualitative interviews and focus groups, or by creating larger-scale measures such as counts or surveys. The choice between these methods often depends on how much is already known about the topic and population and how much precision is necessary. Secondary research is usually used to see what is already known about a topic or target market. Secondary research is often available for free and is relatively easy to access on the Internet or at the library, so all efforts should begin with some secondary research. Because qualitative research usually involves words, qualitative research is often a result of speaking with people, either individually in interviews, or in small groups known as focus groups. Sometimes short questionnaires ask people what they know, feel, or do. This approach is often used to generate new ideas or test intervention ideas. Questionnaires, meanwhile, are most typically used to get a sense of the prevalence of attitudes or behaviors in the audiences and to select a target market (Weinreich, 1996). One strategy is to begin with smaller-scale qualitative research where respondents can help you understand what they already know, how they think about the issue, and the vocabulary they use to discuss the topic, before moving on to apply these insights to understand how common or widespread knowledge, beliefs and behavior are, or how they are distributed in a population.

Commercial marketing often relies on formative research not only to understand the audience but also to test creative promotional concepts. The notion of concept testing can also be applied to social marketing, not only for promoting ideas, but for broader marketing ideas as well. For example, formative research could be used to see where people would think to look for social marketing products such as condoms or tick prevention products. If research shows that people do not look for these things in the right place, then the social marketer might consider offering them in the places where people tend to look.

A critical aspect of consumer-centered social marketing is understanding what people think, feel, and do and what they want to do. It may be best to think of social marketing not as an effort to tell people something, but rather as an effort to help solve the barriers they face in trying to do what they should do (McKenzie-Mohr, 2000, pp. 546–549). For example, formative research was used by the United States National Cancer Institute in a fruit and vegetable campaign to get a baseline measure of how many fruits and vegetables Americans typically ate. This was the basis for the "five-a-day" effort which encouraged people to eat five fruits or vegetables per day. The United States Centers for Disease Control and Prevention's Office of Nutrition and Physical Activity regularly conducts a nationwide Health-Styles survey which revealed that many people wanted to get more physical activity but did not feel they had enough time in their day. The social marketing effort that resulted was to list a variety of physical activities that they could do in the course of their day such as parking further away, taking the stairs at work, taking a walk at lunch, and encouraging employers to provide more opportunities for people to be active at work.

Another example of the value of formative research in social marketing can be seen in Mike Rothschild's "Road Crew" drunk driving efforts in Wisconsin (Rothschild, Mastin, & Miller, 2006). Before starting the program, small focus groups were conducted in bars in small towns where the risk of drunk driving was highest. The results suggested that young men were aware of the risks of drunk driving but did not see any good alternatives to getting home from a bar besides driving, due to the high cost and difficulty of other solutions. As a result of the formative research, the program decided to buy used limousines in order to provide low-cost transportation to and from local bars.

Process Evaluations

After formative research has suggested a strategy and as it is being implemented, the next step is to evaluate the program's progress. Formative evaluation is done before the program, whereas process evaluation is done during the program. It provides information about the ongoing efforts, or the process. Process evaluations can include examining levels of the current awareness and knowledge that arise from ongoing social marketing efforts, examining people's interest in the topic, assessing their motivations to do what is being advocated, learning what opportunities they feel they have to perform the desired behavior, or their current behavior, or any other factor of interest to the program. Often process evaluations are the least expensive type of evaluation research. In commercial marketing, tests are often used to assess the market potential for particular products by introducing the product in trials and measuring sales in a few selected locations. Similarly, commercial advertising research makes use of a variety of methods to assess the effectiveness of advertising. "Broadcast tests" examine memory for the message, often in the form of "day-after recall" measures. Another way to assess the effectiveness of advertising messages is to run the ads in a small area and look at actual behavior rates such as the number of pizza orders after the advertisement is broadcast. In the case of social marketing, at its simplest instantiation, imagine trying to gauge the effectiveness of parenting classes. In this case, you can gain insights into how things are going in a variety of ways including enrollment levels (which may tell you about the appeal of the program or the effectiveness of your promotions), attendance rates (which may speak to people's satisfaction with the form or content of the classes), or asking attendees what they remember (what was learned and retained because what people are learning is a simple evaluation tool in any educational environment).

A more formal evaluation of the process can make use of measures that evaluate awareness and memory for the messages over time. These are called "tracking" questions and are usually done by drawing a sample of people and asking them what they think, feel, or are currently doing. Alternatively, if you are interested in a broader population, process research may involve a survey. You may need to conduct your own survey, though sometimes you can "piggyback" onto another survey that is being conducted by your own organization or by another organization with the same target audience. Surveys can give an estimate of knowledge, attitudes, or behavior of either the target group of the overall population. Rothschild's "Road Crew" effort kept track of the number of rides given to ensure that the program was working and having an immediate impact (Rothschild et al., 2006). Seeing how many people were booking rides provided immediate feedback on the effort. Specifically, they examined if the number of rides being booked, if the general appeal was good, and if people were aware of the effort. If rides were low, additional research should examine awareness of the effort because this would be the easiest to measure (by asking a few people in the targeted bars), and if awareness was high, this would suggest the program was not sufficiently attractive.

Other examples of process evaluations include the National Cancer Institute's use of tracking questions during the five-a-day campaign. They assessed awareness "Do you remember seeing…"; knowledge "How many servings *should* people eat per day," attitudes "Are you interested in…" and actual behavior "Are you trying…" "How many fruits and vegetables did you eat yesterday?" Another process evaluation occurred in an intervention aimed at children called the "Gimme 5" program which attempted to get children to eat more fruits and vegetables (Baranowski et al., 2000). For this effort, the process evaluations included a wide variety of methods including an examination of (1) whether teachers implemented the recommendations contained in each lesson, (2) school lunch offerings on menus and what was actually offered in the cafeteria (which were then compared to reported fruit and vegetables consumption in food diaries), (3) parent telephone interviews that asked about children's mentioning the information or sharing materials, and (4) point-of-purchase events counting store activities, attendance for these activities, and interviewing the produce manager (Baranowski et al., 2000).

Other process evaluations for five-a-day could have examined how the program was working with partners by assessing the number of supermarkets who chose to place the five-a-day logo on their produce bags, and the amount of products sold. In another example, USA's Office of National Drug Control Policy tracked people's concern over children's drug use to evaluate whether their advertising efforts were working and to decide on the optimal level of exposure.

Some social marketing efforts have focused on increasing the availability of important health-related products, often in developing countries. In these cases, knowing product availability is as important as knowing target audience response. For example, several efforts have tried to get people to make use of condoms or mosquito netting. In these cases, process evaluations also involved monitoring the availability of social marketing products to consumers. This is important because efforts to increase the use of condoms and other contraceptives or mosquito netting would have failed if these programs had created interest, but the products were too expensive or unavailable. In these cases, had the social marketing efforts increased consumer interest and demand, even though the initial efforts to raise interest in the products had been successful, this would have been frustrating to consumers, and if judged only by sales or by other post-intervention measures, this would have probably been evaluated as an unsuccessful social marketing effort.

Outcome Evaluations

Finally, the form of research that social marketers are probably most familiar with is outcome evaluations—was the effort effective? Often these outcome measures are done at the behest of the funding agency. These evaluations can include any of the typical measures of what happened as a result of the social marketing effort. These can come in the form of outcome, output, and impact evaluations. Outcome evaluations might examine people's exposure, awareness, knowledge, attitude, or behaviors. Meanwhile, an "output" evaluation might keep track of sales figures such as the number of condoms or mosquito nets that were sold, or the number of pounds of cans, bottles, or papers that were recycled. These two forms of research can be seen as evaluating the efficacy or effectiveness of the social marketing effort. Impact evaluations are more rare and might examine the number of drunk driving arrests or accidents that occurred, or the number of lives that are estimated to have been saved by these efforts, perhaps even in terms of the cost efficiency of the effort. Regardless of what is measured, the goal of an outcome evaluation is to discover how effective the social marketing program was.

One social marketing program that has undergone considerable outcome evaluations is the five-a-day efforts. For example, the evaluation of the "Gimme 5" effort with children evaluated a 7-day food record as well as psychosocial measures from students, telephone interviews with parents, and observational assessments of fruit and vegetable consumption (Baranowski et al., 2000).

One effort at an impact evaluation can be seen in Rothschild's "Road Crew" effort. This program not only kept track of the number of rides but examined some of the efforts. The evaluation showed a significant shift in increases among rides (both output measures), but also demonstrated that the rides were most frequent among the target audience of 21–34 year olds. Perhaps most impressive, the results showed a 17% decline in alcohol-related crashes in the first year, and a projected cost savings of avoiding crashes and the costs of cleaning up after crashes. This type of outcome impact evaluation is very important in encouraging the state government to continue or even expand this program.

Often there is a belief in commercial marketing that the ultimate test of a venture is sales. Relying exclusively on a single outcome measure, however, is problematic for the reasons that can be seen in the contraceptive example in India above. Even if the promotion was wildly successful in generating widespread interest in these products, had the people not known where to buy the contraceptives, had they not been available, or had they been priced too high, this effort would not have resulted in sales of the product. This example demonstrates why relying exclusively on behavior or sales is a risky strategy. Behavior and sales outcomes usually only happen when everything works, so it does not help you diagnose where failures may be occurring. Sometimes behavior change, or sales, can happen for reasons outside of your own efforts. For example, a popular movie might model the behavior change you are advocating. It would be misleading to fully attribute the behavior change to your own social marketing efforts; similarly, sometimes behavior change or sales does not occur as a result of other factors that are outside your control. For example, a neighborhood recycling center might be closed for road construction in the area. It would also be misleading to blame that on your social marketing efforts.

Some excellent outcome evaluations have demonstrated not only behavior change such as product ownership or use, but even more important or "higher-level" outcomes including actual reductions in risk factors or demonstrable health improvements. For example, the "Road Crew" effort showed lowered mortality rates, and other international efforts which involved the low-cost distribution of mosquito netting have been shown to reduce anemia and lower infant mortality (Alden, Basil, & Deshpande, 2011, p. 169). Finally, there are audits that evaluate the cost efficiency of efforts, that is, the value for money. Audits can be done internally or externally but are especially impressive and bound to impress any funding agency which could result in increased funding not only for the program in question but also result in greater recognition of the value of social marketing.

Benchmarking

The name "benchmark" is often used in other fields to refer to baseline measures. However, in 2002, in trying to discern the essential features of social marketing, Alan Andreasen proposed six criteria, he called them "benchmarks," that were important in evaluating or monitoring whether the efforts really constituted a full social marketing program (or simply gave lip service to the term social marketing). These six criteria were: 1. a behavior focus, 2. audience research, 3. segmentation of target audiences, 4. attractive and motivational exchanges, 5. all four Ps of the traditional marketing mix (not just advertising or communications), and 6. consideration of competition (Andreasen, 2002). The evaluation of whether these aspects were used in a program has become a popular approach to assess which program components are critical for program success. Typically, this "benchmarking" is undertaken after the social marketing effort has occurred. It is often used in meta-analyses of published research to compare the strategies that were used with the success of the effort (e.g., Carins & Rundle-Thiele, 2014; Cugelman, Thelwall, & Dawes, 2011; Gordon, McDermott, Stead, & Angus, 2006; Stead, Gordon, Angus, & McDermott, 2007).

Research studies evaluating a social marketing program's success have compared program outcomes to the number or variety of social marketing attributes. Overall the evidence supports the notion that making use of more social marketing strategies within a program is associated with a greater level of success. Therefore, this benchmarking research can be interpreted to say that social marketing is effective in general, and the more social marketing strategies that are employed the more effective the interventions. Perhaps later efforts at benchmarking will eventually be able to identify the most critical aspects of social marketing, or even put them in order of importance for different topic areas. The ultimate goal of these benchmarking analyses is to identify essential program components in order to guide the development of future programs and to increase their potential for success.

Which Type of Research Should I Use?

As a pragmatic field, social marketing should draw on the full range of research data and methods that are available. This should involve making use of both existing secondary data as well as collecting new primary data. This can and should involve both qualitative and quantitative data. We should also make use of any of the other approaches such as content analysis, or even more novel strategies such as visual and physiological approaches as best suits our questions. The strategy here is to have as broad a research toolbox as possible, and to use whichever tool best suits the question at hand. Few people are well-versed in all of these approaches—that is one contribution of a team approach in social marketing. By recruiting a wide variety of contributors, especially researchers, we can bring together various forms of expertise.

When does each form of research make the most sense? A flowchart can provide a helpful heuristic. This flowchart is presented in Fig. 3.1.

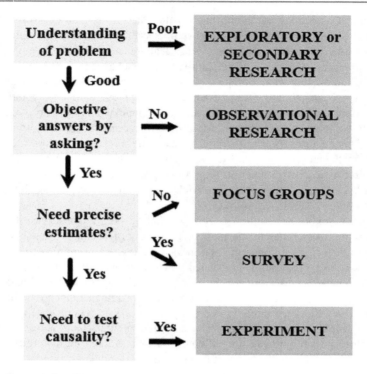

Fig. 3.1 Research flowchart

When little is known about the topic at hand, a literature review is often a good starting point. Starting with what we already know is always advised. A search of existing data or *secondary research* will often turn up a good deal of information on the topic that can be very valuable. In public health, it is common to use epidemiological data or studies to provide an "evidence base" for interventions. Which behaviors are costing the most in terms of years of life, quality of life, or financial costs? Is there evidence for this behavior as being alterable? Next, armed with that information, we often move on to gain an understanding of people's thoughts, attitudes, and behaviors. If we need deeper insights into why behaviors are (or are not) occurring, but we do not need precise measures of how many people are doing this, then *qualitative* research such as interviews often fits the bill. *Interviews* with the public, as Rothschild et al. (2006) did with his "Road Crew" effort, can provide social marketers with a deeper understanding of the issue. Commercial research firms often make use of qualitative research such as focus groups to gain insights into consumer thought processes. If you need a more precise estimate of the prevalence of knowledge, attitudes, or behaviors, that is, you want to estimate what percentage of people think, feel, or act in a certain way, then a larger-scale *quantitative* effort is called for, often in the form of a *survey*. If you want to know about a large segment or the public in general, there are commercial marketing companies that specialize in large-scale surveys that can be used to conduct original research or to "piggyback" a few questions within someone else's survey. If you are concerned about people's ability to remember or tell you what they are doing, often because behavior can be automatic, then observational or visual research may be in order. Several years ago, a toothpaste company was interested in people's teeth brushing. After some initial interviews, the company became skeptical that people could tell them honestly how long they brushed, so the company paid people to install cameras in their bathrooms from which they calculated how often people brushed, for how long, and if this varied across people. Sometimes, instead of asking, you have to *observe*. Then, armed with an understanding of the costs of people's behavior, and an understanding of why people are doing the things they are, social marketers can develop possible programs or interventions. Before fully launching the program, it is helpful to conduct small-scale *experiments* or pilot tests of the intervention. Using few participants, or a smaller town gives you the chance to test out your idea and see what works and what does not.

Appendix: Additional Resources for Research and Evaluation in Social Marketing

Michael Basil

This appendix provides supplementary information for the methods described in Chap. 3. A brief description of the link contents and online links is provided.

1. Formative Research

A primer on formative research, though not focused on social marketing: http://www.endvawnow.org/en/articles/1178-conducting-formative-research.html

An overview of formative research presented by the US National Institutes of Health https://www.ncbi.nlm.nih.gov/pmc/articles/PMC2475675/

2. Research Methods in Social Marketing

An overview of research methods used in a violence against women effort http://www.vawlearningnetwork.ca/research-monitoring-and-evaluating-vaw-social-marketing-campaigns

Another overview provided by Weinreich Communications
http://www.social-marketing.com/planning.html

Slides that review social marketing research methods https://www.slideshare.net/CharityComms/the-role-of-research-in-social-marketing

3. Outcome Evaluations

An overview of evaluation research provided by Weinreich Communications
http://www.social-marketing.com/evaluation.html
How outcome evaluations were used in the VERB campaign: https://www.
ajpmonline.org/article/S0749-3797(08)00254-7/fulltext

4. Social Marketing Benchmarking

A quick overview by the European Social Marketing Association https://
europeansocialmarketing.weebly.com/principles-of-social-marketing.html
National Social Marketing Centre: http://www.thensmc.com/file/234/download?
token=P9Vz-7GO

References

Alden, D., Basil, M., & Deshpande, S. (2011). Communications in social marketing. In *Sage handbook on social marketing*. Thousand Oaks, CA: Sage.
Andreasen, A. R. (2002). Marketing social marketing in the social change marketplace. *Journal of Public Policy & Marketing, 21*(1), 3–13.
Baranowski, T., Davis, M., Resnicow, K., Baranowski, J., Doyle, C., Lin, L. S., et al. (2000). Gimme 5 fruit, juice, and vegetables for fun and health: Outcome evaluation. *Health Education & Behavior, 27*(1), 96–111.
Carins, J. E., & Rundle-Thiele, S. R. (2014). Eating for the better: A social marketing review (2000–2012). *Public Health Nutrition, 17*(7), 1628–1639.
Cugelman, B., Thelwall, M., & Dawes, P. (2011). Online interventions for social marketing health behavior change campaigns: A meta-analysis of psychological architectures and adherence factors. *Journal of Medical Internet Research, 13*(1), e17.
Gordon, R., McDermott, L., Stead, M., & Angus, K. (2006). The effectiveness of social marketing interventions for health improvement: What's the evidence? *Public Health, 120*(12), 1133–1139.
Grier, S., & Bryant, C. A. (2005). Social marketing in public health. *Annual Review of Public Health, 26*, 319–339.
Lefebvre, C. R., & Flora, J. A. (1988). Social marketing and public health intervention. *Health Education Quarterly, 15*(3), 299–315.
McKenzie-Mohr, D. (2000). New ways to promote proenvironmental behavior: Promoting sustainable behavior: An introduction to community-based social marketing. *Journal of Social Issues, 56*(3), 543–554.
Ray, M. L., Sawyer, A. G., Rothschild, M. L., Heeler, R. M., Strong, E. C., & Reed, J. B. (1973). Marketing communication and the hierarchy-of-effects. In P. Clarke (Ed.), *New models for communication research*. Beverly Hills, CA: Sage.
Rothschild, M. L. (1999). Carrots, sticks, and promises: A conceptual framework for the management of public health and social issue behaviors. *The Journal of Marketing, 63*(4), 24–37.
Rothschild, M. L., Mastin, B., & Miller, T. W. (2006). Reducing alcohol-impaired driving crashes through the use of social marketing. *Accident Analysis and Prevention, 38*(6), 1218–1230.

Stead, M., Gordon, R., Angus, K., & McDermott, L. (2007). A systematic review of social marketing effectiveness. *Health Education, 107*(2), 126–191.

For Further Reading

Weinreich, N. K. (1996). A more perfect union: Integrating quantitative and qualitative methods in social marketing research. *Social Marketing Quarterly, 3*(1), 53–58.

Theory in Social Marketing

4

Michael D. Basil

Chapter Overview

As scientists, we try to derive theories to provide predictions on why things operate as they do. That is, we hope to understand a phenomenon by understanding the underlying system. In its most ideal form, we try to understand the general principles which underpin the phenomenon—to allow us to explain not only when something occurs and when it does not, but why. Ideally, this understanding will lead us to be able to make predictions not only about the particularistic phenomenon but lead up to generalizable knowledge about similar phenomena.

Introduction

Theory is important because it can be used in at least two ways. First, a theory is a form of generalized knowledge that allows us to understand important factors and make predictions—something we call "generalizability." That is, we hope that our theory "can be generalized through the design of theory-based interventions that are viable in the real world" and "used as a framework for designing and intervention" (Calder, Phillips, & Tybout, 1981, p. 198). In reference to this practical application of theory, Kurt Lewin, one of the founding fathers of social psychology, is often reported to have said, "There's nothing so practical as a good theory." Secondly, we try to test our theory where "falsification procedures are used to test the intervention under conditions that could cause it to fail in the real world" (Calder et al., 1981, p. 198). Rigorous testing is important because it allows us to see if the theory is

M. D. Basil (✉)
Dhillon School of Business, University of Lethbridge, Lethbridge, Canada
e-mail: michael.basil@uleth.ca

© Springer Nature Switzerland AG 2019
D. Z. Basil et al. (eds.), *Social Marketing in Action*,
Springer Texts in Business and Economics,
https://doi.org/10.1007/978-3-030-13020-6_4

Fig. 4.1 Research process

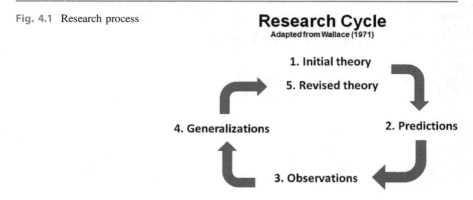

Research Cycle
Adapted from Wallace (1971)

supported. Current thinking in this area is that scientists never actually prove a theory, but simply build up more and more support for it with each test. This is because we realize that in science, the next test might find conflicting results. Popper's basic approach to the scientific method (1959) focuses on the importance of falsification as a critical means to test whether the theory is accurate. Both of these uses of theory are important in social marketing, and it is important to not only draw on theories for guidance, but also to test them in the real world, to see if they hold up under scrutiny. A visual illustration of this approach is shown in Fig. 4.1.

While social marketers draw primarily on commercial marketing strategies, social marketing is also a pragmatic field that is not limited to a single theory, approach, academic discipline, or even a single world view. In 1999, Bill Smith noted that the President of Uganda, when asked how his country dealt with the AIDS crisis said, "when there is a lion in the village, we raise the alarm" to use whatever methods are at their disposal. Similarly, social marketing is a practical field that brings a variety of theories to bear a variety of problems. To this end, this chapter will review some of the primary theories that are applied in social marketing and explain each as well as prepare the reader for the theories that are used in the cases that follow.

Exchange Theory

One of the most fundamental theories underlying the field of social marketing is exchange theory (Peattie & Peattie, 2003; Rothschild, 1999). From its original roots in economics, the notion of exchange is foundational to the field of marketing. According to exchange theory, people are willing to pay the price for things that they believe have value. Kotler (2000: 6–7) argues that there are five underlying requirements of exchange theory: 1. there are at least two parties, 2. each party has something that has value to the other party, 3. each party is free to accept or reject the exchange, 4. each party is willing to deal with the other party, and 5. each party can communicate and deliver on their promises. The notion of exchange can be conceptualized where people "weigh" the costs of a particular choice against the benefits. When the benefits are seen to outweigh the costs, people are likely to purchase the product. This metaphor is illustrated in Fig. 4.2.

Applied to the field of social marketing, the notion of "price" is broadened; however, the central postulate of exchange theory remains the same—that exchanges must be mutually beneficial. Social marketers must demonstrate that the perceived benefits outweigh the perceived costs for the voluntary behavior to become attractive (Maibach, 1993). As a result, exchange theory becomes the foundational theoretical tenant that underlies marketing and social marketing (Luca & Suggs, 2013; Truong, 2014), so we must keep this foundation in mind as we encourage people's behaviors (Rothschild, 1999).

In Chap. 9, Reis-Marques, Lages, and Caminati's case on encouraging entrepreneurship in a developing country proposes that exchange value can best be understood through a value creation wheel. As a result, value corresponds to specific benefits for each stakeholder including customers, suppliers, distributors, employees, shareholders, and other strategic partners. They further "drill down" to suggest that value can be further understood using the "DIANA" and "TIAGO" theoretical frameworks. Casais, Ferreira, and Proença's case on tax evasion in Portugal (Chap. 11) acknowledges that, "In order to encourage the voluntary compliance of invoice request with tax number, exchange theory in social marketing is important to demonstrate that the benefits outweigh the opportunity costs." In Chap. 15's Smile Train case in India by Sivakumar, the use of cleft palate surgery hinges on people's perceptions of the ratio of rewards to costs. By reducing the costs of the surgery, both financial and social, they encouraged more people to take advantage of the surgery. In social marketing, it is important to provide options to people and to do what we can to make the desired behavior more attractive. In "Hand Washing with Soap for a Healthier Vietnam" (Chap. 19), Doan and Truong also invoke exchange theory to understand the logic behind the effort.

Fig. 4.2 Exchange theory

Exchange Theory

There are other commercial marketing theories that are derived from exchange theory that are not as well known in social marketing. For example, Vitartis, Shipley, and March's case on The Bank of Cancer Research (Chap. 8) draws upon product differentiation theory and consumer choice theory. These theories derive from exchange theory and remind us of the importance of consumers' free choice in their actions. Although not stated explicitly, Bürklin's examination of Patagonia's "Better Than New" effort (Chap. 12) may be seen as drawing on the theories of exchange and differentiation to encourage people to stand out in the market and encourage customers to feel a connection to the Patagonia company.

Diffusion of Innovations

Originally developed by sociologists in the 1930s studying the adoption of hybrid corn seed, the theory of diffusion of innovations is an important approach in understanding the adoption of new products (Rogers, 2010). The theory proposes that the decision to adopt a new product or behavior is usually the result of a long series of events that starts with awareness and knowledge, then persuasion, a decision, then implementation and confirmation of that choice. The logic of this theory can be seen as expanding on exchange theory because adoption of a new product or behavior requires people's ability to see its advantages. Products or behaviors that have greater relative advantage, are more compatible with existing practice, less complex, can easily be tried in advance, and whose benefits are more observable are more likely to be adopted. Diffusion theory also makes predictions about the relative effectiveness of different channels of communication at different stages of the adoption process, such as mass communication in building awareness and personal communication in the final decision stage. It also makes predictions about what types of people are likely to be quicker to adopt a new product or practice—innovators, early adopters, the majority, and laggards (Fig. 4.3). The theory proposes the importance of "opinion leaders" in getting an innovation adopted by the majority of the public.

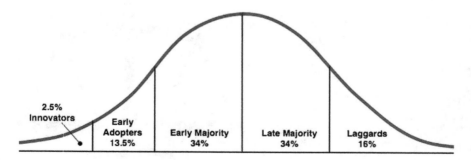

Fig. 4.3 Diffusion of innovations: distribution of adopters

Diffusion of innovations theory is often acknowledged in social marketing. For example, Dearing (2015) illustrated the importance of informal opinion leadership among health workers. Sundstrom (2014) demonstrated that diffusion of innovations theory is useful in understanding how women learn about various health issues. All in all, the diffusion of innovations theory is frequently applied in the social marketing context to understand the process through which behavior change occurs (Truong, 2014).

Diffusion of Innovations: Factors Increasing Adoption of New 'Products'

- Relative advantage over competing products
- Compatible with current behaviors
- Less complex
- Easy to try
- Observable benefits

Hughes, McConell, and Groner, in their case "A Community-Based Social Marketing Anti-Littering Campaign" (Chap. 23), explain the importance of diffusion theory in their efforts by identifying different target segments based on their role in the diffusion process. "Rogers argues that an innovation is communicated through certain channels over time among the members of a social system and different types of adopters accept an innovation at different points in time… In that sense the Green Crusaders, New Adults, and Acceptance Seekers could be likened to Innovators, Early Adopters and Early Majority while Apathetics and Digitally Disengaged are like the Late Majority and Laggards." In Nestlé's "Healthy Kids Programme" in India, the authors propose that, "The pretty low interest of the target audience justifies the need of Nestlé to approach the theory of diffusion of innovations… As a way to implement this scientific approach, Nestlé should foster its effort to raise awareness among teenagers and make them understand that changing behaviors in terms of nutrition is a prior condition for their health in the long run." This strategy draws on the notion of differentially involved publics and therefore the value of targeting particular segments. Reis-Marques, Lages, and Caminati's case on encouraging entrepreneurship in a developing country (Chap. 9) proposes a means to encourage innovation through diffusion via communication, which will result in making people and organizations more aware of the entrepreneurship. Although not explicitly evoked, Kureshi and Thomas's Lifebuoy's "Help a Child Reach 5" (Chap. 17) explained that their effort, "was to bring about a social transformation in villages through hand washing with soap by identifying and mobilizing relevant influencers like mothers, teachers, and community leaders." This notion of reaching important influencers in the community is central to diffusion theory and can be seen as applying principles of that theory to social marketing.

Involvement

Involvement is an important aspect of how people process messages. This theory was uncovered by psychologists and has been applied widely in marketing. Often attributed to Krugman (1965) or Petty and Cacioppo (1979), when people are highly interested or "involved" with a message, they are believed to be more motivated to think about it and process the information more thoroughly; however, when their interest and motivation is lower, they are expected to rely on shortcuts or "heuristics" that simplify their efforts. The notion of involvement has been applied frequently in commercial marketing, often to aspects of the product itself where people are believed to spend more effort considering "high-involvement" products than "low-involvement" products. As a result, different types of messages, especially advertising messages, are used in an effort to match consumer motivation levels. One such application of this approach is the development of a theory of a "hierarchy of effects" where the most effective sequencing of information given to potential customers depends on their involvement with the product or service.

In Jennifer Algie's and Nicole Mean's "Dumb Ways to Die" case on rail safety (Chap. 6) they suggest that the hierarchy of effects model known as Attention, Interest, Desire, Action (AIDA) could also be used to improve the effort by appropriately sequencing the messaging aspects of the effort (Fig. 4.4). They propose that humor and creativity are of more importance in earlier parts of the effort where they can generate attention and interest.

Casting a Wider Net

Although these commercial marketing theories have proven their promise, Peattie and Peattie (2003) believe that there are instances where limiting ourselves to commercial marketing theory has held us back from achieving our full potential. Although the field of social marketing has drawn from commercial marketing

Fig. 4.4 Hierarchy of effects AIDA model

theory, there are many commercial marketing theories that do not have a solid corollary or application in social marketing. One example may be the reliance on the marketing mix or "4 Ps" as an organizing scheme. At times the 4P scheme is a beneficial approach, but at other times it is important to realize that this is more a thought process than a theory, and, as a result, the 4P approach may limit our ability to understanding the full complexity of human behavior in the context of social marketing (Wood, 2008).

Social marketers, especially those working in public health, "tend to be broadly eclectic and intuitive tinkerers in their use of available theory" (Walsh, Rudd, Moeykens, & Maloney, 1993, p. 115). When an alarm sounds, we look to see what we can use. This tendency to use a wide variety of theories from diverse sources is partly the result of some of the limited applicability of commercial marketing theories, and partly the result of the different contexts in which we operate.

A review of the most commonly used theories and models from almost 500 health education and health promotion articles found that the most commonly used theories in social marketing were the health belief model, social cognitive theory, theory of reasoned action, stages of change, and theories of community organization (Glanz, Lewis, & Rimer, 1997, p. 29). These theories are primarily drawn from psychology, making psychology one of the most fruitful fields for social marketing. Often described as attempting to understand human behavior, it is easy to see how many psychology theories would have relevance to social marketing endeavors.

Fear and Efficacy

Two very important concepts from psychology that are often applied in social marketing are fear and efficacy. Fear is an intuitive strategy that is often used in an attempt to alter people's behavior. As early as 1953, psychologists were researching the effects of fear. Early studies on fear appeals found that fear was not always an effective strategy by itself, with findings suggesting that scaring people would often result in them avoiding or counter-arguing the message. One of the earliest studies looked at the effects of fear appeals on brushing teeth. The initial results suggested that moderate levels of fear might be more effective than high fear (Janis & Feshbach, 1953). This study spurred a great deal of additional research in fear appeals. One of the most important factors appeared to be people's sense that that could do something to avoid the danger—what came to be called "efficacy" or "self-efficacy." Bandura (1977) is most recognized for his identification of efficacy in his "social learning theory" and later "social cognitive theory."

Gurviez and Raffin's efforts at encouraging healthier eating habits in France through their VIF and "Les Bonnes Portions" campaign against childhood obesity (Chap. 14) invokes efficacy through Bandura's social learning and social cognitive theory. Starting with some qualitative research which showed low levels of self-belief among canteen employees, the effort aimed to strengthen canteen employees', parents', and students' understanding of appropriate food portions. The first two groups were intended to serve as role models for children, providing appropriate cues and norms around portion sizes. As Lafreniere and Basil observe in their case on the Bicycle Valet (Chap. 20) "The more a person believes in their own capabilities, the more likely they are to complete a desired behavior... In these instances of self-doubt, social marketers have two options to encourage perseverance: (1) they can reassure their target audience of their own competency and the positive feelings associated with completing the action... or (2) they can simply make the desired behavior easier to complete." Fear appeals often attempt more of the first strategy (reassurance) while commercial marketing often relies more on the second (making it easier). In "Hand Washing with Soap for a Healthier Vietnam," Doan and Truong (Chap. 19) also make reference to efficacy and social learning theory to provide some basis for the effort.

Health Belief Model (HBM)

In the 1950s, four psychologists, Codfrey Hochbaum, Stephen Kegeles, Howard Leventhal, and Irwin Rosenstock, became interested in the forces that would propel an individual to act to avoid a disease (Rosenstock, 1974). They proposed that individuals evaluate a variety of factors in deciding whether or not to change their behavior. The factors that were identified were people's perceptions of the susceptibility and the seriousness of the disease as well as the benefits of and barriers to avoiding that disease. The theory also suggested there was often a trigger or other cue to action that caused people to consider their behavior. Self-efficacy, the perceived ability to engage in the recommended action, was later added as an additional factor in the theory. This theory proposes that this mental exercise is how people decide whether or not to follow a recommended course of action. The health belief model is one of the most widely recognized conceptual frameworks in health behavior, focusing on behavioral change at the individual level.

As a result of its utility, the HBM is frequently applied in social marketing, especially in the realm of health (Luca & Suggs, 2013, p. 23; Truong, 2014, p. 24). The theory remains important in understanding how to encourage people to modify their behavior as well as how or when that may happen. The main limitation of the HBM is that it assumes people are always thoughtful, so it is most relevant when people go to some effort in making their health decisions. Kumar and Gupta invoke the HBM to explain how their hand washing program depended on people's willingness to act which hinged on people's attitudes and beliefs. As a result, the effort began with a desire to change those attitudes and beliefs (Fig. 4.5).

Health Belief Model

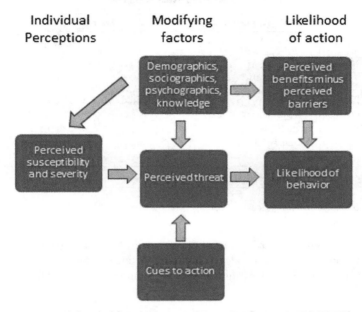

Adapted from Glanz K, Rimer BK & Lewis FM (2002)

Fig. 4.5 Health belief model

The Extended Parallel Process Model (EPPM)

Many of the subsequent theories about fear incorporated the perceptual factors in the health belief model including perceptions of susceptibility, seriousness, and efficacy. Current theories, most notably Kim Witte's extended parallel process model, suggest that fear is only effective when people feel capable in being able to do something to avoid the danger, without which people reject the messages (Witte, 1992). This model is shown in Fig. 4.6.

More recent evidence suggests that efficacy reduces this reactance and increases adaptive coping responses that otherwise arise from fear appeals (Wehbe, Basil, & Basil, 2017). Therefore, the EPPM provides an important theoretical framework for the use of fear appeals. Unfortunately, however, there are many instances of the use of high levels of fear in the absence of efficacy, especially in heath campaigns. The use of simple fear-only appeals raises both practical and ethical concerns (Hastings, Stead, & Webb, 2004; Rotfeld, 1999). Thus, reliance on fear appeals should probably not be the default for social marketing efforts. When fear is used, it should be guided by sophisticated models of human motivation and behavior such as the EPPM.

Extended Parallel Process Model (EPPM)
Adapted from Witte (1993)

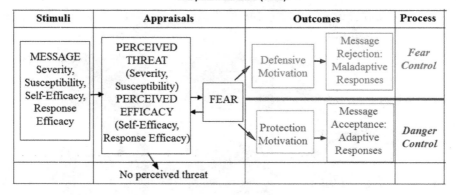

Stimuli	Appraisals	Outcomes		Process
MESSAGE Severity, Susceptibility, Self-Efficacy, Response Efficacy	PERCEIVED THREAT (Severity, Susceptibility) PERCEIVED EFFICACY (Self-Efficacy, Response Efficacy) → FEAR	Defensive Motivation →	Message Rejection: Maladaptive Responses	*Fear Control*
		Protection Motivation →	Message Acceptance: Adaptive Responses	*Danger Control*
	No perceived threat			

Fig. 4.6 Extended parallel process model

Kumar and Gupta (Chap. 13) also invoke the EPPM in their hand washing effort explaining that there is a tendency to overuse fear appeals, and instead they chose to focus on the ease of hand washing which they imply would result in increasing efficacy.

Theory of Reasoned Action (TRA) and Theory of Planned Behavior (TPB)

In 1975, two psychologists, Icek Ajzen, and Martin Fishbein, proposed that people's behaviors could be predicted by understanding people's behavioral intentions. The most important antecedent conditions they proposed were people's beliefs and social norms. This was originally posited as the "theory of reasoned action." Through subsequent research, the acknowledgment of the importance of perceived behavioral control in guiding people's behaviors was added; this augmented theory became the "theory of planned behavior" (Fishbein & Ajzen, 2011; Fig. 4.7). One example of its application can be seen in the "5 A Day for Better Health" program (Lefebvre, 2000). Another example can be seen in an effort to encourage people's willingness to financially support a park (López-Mosquera, García, & Barrena, 2014). The TRA and TPB are frequently applied in social marketing (Truong, 2014, p. 24). Most importantly, the theory of reasoned action and theory of planed behavior are important in understanding the rational human decision-making process that is often relevant to much of what we do in social marketing. Importantly, however, we should be aware that not all of our actions are undertaken so rationally.

Theory of Planned Behavior

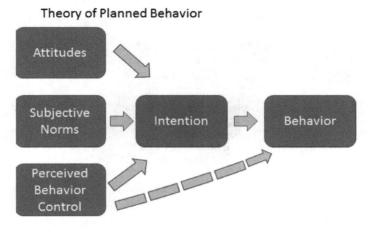

Fig. 4.7 Theory of planned behavior

Jennifer Algie's and Nicole Mean's "Dumb Ways to Die" case on rail safety (Chap. 6) suggests that although the theory of planned behavior may not have been used explicitly in that effort, it is a good way to understand how the effort might affect the public. They explain that the efforts might be explained by the TPB by changing norms around not wanting to be seen as stupid. Similarly, Kureshi and Thomas invoke the TPB in their case on Lifebuoy's "Help a Child Reach 5" Campaign (Chap. 17). They propose that the decision to engage in handwashing was a result of processing and analyzing the available information. They believe success occurred when perception about the value of handwashing outweighed the difficulty it took to perform. Casais, Ferreira, and Proença's case on tax evasion in Portugal (Chap. 11) also acknowledges the importance of social norms. "The phenomena of tax evasion can be connected as a social norm, based on the misperception of community members' acceptance of such attitudes and behaviors… Tax evasion was, in Portugal, misunderstood as a social norm commonly assumed by individuals."

Stages of Change or the Transtheoretical Model

In 1982, two other psychologists, Prochaska and DiClemente (1982), were examining how psychotherapy patients were able to make important changes in their lives, such as quitting smoking. Prochaska and DiClemente proposed that the process of behavioral change could be seen as a sequence of stages. That is, people trying to make changes to their life generally proceeded in a particular sequence that they labeled as precontemplation, contemplation, action, and maintenance. The model is illustrated in Fig. 4.8.

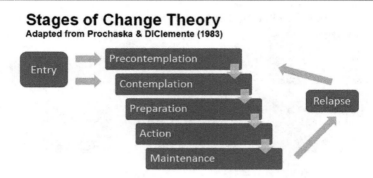

Stages of Change Theory
Adapted from Prochaska & DiClemente (1983)

Fig. 4.8 Transtheoretical model

This "transtheoretical" model has been applied in a large number of efforts in health, including social marketing (Truong, 2014, p. 24). For example, the transtheoretical model has been shown to be effective in helping understand (and later perhaps develop) anti-depression efforts (Levit, Cismaru, & Zederayko, 2016). One of the limitations of the theory, like many of the previous ones, is the assumption that people behave in a careful and thoughtful manner; although this is often the case, many of our behaviors are guided without such careful consideration or by habit. In these situations, the transtheoretical model may not be as helpful.

In the Smile Train case in India, Sivakumar (Chap. 15) explains that the people's decision to take advantage of cleft palate surgery likely proceeded through stages from pre-contemplation to action. Hughes, McConell, and Groner's Anti-Littering Campaign (Chap. 23) was built upon the principles of community-based social marketing. Their approach made use of feedback to create targeted outreach tactics to reach specific audiences. As they explain, "Identifying specific barriers and motivators in behaviors is central to CBSM approaches." Another important aspect of their efforts was the use of multiple perspectives and methodologies from social psychology, behavioral theory, economics, and other social science-based research approaches.

Social Impact and Environmental Psychology

Arising from previous research on the "bystander effect", Darley and Latané (1968) began exploring the importance of other people in the social environment in shaping a person's behavior. This research is probably most known for its recognition of social norms on people's behavior. The general area of norms, especially "correcting" people's inaccurate beliefs of how other people behave has been used in a variety of social change efforts (Schultz, Nolan, Cialdini, Goldstein, & Griskevicius, 2007). This approach is used in a variety of fields. Social norms approaches are likely most familiar to us in social marketing because they are used pervasively in many on-campus alcohol efforts. Similar to the "upstream factors" mentioned above, norms may influence our behavior in instances that are not necessarily a result of rational processes. However, it is important to be careful in using norms, because there are many people whose behavior is "better" than the general norms, so becoming aware of averages can lead these individuals to behave in "worse" ways that they might not have otherwise (Schultz et al., 2007). For example, exposing college students to what is a "typical" level of alcohol consumption can result in the light drinkers drinking more.

Hughes, McConell, and Groner's Anti-Littering Campaign (Chap. 23) raises the issue of social norms. Specifically, they explained that, "Context, or one's social and physical environment, is one of the most significant factors in both driving and curtailing littering behaviors... Precedents set by a friend or known peer's behavior may be indicative of an especially salient social norm... In SGA's youth littering study for KLAB, survey results revealed that the most impactful, non-situational factor in determining individuals' likelihood of littering was the littering habits of their friends. Moreover, friends' behaviors with regard to littering were found to be twice as impactful as the littering habits of their parents."

Community Readiness Model

Another important approach to changing the environment is focused on community change. One social-level theory that has been used in social marketing is termed "the community readiness model" (Oetting et al., 1995). This approach examines developmental readiness for collective action. The theory is about stages, so it bears some similarity to the transtheoretical model, but instead of applying to an individual, it examines this readiness from the perspective of a collective. The theory considers the process to typically involve in recognition of a problem, legitimization by leaders, development of specific plans, decision, and finally action (Kelly et al., 2003). The community readiness model has also been applied to the issue of alcohol reduction among college students (Kelly & Stanley, 2014). The theory is helpful in understanding the careful and thoughtful process that a community might go through in altering social conditions that can encourage or dissuade people from particular acts, for example by banning tobacco from bars in the community. Some recent evidence suggests that Iceland was able to reduce teenage alcohol and drug use through a planned community effort (Arnarsson, Kristofersson, & Bjarnason, 2017). Although the model is helpful in understanding how communities can and often do try to change the environment, there are likely many communities and situations that are not amenable to change, or where targeting particular individuals may be easier or more beneficial.

Silchenko, Simonetti, and Gistri's case on the Italian Food Bank (Chap. 7) is a good illustration of the value of taking a broader socio-environmental perspective. Their social ecological approach is used to design, plan, and execute a multi-player intervention to reduce food waste. Specifically, this intervention involved establishing a collaboration between a variety of stakeholders. The authors argue that connecting the stakeholders enabled them to address two social problems simultaneously. Domegan, McHugh, McCauley, and Davidson's "Co-creating a Sea Change campaign for Ocean Literacy in Europe" (Chap. 26) program invokes their "co-creation" theory which expands on the notion of efficacy at multiple levels to help understand what barriers may limit people's efforts. They propose that, "For co-creation, collaborating, and empowering each of these target audiences together was foundational to Sea Change and its approach to its target markets." This approach suggests that target groups need to develop an understanding of experiences and therefore proposes that social marketers include formal and informal education around the behavior that allows not only individual actions, but supports changes in media coverage and in public policy. Diaz Meneses's case "Social Marketing and Social Media Marketing for Enhancing Health by Means of MOOCs" (Chap. 27) also uses co-creation theory through the inclusion of a variety of participants including researchers, healthcare professionals, and web designers. Their input was central to the development of massive open online courses (MOOCs) tailored to health-related issues including diabetes, pregnancy, and breastfeeding, and aimed at vulnerable groups including children, adolescents, and the elderly. Similarly, Díaz-Perdomo, Álvarez-González, and Sanzo-Perez's case on the Ana Bella social school for female empowerment (Chap. 29) draws on co-creation theory to explain the development of this business-nonprofit partnership. This school is a social project in conjunction with the Danone company that attempts to train and employ women who have suffered from gender violence. As part of the social mandate, it attempts to improve women's economic standing, fulfill some of their social needs, and change the perceived image of these women in society.

Conclusion

In this chapter, we have described the most commonly used theories in social marketing academic publications and in this book. These theories arise from a variety of fields including marketing, psychology, and sociology. Each theory usually focuses on a specific unit of analysis—the exchange dyad situation, the thoughtful individual, or in the context of the community in which the behavior occurs. Despite these differing units of analysis, each theory attempts to explain factors that are important in determining people's behavior. Each can be considered, according to the parable of the three blind men and the elephant, to be explaining a different piece of the elephant.

Several cases in this book draw on more than one theoretical basis to approach the issue. For example, Hughes, McConell, and Groner's Anti-Littering Campaign (Chap. 23) involves, "the introduction of multiple perspectives and methodologies from social psychology, behavioral theory, economics, and other social science-based research approaches." This type of pragmatic approach is not uncommon in social marketing. Often this results from having multiple players at the table, perhaps with each looking at a different part of the elephant, and each contributing their own perspective to the problem. Sometimes the social marketing effort itself, or its evaluation, led to the recognition of other important theories that would have improved the effort or should be tapped into later, as Gurviez and Raffin's VIF and "Les Bonnes Portions" campaign (Chap. 14) acknowledges in their conclusion. Specifically, a discussion question asks, "In line with exchange theory, how can value be jointly created to change the behaviors that lead to negative health outcomes?"

That said, some of the cases in this book do not explicitly identify a particular theory. Importantly, there are also a great many academic articles that either do not identify a particular theory or list a variety of theories (Truong, 2014). Further, it is likely that a good number of social marketing efforts do not explicitly draw on any particular academic theory, but still are trying to understand and guide the behavioral elephant. Deshpande in his case on science teaching in India (Chap. 28) asks the reader, "What underlying theory explains the success of the intervention?" As Smith (2000) acknowledges, there is no single model that unites us, identifies the most important barriers we face or the most important forces that we may muster. Although we run the risk of over-using our favorite theory, as in the parable of the little boy with a hammer, we also have the opportunity of accessing a toolbox full of theories and drawing on the one that makes the most sense in a specific situation at a specific time. Referring back to Smith's article, "when there is a lion in the village we raise the alarm", our variety of theories allows us to take a pragmatic approach to the challenges we face and draw on any of the theories that we hold in our quiver. Our knowledge of these various theories should allow us to analyze the underlying situation and hopefully allow us to reach for the theory or theories most suited to the situation at hand.

Appendix: Theories Used in Social Marketing

Michael Basil
Debra Z. Basil

This appendix provides supplementary information for the theories described in Chap. 4. A brief description of the link contents and a few online links are provided for each theory. We note that on the internet things change rapidly, therefore it is likely that some of the links provided will no longer be working. We hope that the benefit of having a set of curated online resources is worth the risk of frustration in accessing a broken link.

1. Co-creation

This is a short primer on co-creation from the Harvard Business Review. https://hbr.org/2011/02/co-creation.html

This article discusses the value of co-creation, and approaches to take. It is written from a commercial marketing perspective but the concepts can easily be applied to social marketing. https://timreview.ca/article/302

This is a relatively long article from Strategy + Business. It discusses co-creation in quite a bit of detail. It takes a commercial marketing perspective, but the concepts can be easily applied to social marketing. https://www.strategy-business.com/article/18458?gko=f472b

2. Community Readiness Model

This short article from the Rural Health Information Hub provides a clear summary of the community readiness model. https://www.ruralhealthinfo.org/toolkits/health-promotion/2/program-models/community-readiness

This chapter from Community Tool Box summarizes the community readiness model.   https://ctb.ku.edu/en/table-of-contents/overview/models-for-community-health-and-development/community-readiness/main

This short article from the Substance Abuse and Mental Health Services Administration clearly summarizes the nine possible stages of community readiness. https://www.samhsa.gov/capt/tools-learning-resources/stages-community-readiness

3. Diffusion of Innovations

This link from Boston University School of Public Health provides a concise summary of the diffusion of innovations theory, along with limitations of the theory. http://sphweb.bumc.bu.edu/otlt/MPH-Modules/SB/BehavioralChangeTheories/BehavioralChangeTheories4.html

This is an easy-to-read guide from Enabling Change which goes into greater detail on diffusion of innovations. https://twut.nd.edu/PDF/Summary_Diffusion_Theory.pdf

This reader from the Univeritat Hohenheim summarizes Everett Rogers' book on diffusion of innovations, chapter by chapter, on pages 37-53. https://www.researchgate.net/profile/Anja_Christinck/publication/225616414_Farmers_and_researchers_How_can_collaborative_advantages_be_created_in_participatory_research_and_technology_development/links/00b4953a92931a6fae000000/Farmers-and-researchers-How-can-collaborative-advantages-be-created-in-participatory-research-and-technology-development.pdf#page=37

4. Extended Parallel Process Model

This short article from SCE tool provides a brief summary of the extended parallel process model (EPPM). http://wiki.scetool.nl/index.php?title=Extended_parallel_process_model_(EPPM)

This one-page article from the Health Communication Capacity Collaborative offers a concise yet comprehensive overview of the extended parallel process model (EPPM) for fear appeals. It includes a very short case study for illustration. http://www.healthcommcapacity.org/wp-content/uploads/2014/09/Extended-Parallel-Processing-Model.pdf

This one-page article from the Health Compass is similar to the previous example. It also provides a concise summary of the EPPM and includes a short case study for illustration. https://www.thehealthcompass.org/sites/default/files/strengthening_tools/Research%20101%20-%20Extended%20Parallel%20Process%20Model.pdf

5. Health Belief Model

This link from Boston University School of Public Health provides a concise summary of the health belief model (HBM), along with limitations of the model. http://sphweb.bumc.bu.edu/otlt/MPH-Modules/SB/BehavioralChangeTheories/BehavioralChangeTheories2.html
This short article from the University of Twente offers a concise yet complete summary of the HBM. https://www.utwente.nl/en/bms/communication-theories/sorted-by-cluster/Health%20Communication/Health_Belief_Model/
This link from Changingminds.org provides a clear summary of the components of the HBM. http://changingminds.org/explanations/belief/health_belief_model.htm

6. Hierarchy of Effects and AIDA Model

This short article from MBA Skool summarizes the basic principles of the original hierarchy of effects model. Although it is positioned for commercial marketing, the concepts are equally applicable to social marketing. https://www.mbaskool.com/business-concepts/marketing-and-strategy-terms/12173-hierarchy-of-effects-theory.html
This article from MBA Knowledge base offers somewhat more detail regarding the hierarchy of effects. https://www.mbaknol.com/marketing-management/hierarchy-of-effects-model/
This short article by Smart Insights summarizes the AIDA version of the hierarchy of effects model. https://www.mbaknol.com/marketing-management/hierarchy-of-effects-model/

7. Self-efficacy Theory

This short article from Positive Psychology summarizes Bandura's four sources of self-efficacy beliefs. http://positivepsychology.org.uk/self-efficacy-definition-bandura-meaning/
This is a somewhat longer article from the Positive Psychology Program that offers an insightful and accessible understanding of self-efficacy. The article effectively differentiates self-efficacy from related theories. It offers examples and a scale for measuring self-efficacy, as well as useful resource suggestions for further study. https://positivepsychologyprogram.com/self-efficacy/
This article from the American Psychological Association provides background on self-efficacy and applies it to the issue of HIV. It also offers teaching and learning guidance for understanding the concept. http://www.apa.org/pi/aids/resources/education/self-efficacy.aspx

8. Social Cognitive Theory

 This link from Boston University School of Public Health provides a concise summary of the social cognitive theory, along with limitations of the theory. http://sphweb.bumc.bu.edu/otlt/MPH-Modules/SB/BehavioralChangeTheories/BehavioralChangeTheories5.html
 This short article from the University of Twente offers a clear summary of social cognitive theory. It includes a visual model and an example. https://www.utwente.nl/en/bms/communication-theories/sorted-by-cluster/Health%20Communication/Social_cognitive_theory/
 This is a short summary of social cognitive theory from Rural Health Information Hub. It includes links to examples of actual programs which were implemented for behavior change. https://www.ruralhealthinfo.org/toolkits/health-promotion/2/theories-and-models/social-cognitive

9. Social Norms Theory

 This link from Boston University School of Public Health provides a concise summary of social norms theory, along with limitations of the theory. http://sphweb.bumc.bu.edu/otlt/MPH-Modules/SB/BehavioralChangeTheories/BehavioralChangeTheories7.html
 This article from the Brookings institute discusses social norms and their importance in public policy. https://www.brookings.edu/research/social-norms-and-public-policy/
 This very short article from changingminds.org includes a summary of other forms of norms, to allow differentiation between social norms and other types of norms. http://changingminds.org/explanations/theories/social_norms.htm

10. Theory of Planned Behavior

This link from Boston University School of Public Health provides a concise summary of the theory of planned behavior (TPB), along with limitations of the theory. http://sphweb.bumc.bu.edu/otlt/MPH-Modules/SB/BehavioralChangeTheories/BehavioralChangeTheories3.html
 This short article from the University of Twente summarizes the theory of planned behavior and provides a visual model. https://www.utwente.nl/en/bms/communication-theories/sorted-by-cluster/Health%20Communication/theory_planned_behavior/
 This two-page article from the Health Communication Capacity Collaborative offers a clear summary of the TPB and includes a very short case study example. https://www.healthcommcapacity.org/wp-content/uploads/2014/03/theory_of_planned_behavior.pdf

11. Transtheoretical Model

This is a short definition of the transtheoretical model from the Oxford Research Encyclopedia. http://communication.oxfordre.com/view/10.1093/acrefore/9780190228613.001.0001/acrefore-9780190228613-e-324

This link from Boston University School of Public Health provides a concise summary of the transtheoretical model, along with limitations of the model. http://sphweb.bumc.bu.edu/otlt/MPH-Modules/SB/BehavioralChangeTheories/BehavioralChangeTheories6.html

This article from Pro Change offers a clear summary of the transtheoretical model. It includes assumptions of the model and a brief historical overview of model advancement. https://www.prochange.com/transtheoretical-model-of-behavior-change

12. Utility of Theory

United States National Institutes of Health, Office of Behavioral and Social Sciences Research:
  http://www.esourceresearch.org/tabid/724/default.aspx
  University of Southern California:
  http://libguides.usc.edu/writingguide/theoreticalframework

References

Arnarsson, A., Kristofersson, G. K., & Bjarnason, T. (2017). Adolescent alcohol and cannabis use in Iceland 1995–2015. *Drug and Alcohol Review*.

Bandura, A. (1977). Self-efficacy: Toward a unifying theory of behavioral change. *Psychological Review, 84*(2), 191–215.

Calder, B. J., Phillips, L. W., & Tybout, A. M. (1981). Designing research for application. *Journal of Consumer Research, 8*(2), 197–207.

Darley, J. M., & Latané, B. (1968). Bystander intervention in emergencies: Diffusion of responsibility. *Journal of Personality and Social Psychology, 8*(4), 377–383.

Dearing, J. W. (2015). The use of informal opinion leader-based strategy for the diffusion of public health services among international workers in South Korea. *Health Communication, 12*, 115–148.

Fishbein, M., & Ajzen, I. (2011). *Predicting and changing behavior: The reasoned action approach*. New York: Taylor & Francis.

Glanz, K., Lewis, F. M., & Rimer, B. K. (1997). *Health behavior and education* (2nd ed.). San Francisco: Jossey-Bass.

Hastings, G., Stead, M., & Webb, J. (2004). Fear appeals in social marketing: Strategic and ethical reasons for concern. *Psychology and Marketing, 21*(11), 961–986.

Janis, I. L., & Feshbach, S. (1953). Effects of fear-arousing communications. *The Journal of Abnormal and Social Psychology, 48*(1), 78–92.

Kelly, K. J., Edwards, R. W., Comello, M. L. G., Plested, B. A., Thurman, P. J., & Slater, M. D. (2003). The community readiness model: A complementary approach to social marketing. *Marketing Theory, 3*(4), 411–426.

Kelly, K. J., & Stanley, L. (2014). Identifying upstream factors using the community readiness model: The case of reducing alcohol use among college students. *Journal of Social Marketing, 4*(2), 176–191.

Kotler, P. (2000). A framework for marketing management. Prentice-Hall, Upper Saddle River, New Jersey.

Kotler, P., & Levy, S. J. (1969). Broadening the concept of marketing. *Journal of Marketing, 33* (January), 10–15.

Krugman, H. E. (1965). The impact of television advertising: Learning without involvement. *Public Opinion Quarterly, 29,* 349–356.

Lefebvre, R. C. (2000). In P. N. Bloom & G. T. Gundlach (Eds.), *Handbook of marketing and society*. Newbury Park, CA: Sage.

Levit, T., Cismaru, M., & Zederayko, A. (2016). Application of the transtheoretical model and social marketing to antidepression campaign websites. *Social Marketing Quarterly, 22*(1), 54–77.

López-Mosquera, N., García, T., & Barrena, R. (2014). An extension of the theory of planned behavior to predict willingness to pay for the conservation of an urban park. *Journal of Environmental Management, 135,* 91–99.

Luca, N. R., & Suggs, L. S. (2013). Theory and model use in social marketing health interventions. *Journal of Health Communication, 18*(1), 20–40.

Maibach, E. (1993). Social marketing for the environment: Using information campaigns to promote environmental awareness and behavior change. *Health Promotion International, 8*(3), 209–224.

Oetting, E. R., Donnermeyer, J. F., Plested, B. A., Edwards, R. W., Kelly, K., & Beauvais, F. (1995). Assessing community readiness for prevention. *International Journal of the Addictions, 30*(6), 659–683.

Peattie, S., & Peattie, K. (2003). Ready to fly solo? Reducing social marketing's dependence on commercial marketing theory. *Marketing Theory, 3*(3), 365–385.

Petty, R. E., & Cacioppo, J. T. (1979). Issue involvement can increase or decrease persuasion by enhancing message-relevant cognitive responses. *Journal of Personality and Social Psychology, 37,* 1915–1926.

Popper, K. R. (1959). *The logic of scientific discovery*. New York: Harper Torchbooks.

Prochaska, J. O., & DiClemente, C. C. (1982). Transtheoretical therapy: Toward a more integrative model of change. *Psychotherapy: Theory, Research & Practice, 19*(3), 276–288.

Rogers, E. M. (2010). *Diffusion of innovations*. New York: Simon and Schuster.

Rosenstock, I. M. (1974). Historical origins of the health belief model. *Health Education Monographs, 2*(4), 328–335.

Rotfeld, H. J. (1999). Misplaced marketing commentary: Social marketing and myths of appeals to fear. *Journal of Consumer Marketing, 16*(2), 119–121.

Rothschild, M. L. (1999). Carrots, sticks, and promises: A conceptual framework for the management of public health and social issue behaviors. *Journal of Marketing, 63,* 24–37.

Schultz, P. W., Nolan, J. M., Cialdini, R. B., Goldstein, N. J., & Griskevicius, V. (2007). The constructive, destructive, and reconstructive power of social norms. *Psychological Science, 18* (5), 429–434.

Smith, B. (2000). There's a lion in the village: The fight over individual behavior versus social context. *Social Marketing Quarterly, 6*(3), 6–12.

Sundstrom, B. (2014). Breaking women's health taboos: Integrating diffusion of innovations theory with social marketing. *Social Marketing Quarterly, 20*(2), 87–102.

Truong, V. D. (2014). Social marketing: A systematic review of research 1998–2012. *Social Marketing Quarterly, 20*(1), 15–34.

Walsh, D. C., Rudd, R. E., Moeykens, B. A., & Maloney, T. W. (1993). Social marketing for public health. *Health Affairs* (Summer), 104–119.

Wehbe, M. S., Basil, M., & Basil, D. (2017). Reactance and coping responses to tobacco counter-advertisements. *Journal of Health Communication, 1–8.*

Witte, K. (1992). Putting the fear back into fear appeals: The extended parallel process model. *Communications Monographs, 59*(4), 329–349.

Wood, M. (2008). Applying commercial marketing theory to social marketing: A tale of 4Ps (and a B). *Social Marketing Quarterly, 14*(1), 76–85.

A Brief History of Social Marketing

5

Gonzalo Diaz-Meneses and Michael D. Basil

Chapter Overview
Learning from the past can help increase our chances for success in the future. Savitt (1980) believes that marketing scholars have not paid sufficient attention to our history, and this is important for social marketing. There are many benefits to be gained from examining our history. In this chapter, we provide a brief history of social marketing, to help us understand where we have been, how we got here, and to orient our social marketing practice for the future. There are several specific benefits of reviewing our history. First, understanding the history of social marketing helps delimit the concept and scope of the enterprise. Historical analysis illuminates the use of technical terms and identifies the boundaries of its application. Therefore, a review of history strengthens our general understanding of the field. Second, the study of our history facilitates informed discussions, critical reflections, and analytical thought that the development of any discipline needs (Domegan, 2010). That is, history is a vehicle for diagnosing the current context and understanding changes with the aim of imbuing our potential praxis with meaning. Third, as long as we learn from experience, the past can provide a source of wisdom and good sense. As a result, this can help us improve social marketing tools' efficacy and efficiency in future endeavors. Though our history may not progress linearly, advances are unlikely if they are not based on a firm knowledge of where we have been. An understanding of our history allows us to of bridge the past, present, and future (Domegan, 2010).

G. Diaz-Meneses (✉)
Faculty of Economy, Management, and Tourism, University of Las Palmas de Gran Canaria, The Canary Islands, Las Palmas, Spain
e-mail: gonzalo.diazmeneses@ulpgc.es

M. D. Basil
Dhillon School of Business, University of Lethbridge, Lethbridge, Canada
e-mail: michael.basil@uleth.ca

© Springer Nature Switzerland AG 2019
D. Z. Basil et al. (eds.), *Social Marketing in Action*,
Springer Texts in Business and Economics,
https://doi.org/10.1007/978-3-030-13020-6_5

A Look Back

The establishment of what we call social marketing can be traced to several possible points. One event was Wiebe's 1952 article that asked, "Why can't you sell brotherhood like you sell soap?" The value of his idea is reflected in the United States Agency for International Development's (USAID) variety of communication efforts to improve people's lives in developing countries. These efforts included radio programs on topics such as family planning and rural math education (Khan & Choldin, 1967; McAnany, 1973; Schramm, 1968). Similar communication efforts were instigated around the world on behalf of the UK, Germany, and the United Nations (Cairns, Mackay, & MacDonald, 2011).

In 1969, Kotler and Levy identified the relevance of the marketing approach to a wide variety of non-commercial efforts including political campaigns and marketing of non-profit ventures such as universities. Using marketing strategies, they argued, would make these efforts more successful. Two years later, Kotler and Zaltman further explained the limitations of traditional communication-only approaches, such as family planning efforts in India, and delineated how a marketing-based approach could improve these efforts. They termed this "social marketing."

Although we can point to particular milestones, is there a better way to understand the history of social marketing? One strategy is to look for distinguishing events and classify the field's development into "periods." Several academics have attempted to identify the phases and events, and their efforts have resulted in the derivation of particular periods, milestones, and turning points. Although it offers a welcome simplification, there are several limitations of periodization. First, it may introduce possible problems such as oversimplification. Second, it may suggest an artificial consistency between the history of social marketing practice and the history of social marketing thought. Third, it may even offer a false sense of progress (Hollander, Rassuli, Jones, & Farlow, 2005). However, since the main objective of this chapter is to shed light on general social marketing trends, we believe that paying attention to historical divisions can provide insights into our history.

The following periodization identifies several stages in the development of social marketing, its conception in the 1950s, its birth in the 1960s, early development in the 1980s, adolescence in the 1990s, and finally adulthood in the new century (Andreasen, 2003). These stages are seen in Table 5.1.

This chapter will attempt to identify theoretical and scientific tensions and debates that have practical and professional implications. Finally, the chapter will also try to bring into focus current tendencies and trends.

Trends and Tensions in the Theoretical World

Like most fields, the discipline and practice of social marketing have faced hindrances throughout its evolution that have impeded its development (Andreasen, 2002). In social marketing's case, there were problems related to formulating a

Table 5.1 Periodization of history with milestones and turning points

Periods	Milestones and turning points
Conception (1950s)	Wiebe (1952) asked, "Why can't you sell brotherhood like you sell soap?"
Birth (1960s–1970s)	Kotler and Levy (1969) propose that commercial marketing strategies can also be applied to non-profit and public policy issues
	Kotler and Zaltman (1971) distinguish the additional contribution of social marketing over other social science approaches such as mass communication, especially the importance of the acceptability of ideas
Early development (1980s)	Kotler and Roberto (1989) explain the steps that can be used to apply social marketing to a wide range of social problems
Adolescence (1990s)	1994. Social Marketing Quarterly is the first journal dedicated specifically to the practice of social marketing.
	Andreasen (1995) explains that the mission of social marketing is changing behaviors and puts forward the benchmarks that distinguish social marketing from other social science approaches. He explains social marketing upstream, midstream, and downstream efforts
	MacKenzie-Mohr (1999) explains a system-based approach to social marketing
Adulthood (2000s)	2006. With the establishment of the National Social Marketing Centre, social marketing is institutionalized. It is implemented by consultants and public policy organizations. Professionalism and a common vision are laid out
	The planning process is explained as a series of 10 steps
	2011. Our second social marketing journal—Journal of Social Marketing—is established, providing a more international focus

Source Dibb and Carrigan (2013), Andreasen (2003), Brychkov and Domegan (2017)

definition, identifying the field, and developing a solid theoretical basis. Although some problems may have occurred at a specific point in time, there are other issues that continue to be important.

Confusion about the nature of the field was common from the birth of the field in the 1960s through its early development in the 1970s (Kotler, 2017). As social marketing was born from commercial marketing, there was a tendency to retain the old paradigms, such as the four Ps (Wood, 2012) and exchange theory (Hastings & Saren, 2003), and some social marketing scholars have argued that these concepts don't match well with the current practice and positioning of social marketing.

A struggle for self-identity arose primarily during the field's adolescence in the 1980s. There seemed to be a lack of consensus in drawing a distinct boundary between what might be considered a social marketing approach versus other kinds of social science approaches including social advertising, education, and persuasion. There was a conflict between those upholding the view of social marketing as a marketing of ideas versus those highlighting the importance of changing behaviors (Dinan & Sargeant, 2000). This generated an identity crisis, partly as a result of an ambiguous subject matter and a lack of boundaries with other disciplines (Andreasen, 2003; Shaw & Jones, 2005). Finally, different terms were used whose meanings were confused for social marketing, such as societal marketing, socially responsible marketing, and non-profit marketing (McDermott, Stead, & Hastings, 2005). In this respect, the term "social marketing" was often applied incorrectly and in inappropriate areas (Andreasen, 1994).

Part of the difficulty in delineating social marketing from other fields can be traced back to the original interdisciplinary nature of marketing. Marketing draws from economics, psychology, sociology, and anthropology. Drawing from these disciplines made social marketing richer and more complex, but it also resulted in less clarity and precision about the disciplinary boundaries. It was difficult to import such divergent theories and approaches while forming a unique perspective (Bartels, 1976). As a result, researchers and practitioners sometimes found it hard to adapt their methods and forge them into a coherent discipline (Brennan, Voros, Brady, 2011). Social marketers were confused with health educators, mass communicators, social mobilisers, social advertising creators, and so on (Dinan & Sargeant, 2000), so social marketing efforts were often mislabeled. Social marketers were not easily recognized as being part of one unified profession; therefore, academics and practitioners were not working together as a single integrated force. As a result, advances in building an academic and professional home were slow. Until recently, there were no academic degrees granted in "social marketing"; the discipline is typically housed under other academic umbrellas such as business and engineering (Truong & Dietrich, 2018) and social advertising (Smith, 2011). So, even in what should be adulthood, social marketing students still do not have a common home, but instead graduate from many different departments rather than sharing a common discipline. The geographic location and disciplinary homes of social marketing theses are shown in Fig. 5.1.

The variety of theoretical approaches, plus the lack of professional accreditation, often led to the value of social marketing being questioned or underrated. Some critics accused the commercial marketing profession of not acting with integrity, and denigrating its knowledge, claiming the field is "ethically challenged" (Bartels, 1976). The negative reputation of commercial marketing bled into the reputation of social marketing, which spurred some social marketers toward a critical approach. As a result, they have developed what is called "critical marketing." On the one hand, critical marketing represents a sign of integrity as it emphasizes the rationality over emotionality of consumers and denounces the propaganda, deplores the worst side of competition, reveals the deceiving myth of beauty, and advocates some ground for ethics. On the other hand, critical marketing disparages marketing and so, to some extent, joins forces with those reluctant to accept this new field, reinforcing the negative aspects of the field's reputation (Tadajewski, 2010).

Although the negative reputation of social marketing may be somewhat undeserved, it is probably not entirely without warrant when the above shortcomings are considered. Specifically, by associating social marketing with commercial marketing, links are formed with the manipulative perceptions of commercial marketing; the lack of a separate identity with respect to commercial marketing did not help to improve the picture. In addition, the undeveloped theoretical framework as

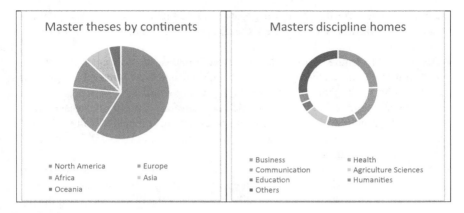

Fig. 5.1 Indicators of the interdisciplinary background of social marketing education. *Source* Truong and Dietrich (2018)

well as a lack of professional identity and formalization is still actively undermining it. In fact, some authors interpret social marketing as being as self-serving and self-interested as commercial marketing by supposing that behind any advocacy for a social cause lay the interests of the lucrative industries of condoms, recycling, sport, insurance, and so on (Fox & Kotler, 1980).

Trends and Tensions in the Applied World

It is worth noting that social marketing was not free of imperfections in its implementation either. In the early 1980s, social marketing showed sluggish progress and there was a glaring difference between its potential and real implementation, between theoretical efficacy and real obtained outputs. Not all of these barriers have been overcome today. Specifically, according to Bloom and Novelli (1981) and Fox and Kotler (1980), there were seven categories of problems, as follows:

- Market analysis complications resulted from the scant secondary sources of information as well as the lower financial resources associated with the vast majority of the non-profit causes. In addition, the determinants of human behavior are more complex and so it is harder to measure the key variables with reliability and validity.
- Segmentation is often maligned because they appear to be in conflict with egalitarian rights that act against discrimination. This complicates segmentation and treating people differently. For example, in many segmentation schemes, the

segments with priority are those groups with a higher level of risk; however, many public health agencies are expected to provide treatment for all of their clients.

- The intangible nature of much behavior often makes the concept of the product more difficult to articulate. Product formulation can also be limited by regulations of the authority in charge of the social marketing campaign.
- In some cases, price is often intangible and therefore can only be measured and explained through external expressions such as the monetary value. At other times, price is a 'non-controlled' variable which cannot be set by the social marketing campaign itself.
- Location (Place) is often problematic because intermediaries are under less control by the social marketer than they are in the commercial field.
- Promotion is often more complicated because we typically cannot afford the high cost of advertising. Also, the messages often need to convey intense content such as fear. As a result, social marketers often need to steer clear of innovative or potentially controversial appeal strategies such as using humor.
- The planning function is often performed by organizations who do not have a good understanding of or appreciation of marketing. Similarly, their evaluations often are not oriented toward measuring results. These evaluations are often further complicated when the results are in more abstract form such as an idea, as invisible as people's values and attitudes, or as intangible as a behavior, compared to more direct measures such as sales or deaths.

After two decades of social marketing practice, many of the problems seem to persist and demonstrate the same difficulties in planning as well as the marketing mix and strategic functions (Dibb & Carrigan, 2013; Stead, Gordon, & Angus, 2007).

Merritt, Kamin, Hussenöder, and Huibregtsen (2017) explain the delay by arguing several factors, such as the general skepticism about marketing, language barriers, and the tradition of other disciplines presented direct and fierce competition for social marketing. Finally, there were very few developments in social marketing in Africa, Asia, and Latin America (White, 2018; Truong & Dietrich, 2018).

As a result of the trends identified above, some believe that social marketing thought has not moved forward as rapidly as it should. Because the theories and the practice of social marketing have evolved differently from commercial marketing, some believe that social marketing has not kept pace with that of commercial marketing. The practice of social marketing also differs depending on the level of economic development across countries where it is applied. Specifically, in developing economies the concerns have often focused on products and services linked to health while in developed economies social marketing has focused on the prevention and reduction of the risk behaviors related to chronic diseases and addictions (Lefebvre, 2011). As a result of these factors, the adoption and advancement of social marketing have been quite varied, perhaps more than that of commercial marketing. There seem to be specific tensions and discussions that account for this particular evolution around the dichotomy between the nature of social marketing efforts in developed and developing countries (Lefebvre, 2011).

Social Marketing and the New Millennium

As the discipline of social marketing reaches maturity, social marketing has begun to establish a unique identity to distinguish itself from other social sciences. Part of this identity may have been a result of Andreasen's six benchmarks of social marketing (Andreasen, 2003; McDermott et al., 2005). These benchmarks put emphasis on the following essential criteria: behavior change, audience research, segmentation principles, motivational exchange, four Ps, and competition.

Research in social marketing began to flourish as a result of the establishment of two specialized journals—Social Marketing Quarterly and the Journal of Social Marketing. Providing a unique home has helped to establish the name and boundaries of social marketing. In addition, there were a number of special issues by the European Journal of Marketing, the Journal of Macro Marketing, and the Journal of Marketing Management which helped recognize and identify social marketing (Truong & Dietrich, 2018). These publications were also important as they resulted in substantial knowledge generation. These factors, in turn, may have also been important in the development of social marketing courses around the world (Kelly, 2013).

In the professional arena, new social marketing centers were established, initially in the English-speaking world, especially the USA, and social marketing was applied to solving a wide range of social problems by governmental agencies and consultants (Andreasen, 2003). Similarly, professional associations dedicated to Social Marketing flourished all over the world, such as the International Social Marketing Association, European Social Marketing Association, Australian Association of Social Marketing, Social Marketing Association of North America, Finish Social Marketing Association, and International Association on Public and Non-Profit Marketing (Truong & Dietrich, 2018). This growth reflects the achievement of a significant level of maturity by the field (Lefebvre, 2012).

Furthermore, at the dawn of the new century, social marketers began to gain a reputation for providing an effective managerial tool that could deal with a variety of problems such as sedentary lifestyles, binge drinking, and drug consumption. This effectiveness was a result of the social marketing approach comprising downstream, midstream, and upstream interventions as well as the acknowledgment of competitive forces (Stead et al., 2007). These advances were partly achieved as a result of new planning tools that were developed through pooled contributions from both the academic and professional worlds (Dibb & Carrigan, 2013). This planning process was typically divided into 10 steps, as follows: (1) background, purpose, and focus, (2) situation analysis, (3) target market profile, (4) marketing objectives, (5) barriers, benefits, and competition, (6) positioning, (7) marketing mix, (8) evaluation, (9) budget, and (10) implementation (Dibb & Carrigan, 2013).

Current Tendencies and Budding Trends

What are the new tendencies and trends in the field of social marketing? Nowadays, the definition of social marketing and its theories are being rebuilt to (1) assimilate upstream and midstream interventions (Dann, 2010; Truong, 2014), (2) expand social marketing's scope beyond mere transactional terms so that it falls into a more relational perspective that highlights interest groups, quality, and sustainability (Hastings, 2003), and (3) provide more consideration of coopetition, including the notion of cooperation with what could be traditionally seen as competition. Social responsibility has also become important to commercial marketing. As a result, social marketers can sometimes join forces with commercial marketers to achieve their goals. For example, fast food companies may be persuaded to provide healthier alternatives that meet with social marketing approval. In this way, social marketing has the potential to become part of a total market approach (Lefebvre, 2011) in which networking, macro marketing, systems, and ethics take center stage and serve as a force behind a highly integrative understanding and way of marketing.

The recognition of social responsibility has meant that educators of marketing need to teach not only technical tools, but also about more critical and ethical issues. Tadajewski (2010) argues that commercial marketers are exploring beyond the traditional sources of marketing and realizing how important it is to consider the consequences of certain techniques and tools. Commercial marketing, from the inside, is making efforts to distinguish between real and fake needs, reveal the fetishism associated with maladaptive consumption, interrogate the genuine nature of satisfaction, and propose social amelioration, responsibility, and distributive justice. Thus, social and commercial marketing are assuming critical marketing sensibility and the education of marketing studies is becoming more transformative. Layton (2017) advocates a search for meaning in marketing since technology is not sufficient. Ethics education in marketing is too often a mere training activity, but as commercial marketing education is becoming more ethical and principled, social marketing education can play an important role.

Social marketing is also learning from new technologies and so transforming its theory and practice toward social innovation, design thinking, and social media (Lefebvre, 2012). As a consequence, the research methods used within social marketing are changing toward encompassing more combined procedures that employ qualitative techniques such as in-depth interviews in conjunction with quantitative techniques such as surveys (Truong, 2014).

As mentioned earlier, until quite recently there was neither a specialized social marketing master's program nor a social marketing degree title anywhere in the world. This may have played a role in holding social marketing back from reaching its full potential. Now that social marketing has achieved some status, it is important for new social marketing initiatives to be infused with social marketing theory and implemented by highly qualified marketers. Partly as a result of social marketing's late arrival, the sense of belonging to the same profession is also in its infancy. However, as social marketing becomes more mainstream and starts to build alliances with commercial marketing, the profession of social marketer will become more distinct and accredited. Hastings and Saren (2003) affirm that not only is there a mutual influence between commercial and social marketing, but also critical marketing plays a key role for achieving this influence. In fact, social marketers and commercial marketers are strengthening their collaborations (Dibb & Carrigan, 2013). Unfortunately, commercial marketing has been in the center of the recent financial and real estate crisis (Dibb & Carrigan, 2013) and the word marketing is associated with the four Ms, as follows: manipulation, materialism, malevolence, and misrepresentation. For this reason, a branding campaign for social marketing is still necessary if we want to have a stronger, more distinct, and better professional positioning (Andreasen, 2002).

After analyzing the new tendencies and trends in social marketing, we should raise our voices to ask for inclusion in the historical perspectives in marketing. Schwarzkopf (2015) states that historians have overlooked the history of social marketers and their target audiences as authentic co-creators. The time is opportune to enrich the traditional approach from the mere description of social marketing to include the intellectual thought processes. Therefore, the discipline of marketing history should be renewed so that the study of social marketing can enhance marketing's frameworks, common vision, and implementations. In short, the new history of social marketing should be developed to embrace a broader variety of both theories and methods while driven by a critical and constructive rigor.

In conclusion, the story of marketers and consumers is the nature of marketing. In the search for meaning, history is always crucial, but we believe that a broader approach to marketing is in order. While the current trajectory of marketing is rooted in history, the field is rapidly evolving toward a more digital, technical, and commercial approach. The same is occurring in social marketing. Social marketing is also developing its reputation both inside and outside the academy. For this reason, we hope that one day when asking consumers about the reputation of marketing, they will speak more positively, because the reputation of commercial marketing is intricately intertwined with the reputation of social marketing.

Ultimately, we hope this book on social marketing will become a source of inspiration for social marketers and for those who interact with social marketers. We hope that both academics and practitioners of social marketing will find value here.

Appendix: Additional Resources for the History of Social Marketing

Michael D. Basil

This appendix provides supplementary information for the history described in Chapter 5. A brief description of the link contents and online links is provided.

Other histories of social marketing:

Andreasen (2003). This article summarizes the history of social marketing. http://citeseerx.ist.psu.edu/viewdoc/download?doi=10.1.1.1000.3024&rep= rep1&type=pdf

Fox and Kotler (1980). This academic article from the Journal of Marketing outlines the first 10 years of social marketing. https://archive.ama.org/archive/ ResourceLibrary/JournalofMarketing/documents/4997928.pdf

Honeyman (2008). This article from Population Services International summarizes the highlights in social marketing from 1969 through 2000. https://www. shopsplusproject.org/sites/default/files/resources/5009_file_Historical_ Highlightshonemanp3.pdf

Wikipedia: https://en.wikipedia.org/wiki/Social_marketing

References

Andreasen, A. (1994). Social marketing: Its definition and domain. *Journal of Public Policy & Marketing, 13,* 108–114.
Andreasen, A. R. (1995). *Marketing social change: Changing behavior to promote health, social development, and the environment.* San Francisco, CA: Jossey-Bass.
Andreasen, A. (2002). Marketing social marketing in social change market place. *Journal of Public Policy, 21,* 3–13.
Andreasen, A. (2003). The life trajectory of social marketing: Some implications. *Marketing Theory, 3,* 293–303.
Bartels, R. (1976). *The history of marketing thought. Grid series in Marketing.* Columbus.
Bloom, P., & Novelli, W. (1981). Problems and challenges in social marketing. *Journal of Marketing, 45,* 79–88.
Brennan, L., Voros, J., & Brady, E. (2011). Paradigms at play and implications for validity in social marketing research. *Journal of Social Marketing, 1,* 100–119.
Brychkov, D., & Domegan, C. (2017). Social marketing and systems science: Past, present and future. *Journal of Social Marketing, 7*(1), 74–93.
Cairns, G., Mackay, B., & MacDonald, L. (2011). Social marketing and international development. In *The SAGE handbook of social marketing* (330–342).
Dann, S. (2010). Redefining social marketing with contemporary commercial marketing definitions. *Journal of Business Research, 63,* 147–153.
Dibb, S., & Carrigan, M. (2013). Social marketing transformed: Kotler, Polonsky and Hastings reflect on social marketing in a period of social change. *European Journal of Marketing, 47,* 1376–1398.
Dinan, C., & Sargeant, A. (2000). Social marketing and sustainable tourism, is there a match? *International Journal of Tourism Research, 2,* 1–14.
Domegan, C. (2010). The history of marketing thought: A teaching reflection. *Journal of Historical Research in Marketing, 2,* 457–466.
Fox, K., & Kotler, P. (1980). The marketing of social causes: The first 10 years. *Journal of Marketing, 44,* 24–33.
Hastings, G. (2003). Relational paradigms in social marketing. *Journal of Micromarketing, 23*(1), 6–15.
Hastings, G., & Saren, M. (2003). The critical contribution of social marketing: Theory and application. *Marketing Theory, 3,* 305–322.
Hollander, S., Rassuli, K., Jones, B., & Farlow, L. (2005). Periodization in marketing history. *Journal of Micromarketing, 25,* 32–41.
Kelly, K. (2013). Academic course of offerings in social marketing: The beat continues. *Social Marketing Quarterly, 19,* 290–295.

Khan, A. H., & Choldin, H. M. (1967). Application of a theory of rural development to family planning in East Pakistan. In *United Nations. Dept. of Economic and Social Affairs. Proceedings of the World Population Conference, Belgrade, 30 August–10 September 1965. Vol. 2. Selected papers and summaries: Fertility, family planning, mortality* (pp. 282–285). New York: UN. Available at https://www.popline.org/node/516720.

Kotler, P., & Roberto (1989). *Social marketing: Strategies for changing public behavior.* Sage Publications.

Kotler, P. (2017). Philip Kotler: Some of my adventures in marketing. *Journal of Historical Research in Marketing, 9,* 203–208.

Kotler, P., & Levy, S. (1969). Broadening the concept of marketing. *Journal of Marketing, 33*(1), 10–15.

Kotler, P., & Zaltman, G. (1971). Social marketing: An approach to planned social change. *Journal of Marketing, 35*(3), 3–12.

Layton, R. (2017). My search for meaning in marketing. *Journal of Historical Research in Marketing, 9,* 217–243.

Lefebvre, R. (2011). An integrative model for social marketing. *Journal of Social Marketing, 1,* 54–72.

Lefebvre, R. (2012). Transformative social marketing: Co-creating the social marketing discipline and brand. *Journal of Social Marketing, 2,* 118–129.

MacKenzie-Mohr, D. (1999). *Fostering sustainable behavior: An introduction to community based social marketing program.* New Society Publisher.

McAnany, E. G. (1973). *Radios role in development: Five strategies of use.* Available at https://eric.ed.gov/?id=ED086155.

McDermott, L., Stead, M., & Hastings, G. (2005). What is and what is not social marketing: The challenge of reviewing the evidence. *Journal of Marketing Management, 21,* 545–553.

Merritt, R., Kamin, T., Hussenöder, F., & Huibregtsen, J. (2017). The history of social marketing in Europe: The story so far. *Social Marketing Quarterly, 23,* 191–301.

Savitt, R. (1980). Historical research in marketing. *Journal of Marketing, 44,* 52–85.

Schramm, W. (1968). Ten years of the radio rural forum in India. *New Media, 1,* 107–134.

Schwarzkopf, S. (2015). Marketing history from below: Towards a paradigm shift in marketing historical research. *Journal of Historical Research in Marketing, 7,* 295–309.

Shaw, E., & Jones, D. B. (2005). A history of schools of marketing thought. *Marketing Theory, 5,* 239–281.

Smith, W. (2011). Social marketing: A future rooted in the past. In *The SAGE handbook of social marketing* (p. 419).

Stead, M., Gordon, R., & Angus, K. (2007). A systematic review of social marketing effectiveness. *Health Education, 107,* 126–191.

Tadajewski, M. (2010). Towards a histoy of critical marketing studies. *Journal of Marketing Management, 26*(9–10), 773–824.

Truong, V. (2014). Social marketing: A systematic review of research 1998-2012. *Social Marketing Quarterly, 20,* 15–34.

Truong, D., & Dietrich, T. (2018). Master's thesis research in social marketing (1971–2015). *Journal of Social Marketing, 8,* 58–98.

White, L. (2018). Social marketing in the Caribbean: Philosophy, programs, projects, and pedagogy. *Social Marketing Quarterly, 24,* 35–44.

Wiebe, G. (1952). Merchandising commodities and citizenship on television. *Public Opinion Quarterly, 15,* 679–691.

Wood, M. (2012). Marketing social marketing. *Journal of Social Marketing, 2,* 94–102.

Part II
Social Marketing Cases: Social Welfare

Fun Ways to Engage with Rail Safety Through the Dumb Ways to Die Social Marketing Campaign

Jennifer Algie and Nicole Mead

Chapter Overview

"Dumb Ways to Die, so many Dumb Ways to Die"—can you hear the song? It will be stuck in your head all day now! This case examines a world renowned viral campaign with an underlying message about "being safe around trains." Metro Trains Melbourne chose a unique approach to connecting with train passengers, and this innovative campaign, created by McCann Agency, has reached millions of people worldwide. The humorous and fun message represents a completely different tactic to the often-used serious and/or fear-based messages adopted by social marketers aiming to improve rail safety. Despite the campaign's success in regard to evaluative measures of the number of YouTube video views and app downloads, there is debate surrounding the translation of these measures into actual behavior change. This case study centers upon exploring the case from a social marketing program perspective, so, all aboard!

Campaign Background

Dumb Ways to Die (DWTD) was an Australian Public Service Announcement (PSA) Campaign by Metro Trains in Melbourne, Victoria, in 2012 to promote rail safety (DumbWaystoDie.com, 2017). Metro Trains is Melbourne City's privately operated metropolitan rail service, with 210 six-carriage trains across 15 lines and 869 km of track. With 218 stations, Metro Trains transport 415,000 customers each day, seven days a week (metrotrains.com.au, 2017).

J. Algie (✉) · N. Mead
School of Management, Operations and Marketing Prior,
University of Wollongong, Wollongong, Australia
e-mail: jenni@uow.edu.au

© Springer Nature Switzerland AG 2019
D. Z. Basil et al. (eds.), *Social Marketing in Action*,
Springer Texts in Business and Economics,
https://doi.org/10.1007/978-3-030-13020-6_6

Metro Trains Melbourne created the campaign in response to concerns about the number of passenger-related accidents on and around its train platforms. While from an infrastructure perspective, Victoria has the highest number of level crossings, which in of themselves pose serious risks, reckless behaviors were often recorded in CCTV and security camera footage, which included teenagers sprinting over tracks as trains approached, and impatient drivers circumventing level crossing gates after they were already lowered. In many cases, young people's perceptions of invincibility led to poor decision making that showed no signs of abating.

With increased public transport use year after year, both the number of people using the Metro Trains system and the frequency of that use indicated heightened risk factors for the general public (Fig. 6.1).

Examples of unsafe behaviors around trains leading to fatalities include incidents of "coupler riding" (hanging on to the outside of the train) and train surfing incidents. There has been concern expressed by local police that Melbourne has a growing "culture" of unsafe behaviors around trains (Table 6.1).

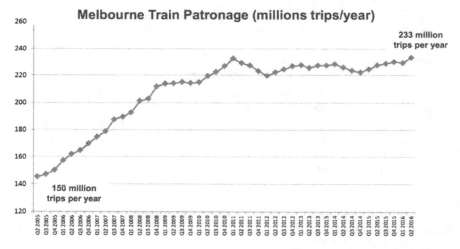

Fig. 6.1 Melbourne Train Patronage (million trips/year) *Source* Presentation by Neal Lawson, Deputy CEO, Metro Trains Melbourne http://www.icn.org.au/sites/default/files/Avalon%20Airshow%20-%20Rail%20-%20MTM_0.pdf

Table 6.1 Coupler riding and train surfing incidents, Metro Trains 2009–2016

Year	2009	2010	2011	2012	2013	2014	2015	2016
Coupler riding incidents	9	48	132	118	67	117	131	130
Train surfing incidents	1	3	7	10	8	9	5	8
Total	10	51	139	128	75	126	136	138

Source Jefferson (2017)—http://www.heraldsun.com.au/news/victoria/metro-trains-train-surfing-coupler-riding-in-melbourne/news-story/3075c4b565c57bd6de3ec07ec040a2f9

The McCann Agency helped Metro Trains develop a new style of public service campaign, and with a budget of just $200,000, focused on a train safety message that would resonate with a young, skeptical audience.

The Dumb Ways to Die Campaign

Campaign Web site: www.dumbwaystodie.com

Agency Web site: http://mccann.com.au/project/dumb-ways-to-die/

The Dumb Ways to Die Campaign, created by McCann Agency for Metro Trains Melbourne and launched on November 16, 2012, represented a fresh approach to traditional public safety messages. With "a mix of offbeat humour, a catchy tune and a collection of amiable animated characters" (McCann, 2016) to communicate rail safety messages, the campaign achieved the elusive viral status and has amassed over 316 million views (Mendes, 2018), and is the third most shared ad of all time. Following on from the original launch, the campaign life has been extended through character licensing and merchandising, a children's book, and interactive gaming developments and extensions (Fig. 6.2).

Fig. 6.2 © Metro Trains Melbourne Pty Ltd, Dumb Ways to Die ™ All rights reserved. *Image Source* You Tube (https://www.youtube.com/watch?v=IJNR2EpS0jw)

Past Efforts and Environmental Context

Rail safety messaging has been a constant theme in Victoria for many years. The annual "Rail Safety Week (RSW) is an Australasian Railway Association (ARA)/ TrackSAFE initiative that has been running since 2006. RSW aims to improve education and awareness around railway level crossing and track safety" (http:// tracksafefoundation.com.au/about, 2017).

Traditional approaches to rail safety have included educational messages, slogans encouraging personal responsibility, adopting warning-, fear-, and shock-based messaging with confronting imagery that focused on deaths or maiming that resulted from such risky behaviors. Over time people have generally become desensitized to these kinds of messages and often ignore them.

Another successful campaign regarding rail safety was Yarra Tram's "Beware the Rhino" campaign. Further information can be found here: https://ridetheg.com. au/rhino/, and the campaign can be viewed here: https://www.youtube.com/watch? v=w72R4zlgozY.

SWOT Analysis

Strengths

- **Content creativity and appeal**—The "catchy" song (Egan, 2012) and universally appealing characters that are not representative of any one demographic and with overall entertainment value showed that a serious safety issue can be communicated in a non-threatening manner to engage to a wider audience.
- **Adaptability**—By creating elements that encouraged interactivity and sharing capability, the campaign elements allowed wider distribution and facilitated the viral platform (Kissane, 2015).
- **Call to Action**—Included a strong call to action ("pledge" to be safe around trains) which required engagement (Caroll, 2016).
- **Effective Distribution**—Use of multiple mediums with consistent execution proved that for all creative ideas, "distribution is equally as important as creative" (Roper, 2014).
- **Appropriate Media Selection**—Using Tumblr, YouTube, and iTunes—all social channels and sites frequented by the target audience.
- **High Sharing Capability**—By creating mini clips and facilitating sharing on Tumblr and making the song available for purchase on iTunes, the content's humor coupled with effective delivery facilitated the viral nature of the campaign.

Weaknesses

- **Overpowering Creative**—The creativity of the campaign had the potential to overpower the main message of the campaign—which is safety around trains.
- **No Changes to Physical Environment**—The campaign is mainly about promoting a message and does not change the physical environment to make people safer around trains (many countries have better infrastructure—for example, barriers to help passenger safety).
- **Budget**—Limited initial budget (reported to be around $200k)—so longevity of message not guaranteed.
- **Target Market**—Creative execution appears to appeal to a younger demographic than stated target market (18–29).

Opportunities

- **Concept Extension**—To extend the messaging and concept beyond the original young audience.
- **Linkages**—To tighten the link between the concept and rail safety (many young people viewed it as a gimmick/game) and did not take away the original message intent.
- **Licensing** to other countries.
- **Budget extension (created from content sales)**—Additional budget may allow the extension of the campaign in duration (longer periods of activity) and reach (tapping into new markets through extended activity), and exploring new media opportunities (outside of channels utilized—e.g., VR, etc.).

Threats

- **Life span**—The nature of viral campaigns is they can become dated and the target audience quickly moves onto the next "craze."
- **Competitive Creative Environment**—Adoption of alternative messaging strategies by other agencies, which reduce the novelty and effectiveness of this one.
- **Ingrained Unsafe Behaviors**—People return to their former unsafe behaviors without continual reminders.
- **Peer Pressure**—Train surfing and other unsafe behaviors being shown and shared on social media as fun and funny activities to engage in.

Target Audience

The Dumb Ways to Die campaign is claimed to be targeted at predominantly 18–29-year-old public transport users (Chan & Mills, 2013). This audience is digital natives, who consume digital media when and where it suits them, and content needs to have unique, authentic appeal to be "shareworthy." The audience has a high ownership rate of digital devices, and also a high usage of social media, demonstrated in the following link—https://www.acma.gov.au/theACMA/engage-blogs/engage-blogs/Research-snapshots/Aussie-teens-and-kids-online.

While the stated target market displayed all the desirable media behaviors, the creative and media buy extensions beyond the original placement have appeared to resonate more with a younger target audience (aged 12–18), particularly the gaming permutations. Some critique can therefore be applied to the creative strategy to question whether the execution properly resonated with the stated target market.

John Mescall, Executive Director at McCann and the copywriter on the DWTD campaign, has said, "We didn't preach, we didn't threaten, we didn't lecture. We wanted to engage a young audience who are wired to resist lectures and warnings from authorities, but would share recommendations peer to peer. It allows you to call out your friends without losing your cred" (Quelch, 2016).

Campaign Objectives

According to the submission to the Communications Council for the Australian Effie Awards in 2013 (Ward, 2015), the campaign objectives for the Dumb Way to Die Campaign were to:

1. Increase public awareness and engagement with rail safety.
2. Generate PR, buzz, and sharing around our message.
3. Invite a commitment to be safe around trains (with a target of 10,000 local pledges via the Web site in 12 months).
4. See a 10% reduction of near misses and accidents at level crossings and station platforms over 12 months.

It seems to some extent that these objectives may have been retrofitted for the purposes of an advertising awards submission, rather than a carefully planned campaign brief in advance. That is not to say that Metro Trains did not specify business objectives when approaching McCann to create the advertising, but those have not been made available to the public. Ideally, each objective should have been "SMART" (Specific, Measurable, Actionable, Relevant, and Time Bound) so it could be assessed post implementation for success.

Utilizing the DAGMAR advertising model (DAGMAR = Defining Advertising Goals for Measured Advertising Results), objectives could have been framed in a way that provided specific communication benefits around awareness, comprehension, conviction, and action, with measureable outcomes that can be benchmarked for success measurement.

There are a few issues with the DWTD campaign, as specified in the awards brief.

(1) **Local Client/Local Campaign**: Metro Trains did not aim to educate "all of Australia, or the world" when it set the budget and commissioned the advertising strategy. The viral nature is somewhat of a "happy accident." The objectives should have reflected local measures, and the campaign success should ultimately be assessed against what it delivered in the intended market.

(2) **Marrying Source Data, Target Market Selection, and Objectives**: While individual operators collect and report data (such as near misses and accidents) to governing bodies (such as the Office of National Rail Safety Regulator or Transport Safety Victoria (TSV)), public records only show rolled-up state-based data, not specific to just one provider. There is also no overt connection to a specific data source to assess success of these objectives. Mention is often made of a "reduction in near misses," but the before and after comparisons are not readily available to validate this information.

While the success of the DWTD campaign is certainly impressive and boasts some "big numbers," it is important to assess success based on the client's original specified brief and their business-related objectives. Because Metro Train's brief has not been disclosed, definitive confirmation of success cannot be made.

Positioning

In contrast to previous fear-based attempts at making safety around trains desirable via a competition-focused positioning strategy (Lee & Kotler, 2015), the Dumb Ways To Die campaign was a unique and fresh approach to making the behavior distinctive in its target audience's minds. Other similar attempts in the field of social marketing to the approach used by the Dumb Ways to Die campaign are Road Crew (NSMC, 2018) and The Truth Campaign (https://truthinitiative.org/). Using Kotler's positioning strategies (Lee & Kotler, 2015), the Dumb Ways to Die campaign could be classified as a "re-positioning" strategy—with Metro Trains making the behavior of being safe around trains attractive (and younger people not wanting to be seen by others to be "dumb").

The positioning of the behavior was also supported through the selection of an approach to persuasion that contained entertaining content that people were comfortable with sharing among friends/peers. The use of humor provided success for the peer-to-peer sharing of the campaign.

The Dumb Ways to Die campaign was a non-threatening, non-authoritarian, unique, and fun persuasive approach to changing how the target audience views *rail safety*. The campaign attempts to shift a social norm for young people from being foolish around trains as funny and cool to being socially unacceptable. An

Australian road safety campaign called the "Pinkie" campaign (NSW Government, 2013) and the Canadian anti-smoking campaign of "Social farting" (an Ontario Health Ministry advertisement) are similar examples of shifting social norms.

Supporting Theories

The prominent and repetitious use of the word "dumb" in this campaign attempts to influence an individual's behavioral beliefs (that is, components of an attitude) about their safety behavior around trains. Furthermore, the emphasis placed on "dumb" behavior largely effects the normative beliefs and motivation to comply with these normative beliefs that comprises the Theory of Planned Behavior's (TPB) *subjective norm* (Ajzen, 1991). The premise of this campaign is to make people feel social pressure not to be judged as stupid by behaving dangerously around trains but instead to be "safe around trains" and avoid social judgement by peers and other members of the community. There is, however, no emphasis in the DWTD campaign on the perceived behavioral control component of the TPB (Fig. 6.3).

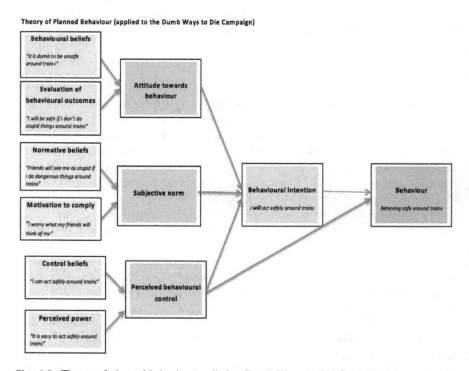

Fig. 6.3 Theory of planned behavior (applied to Dumb Ways to Die Campaign)

A hierarchy of effects model known as Attention Interest Desire Action [AIDA] (Priyanka, 2013) could also be applied to the campaign, given the predominant reliance on the messaging (social advertising) component of this campaign. The humor and creativity of the campaign was particularly effective in generating attention and interest (the first two steps of the model), supported by the sharing capability and reach of the campaign.

Marketing Strategy

Product (or "Proposition")

Instead of "Product," social marketing campaigns offer a "Proposition" (S. Peattie & K. Peattie, 2003), which in the case of the Dumb Ways to Die campaign is the notion of *being safe around trains*. In essence, the campaign outlines a range of obviously unsafe behaviors which may cause death, of which standing on the edge of a train station platform, driving around the boom gates at a level crossing, and running across the tracks are listed as the "Dumbest Ways to Die."

In this case, the principal benefit recipient is the individual, with the timescale being at the point of encounter on a platform or level crossing. The persuasiveness of the message it is hoped will be recalled at the key location the normally risky behaviors occur and results in the individual considering alternative safer actions. There is little customization in the message, and it is hoped the broad-brush approach will equally apply to any person in the target demographic.

Price (or Costs of Involvement/or Behavior Change)

The "Price" element is often referred to as the "Costs of Involvement" (S. Peattie & K. Peattie, 2003) with the proposition, or behavioral change. The cost of involvement includes the physical effort expended on being safe around trains, such as walking across a rail bridge versus jumping the tracks. Additionally, there is the inconvenience and time cost of waiting at a level crossing. There is also the lack of exhilaration for some thrill-seeking members of the population. For this target market, there also could be a social or reputational cost of being safe—and not being seen to be socially acceptable to the peer group—by not partaking in risky behaviors.

Place (or Accessibility of Proposition)

"Place" for social marketing involves "accessibility and the locations involved in either the behavior under consideration or the interventions aimed at changing it" (S. Peattie & K. Peattie, 2003, p. 374).

Metro Trains could consider other infrastructure-related improvements to additionally improve passenger and safety. Compared to many Asian rail systems, Australian rail networks have a higher incidence of level crossings, and fewer barrier-based structures integrated into platforms. The Victorian Government have already committed investment to overhaul the level crossing infrastructure, so this is likely to contribute to safety improvements in the coming years.

Promotion

The genius of the DWTD campaign was how, as John Mescall, Creative Director at McCann Melbourne said, it embraced the "content model, rather than advertising model" (Diaz, 2013) and the design and development approach to create something "people would want to pay for." The campaign launch centered around a "melodic music video featuring animated creatures who die in comically unintelligent ways before highlighting that death due to contact with trains is quite possibly the dumbest way of all" (Roper, 2014).

In keeping with the content model, the song recorded was downloadable from iTunes (generating revenue), and the music video was shared on YouTube. An interactive Web site and Tumblr page was created with sharable GIFs and over time additional offline support (like radio, outdoor, and ambient media) also focused on how to harness other social media like Facebook and Instagram with user-generated content and enhanced sharing capability. To extend the campaign's longevity, a gaming app was created, and a children's book published. Character licensing and merchandising is also being explored as the organization now sees the concept as a "franchise" that can be leveraged for greater long-term impacts. Both the children's book and character licensing direction is an interesting move toward a younger audience—and raises ethical considerations about the audience's ability to distinguish the satire and humor of the approach.

In the Metro Trains message, the locations where the highlighted risky behaviors occur are near rail crossings and on platforms. Metro Trains addressed this by integrating the campaign messaging into the environment in question. Playing the DWTD song over platform speaker systems and also having outdoor advertising (billboards) on platforms reinforces the safety message in the actual environments. Otherwise, the media choices were selected for the campaign and to be consistent with convenience devices for the target market. Many elements were designed to be played on mobile phones (given the high ownership rate among the audience), and the gamification of the concept encouraged repeated exposure to the message.

People and Processes

Metro Trains platform and customer service staff were key influencers in the identification of the customer insight that led to the DWTD campaign creation. By knowing their contribution was valued, staff bought into the campaign from the start. Metro Trains did not seemingly implement any process changes to their services to accompany the DWTD campaign.

Campaign Evaluation

Some of published and accessible results achieved include:-

- Within 24 h of its launch on November 16, 2012, the DWTD song reached the **top 10 chart of iTunes** and was ranked number six on the singer/songwriter category on the global iTunes chart just 48 h later. (McCann 2016) It sold over 100,000 copies (Mendes, 2016).
- The DWTD YouTube channel video has now amassed **316 million views** (Mendes, 2018). In February 2015, Dumb Ways to Die was the **third most shared ad of all time** (Mendes, 2016). McCann (2016) reports that "supported by an integrated advertising campaign, it spawned a plethora of global parodies and spin-offs with over 35 million combined views, attracting massive global media attention for Metro Trains and its safety message."
- The **first app**, Dumb Ways to Die, climbed to number one in 22 countries including the USA, UK, Canada, and Australia after it launched in May 2013. It now **has over 319 million app downloads and 6.8 billion app sessions plays** coming from every country in the world (Mendes, 2018).
- Earned **$60 million in media impressions within 6 weeks** and **reached 46% of the target audience in a month.**
- **126 million pledges** from people to be safer around rains via the Web site and apps (Mendes, 2018).
- 20% reduction in railway accidents or near misses year on year (Diaz, 2013).

Metro Trains claims that it has achieved its rail safety aims, too: Over 44,000 Melbournians pledged "not to do dumb things around trains" in the four months after the campaign launched. Also, for the November to January period, the operator claimed it had seen a year-on-year reduction in the number of "near misses," from 13.29 to 9.17. (https://www.campaignlive.co.uk/article/dumb-ways-die-story-behind-global-marketing-phenomenon/1187124?src_site=marketingmagazine_)

It is important for marketers to relate their success measures back to the stated campaign objectives. Much of the cited "success" of the DWTD campaign was "big numbers" from the viral nature of the campaign.

Revisiting the stated objectives, being:

1. Increase public awareness and engagement with rail safety: The fact that the campaign "went viral" significantly improved the claimed performance in this area—certainly the creative and novel approach did indeed increase public awareness of the campaign—although whether this definitively extended to rail safety awareness was not explicitly measured.

2. Generate PR, buzz and sharing around our message: This unquestionably was a success and achieved. Defining the success by video views, song downloads, and "earned media" (PR benefits) readily results in achievement of this objective.
3. Invite a commitment to be safe around trains (with a target of 10,000 local pledges via the Web site in 12 months): Again, the viral nature of the campaign ensured that this objective was achieved. There were claims that local representation of this objective was also exceeded.
4. See a 10% reduction of near misses and accidents at level crossings and station platforms over 12 months: The exact numbers and source of measurement of this metric could not be identified, yet claims were made that a 20% reduction in railway accidents or near misses occurred. (Unsubstantiated by the authors due to source data confusion.)

The stated objectives were somewhat weak (and potentially skewed for the purpose of the awards submission), and therefore, the post implementation review is weakened by not having independent and consistent measures in place. Undoubtedly, being one of the most "viewed" campaigns of all time, this campaign achieved incredible results. Creatively, it pushed boundaries and achieved incredible cut-through. The way the campaign became "self-funding" from the revenue generated from song and game downloads was innovative and ground-breaking— providing content that people are prepared to "pay for" a unique approach. From a business perspective though, unless the results in the local market are definitively achieved, no matter what the "global interest" in the campaign, it cannot be hailed as a success if it did not overwhelmingly achieve on business performance results.

Discussion and Lessons Learned

Undoubtedly, the Dumb Ways to Die clip was a memorable and highly sharable piece of entertainment. However, the question remains if this clip should be considered a successful social marketing campaign or simply entertainment?

The safety message is contained in the final 20 seconds of a 3.05-minute clip. Given the target audience's resistance to viewing messages from authorities, it is understandable why the Metro Trains brand is not shown until the final five seconds of the clip. However, the absence of the brand throughout the clip reduces the memorability of the sponsor of the "advertisement" for rail safety. The strength of fun and entertainment created by the clip actually dilutes or interferes with the brand's linkage with the campaign. Similar criticisms have been cited in the literature investigating the use of sex appeals and humor appeals in advertising (Gelb & Zinkhan, 1986; Severn, G. E. Belch, & M. A. Belch 1990).

The extent of pledging to be safe around trains, however, does demonstrate that some viewers of the clip did understand the intent and message of the campaign. Asking for pledges is an effective persuasive tool, referred to as the "*foot in the door"* technique (Freedman & Fraser, 1966), and has previously been used by environmental and prosocial causes (cf Katzev & Johnson, 1983; Pallak, Cook, & Sullivan, 1980).

The campaign was capable of taking people on a journey, with the first step being viewing an engagingly funny video (*exposure and processing*), with some viewers following on with their journey by either making a pledge and/or downloading a digital application (app) containing entertaining games involving unsafe behavior scenarios (*taking some action and further processing*). The ultimate stage of the journey for the creators of the campaign is for people to act on the message—when faced with a choice—to be safe around trains (*taking action in the form of actual behavior change*).

It could be contended that the gamification of the campaign is more "on message" than the original three-minute clip, with the "*be safe around trains*" motif explicitly displayed on the gaming site. Google Play reports "Dumb Ways to Die 2: The Games has taken the world by storm; launching to the #1 spot in 83 countries with 75 million downloads and over 1.2 billion unique plays to date" (accessed January 7, 2018). A leading gaming Youtuber, DanTDM, featured the new edition of the game, Dumb Ways to Die 2, on January 6, 2017, amassing 5 million views and 72,000 likes to date. The features of the game resonate with its target audience, with DanTDM commenting that the name of the section "AREA FIFTYDUMB" was funny (which it is!). The gamification component has sustained interest in the concept and with that interest comes incidental learning which—for younger people —is a highly effective way of ingraining new attitudes toward safety behaviors. While many of the games within both the original edition and new edition are not rail-safety-specific (as noted in a user's review below), the game attracts attention and interaction with a message that was previously resisted by many young people (Fig. 6.4).

Fig. 6.4 © Metro Trains Melbourne Pty Ltd, Dumb Ways to Die ™ All rights reserved. *Source* http://apk-dl.com/dumb-ways-to-die-2-the-games

Apple iTunes CUSTOMER REVIEWS (Accessed January 7, 2018)
What??? by Michaela Quilliam
I love the game don't get me wrong but some of the deaths have nothing to do with trains when the game is designed to tell people how to be safe around trains but apart from that I love the game! ♥

In the context of social marketing, with most social causes constrained by limited funding due to small budgets, the Dumb Ways to Die campaign is a tremendous feat—for rail safety and beyond (that is, other social and health behaviors, particularly those that are safety focused).

An executive from McCann presented on the DWTD campaign at a Health Symposium hosted by the Queensland University of Technology during 2016. The executive indicated that the concept of the Dumb Ways to Die campaign was one that the ad agency felt might be a "tough sell" to Metro Trains. The client had asked for a message about rail safety and what McCann were about to deliver as the creative brief was far from the typical safety messages traditionally implemented in this field. A three-minute message versus a 30-second radio or TV ad! A fun and entertaining cartoonish concept! How would the management at a Metro Trains respond to such a different approach in communicating about rail safety? Fortunately, for both Metro Trains and McCann the risks involved in using a completely innovative campaign were worth it.

The intended target audience was Melbournians—specifically young residents of the second largest city in Australia. The viral capability of online content has dramatically altered the intended reach of this particular campaign. An unintended, yet *positive*, consequence arising from the success of the clip for Metro Trains Melbourne was the far-reaching expanse of the message, flowing through to rail travelers worldwide. It also gained traction in pop culture, and with this, further reach through numerous parodies created on YouTube. Examples include a popular online game in 2013, DayZ, adapting the song to instances in their game and a more recent, 2017 published YouTube clip, featuring examples of the Dumb Ways to Die accidents animated in Minecraft.

It also could be said that another unintended, yet *negative* consequence of the campaign was the accessing of the clip by so many young children due to the attraction of funny cartoon characters. Children aged 2–13 years of age comprised a lot of the viewership of the clip. Unfortunately, dangerous behaviors shown in the clip, like sticking a fork in a toaster, could be modeled through observational learning and copied by children who do not have the cognitive development of the intended target audience for the campaign.

There are some caveats to this case study. First, Metro Trains are a consortium of private businesses; thus, the campaign technically should be deemed as either *prosocial marketing* or a *corporate social responsibility* initiative. For the instance of this casebook, "safety around trains" is essentially a social marketing cause and therefore should be examined in this light. Additionally, and more importantly, social marketing requires more than just a message—a comprehensive program should be designed to support the behavior change. Upstream measures, including investment in infrastructure, such as the level crossing program, need to be implemented to reduce rail-related injuries and fatalities.

In conclusion, social marketers aspire to producing campaigns that have an impact—typically expecting their message to reach a certain percentage of their target audience and then hoping for actual behavior change from a much smaller percentage of their target audience, given that many types of behavior are ingrained and hard to change. Most campaigns come and go in a time period of 10–12 weeks. The viral spirit and subsequent pervasive (earworm!) nature of the song has created a much longer life span for the campaign. It could be argued that the pure reach of this clip, on a global scale, and the longstanding duration of the campaign and gamification of the concept, can be used to deem it a highly successful campaign.

Discussion Questions

Question 1　Should other social causes, such as reducing mobile phone use when driving or encouraging children to wear a bike helmet, use a similar approach to promote their cause? Why/Why not?

Question 2　If you were Product Manager for Metro Trains and wanted to create a PSA campaign from scratch, what would be some campaign objectives you would consider important? Think about how you would identify the problem to be solved (and what data sources could be used and remember to frame each objective using SMART objectives framework).

Question 3　Do you feel that there are ethical issues with treating safety around trains in a humorous/fun way?

Question 4　Ask your friends, family, and/or work colleagues if they can name the organization promoting the DWTD message and/or the behavior that is recommended at the end of the song? Compare your results within your class, and discuss if there is a risk of the creativity of the campaign overpowering the message from Metro Trains Melbourne?

Question 5　Find four successful viral campaigns, and determine if they have any factors in common. Could these factors be applied to other social and health behaviors (e.g., reducing mobile phone use when driving or encouraging people to wear a bike helmet)?

Question 6　What elements do viral campaigns share?

Question 7　What are some considerations that social campaigns can learn from viral/corporate marketing?

Question 8 Social marketing should be more than social advertising—it should be a comprehensive program beyond the promotion of a message. Do you feel that the Dumb Ways to Die campaign is an example of social marketing or social advertising? Do you have suggestions for further improving the campaign?

References

Ajzen, I. (1991). The theory of planned behavior. *Organizational Behavior and Human Decision Processes, 50*(2), 179–211.

Berger, J. (2013). *Contagious: Why things catch on.* Later Printing Edition: Simon & Schuster.

Brownsell, A. (2013). *Dumb Ways To Die: The story behind a global marketing phenomenon.* Retrieved from http://www.campaignlive.co.uk/article/1187124/dumb-ways-die-story-behind-global-marketing-phenomenon/. Accessed September 13, 2016.

Cain, J. (2016). *Finding the right vehicle(s) for your mission.* Retrieved from http://www.philanthropyroundtable.org/topic/donor_intent/finding_the_right_vehicles_for_your_mission/. Accessed September 22, 2016.

Caroll, J. (2016). What CEOs Can Learn from "Dumb Ways to Die". Retrieved from http://www.callboxinc.com/strategy/dumb-ways-to-die-marketing/. Accessed September 20, 2016.

Chaffey, D., & Ellis-Chadwick, F. (2016). *Digital marketing.* Harlow: Pearson, Print.

Chan, D., & Mills, A. (2013) "Dumb Ways to Die", *The Australian Effie Awards Nomination Form—EFFIE Awards 2013, Entry No 95*, to the Australian Association of National Advertisers and the Communications Council.

Commonwealth of Australia (2016). *Let's stop it at the start campaign.* Retrieved from https://www.respect.gov.au/. Accessed September 13, 2016.

Cruz, D., & Fill, C. (2008). Evaluating viral marketing: Isolating the key criteria. *Marketing Intelligence & Planning, 26*(7), 743–758.

Diaz, A. C. (2013a). *How 'Dumb Ways To Die' won the internet, became the no. 1 campaign of the year.* Retrieved from http://adage.com/article/special-report-the-awards-report/dumb-ways-die-dissected/245195/. Accessed September 13, 2016.

Diaz, A. C. (2013b). *Smart lessons from 'Dumb' marketers.* Retrieved from http://adage.com/article/the-awards-report-2013/smart-lessons-dumb-marketers/245213/. Accessed September 20, 2016.

Dumb Ways To Die website (2016). Retrieved from www.dumbwaystodie.com. Accessed September 13, 2016.

Egan, V. (2012). *Dumb Ways to Die, smart ways to do viral.* Retrieved from https://econsultancy.com/blog/11204-dumb-ways-to-die-smart-ways-to-do-viral. Accessed. September 13, 2016.

Foong, L. (2014). *Interesting Infographics: How to make your content go viral.* Retrieved from http://www.business2community.com/content-marketing/interesting-infographics-make-content-go-viral-0898700#P1dYHgMev7RKu7Q0.99. Accessed September 13, 2016.

Freedman, J. L., & Fraser, S. C. (1966). Compliance without pressure: The foot-in-the-door technique. *Journal of Personality and Social Psychology, 4*(2), 195–202.

Gelb, B. D., & Zinkhan, G. M. (1986). Humor and advertising effectiveness after repeated exposures to a radio commercial. *Journal of Advertising, 15*(2), 20–34.

Helm, S. (2000). Viral marketing: Establishing customer relationship by 'word-of-mouse'. *Electronic Markets, 10*(3), 158–161.

Jefferson, A. (2017, June). Railway roulette. *Herald-Sun, 2*, 16, Australia.
Juvertson, S. (2000). *What is viral marketing?* Retrieved from http://dfj.com/news/article_25.shtml. Accessed September 15, 2016.
Katzev, R. D., & Johnson, T. R. (1983). A social-psychological analysis of residential electricity consumption: The impact of minimal justification techniques. *Journal of Economic Psychology, 3*(3–4), 267–284.
Kissane, D. (2015). *Dumb ways to die and lessons for going viral.* Retrieve from http://www.doz.com/media/dumb-ways-to-die. Accessed September 13, 2016.
Lake, C. (2009). *10 Ways to measure social media success.* Retrieved from https://econsultancy.com/blog/3407-10-ways-to-measure-social-media-success/. Accessed September 13, 2016.
Lee, N. R., & Kotler, P. (2015). *Social marketing: Influencing behaviors for good* (5th ed.). Sage.
McCann (2016). McCann Australia. Available at www.mccann.com.au. Accessed 20 September, 2016.
Mendes, D. (2016). *Head of Digital Ways to Die, Metro Trains, Email correspondence.* 11 October 2016. Dumb Ways To Die (2016).
Mendes, D. (2018). *Head of Brand and Marketing, Metro Trains, Email correspondence.* 10 September, 2018.
Nicastro, D. (2013). *5 Barriers to successful digital marketing.* Retrieved from http://www.cmswire.com/cms/customer-experience/5-barriers-to-successful-digital-marketing-023544.php. Accessed September 20, 2016.
NSW Government. (2013). *Premier and cabinet: Behavioral insights unit.* Retrieved from https://bi.dpc.nsw.gov.au/blog/case-study-series-pinkie-challenging-masculine-social-norms-on-nsw-roads-transport-for-nsw/. Accessed January 13, 2018.
Pallak, M. S., Cook, D. A., & Sullivan, J. J. (1980). Commitment and energy conservation. *Applied Social Psychology Annual, 1*, 235–253.
Peattie, S., & Peattie, K. (2003). Ready to fly solo? Reducing social marketing's dependence on commercial marketing theory. *Marketing Theory, 3*, 365–384.
Priyanka, R. (2013). AIDA marketing communication model: Stimulating a purchase decision in the minds of the consumers through a linear progression of steps. *International Journal of Multidisciplinary Research in Social Management, 1*, 37–44.
Quelch, J. A. (Ed.) (2016). *Consumers, corporations, and public health: A case-based approach to sustainable business.* Oxford University Press, ProQuest Ebook Central. https://ebookcentral-proquest-com.ezproxy.uow.edu.au/lib/uow/detail.action?docID=4310730.
Roper, P. (2014). *Case study—Metro Trains' dumb ways to die, the best of blobal digital marketing.* Retrieved from http://www.best-marketing.eu/case-study-metro-trains-dumb-ways-to-die/. Accessed September 13, 2016.
Rothschild, M. (2018). *NSMC showcase study, road crew.* Retrieved from http://www.thensmc.com/resources/showcase/road-crew. Accessed January 13, 2018.
Ruehl, M. (2013). *Smart ways to advertise: Lessons from dumb ways to die video.* Retrieved from http://www.afr.com/business/media-and-marketing/smart-ways-to-advertise-lessons-from-the-dumb-ways-to-die-video-20130730-jyvtn. Accessed September 13, 2016.
Severn, J., Belch, G. E., & Belch, M. A. (1990). The effects of sexual and non-sexual advertising appeals and information level on cognitive processing and communication effectiveness. *Journal of Advertising, 19*(1), 14–22.
Turnbull, N., & Algie, J. (2015). A qualitative analysis of young drivers' perceptions of driver distraction social marketing interventions. In *World Social Marketing Conference*, Sydney, Australia.
Ward, M. (2015). *Has Dumb Ways To Die Been Effective?* Retrieved from https://mumbrella.com.au/dumb-ways-die-stopped-dumb-behavior-around-trains-270751. Accessed September 13, 2016.

Resources and Websites

http://www.metrotrains.com.au/.
http://mccann.com.au/project/dumb-ways-to-die/.
http://mccann.com.au/project/dumb-ways-to-die-the-games/.
https://www.youtube.com/watch?v=IJNR2EpS0jw.
https://ridetheg.com.au/rhino/.

The Second Life of Food: When Social Marketing Bridges Solidarity and Waste Prevention

7

The Case of the Italian Food Bank

Ksenia Silchenko, Federica Simonetti and Giacomo Gistri

Chapter Overview

Building on the social ecological framework, the case of the Italian Food Bank sheds light on how multi-level social marketing strategies and synergistic collaborations between various groups of stakeholders could create an enabling environment for change that eventually benefits the individuals, communities, environment, and society at large. The Italian Food Bank has been recovering the food that would otherwise end up in landfills in order to redistribute it to charitable organizations for the benefit of those in need since 1989. It further takes an active role in public policy advocacy, spreading the best industry practices and public awareness-raising initiatives aimed at curbing food waste in collaboration with food producers, retailers, public institutions, and other non-profits. In this way, by bridging two urgent social problems—food waste and food insecurity—as well as connecting public, non-profit, and for-profit organizations, it eventually transforms "food recovery" from a cost to a multiplied value, thus creating a win–win and a virtuous circle for all stakeholders involved.

K. Silchenko (✉) · F. Simonetti · G. Gistri
Department of Political Sciences, Communication and International Relations,
University of Macerata, Macerata, Italy
e-mail: k.silchenko@unimc.it

F. Simonetti
e-mail: f.simonetti4@unimc.it

G. Gistri
e-mail: giacomo.gistri@unimc.it

© Springer Nature Switzerland AG 2019
D. Z. Basil et al. (eds.), *Social Marketing in Action*,
Springer Texts in Business and Economics,
https://doi.org/10.1007/978-3-030-13020-6_7

Theory

Change of behavior is a complex process, where individual willpower alone is often not sufficient to lead to a relevant and sustainable improvement of individual and social welfare. In a response to criticism of social marketing approaches being predominantly focused on the individual (Basil, 2015; Helmig & Thaler, 2010; Rothschild, 1999), the range of theoretical frameworks applied to solving the problems of concern to social marketing has been expanding to embrace wider socio-environmental perspectives. In particular, a social ecological approach has been proposed as a framework useful in design and planning (Collins, Tapp, & Pressley, 2010), as well as execution and evaluation (Gregson et al., 2001; Lindridge, MacAskill, Gnich, Eadie, & Holme, 2013) of social marketing strategies. Originating from the ecological theory developed by Bronfenbrenner (1974), social ecological framework essentially focuses on how behavior and its change are simultaneously affected by multiple levels of interaction and social contexts (Collins et al., 2010; Gregson et al., 2001; Lindridge et al., 2013). First, at the *microsystem* level, we are talking about direct and immediate, often face-to-face interpersonal interactions and respective social roles that affect one's behavior. Second, the *mesosystem* level represents links between multiple microsystems in which behavior can be affected by social rules and formal structures. Third, *exosystems* represent aspects within wider social structures that go beyond individual control or involvement (e.g., policy, economic factors, the media, material structures, and facilities) and thus impact behaviors indirectly. Forth, *macro-systems* or generalized sociocultural factors represent an overarching configuration of behaviors within a certain culture and functioning at the level of belief systems, customs, lifestyles, etc. Another, slightly less prominent, element from Bronfenbrenner's original ecological theory, *chronosystem*, focuses on the component of temporality, transitions, and sequences of events, which in a social marketing perspective suggests that efforts oriented at behavior change need to be fairly regular or otherwise consistent over extended periods of time (Shaw, 2014).

Social marketing strategies that are based on the social ecological framework thus stress not only the importance of taking into consideration various economic, environmental, and social influences relevant for a targeted behavior change, but also the need to design multiple-component programs consisting of interventions on multiple levels of social environments that work in a complementary and synergistic manner (Moore, de Silva-Sanigorski, & Moore, 2013). This can be achieved by involving a wider range of stakeholders and establishing closer collaborations between community, social, institutional, and policy approaches (Lindridge et al., 2013).

In this study, building on the social ecological framework, we present the case of a multi-level initiative by the Italian Food Bank that creates an enabling environment for change by synergistically addressing two vital social problems and connecting various groups of stakeholders.

Campaign Background

Two Global Problems of the Food Domain

Nowadays, the world lives a paradoxical situation when it comes to food. On the one hand, abounding warnings about the obesity epidemic suggest that the most challenging and urgent problems, at least in the Western world, are linked to the affluent diets and the overall abundance of food. The other face of abundance of choice is the so-called surplus food issue, i.e., generation of stocks of edible food products that for various reasons are not purchased, consumed, or otherwise (re) used and thus go to waste at different stages of the food supply chain (Garrone, Melacini, & Perego, 2012). Food waste amounts to about 1.3 billion tons globally and about 88 million tons in Europe. Translated in per capita rates, consumers in Europe and North America throw away around 95–115 kg of food per year. The costs of such losses are estimated at US\$680 billion in industrialized countries and €143 billion in European Union alone (European Commission, 2012; FAO, 2011).

On the other hand, food poverty and insecurity are far more common than usually thought about. Though out of 815 million people in the world that go hungry, only a small share is in Europe and North America, milder cases of food insecurity, such as worrying about obtaining food, compromising quality and variety, reducing quantities or skipping meals, are getting more and more commonplace (FAO, IFAD, UNICEF, WFP, & WHO, 2017). In Europe, for instance, 23.7% of the population (ca. 119 million people) are considered at risk of poverty or social exclusion and some of them (ca. 8% of the population) live in such a state of material deprivation that they cannot afford a quality meal every second day (Eurostat, 2015).

The two food problems have a significant impact on the individuals and on social, economic, and environmental welfare and therefore are the objects of public policy concern, non-profit organizations' work, as well as numerous social marketing initiatives. With different targets for behavioral change outcomes, the two problems are often addressed by different sets of initiatives. In contrast, a number of organizations around the world, known as food banks, treat the two problems as a source of mutual benefit and implement the mission of reducing food insecurity through the fight against food waste. This case will focus on one of such organizations' social marketing efforts—the Italian Food Bank, *Banco Alimentare*.[1]

---

[1]The case is based on the documents available from the Italian Food Bank and its partners' websites, mass media, policy documentation, and other information kindly provided by the Secretary-General, Liaison Officer to the Secretary-General for EU and International Relations, and Communication Manager of the *Fondazione Banco Alimentare Onlus*.

Banco Alimentare Initiative: Reducing Food Insecurity Through the Fight Against Food Waste

Banco Alimentare was established as a non-profit organization in 1989, following in the steps of the first food banks in the USA (1967), France (1984), and Spain (1987) with the purpose of recovering the food that would otherwise end up in the landfills in order to redistribute it to the charitable organizations for the benefit of those in need. More specifically, it coordinates the recovery of surplus food at all stages of the food supply chain (agriculture and primary production, food processing, distribution, retail, and foodservice) and its transportation to the regional food banks, where food is controlled, selected, and reconditioned when necessary, and then redistributed to the network of charitable organizations (food pantries, soup kitchens, etc.) located all around Italy and in constant direct contact with the local communities.

Since 2008, the coordination of the network consisting of 21 regional food banks is carried out by the Milan-based Foundation (*Fondazione Banco Alimentare Onlus*). As a second-level entity, the Foundation carries out the overall guidance and coordination of the network including logistics, financing, legal aspects, and public policy advocacy, as well as social marketing activities, while the local food banks establish closer and more personal ties with the local populations and frontline charitable organizations. As of 2016, the *Banco Alimentare* network provides food to over 8035 charitable organizations that in their turn reach around 1.6 million of people in the state or at risk of food poverty.

Starting from its earliest days, *Banco Alimentare* was oriented at bridging the gap between the industry and the world of non-profits. Instead of targeting on–off donations, it preferred to invest into establishing long-term relationships between charitable organizations in need of food supply and the food business operators in possession of surplus destined to end up in the landfills. By demonstrating sensibilities for a whole range of human, societal, economic, and environmental issues, the Italian Food Bank managed to build a strong intersectorial network of various stakeholders engaged at a number of levels and in different contexts.

SWOT Analysis (Strengths, Weaknesses, Opportunities, Threats)

Strengths
Banco Alimentare's multi-level approach is uniquely positioned to address several food-related issues through a double "win–win" logic: While it provides food resources for the charitable organizations for free, it also enables the actors along the food supply chain to reduce their food waste, optimize their inventories, minimize their disposal costs, benefit from tax deductions and fiscal incentives, and strengthen their reputation (with consumers and stakeholders). In other words, it contributes to reducing the overall food waste and directly helps the vulnerable

individuals by providing food, which is also a first step toward social inclusion (Riches, 2002).

Another strength lies in *Banco Alimentare*'s strong and lasting relationships with volunteers, public, non-profit, and for-profit organizations both on interpersonal and institutional levels.

The extended network of regional food banks coordinated by *Banco Alimentare* is advantageous not only from the perspective of logistics, but also in a relational perspective as regional hubs take advantage of more direct personal networks with local communities and charitable organizations.

Weaknesses

The amount and the typology of food products available for recovery and redistribution coordinated by *Banco Alimentare* are constrained by a number of legal, operational, and transportation factors. More importantly, the amount of redistributed food destined for human consumption is only a small fraction of the overall volume of surplus food, most of which still goes to waste. In Italy, out of 5.6 million tons of surplus food, 91.4% or 5.1 million tons goes to waste (Garrone, Melacini, & Perego, 2015).

As is the case with other food banks (Tarasuk & Eakin, 2005), *Banco Alimentare* is dependent on partner organizations on both the donation and distribution sides.

Opportunities

Banco Alimentare operates in a macro-context of increasing food poverty in need for collective action: Italy is one of the countries that overindexes (vs. the EU average) on the risk of poverty or social exclusion with 30% of the population being at risk (around 18 million in 2016, +1.3% from 2015) (Istat, 2016).

Culturally, there is growing social consciousness manifesting in companies' CSR initiatives, increasingly treated as a matter of businesses' economic survival (Lubin & Esty, 2010), on the one hand, and growing awareness in the general population about food waste and its social, economic, and environmental implications, on the other (European Commission, 2012).

The opportunity at the exosystem level is characterized by a favorable legal climate oriented at fostering the surplus food donations via incentives and overall simplification of the donation process for the food business operators in Italy.[2]

Threats

On the macro-level, the awareness of food poverty in developed countries like Italy lags behind awareness about food waste (FAO et al., 2017).

The proportion of surplus food and the degree of its recoverability varies according to the different stages of the food supply chain and the different categories of products and thus creates different levels of costs and barriers for interventions and behavior change.

---

[2]Compare to the French example based on penalizations instead (Chrisafis, 2016).

Stringent criteria for food safety, food hygiene, consumer information and liability, and other legal and operational barriers on the exosystem level restrict surplus food recoverability and increase the complexity of redistribution operations.

Target Audience

As a multi-level, multifaceted, and multi-site initiative, *Banco Alimentare* targets various groups of stakeholders. Its primary target consists of the food business operators, based on the fact that they produce 57% of food surplus (of which 64% in primary production, 5% in food processing, 24% in retail and distribution, and 7% in foodservice) and, unlike households responsible for the remaining 43%, provide better opportunities for recoverability—understood as the ability to recover food that is safe for human consumption using the minimum level of intervention (highest for food processing and retail sectors) (Garrone et al., 2015). As of 2016, *Banco Alimentare* works with 1387 food companies, 929 retailers, and 367 foodservice operators that regularly donate their surplus food and support its operations in other ways.

In order to support the change of behavior for its primary target, *Banco Alimentare* also targets those who more or less directly influence whether or not food businesses intervene to curb food waste by donating food surplus for the benefit of people in need. On the one hand, following the exosystem logic, *Banco Alimentare* invests in the relationship with public institutions for the sake of promoting food-related policies and legislation at the national and the EU level. As a result of policy advocacy, the Italian Food Bank contributed to Law No 155/2003, the so-called Good Samaritan Law, which enabled the launch of the *Siticibo* program that rapidly (within 24 h from the first preparation) recovers and redistributes chilled food products and ready-to-eat meals from foodservice venues to soup kitchens. In 2016 alone, the program redistributed 326 tons of fruit and vegetables, and 1188,466 portions of ready meals (178 tons), which was simply not possible without the policy. More recently, thanks to the Law No 166/2016, known as the "Gadda Law," the network of foodservice partners for ready-to-eat meal recovery was expanded to include fast food restaurants and cruise ships.

On the other hand, and from a more macro-perspective, *Banco Alimentare* pursues overall social mobilization in regard to both food waste and food insecurity issues. In the times of ubiquitous appeal of CSR and triple bottom line orientation,[3] more and more business operators in the food supply chain are guided by consumer values and aspirations in regard to social justice and environmental sustainability, which makes increased public awareness a pragmatic argument used to convince

---

[3]The term "triple bottom line" (Elkington, 1997) refers to managerial imperative to reorient from solely profit- and shareholder-orientation toward generation of stakeholder value and managing simultaneously for company's total social, environmental, and economic impact. To achieve such "triple bottom line" goal, companies engage in corporate social responsibility (CSR) activities considered today as a form of ethical accountability (Roberts, 2003, p. 256 cit. in Herrick, 2009).

more and more food businesses to adhere to *Banco Alimentare*'s initiative. Moreover, it creates a cultural climate that helps promote and enable change in the direction of anti-waste and social inclusion behavior.

Social Marketing Objectives

Banco Alimentare conceives of its main objective as consisting of four ambitious dimensions. First, its core objective in terms of *social benefit* is to alter the typical behavior of food businesses and save edible surplus food from waste by giving it a "second life" in the hands of charitable organizations. Second, from the perspective of *economic sustainability*, food donations facilitated by the food banks' network enable recirculation of value within the economic system and optimization of spending behavior by both profit and non-profit organizations. Though food companies give away their products without any compensation, they gain material (saved costs of storage and disposal) and immaterial (reputation) value. The charitable organizations that receive food donations for free then can also invest the saved funds into the implementation of other needed social initiatives. Third, by restructuring the overall food supply flows and preventing food waste, *Banco Alimentare* aims at overall energy conservation and reduction of harmful CO_2 emissions as an *environmental benefit*. Finally, the overarching *educational goal* of the food banks' operations is to raise awareness about food waste and food poverty and foster a collective action in order to address both of them. On a moralistic level, such education aims at the promotion of solidarity and social coherence. The food banks' network structure thus targets cognitive change and creation of social ties between a vast number of actors based on the value of charity, understood as both an act (of giving) and a feeling (of goodwill).

Barriers, Benefits, and Competition

Due to operational, legal, logistical, economic, and safety barriers, the food recovery initiative is a costly enterprise. The cost of food recovery for the businesses ranges from €0.05 to €0.1 per kg for food processing companies, from €0.4 to €0.8 per kg for food retailers, and from €1.5 to €2 per kg for foodservice, excluding the costs of the Food Bank's operations (Garrone et al., 2015). The issue of costs is the primary reason why some food businesses do not engage in recovery and stick to a more conventional (but less socially and environmentally advantageous) option of disposal. Moreover, some food businesses are not equipped with technological or business management tools to efficiently identify "moments" and "places" where food can be recovered for further redistribution. For this reason,

Banco Alimentare's collaborates with a number of Italian universities to study "best-in-class" business practices[4] and to promote them among food business operators.

On the other hand, the benefits of collaborating with the Food Bank are not limited to the philanthropic enterprise of the fight against food waste and helping the poor: Surplus food represents a considerable economic cost (storage, disposal) to the food business operators that they can reduce through donations. Furthermore, the food businesses gain from tax benefits and the overall boost in reputational terms due to a stronger CSR profile that nowadays is essential for attracting consumers.

Positioning

By bridging two urgent social problems as well as connecting various stakeholders on both profit and non-profit sides, *Banco Alimentare* markets donations of surplus food as essentially a "profit-making" activity. Even though food recovery, on average, has a cost of €0.2–2 per kilo, on the receiver's and end user's ends (charitable organizations and people in need), it has a much greater value ranging from €2.5 to 6.5 per kg (Garrone et al., 2015). In this way, food recovery is positioned as not only "zeroing out" of storage and disposal costs for food-donating businesses, but also as an action that eventually multiplies the use-value of food by 3–10 times, thus creating a win–win and a virtuous circle for all stakeholders involved.

Research

The Italian *Banco Alimentare* initiative was established following the benchmark model of the Barcelona-based Spanish Food Bank. In terms of research, both today and in its earlier days, it relies on secondary data about population, its food insecurity and food waste-related trends. Qualitative insights obtained through what can best be termed as expert knowledge-exchange sessions have also been an important source of information needed to explore the context and design its initiatives. As a matter of fact, *Banco Alimentare* was first founded in collaboration between two experts coming from two different backgrounds and with different sets of expertise in regard to food. One was a Catholic theologian and educator Luigi Giussani involved in the world of charitable organizations providing food for those in need.

---

[4]"Best-in-class" food processing companies recover up to 80% of their food surplus (vs. 42% on average) and retailers up to 30% (vs. 10% on average) thanks to systematic engagement in food surplus assessment, the existence of formalized procedures to do so, a high level of coordination between various business units, and transparent processes and mechanisms of collaboration with the external organization in charge of recovery and redistribution (Food Bank) (Garrone et al., 2015).

And another was the founding partner of the bouillon cube company, Star, Danilo Fossati, who had firsthand experience with food surplus and food waste issues in the industry.

Marketing Strategy

Product

Banco Alimentare operates by the measure of kilos of surplus food saved from waste and transformed into a number of meals provided to charitable organizations for the benefit of those in need. On the receiver's end, food is provided either in the form of care packages or soup kitchen meals.

The opportunities for surplus food recovery exist at all stages of the food supply chain, but are generally higher in case of products nearing (or sometimes exceeding) the "sell-by," "best before" or "use-by" date; aesthetic problems (product color, size, shape variations) and packaging defects (incorrectly labeled or damaged); supply inefficiencies (oversupplied items, product returns, or shipping errors); and unsold stocks (outdated promotional or seasonal items, discontinued products). Upon recovery, the food banks ensure that the donations have sufficient remaining product life and are compliant with hygiene, safety, and labeling standards for human consumption.

In addition to food-raising, *Banco Alimentare* runs by a more standard form of fund-raising, collecting donations of money from the supporters by means of direct deposits, donations of resources (e.g., vans, boxes, food containers, pallets, fridges, and other equipment), pre-tax and payroll donations, or purchase of small solidary goods (e.g., party favors, gift cards, calendars).

The food supply comes from national and European aid programs (35.4%, 23,563 tons), fruit and vegetable produce (16.8%, 11,155 tons), food processing companies (21.7%, 14,428 tons), retail (7.5%, 4966 tons) and wholesale (3.9%, 2594 tons), and foodservice (0.8%, 504 tons). A smaller share of food comes from private persons' donations during food collections (14%, 9268 tons).[5]

Price

As was explained before, the cost of the behavioral changes for the businesses includes organizational, operational, and some monetary sacrifices, which *Banco Alimentare* tries to "zero out" (by spreading best practices, implementation of larger-scale interventions, policy advocacy, etc.) and transform into a multiplied

---

[5]All data here refer to 2016.

value by taking into consideration a total of environmental, economic, and social benefits.

The same principle of mutually beneficial exchange (Rothschild, 1999) achieved through a "multiplication of value" effect is at work in case of volunteer and general public involvement at the microsystem level.

Founded on the values shared by all food banks, such as giving, sharing, solidarity, and fight against food waste, the Italian Food Bank—rooted in strong Catholic values—also embraces the value of charity in the double sense of the word as not only an act of helping those in need, but also as expression of goodwill and love of humanity. Targeting volunteers through these values, *Banco Alimentare* encourages them to donate their time in order to experience the feeling of social cohesion and the transformative power of giving.

Among other initiatives, *Banco Alimentare* encourages its food business partners to lend their employees as volunteers for a day, which not only helps the daily redistribution flow, but also serves as a corporate team building exercise, helps spread their core values, and brings closer together the giving and the receiving ends of the network. As of 2016, there are 1878 volunteers (and 119 staff members) who ensure the daily operations of food recovery, management, storage, preparation, and delivery to the charitable organizations.

Place

The coordinator of the food banks' operations, the Foundation is placed at the center of a network of networks. On the one hand, it manages the network of donors from the food supply chain, for which *Banco Alimentare* provides a solution to their food waste problem. On the other, there is a network of frontline charitable organizations that protect the vulnerable individuals and communities from food poverty and social exclusion, for which *Banco Alimentare* provides an ongoing supply of food resources.

In such a complex network, the breadth of reach is supported by the specialization of the individual actors, which eventually enables a time- and costs-effective transition of even short-life perishable foods from the donors to those in need. Geographically speaking, this network has expanded from the first and only warehouse in the Milan area in 1989 to 21 regional food banks in 18 Italian regions. The network is also a valuable source of touch-points for the initiatives aimed at raising the awareness around food waste, food poverty issues, and *Banco Alimentare*'s core values.

Promotion

Besides marketing its food waste reduction program directly to food businesses, *Banco Alimentare* runs several coordinated promotional strategies that help communicate its initiatives to the (present and future) volunteers, general supporters of its cause, and policymakers, as well as much wider categories of consumers.

Partnering with Food Business for Cause-Related Marketing

Banco Alimentare partners with the food businesses in creation of various promotional campaigns, when consumers are invited to purchase a certain product and, by doing so, contribute to the donation to the food banks' network. As a rule, the companies make a promise to contribute a certain sum of money or amount of food products to the food banks for every item sold during the designated campaign.

The previous campaigns involved both food brands, such as Coca-Cola, Kellogg's, Giovanni Rana (stuffed pasta), Oro Saiwa (cookies), Monini (olive oil), Naturelle (eggs), Rio Mare (canned tuna), Berna, Carnini, Sole, Torvis, Oro (local milk brands by Parmalat), Nipiol (baby food), etc., as well as non-food brands and products, including food containers (Cuki), cosmetics and personal care (L'Oréal Paris, Garnier, L'Erbolario), household goods (Viakal, Dash), cellphone operators (Wind), financial institutions (Esperia bank, Deutsche Bank), and transportation companies (Trenitalia).

While the food banks' network is always a beneficiary (not a promoter) of such campaigns, they serve both social and regular marketing purposes as they increase sales, recognition, and identity of the advertising brand, as well as awareness of *Banco Alimentare*'s causes.

Visual Identity

While *Banco Alimentare* does not have a single slogan, its visual identity is uniform across regional food banks, various operational units (e.g., *Siticibo*) and individual campaigns since the introduction of its current logo (see Fig. 7.1). Reportedly, it was inspired by a picture of a round bread loaf (centerpiece) and enhanced with the graphical representation of the circular economy flow of food surplus feeding in the flow of charity.

Fig. 7.1 Logo of Banco Alimentare, the Italian Food Bank

Social Media

Though present on Facebook since 2008, *Banco Alimentare* started implementing a deliberate social media strategy since 2013, with the purpose of growing the awareness about *Banco Alimentare* and extending the community of followers from the volunteers toward, more generally, supporters of its causes. In the 5 years following the setup of an editorial plan structured around a number of overarching topics leading to Calls-to-Action, a codified workflow and a scalable team structure for the social media, the amount of followers grew almost threefold. Social media presence is now expanding to other channels (LinkedIn, Twitter, YouTube, and Instagram).

Annual National Food Collection Day

Every year since 1997, the *Banco Alimentare* network arranges a one-day national solidarity campaign that takes place in a vast range of retail outlets around Italy and targets their regular customers. The volunteers meet the shoppers and ask them to contribute to the fight against food poverty by donating some non-perishable foods, such as baby food, tomato sauce, canned tuna, oil, rice, canned vegetables, biscuits, etc.

This event is in fact an atypical source of food supply for the *Banco Alimentare* network (responsible for ca. 14% of the annual total), since it does not recover surplus food otherwise destined to go to waste, but simply collects regularly purchased food from those willing to participate.

The annual collection day, however, represents a large-scale double awareness campaign. On the one hand, it is another occasion to increase the level of public education on the matters of food poverty. On the other, it is a prominent event that raises the awareness of the brand of *Banco Alimentare* itself. More specifically, it promotes its core values of solidarity and social cohesion considering the involvement of 145,000 volunteers for one day in direct contact with ca. 5.5 million shoppers. Additionally, it is a chance to communicate about the food banks' daily operations and struggles, thus driving consumers on other days of the year to make donations themselves, choose brands that donate to the *Banco Alimentare* network, and volunteer, at least occasionally, to help the local food banks.

Program Evaluation

The case of the Italian Food Bank sheds light on how multi-level social marketing strategies and synergistic collaborations with public, non-profit, and for-profit organizations could encourage changes in companies' and consumers' behaviors that eventually benefit individuals, communities, environment, and society at large.

Food Recovery and Redistribution[6]

Banco Alimentare contributes to alleviating food poverty by giving food to close to 1.6 million of people every year by redistributing around 66.5 kilotons of products, an equivalent of 364,263 meals a day. Overall from 1994 to 2016, the organization provided a total of 1,137,261,363 kg of food for the benefit of charitable organizations.

It further contributes to reduction of food waste by saving 33,647 tons of surplus food otherwise destined to end up as waste, which also reduces CO_2 emissions by 84,118 tons per year.

Growth and Reach

Banco Alimentare's overall progress has been remarkable. While in 2000 the Food Bank network was able to reach around 5400 charitable organizations and provide food to about 900,000 people in need, it is now constantly present in more than 8000 organizations reaching up to 1.9 million disadvantaged individuals every year.

The intensity with which food surplus is now recovered and redistributed in the Italian food industry has grown from 7.5% in 2012 to 9% in 2015 (Garrone et al., 2015).

The Italian experience has also become a useful model to follow in case of Paraguayan and Argentinian food banks, especially when it comes to fund-raising, volunteer training, and coordination of collection days. More recently, *Banco Alimentare* became one of the partners of the EU-promoted LIFE-Food.Waste. Stand-up project, which advances the *Banco Alimentare*'s synergistic and multi-level orientation at creating collaborations between food producers, retailers, and consumers at a larger institutional and national scale.

Public Awareness

The public awareness about food issues in Italy is as high as ever with 84% of Italians being aware of economic, environmental, and ethical consequences of food waste (Waste Watcher, 2016); 58% taking action to reduce it (by reutilizing the ingredients of the unconsumed meals, paying attention to the expiration date, etc.) (Coldiretti/Ixe', 2017); and 64% willing to boycott the companies that do not demonstrate sensibilities for environmental or social sustainability (Findomestic, 2017). Though increase in public awareness is certainly a complex enterprise that involves a large number of players and forces, the work of the Italian Food Banks'

---

[6]All data here refer to 2016.

network—in terms of the information outreach and delivering value by saving food from waste and helping people in need—has been of significant impact.

Increase in Exposure

The proper brand of *Banco Alimentare* has gained considerably greater exposure[7] in the latest period (2015–2017). For instance, it was recently featured in the nationwide pre-Christmas campaign #nataleperglialtri (*Christmas for others*) by Coca-Cola, on the onboard meals distributed by the main Italian train carrier Trenitalia, in the nationwide CSR-focused campaign by the stuffed pasta brand Giovanni Rana, and in a video broadcasted to the visitors of the main entrance Pavilion Zero at Expo 2015, the universal exposition in Milan visited by more than 22 million people.

Discussion and Lessons Learned

By bridging two urgent societal problems and trying to solve one through another, the Italian Food Bank not only found a way to provide food to a considerable fraction of those in need, but also contributed to a change of businesses' and some consumers' behavior that benefits the economy, environment, and society at large. Thanks to its long and consistent presence on the Italian non-profit scene, efficient network structure skillfully coordinated by the Foundation, effective public policy advocacy, thought-provoking awareness-raising initiatives, campaigns in collaboration with highly visible food and non-food brands, *Banco Alimentare* managed to grow its own brand that embodies the fight against food waste and values of social cohesion, and thus create an enabling environment for gradual behavior change.

In the current setting of increasing awareness, consumer pressure for responsible business conduct, legal climate of incentives, many more substitutable ways are becoming available for the food industry and the individuals to contribute to the social causes of food waste prevention and alleviating food insecurity. For this reason, the next step for the Italian Food Banks' network will likely be to find the strategies to operate in the conditions of a higher level of competition among social marketers for both recourses and the targets' attention.

---

[7]According to an advertising effectiveness framework DAGMAR (Colley, 1961), greater exposure intrinsically leads to raising consumer awareness as the first fundamental step in convincing them to take action. It is then followed by comprehension and conviction mind states, all of which are enabled by efficient communication.

Discussion Questions

1. What approaches might *Banco Alimentare* use to further grow the amount of recovered and redistributed food?
2. In what other ways (beyond the amount of recovered and redistributed food) can *Banco Alimentare* deliver on its social marketing objectives?
3. What can *Banco Alimentare* do to further increase its volunteer base?
4. In what other, currently underexploited ways, can *Banco Alimentare* utilize its nationwide network of food banks?
5. In what ways can *Banco Alimentare* capitalize more on its social media presence?
6. What other initiatives can *Banco Alimentare* implement to enhance its own brand?
7. Which slogan or other verbal cues can be added to support the visual identity of *Banco Alimentare*?

References

Basil, M. (2015). Introduction to the special issue. *Journal of Social Marketing, 5*(4). https://doi.org/10.1108/JSOCM-09-2015-0064.

Bronfenbrenner, U. (1974). Developmental research, public policy, and the ecology of childhood. *Child Development, 45*(1), 1–5. https://doi.org/10.2307/1127743.

Chrisafis, A. (2016, February 4). French law forbids food waste by supermarkets. *The Guardian.* https://www.theguardian.com/world/2016/feb/04/french-law-forbids-food-waste-by-supermarkets. Accessed December 28, 2017.

Coldiretti/Ixe'. (2017, May 23). Consumi: Coldiretti, 6 italiani su 10 tagliano sprechi alimentari. https://www.coldiretti.it/coldiretti-it/consumi-coldiretti-6-italiani-su-10-tagliano-sprechi-alimentari. Accessed December 28, 2017.

Colley, R. H. (1961). *Defining advertising goals for measured advertising results.* New York, NY: Association of National Advertisers.

Collins, K., Tapp, A., & Pressley, A. (2010). Social marketing and social influences: using social ecology as a theoretical framework. *Journal of Marketing Management, 26*(13–14), 1181–1200. https://doi.org/10.1080/0267257X.2010.522529.

Elkington, J. (1997). *Cannibals with forks: The triple bottom line of 21st century business.* Oxford: Capstone Publishing Ltd.

European Commission. (2012). *Food waste.* https://ec.europa.eu/food/safety/food_waste_en. Accessed December 28, 2017.

Eurostat. (2015). *People at risk of poverty or social exclusion.* http://ec.europa.eu/eurostat/statistics-explained/index.php/People_at_risk_of_poverty_or_social_exclusion. Accessed December 28, 2017.

FAO. (2011). *SAVE FOOD: global initiative on food loss and waste reduction.* Rome. http://www.fao.org/save-food/resources/keyfindings/en/. Accessed December 28, 2017.

FAO, IFAD, UNICEF, WFP, & WHO. (2017). *The state of food security and nutrition in the world 2017.* Rome. http://www.fao.org/3/a-I7695e.pdf. Accessed December 28, 2017.

Findomestic. (2017). *L'osservatorio Findomestic. Consumi. I mercati dei beni durevoli e le nuove tendenze di consumo.* http://www.osservatoriofindomestic.it/media/Osservatorio_Consumi_ 2017_Tendenze.pdf. Accessed December 28, 2017.

Garrone, P., Melacini, M., & Perego, A. (2012). *Dar da mangiare agli affamati: le eccedenze alimentari come opportunità.* Milano: Guerini e associati.

Garrone, P., Melacini, M., & Perego, A. (2015). *Surplus food management against food waste.* Milano: La Fabbrica.

Gregson, J., Foerster, S. B., Orr, R., Jones, L., Benedict, J., Clarke, B., et al. (2001). System, environmental, and policy changes: Using the social-ecological model as a framework for evaluating nutrition education and social marketing programs with low-income audiences. *Journal of Nutrition Education, 33,* S4–S15. https://doi.org/10.1016/S1499-4046(06)60065-1.

Helmig, B., & Thaler, J. (2010). On the effectiveness of social marketing—What do we really know? *Journal of Nonprofit & Public Sector Marketing, 22*(4), 264–287. https://doi.org/10. 1080/10495140903566698.

Herrick, C. (2009). Shifting blame/selling health: Corporate social responsibility in the age of obesity. *Sociology of Health & Illness, 31*(1), 51–65. https://doi.org/10.1111/j.1467-9566. 2008.01121.x.

Istat. (2016). *Condizioni di vita, reddito e carico fiscale delle famiglie.* https://www.istat.it/it/ archivio/207031. Accessed December 28, 2017.

Lindridge, A., MacAskill, S., Gnich, W., Eadie, D., & Holme, I. (2013). Applying an ecological model to social marketing communications. *European Journal of Marketing, 47*(9), 1399–1420. https://doi.org/10.1108/EJM-10-2011-0561.

Lubin, D. A., & Esty, D. C. (2010). The sustainability imperative. *Harvard Business Review, 88* (5), 43–50.

Moore, L., de Silva-Sanigorski, A., & Moore, S. N. (2013). A socio-ecological perspective on behavioral interventions to influence food choice in schools: Alternative, complementary or synergistic? *Public Health Nutrition, 16*(6), 1000–1005. https://doi.org/10.1017/ S1368980012005605.

Riches, G. (2002). Food banks and food security: Welfare reform, human rights and social policy. Lessons from Canada? *Social Policy and Administration, 36*(6), 648–663. https://doi.org/10. 1111/1467-9515.00309.

Rothschild, M. L. (1999). Carrots, sticks, and promises: A conceptual framework for the management of public health and social issue behaviors. *Journal of Marketing, 63*(4), 24–37. https://doi.org/10.2307/1251972.

Shaw, A. (2014). How to enhance the Social Ecological Framework by incorporating Bronfenbrenner's Process, Person, Context and Time Model. *Academy of Marketing Conference* (pp. 1–9). Bournemouth: Bournemouth University.

Tarasuk, V., & Eakin, J. M. (2005). Food assistance through 'surplus' food: Insights from an ethnographic study of food bank work. *Agriculture and Human Values, 22*(2), 177–186. https://doi.org/10.1007/s10460-004-8277-x.

Waste Watcher. (2016). *Rapporto sullo spreco domestico.* http://www.lastminutemarket.it/media_ news/waste-watcher/. Accessed December 28, 2017.

The Bank of Cancer Research: Applying Social Marketing to Provide Sustainable Funding for Cancer Research

8

Peter Vitartas, Nicholas Shipley and Aaron March

Chapter Overview

This case study presents a concept for raising funds that would lead to sustainable funding for cancer research. The concept draws on the idea of a purpose entity, in the form of the Bank of Cancer Research (BCR), that would use its profit as a revenue stream for cancer research. The approach also includes aspects of cause-related marketing, where a profit and non-profit organization work together for mutual benefit. The BCR concept has significant benefits for customers, the bank, cancer research, and society more broadly; however, it is not without its limitations, namely how is the funding for a bank able to be obtained? Details of the concept are presented and who should be targeted together with campaign objectives and considerations for positioning of the bank. While the concept is still at an embryonic phase, the case provides the reader with much to consider in the establishment of a new venture concept and the opportunities for applying social marketing theory.

Campaign Background

Aaron March had always thought about how he could lead a life with purpose. He thought about what was the biggest problem the world faced and identified cancer as a cause worthy of his efforts. At the time he realized the only way that this problem could be solved was through research, in particular cancer research.

P. Vitartas (✉) · N. Shipley
La Trobe Business School, Melbourne, Australia
e-mail: p.vitartas@latrobe.edu.au

A. March
Bank of Cancer Research, Melbourne, Australia
e-mail: amarch@bankofcancerresearch.com

© Springer Nature Switzerland AG 2019
D. Z. Basil et al. (eds.), *Social Marketing in Action*,
Springer Texts in Business and Economics,
https://doi.org/10.1007/978-3-030-13020-6_8

However, in order to do cancer research, researchers needed funding. And so, he saw the solution as being the ability to fund research to unprecedented levels in order to find cures for cancer. So, he started thinking about new and novel strategies of how to fund cancer research. At the time, there were a lot of reports in the media about the very high profits made by the banking industry and he wondered if banking profits could be used to fund research. From that idea, the concept of the Bank of Cancer Research (BCR) was born.

BCR is the concept for a bank, identical to existing banks, however with one important difference that all available profits are used to fund open-source cancer research.

In the USA, the top ten banks made profits of over \$115 billion annually (Onaran, 2017) and he thought about the impact that amount of money would have if it could be applied to cancer research. But he also realized that there would be other benefits as well. For example, staff in the banking industry would immediately have a social purpose in their careers and customers would recognize that every time they use the bank that they are effectively funding cancer research. The scientists and researchers will benefit from the additional funding as well. They will not have to spend time completing grant applications and seek other funding—the bank would sustainably fund their research year on year. In effect, it would allow the best scientists to focus on getting the job done. And what about supporters of existing cancer research? The current problem is that when money is donated to research, it is used up straight away and new donations are required thereafter. However, this concept provides a philanthropic investment that can grow over time and fund the cause for years to come. And for the public, everyone will benefit from improvements in cancer research and cancer treatments that are generated from the research. Under this model, everyone is better off.

The theory behind the model is based on three elements: the purpose entity (Wan & Sidoti, 2016), product differentiation theory (Sharp & Dawes, 2001), and consumer choice theory (Browning & Zupan, 2014). In our economy, we typically have two types of enterprises—those that operate for-profit and those that are not-for-profit. BCR is created as a purpose entity, which is also referred to as a *Special Purpose Entity*, which is a legal term referring to a not-for-profit company set up for a special purpose, such as funding a cause. The bank's social marketing efforts can be likened to cause-related marketing (Varadarajan & Menon, 1988). Cause-related marketing is where a for-profit organization works with a not-for-profit to promote a cause. It follows a very simple formula that can be applied to almost any business and to any cause. By having the sponsor (for-profit) promoting the cause, it receives benefits such as higher sales or a positive image while the cause (not-for-profit) benefits from greater exposure and funding. However, in this case, the Bank of Cancer Research as a not-for-profit acts as the sponsoring organization as well as the not-for-profit promoting the cause of funding cancer research. The social marketing effort, and resultant behavior change desired for consumers, is to adopt BCR as the preferred bank instead of using a traditional bank.

The second element relates to how profit is used to be a differentiator for the business. Consider two products that are identical. Marketers use the four "P's" to make their products different (Lee & Kotler, 2016), for example, by having additional features; by setting different pricing levels; the way the product is distributed and branded; or how the product is promoted. In this case, the bank would be differentiated through the use of its profits. By having comparable services, the point of difference is made by letting customers know how the excess returns made by the bank are used to fund cancer research. Product differentiation theory tells us that when there are two products that are identical, the differential use of the profits will differentiate the organization and determine the purchase decision. Finally, when applied correctly, product differentiation theory enables the consumer to make a choice decision based on how the organization allocates its profits. It creates a powerful statement—our bank supports cancer research, what does your bank do?

The purpose model provides four outcomes. In the first instance, customers become philanthropists through their use of the bank. By using the bank's services, the profits that would normally be generated by the bank are donated to charity. In Australia alone, the banking industry generates over $31 billion of profit annually (Yeates, 2017). This equates to approximately $1250 per person per year. In effect, the purpose model moves the point of donation for the consumer without any out-of-pocket expense—instead of giving this money to the "for-profit" banks, the customer is now donating the money to cancer research. The model has the power to give people of all levels of wealth a voice in the market, and it has the power to raise the volume of all the voices in the market.

The second outcome is that banking employees are provided employment with purpose. In many jobs today working for an employer is effectively working for the people who own the business and receive the profits. For many businesses with purpose-focused employees, a trade-off is made by the employee whereby they take a lower salary to work with the organization, sometimes even volunteering or not receiving a salary. BCR employees would be paid at the same rate as the competitor banks and not have to sacrifice salary or working conditions. In addition, they can see that their efforts are helping to fund cancer research through their employment. The bank then becomes an attractive employer to people in the industry who wish to work for a purpose, and it means that the bank has a richer pool of potential employees.

Third, the bank creates sustainable funding for cancer research. Once the bank is established, there will be no need to seek government funding or donations from the private sector to fund research as the bank will actively generate their own profits. The best way to explain the concept is to consider the old saying "Give a man a fish, and he will eat for a day, teach a man to fish and he will eat for a lifetime!"

Finally, BCR has one goal which is to cure cancer. Unlike many others in the field, there is no requirement to make a financial return from any medical breakthroughs that are achieved. The requirement not to profit from research gives BCR the opportunity to share its research with the world and contribute to open-source research.

Why Cancer?

Cancer has one of the greatest impacts in the world and means that its cure would provide the greatest return on the investment. Cancer is a leading cause of death globally and was responsible for 8.8 million deaths in 2015 (WHO, 2018). Globally, nearly 1 in 6 deaths are due to cancer. Further, approximately 70% of deaths from cancer occur in low- and middle-income countries (WHO, 2018). Cancer was chosen because the disease regularly results in death. Consequently, finding a cure for cancer will deliver the greatest social return for the effort.

Why a Bank?

Banks were chosen because they have a long history of being highly profitable. Banks have a strong ability to turn their accounting profits into cash profits which is demonstrated by their high dividend payout ratios. In the Australian market, banks often achieved a dividend payout ratio of 75% and higher (Yeates, 2017). This is important as it is the dividend or excess cash profits that are to be used to fund cancer research. Also, the profits they generate are largely cash. Secondly, the product differentiation theory applies more easily to service businesses. The model of banking is straightforward, and the fact that it is very easy to replicate the service and the profit differentiation theory suggests that making the product similar to other banks in the marketplace would allow the BCR to differentiate on the use of the product. Finally, in today's modern world, a bank is widely considered an essential service, so consumers must make a choice as to which bank they choose. The BCR provides the consumer a highly differentiated option where they can see their efforts are being used for a social purpose.

Currently, there are four major banks in Australia: The Commonwealth, National, Westpac Australia, and New Zealand Bank (ANZ). However, these four banks have some of the largest capitalization on the Australian stock market and are unlikely to be considered as potential options for the BCR. There are, however, several other financial institutions such as credit unions or smaller banks including the Bank of Melbourne (ME bank), Bank of Queensland, Bendigo Bank, or BankSA. Some, such as Bendigo Bank, also offer community development and other socially oriented financial support as a part of their value proposition.

At a national level, there are no major not-for-profit banking organizations in Australia; however, this is not the case at the international level. Charity Bank, for example, is a not-for-profit banking business that operates out of the UK. Charity Bank strives to support various charitable activities as well as helping people save and "do good" (https://charitybank.org/). While it does not have an identical model to BCR, it is possible there are other organizations similar to Charity Bank that could act as competitors to BCR.

Concept Implementation

To make BCR work, it is proposed that philanthropic money will be obtained of sufficient quantity to fund the purchase, either outright or partially, of an existing banking institution. The quantum of funds required for the project would be significant, however once obtained the profits due to the investment would form the basis for an ongoing cash flow to fund cancer research. Details of how the funding will be achieved are outlined later in the document.

SWOT Analysis (Strengths, Weaknesses, Opportunities, Threats)

A SWOT analysis of the BCR as a conceptual organization provides an insight into the company's current and future potential.

Strengths

Strong appeal to the public's emotions;
Appeal to fear based on the consequence of not acting;
Career and job creation opportunities;
A more motivated workforce as employees at BCR will have careers with purpose;
Attracting customers and employees who have an emotional connection with cancer or who have in interest in medical research;
Potential benefits of new products from cancer research;
Benefits can be ascribed to all;
Leverage off the reputations and networks of the BCR's investors;
A more positive public image when compared to its competitors.

Weakness

Unproven concept;
Little experience;
No collateral;
Lack of public trust.

Weaknesses will also arise whenever the Profit Differentiation Theory (PDT) is not applied correctly, i.e., whenever BCR's operations differ materially from the operations of competitors. Examples of areas where potential weaknesses could arise if the PDT is not applied correctly include:

Product and service offering;
Employment and remuneration offering;
Internal operations including information systems.

Opportunity

Development of a cure for cancer;
Research can be extended to other illnesses;
BCR will have the opportunity to use its annual profit announcement as a major marketing event. This event could be used to communicate what BCR is trying to achieve and prove to the market that they are delivering on their promise, which would further assist the bank in attracting customers and employees. All stake-holders would be welcomed to share in the event and to share in the joys of philanthropy as it is the stakeholders whose efforts and contributions that have created the profit and therefore the amount to be invested in cancer research;
There is also an opportunity to announce improvements in cancer treatments at the annual meeting in a similar way that IT companies release new products;
Global Expansion—BCR could seek to disrupt the traditional banking market by establishing a fully online international bank. Note this option may be more cost-effective than purchasing a bank.

Threats

Philanthropic donors preferring alternative causes;
Other illnesses or causes becoming more important than cancer;
Other banks and competitors make financial donations to cancer researchers;
Consumer loyalty of customers toward their banks;
Lack of public awareness and customer apathy;
Advancements in technology that disrupt the market and BCR's strategy.

Target Audience

There are currently no current customers; however, the following section outlines potential opportunities for future customers and a profile of individual customers.

The products which BCR provides form a service; intangible, perishable, and inseparable performance that one party provides to another to satisfy their needs. BCR could offer many services to individuals to make their day-to-day transactions much more convenient and manage their investments more effectively. However, the banking market also comprises a significant business sector consisting of business owners who require professional financial services such as loans for businesses, digital card services, payroll, and merchant services. To maximize profit, both groups would need to be targeted with appropriate products and communications. The following section focuses on the consumer market as the largest potential market in terms of numbers; however, this is not to say that the appeals discussed below would not also appeal to business owners and operators.

Market segmentation undertaken via demographic, geographic, psychographic, and behavioral segmentation categories provides the basis for target market selection. As BCR is a purpose entity, the most suitable segmentation criteria are believed to be psychographic segmentation. This approach categorizes the consumer based on psychological and demographic factors. Using the VALS framework (Yankelovich & Meer, 2006), potential markets can be identified such as those who have a mindset that needs to be involved in philanthropic activities. According to the VALS frameworks, the BCR's potential consumers could be identified as Thinkers, Achievers, Experiencers, and Believers. Among these segments, BCR could target Believers because they believe in good ethics, differentiate right and wrong, seek a friendly community, and are very loyal. BCR would also need to consider customers who believe in morality and philanthropy as values, are financially stable and willing to experience new products. These customers would respond to all the services provided by BCR while responding positively to their contributions for cancer research.

Demographic

The demographic characteristics of potential customers would be anyone who can make the decision about the choice of their bank. More specifically, a target group would be people over 25 years of age, because it is the time most people are looking to establish their banking credentials and thinking about a housing loan. The gender would be both males and females, and the income group would be households earning over AU$100,000 per annum.

Geographic

Initially, BCR would focus on major Australian cities because they account for the largest proportion of the population. However, it is expected that an online banking service would be provided by the bank which would provide improved access and geographic coverage.

Product Usage Characteristics

The usage characteristics of potential customers would be current bank and home loan account holders looking for better services and who wish to support cancer patients or have been affected by cancer through personal experiences of their own or those of loved ones.

Campaign Objectives

As outlined in the introduction, the BCR is only a concept. The plan is very ambitious. The aim of the campaign is to raise sufficient funds from philanthropy to purchase an existing bank and instantly make BCR a reality. The first stage of the plan is to raise the capital from a group called "The Giving Pledge."

The Giving Pledge are a group of philanthropists established by Bill Gates and Warren Buffett in 2008. It is a group of the world's wealthiest individuals and families who have a combined net worth of over $730 billion and who have made a commitment to dedicate part of their wealth to philanthropy. The group totals more than 150 signatories and is growing. This group has the financial capacity and philanthropic mindset to purchase an established bank and instantly make the BCR a reality. At this stage, members of The Giving Pledge operate independently. The idea would be to attempt to bring a number of these people together to combine their resources, or a portion of them, in order to be able to purchase a bank.

However, at the same time, it is recognized that there is a role for the general public by educating them about the concept so that they may appreciate the approach and be willing to change their banking when the bank is established. Therefore, the second stage of the plan is to undertake a social marketing campaign that seeks to raise broad general awareness and a positive attitude toward the BCR concept with the behavior change being for banking consumers to make a pledge to move their banking (savings and loans) to BCR.

Positioning

The BCR clearly targets people who have philanthropic ideals. It uses a clear long-term vision of investing in cancer research to the benefit of society as its common goal that appeals to all stakeholders. To establish the bank, it is targeting the world's most financially successful people who have a passion for philanthropy to donate the initial capital to purchase a bank. The target group have significant influence and business networks that are unrivaled anywhere in the world, and they understand the value of making investments that can generate sustainable income for cancer research.

For BCR to be successful, it is the second stage of the plan that targets consumers that needs to be successful. In appealing to banking customers, BCR's positioning requires consistency in its messages and approach. This is achieved by providing the same services as traditional banks but investing all profits in cancer research and "doing good" for society.

Marketing Strategy (the Extended 7P's of Marketing: Product, Price, Place, Promotion, People, Process, and Physical Evidence)

To achieve BCR's first goal, there is a second supporting and longer-term goal, which is to raise public awareness and support for the concept that results in a behavioral change by banking customers—to move their banking (savings and loans) to BCR. Building public support provides two outcomes. Firstly, it attracts the attention of the signatories to The Giving Pledge which could lead to an opportunity to meet with them. Secondly, by raising public support and having banking customer pledges, it will prove that there is a market for BCR, which will make any investment decision by the signatories to The Giving Pledge easier.

In considering the marketing mix, Boom & Bitner's (1981) extended marketing mix is used as the basis for the marketing strategy (see also: http://marketingmix.co.uk/). The 7P's framework extends the traditional 4P's framework by including people, processes, and physical evidence. It was proposed for services marketing in response to the unique characteristics of services—namely intangibility, heterogeneity, inseparability, and perishability.

While offering competitive banking services along the lines of traditional banking products, the 4P's will be augmented by BCR's purpose, with the focus on the benefits of adopting a social-based bank that supports research into cancer. The cost of loans (pricing) will also be competitive with traditional banks; however, it is recognized that the price for new customers will also be the effort in transferring loans and setting up accounts. BCR will need to make this transfer as simple as possible as traditional banking customers are generally entrenched in their practices and find it difficult to make the transition to a new bank. The use of special offers, incentives, and one-to-one support in completing transfer forms would be important. Trust is a further element that may cause resistance and be seen as a cost by consumers. Having a strong reputation will be critical, and this could include considerations for personnel leading and working in BCR. The bank would offer, as close as possible, a competitive marketing offering. It could be argued that this approach is not dissimilar to the approach used by traditional banks. A further point of difference would appear in the promotional appeal—or in the bank's case, the "purpose."

In relation to the last three P's in the 7P's framework, process and physical evidence would also be similar to traditional banks. However, as mentioned earlier, the people or staff of the bank would help differentiate the bank from competitors.

Staff who are attracted to work for a bank with a social purpose would be attracted to the purpose and as a result be more suited to working for the bank and with its customers who share the same values.

Aaron is using Ted Talks and speaking engagements, combined with social media, to spread the message about the BCR. These media are credible sources that appeal to an educated market with social values. Aaron imagines that if there were one or potentially two million people ready to sign up for a BCR account, then it would create a level of safety for the philanthropists and encourage them to become involved.

Program Evaluation

At this stage, Aaron has not been able to obtain the support of any member of The Giving Pledge. He has been able to speak to a small number of members who have been supportive and provided him with guidance and advice regarding the concept.

In terms of the second objective, Aaron has been more successful. Through his social media activity, he has increased the number of followers to his Twitter and Facebook accounts and the number of hits on his YouTube videos grows daily (see links below). Generally, people are supportive and can see the value of the program, however without the ability to provide people with bank accounts he is not in a position to establish the bank.

Discussion and Lessons Learned

Aaron has been particularly fortunate to be the beneficiary of other people's kindness, with many people committing a lot of their time to help improve the BCR concept. Their assistance supports the view that where there is a social outcome people are willing to "jump on board and help you, often without expecting a return." He has learned a great deal from his project. "I have also learned that there is a healthy skepticism out there especially in relation to charitable or social causes and the best way to overcome the skepticism is through being able to explain in detail the theory behind the business plan."

"I started BCR because I want to live a life that had a purpose and throughout the journey there have been times where I have felt that I have been achieving this goal," he explained. The greatest part of his experience to date has been the challenge and the ability to personally explore the purpose model in great detail. He has identified three key findings from his work:

The BCR model is a step toward delivering a more creative capitalism which can better align market forces to provide people with what they need, a cure for cancer, as opposed to providing what people with large market power demand, such as a fast car.

The purpose model allows customers to donate to cancer research while not incurring any additional costs compared to the same service offered at a competitor. In this way, the model has the power to give people of all wealth levels a voice in the market and has the power to "...raise the volume of all the voices in the market. I refer to this voice in the market as a consumer's Economic Voice," Aaron explained.

The model also has the power to address elements of wealth distribution as it provides people the opportunity to decide the outcome of business profits.

Aaron has also found when seeking funding that "you need to know your desired outcome, how you are going to get there and all aspect of your business plan." He also adds "don't get disheartened when people doubt your concept." Someone once told him "there is lots of money in the world, if the idea is good enough the money will come."

Discussion Questions

1. What is your view of the BCR concept?
2. What would you do to (1) contact signatories to The Giving Pledge and (2) how would you get their attention?
3. What other products could be used for a purpose entity? What are the important elements of a purpose entity?
4. How are competitors in the banking industry likely to respond to the BCR if established?
5. Aaron believes that proof-of-concept for the BCR and evidence of consumer propensity to switch services is required in order to attract philanthropic funding for purchase of an existing bank. What alternative means of establishing demand for BCR services could Aaron use? What customer behavioral challenges will BCR face attracting customers?
6. What are the challenges of using VAL's typologies for targeting purposes? How will BCR be able to use these to accurately forecast the size of the target audience and consumer demand?

Additional Resources

The following additional background information is available on the BCR.

Videos for Social Media

Bank of Cancer Research—The Cure for Cancer Within Our Lifetime? https://www.youtube.com/watch?v=HpgYPl2zdcA&t=318s
Bank of Cancer Research—Anything is Possible. https://www.youtube.com/watch?v=GoWrsd-iaUM
Bank of Cancer Research—Global Financial Crisis. https://www.youtube.com/watch?v=Uy7nGKXwkKw
Bank of Cancer Research—Tell Someone Else. https://www.youtube.com/watch?v=xzGi8bLIjhg
Press release to American News outlets
Please click on the link below to see the press release sent to 800 American news outlets:

https://gallery.mailchimp.com/f4c5adf0f592fae24046d797a/files/Bank_of_Cancer_Research_Press_Release.pdf

Blogs and Memes on Social Media

Instagram https://www.instagram.com/bankofcancerresearch/; @bankofcancer research
Website www.bankofcancerresearch.com
Facebook Page: Bank of Cancer Research https://www.facebook.com/Bank-of-Cancer-Research-183489708376431/?fref=ts
Twitter: @BankofCancer https://twitter.com/BankofCancer
YouTube Channel https://www.youtube.com/channel/UCkNNk0QXPKgulQSd72
DtZIg Instagram: @bankofcancerresearch

References

Booms, B., & Bitner, M. (1981). Marketing strategies and organizational structures for service firms. In James H. Donnelly & William R. George (Eds.), *Marketing of services* (pp. 47–51). Chicago: American Marketing Association.
Browning, E., & Zupan, M. (2014). *Microeconomics: Theory and applications* (12th ed.). ISBN: 978-1-118-75887-8.
Lee, N., & Kotler, P. (2016). *Social marketing: Changing behaviors for good* (5th ed.). ISBN: 978-1-452-29214-4
Onaran, Y. (2017). US Mega Banks are this close to breaking their profit record. *Bloomberg Markets*. Retrieved from: https://www.bloomberg.com/news/articles/2017-07-21/bank-profits-near-pre-crisis-peak-in-u-s-despite-all-the-rules. Accessed March 15, 18.

Sharp, B., & Dawes, J. (2001). What is differentiation and how does it work? *Journal of Marketing Management 17*, 739–759. https://doi.org/10.1362/026725701323366809

Varadarajan, P. R., & Menon, A. (1988). Cause-related marketing: A coalignment of marketing strategy and corporate philanthropy. *Journal of Marketing, 52*(3), 58–74.

Wan, A., & Sidoti, J. (2016). Why 'special purpose entities' are so special. Crowdfund Insider. Retrieved from: https://www.crowdfundinsider.com/2016/09/90049-special-purpose-entities-special/. Accessed March 15, 18.

WHO (World Health Organization). (2018). *Cancer: Fact sheet, February 2018*. Retrieved from: http://www.who.int/mediacentre/factsheets/fs297/en/. Accessed March 20, 18.

Yankelovich, D., & Meer, D. (2006, February). Rediscovering market segmentation. *Harvard Business Review*, pp 1-11.

Yeates, C. (2017, October 23). Big four banks set to rake in $31b in profits, boosted by rate hike 'tailwind'. *Sydney Morning Herald*. Retrieved from: https://www.smh.com.au/business/banking-and-finance/big-four-banks-set-to-rake-in-31b-in-profits-boosted-by-rate-hike-tailwind-20171020-gz4o4l.html. Accessed March 20, 18.

VCW for Social Impact in a Developing Country: Personal Development and Entrepreneurship in a Leadership Academy

9

Carlos Reis-Marques, Luís Filipe Lages and Valentine Vix Caminati

Chapter Overview
The Value Creation Wheel (VCW) is a new way of thinking for key decision makers (KDMs) to find solutions for their challenges. The VCW can be integrated, integrate and/or complement other projects and/or tools to solve both individual and organizational challenges. This case study describes, first at the individual level (myVCW), the application of the VCW to a set of social entrepreneurship projects driven by young women who wish to become leaders in projects with world impact. It highlights how the benefits brought by the VCW training was of great help to solve different challenges associated with individual insecurities and hesitations, helping people to define their value proposition and market approach to fulfill their vocation. Second, at the organizational level, this case explains how the VCW can be used to support social organizations (socialVCW) to tackle the challenges of their own targets. The VCW project supported the Leadership Academy Program, promoted by Girl Move Foundation, a social organization operating in the region of Nampula, Mozambique. The goal of the program is to stimulate personal development and encourage women to make life decisions in a developing country. The training and empowerment of young women will foster

C. Reis-Marques (✉)
Nova Information Management School, Lisbon, Portugal
e-mail: crmarques@novaims.unl.pt

L. F. Lages
Nova School of Business and Economics, VCW Center at Nova, Carcavelos, Portugal
e-mail: lflages@novasbe.pt

V. V. Caminati
ROFF Consultancy, Lisbon, Portugal
e-mail: valentine.vixcaminati@gmail.com

© Springer Nature Switzerland AG 2019
D. Z. Basil et al. (eds.), *Social Marketing in Action*,
Springer Texts in Business and Economics,
https://doi.org/10.1007/978-3-030-13020-6_9

leadership and entrepreneurship competencies, and consequently will have a social impact. This is an excellent social context in which to apply the VCW, socialVCW, and myVCW.

Theoretical Background

Social Marketing, Leadership, Innovation, and Value

This case-study presents a VCW social project promoted by Girl Move Foundation in Mozambique. The participants of Girl Move Leadership Academy applied the VCW to support personal development and transformation from a social marketing perspective. Social marketing was first defined by Kotler and Zaltman (1971, p.5) as the "design, implementation and control of programs calculated to influence the acceptability of social ideas and involving considerations of product planning, pricing, communication, distribution and marketing research". Understood as the set of marketing processes able to identify, create, and deliver social value in a way that generates acceptance and influences voluntary behavior on the part of target audiences to improve their personal welfare and the society in which they live, social marketing has been applied throughout the years in different fields, both in personal and organizational contexts, with a high degree of acceptance (Andreasen, 1994).

The application of social marketing procedures was fundamental for the enlargement of social innovation initiatives that have leveraged the development of policies and practices associated with health, education, employment, and social security while fighting social exclusion. The "Guide to Social Innovation", published by the European Commission, defined social innovation "as the development and implementation of new ideas (products, services and models) to meet social needs and create new social relationships or collaborations... that are social in both their ends and their means... [and] that are not only good for society but also enhance individuals' capacity to act" (European Commission, 2013, p.6).

In this case study, the Value Creation Wheel (VCW) is used to enhance entrepreneurship skills and personal development (i.e., myVCW) of young women's ability to solve their challenges and become leaders having a social impact in the world. During the VCW training, different leadership styles (Goleman, 2017) are presented and it is explained how social leaders can become a source of ethical guidance and how ethical leadership is related with important outcomes such as consideration behavior, honesty, trust in the leader, and interactional fairness. It is emphasized how ethical leadership predicts outcomes such as perceived effectiveness of leaders, followers' job satisfaction and dedication, and their willingness to report problems to management (Brown, Treviño, & Harrison,

2005). Moreover, a special focus is also given to bottom-up approaches and guidelines about how employees can manage relationships with their bosses (Gabarro & Kotter, 1980).

The identification of innovation and value in social projects is a common challenge that is often associated with a vague approach. The way to address that issue is especially important in light of the lack of processes/systems to support such an endeavor. In fact, many of the popular frameworks used during the twentieth century (e.g., Ansoff Matrix, BCG Matrix, Business Plans, Cooper Stage-Gate Model, McKinsey Matrix, and Porter Generic Strategies) are no longer adjusted to new market demands and personal challenges. Today's dynamic paradoxes (experimentation, challenge, interaction, and flexibility) have become paradigms questioning the traditional management processes based on static trade-offs (Lages, 2016). A way to address social innovation and assure its adoption by society is related with the implicit process of communication, making it closer to people and organizations. Rogers (2003) developed the Diffusion of Innovations (DOI) theory, in which he says that "Diffusion is the process in which an innovation is communicated through certain channels over time among the members of a social system." Over time, the DOI theory was verified across different fields, including social initiatives. As mentioned by Kotler and Keller (2012), social marketing organizations should evaluate program success using criteria such as "incidence of adoption, speed of adoption, continuance of adoption, low cost per unit of adoption, and absence of counterproductive consequences." (pp. 662)

The Value Creation Wheel Meta-Framework

The Value Creation Wheel (VCW) is a problem-solving meta-framework that has been used during the last two decades to solve a wide range of challenges of Fortune 500, very large firms, and business groups such as Airbus, Axa, Cathay Pacific Airways, Credit Suisse, Eurocopter, Four Seasons, Jerónimo Martins, Lufthansa Technik, Mastercard, McDonald's, Otis, Philips, Rio Tinto Alcan, Santander, Thomson Reuteurs. Additionally, the VCW has been applied to solve the challenges of several large and SMEs (e.g., Alphamega Supermarkets, INCM Portugal, Universal Life Insurance Cyprus), franchises (e.g., Flying Tiger Copenhagen), associations (e.g., League of Professional Portuguese Soccer), cities (e.g., Forbach), governments (e.g., Lisbon), hospitals (e.g., IPO Porto), innovation camps (e.g., thecamp), foundations (e.g., Aga Kahn), non-profit and non-governmental organizations (e.g., Acredita Portugal, ReFood), start-ups (e.g., WhyMob), trade associations (e.g., Nerlei), primary schools (e.g., CSCM), faculties (e.g., CIIM), and universities (e.g., Marseille University).

The VCW can be integrated, integrate and/or complete other methodological approaches (e.g., blue ocean strategy, customer development process, design thinking, creative problem solving, lean). Rather than competing with them, very often it triggers the decision to use them. The VCW can also be combined with other tools (e.g., SWOT, PESTEL, Porter 5 Forces, Ansoff Matrix, STP Approach), as well as specific tools developed by Lages and colleagues, such as the POKER method for concept-purifying—consisting of informing, validating, refining, multiplying, and/or discarding the ideas and filters generated (Lages, 2016; Lages, Fonseca, & Paulino, 2018)—and the Lag-User method, a process used to stimulate, involve, and implement skeptical targets and late-adopters in the generation of ideas and filters (Jahanmir & Lages, 2015). Rather than depreciating the value of laggards (Rogers, 2003), the VCW identifies the relevance of their opinion/contribution for the innovation process. This is especially important in projects that include contributions from a wide range of stakeholders, including those resistant to innovations and those with fewer competencies than the key decision makers (e.g., participant's parents).

The main pillar of the VCW is value. Value corresponds to the benefit created by and for all the stakeholders, such as customers, suppliers, distributors, employees, shareholders, and strategic partners. It involves processes of co-creation in which multiple stakeholders wish to create value together through knowledge sharing and interaction. In a dynamic context in which management strategy is often associated with past and future organizational performance (Lages, Jap, & Griffith, 2008), the decisions of the key decision makers play a critical role (Fonseca, Lages, & Kim, 2018; Lages, 2016). The significance of value and its perception, taking into consideration the customer (Ranjan & Read, 2016) and other stakeholders, is vital to establish a value proposal associated with each project and define a go-to-market strategy (Service, 2016).

Innovation is another pillar of the VCW. Innovation is an excellent way to improve value for social organizations, firms, and governments. It needs to be approached with a clear strategy concerning the demands emerging from a dynamic world and digital enablement (Reis-Marques & Popovic, 2016). Inspired by the need to revisit the twentieth-century-based static tools used in the business environment, the VCW has two components: the "DIANA" theoretical framework and the "TIAGO" customizable method for implementation (see Fig. 9.1).

DIANA stands for Define, Increase, Assess, Narrow, and Act. DIANA provides an overview of the supporting theory that will be used to solve problems and address challenges across the five phases. DIANA posits that value is created whenever there is any purely two-party exchange transaction and there is a Pareto improvement, which leads to an increase in net benefits (Jones et al., 2016; Windsor, 2017). Moreover, all of the various stakeholders might play a critical role for value creation (Berman, Wicks, Kotha, & Jones, 1999). However, in the case of some specific projects, customers might assume a more active role and be more willing to create value together with the organization (Prahalad & Ramaswamy, 2004) through direct and indirect collaboration, across one or more stages of production and consumption (Hoyer, Chandy, Dorotic, Krafft, & Singh, 2010; Payne, Storbacka, & Frow, 2008; Payne, Storbacka, Frow, & Knox, 2009).

TIAGO is the acronym of Tap, Induce, Analyze, Ground, and Operate. It incorporates all of the possible tools that allow for implementing the abovementioned meta-framework across those five phases. The combination of both theoretical and practical components offers a flexible solution that is adaptable to different kinds of trends and requirements (Lages, 2016).

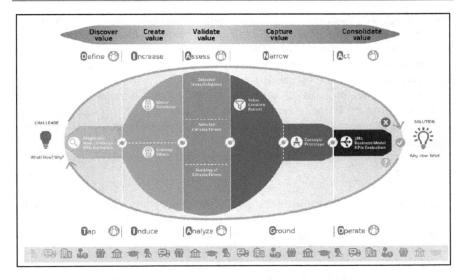

Fig. 9.1   Value Creation Wheel (VCW). *Source* adapted from Lages (2016)

The VCW has five phases:

VCW helps to discover value, characterize the context, identify the challenge, and establish KPIs;

VCW allows for creating value through a stream of solutions (phase 2a) and filters (phase 2b) using a wide range of methods (e.g., brain writing, brainstorming, literature review, surveys, questionnaires, interviews, search engines);

Then, the VCW allows for validating the previously created value by refining the outcomes of the previous phase and involving the key decision makers to validate solutions (phase 3a) and filters (phase 3b) and establish a ranking of filters (phase 3c);

In order to capture value, the VCW applies the filters using the Value Creation Funnel (VCF) (phase 4a) and helps to prepare a concept or prototype of the solutions (phase 4b) that have the greatest potential;

Finally, in order to consolidate value, the VCW enables organizations/projects to develop an action plan (e.g., 3Ms, business plan) and analyze its impact.

The Use of VCW as a Tool to Support Social Marketing Initiatives

Over the years the VCW has been used to create value for several social organizations while addressing a wide range of market challenges such as: how the VCW can be used to help enter an international market, identify the most attractive city for expansion, expand a network of non-qualified and highly qualified volunteers, find funding, stimulate social entrepreneurship, build brand image and reputation, identify the right value proposition, and foster positive solutions for unemployment.[1] Within a social marketing context the VCW has been used as a tool that establishes a virtuous cycle of value, from the identification of the market problem/pain to the final market delivery.

The VCW can be used as a tool to support the traditional marketing-mix approach (Product, Price, Promotion, and Place) and the formulation of a go-to-market strategy (Positioning, Segmentation, and Targeting) in a social marketing context.

In the present case study, the VCW accomplished such achievements through its five phases.

Discover Value—during this first phase, the participants began to identify the market needs/opportunities and the skills and competencies needed to address their professional challenge. They were challenged to use the VCW to develop a professional activity having a social impact. Stakeholders' opinions were also collected.

Create Value—during this second phase, participants listed a number of ideas/solutions as well as the criteria/filters to give them a more accurate perception of the associated value. Stakeholders' contributions were also collected.

Validate Value—during this third phase, while working jointly, participants analyzed the various solutions and criteria. The key decision maker decided on the ranking of filters for her own project.

Capture Value—during this fourth phase, each participant refined the final challenge, and while applying the ranked filters to the ideas having greater potential, arrived at the final concept. While taking into consideration the expected value and products/services to deliver associated with the final activity, participants defined the market, namely market segmentation, positioning, target audience, and the main partnerships to establish.

Consolidate Value—during the fifth phase, participants elaborated and consolidated a business model and established the key principles concerning price policies, expected revenues, and associated costs. This phase ends with a pitch for the Girl Move Leadership Academy Board that has evaluated each project in reference to its go-to-market potentialities.

Campaign Background

Case Study/Project Specification

The VCW project addressed in this case study occurred in February 2017. The VCW was part of a group of 23 personal projects promoted by a social

---

[1]www.openVCW.com.

organization (Girl Move Foundation) in one of the poorest countries in the world. Mozambique occupies the 181st position in the ranking of 188, of the Human Development Index (HDI).[2] When we refer to the project, or case study, we mean the application of the VCW meta-framework and its specifications to leverage Girl Move Leadership Academy results as a consequence of the success emerging from each participant's personal project. The Girl Move Leadership Academy participants directly applied the VCW to support personal development and personal transformation from a social marketing perspective. During the VCW co-creation journey, participants identified their soft and hard skills, strengths, and weaknesses, generated ideas and selection criteria to explore market opportunities and overcome threats, defined possible market segments and targets, generated a clear positioning and value proposition, and concluded with a go-to-market strategy. These participants were the target audience for the project (beneficiaries). The Girl Move Foundation was the client that bought the VCW solution, which was provided through the VCW Center at Nova School of Business and Economics, Portugal. Each of the 23 participants that applied the VCW identified specific elements related with her own project. These specific elements are not discussed in the case study due to confidentiality issues and limitations of space.

The Context

Alexandra Machado, Executive Director of Girl Move Foundation, had one precise objective: help young girls to realize their dreams despite unfavorable environmental conditions and foster female leadership in developing countries. In recent years, Girl Move began helping young Mozambican women to define their career path and realize their professional projects. With this purpose, the Girl Move Leadership Academy was founded in Nampula (Mozambique) with a program dedicated to recently graduated young women. In her search to find solutions and partnerships to assure the development of participants' social entrepreneurship ideas and leadership skills, Alexandra coincidentally encountered and joined forces with her close friend Rita, who had found a disruptive, innovative methodology that helped her to solve a personal challenge: to address the uncertainty and hesitations about the right career choice. To overcome her doubts, Rita applied a tool that she had discovered during her studies at the Doctoral School of the Universidade Nova de Lisboa: the Value Creation Wheel (VCW). Thanks to the VCW method, Rita could reinvent her professional career, and she presented her wonderful experience in a VCW Conference.[3]

After Rita shared her experience with Alexandra Machado and Ana Avilez, Director of Girl Move in Lisbon, they decided to further explore the application of the VCW. Convinced by the results obtained in other social cases, they contacted Luís Filipe Lages, Creator of the VCW framework and VCW Lab, Founder and

---

[2]http://hdr.undp.org/en/composite/HDI.
[3]https://youtu.be/FUzfCfNTSV4.

Director of the VCW Center at Nova, and Carlos Reis-Marques, Co-Founder and Executive Director of the VCW Center at Nova, Portugal. After analyzing the extensive portfolio of VCW projects with social impact around the world developed over several years,[4] Alexandra and Ana decided to add the VCW as one of the components of the Girl Move Advanced Program for Leadership and Social Entrepreneurship (Leadership Academy)[5] to help participants identify a professional activity having a social impact. A 24-h VCW program was planned for running in Nampula, confronting each of the future participants with a common challenge: how to design a successful social entrepreneurship business having an impact in the world? Subsequently, Luís Filipe became the VCW Scientific Advisor and Carlos became VCW Project Director in Girl Move's Leadership Academy program. Girl Move launched the second edition of its Leadership Program, using the VCW as the main methodology for future participants to acquire social marketing, entrepreneurial, and leadership skills.

Through the Leadership Academy Program, Girl Move developed new ideas and solutions for social problems rooted throughout Mozambican society supported by a strong and innovative value proposition concerning target market, services, and local partnerships. Protocols were established with the Lurio University, citizens' communities, and the Mwarusi Project[6] dedicated to young girls of the fifth, sixth, and seventh grades living in conditions of potential vulnerability in the Marrere neighborhood of Nampula, among others. Problems were related to the low level of economic development motivated by social and cultural issues demand for social innovation initiatives with a clear value proposition that can be diffused and adopted at the national scale.

The social impact generated by Girl Move projects emerging from social innovation, entrepreneurship, and value creation is increasing the public interest and leveraging partnerships with social impact,[7] which will empower its outcomes.

SWOT Analysis (Strengths, Weaknesses, Opportunities, Threats)

Strengths of this VCW Project

VCW helps key decision makers (people and executives of organizations) to face their challenges and develop their leadership skills;

VCW is a new way of thinking that contributes to problem-solving and helps to answer challenges, namely those emerging from social innovation demands;

VCW is a flexible tool that can be applied to a very wide range of situations/projects, as well as different cultural environments;

---

[4]https://youtu.be/k5b9ivLK55w.
[5]http://www.girlmove.org/eng/academy.html.
[6]http://www.girlmove.org/eng/mwarusi.html.
[7]https://bit.ly/2Jh0Ua6.

VCW combines individual activities with group work activities;

VCW provides an innovative process that includes a wide range of tools to stimulate idea generation and problem-solving;

VCW encourages the collection of the greatest number of ideas/solutions and criteria/filters, and without typical restrictions;

VCW sources as widely as possible while combining top-down and bottom-up approaches;

VCW helps to overcome paradoxes and possible tensions or confrontations between conflicting mindsets: too many options versus lack of options, solution-driven versus problem-driven, technology-push versus market-pull, shareholder-orientation versus customer-orientation, cost reduction versus added value.

Weaknesses/Challenges for this VCW Project

The second edition of the Girl Move Leadership Academy Program was the first VCW application with the first stage developed at a distance. The local promoter did not have past experience with the VCW, which could mitigate the associated risk;

Before this project, the VCW was applied in over twenty countries but had never been applied in developing markets geographically distant from the place where the process management occurred;

VCW had never been applied for such a homogeneous group of key decision makers (KDMs), who had a common vision (becoming leaders of social projects and having social impact) and at the same time addressing individual challenges;

VCW is not the "theory of everything". For example, it should not be used when KDMs are not strongly involved. It should not be implemented when KDMs have no willingness to change, innovate, being both flexible/agile and/or structured/organized, and share feedback/inputs from different stakeholders.

Market Opportunities for this VCW Project

As mentioned in the "Demographic and Health survey" (INE, 2013):

Mozambique is a young, dynamic country where 50% of the population is less than 15 years old;

There are 3 million girls aged 10–19 and 10 million teenage girls and women under the age of 30—which is 37% of the population;

The economic and cultural environment is unfavorable to the pursuit of secondary and post-secondary studies, and school dropout is very high in the geographical area. Among girls, 33% do not continue to go to school after the fifth grade—and 19% of boys stop attending classes after the fifth grade, which reveals a gender-related inequality;

Only 35% of girls between 15 and 24 years old complete primary education, 8% finish secondary education, and the proportion who enroll in higher education is as low as 2%;

Early marriages and pregnancies are widespread situations, and are a further obstacle to the realization of young women's aspirations to continue studies or begin the career of their choice. 48% of women marry before the age of 18, 14% before 15 (Bocquenet et al., 2016).

Market Threats for this VCW Project

Complex social reality with a possible latent lack of market orientation;

First time interaction with the VCW and its team;

Social entrepreneurship context in a developing country with low level of professional working opportunities, especially for women;

Non-existence of data related with local business opportunities;

Insufficient Internet access, complemented by a lack of technological devices, namely at personal level, to promote further and complementary research;

VCW has challenging features not previously tested in developing countries (e.g., requires the full commitment of KDMs at critical steps, promotes partnerships through the involvement of angel's and/or devil's advocate, internal and/or external stakeholders);

VCW is a meta-framework that can be integrated, complement and/or integrate other theories, models, tools, and frameworks (e.g., 5WHYs, situational analysis, TOWS, brainstorming, design thinking, strategic triangle, SCAMPER, BMC) that demand some background knowledge during VCW application.

Project Goals

The fundamental goal of the project was directly aligned with the Leadership Academy mission, which is to stimulate vocational development, to generate individual projects, and to allow the participants to build a satisfying professional career and reach their personal goals while personally managing possible decision-making styles, i.e., rational, intuitive, dependent on others, avoidant and spontaneous decision-making styles (Scott & Bruce, 1995).

Concerning the VCW application, a common goal was defined: how to design a successful social entrepreneurship business having an impact on the world? To that, the following specific objectives were established:

- Creation by the key decision maker (KDM) of a "Who I am profile", listing personal values, and soft and hard skills. This profile should result from individual reflection and stakeholders' perspectives;
- Generation of a set of possible business activities, according to personal profile and professional challenges (incorporating individual reflection and stakeholders' perspectives);
- Generation of a set of selection criteria;
- Analysis and synthesis of solutions for the personal challenge and associated decision criteria;
- Establishment of the ranking for the selected filters/criteria;
- Analysis and decisions regarding the solution(s) having the best value proposal, through the application of the Value Creation Funnel;
- Conceptualization and/or prototype of "final value proposition" and business proposal;
- Implementation of the business model and go-to-market strategy.

Target Audience

Young Mozambican women, recently graduated or completing their graduation, with leadership potential and who have a strong willingness to be an element of change and social development. These women are between 21 and 28 years old and come from different social groups. Some face demanding challenges associated with the fact of being single mothers or coming from unstructured families. Members of this group came from different cities and the participants had earned their degrees in different universities. These young women had graduated with bachelor's degrees in one of several fields: (i) Education Sciences—9; (ii) Management/Economics—5; (iii) Law—4; (iv) Agronomy—3; (v) Biology and Health—2; (vi) Environmental Sciences—2; (vii) Social Sciences—2.

Most of the group's members came from the region of Nampula. Girl Move Foundation provided the lodging for those coming from other regions for the Leadership Program.

Barriers and Benefits

Several barriers were found during the implementation of the VCW in Nampula:

- Cultural barriers, emerging from differences associated with the use of certain speech patterns and references not common for the audience;
- Knowledge barriers, emerging from the fact that the audience backgrounds were different, often with a low level of management and marketing knowledge and no experience in these fields;

- Time constraints related to the fact that the VCW program was very compact and intense, putting pressure on the amount of work done during the sessions as well as at home;
- Technological resources, which are difficult to ensure in developing countries, namely concerning reliable access to computers and Internet.

The follow-up conducted after the course revealed that the benefits for each of the participants were significant. After this program, barriers were overcome and the 23 participants that concluded the VCW program presented a project. This was done to increase value and consolidate their market proposal, and as a tool to help the participants address other personal challenges.

The risk that participants might lose the sense of the VCW's utility did not occur. The VCW became the reference methodology for them. Naturally, some possible explanations are that the methodology is credible and that they have not been exposed to other solid alternatives (e.g., other problem-solving methodologies). Testifying to this impact is the fact that three participants were hired by the Girl Move Foundation. All of them mentioned that the VCW was fundamental for their success. Still today, several of them continue to apply the VCW in their daily life. One of the participants mentioned that she has already applied the VCW seven times following the course.

Positioning

Following the conclusion of the project, the relationship with Girl Move was deepened and contact with participants was established on certain occasions. A video was produced with images collected during the sessions.[8] Posts were also published on social network sites to demonstrate the success of this partnership initiative and disseminate it.[9]

Girl Move participated in the VCW17 Conference, subordinated to the topic of Social Impact, and a testimonial of the VCW project in Mozambique was given by Alexandra[10] to an audience of over 700 people. Contacts with the participants occurred during their international internship in Lisbon. Complementary contacts were made during the third edition of the program, in 2018. During these contacts, the participants confirmed the value of the VCW in their lives. The success of the 2017 project and the recognized added value it brought motivated the Girl Move Foundation to invite VCW to be present during the 2018 edition. After the success of the 2018 edition (which occurred in February 2018), the VCW was recognized once again as able to deliver the expected value and was invited, once again, to the 2019 edition.

---

[8]http://bit.ly/2pbv0zP.
[9]https://www.facebook.com/girlmove; http://bit.ly/2GoagwH.
[10]http://bit.ly/2Dsy1Ru.

In summary, the Leadership Academy has gained greater differentiation through the application of VCW, becoming a program with remarkable competitive advantages in relation to possible competitors, considering, in particular, the core competencies that comprise it.

Research

The project was previously prepared concerning the collection of associated data and registration of experiences, as shown in the video produced.[11] The results gained from the data are discussed below. During the 2018 edition, the preparation replicated what was considered positive in the initial experience and some improvements were realized, including the way to gather information from participants' stakeholders. As a result of the feedback of the 2017 experience, 8 hours were added to the 2018 edition, thereby raising the program to a total of 32 hours.

VCW Project Marketing Strategy

We now present the marketing strategy for this project.

Product/Service Definition, Process, and Delivery

In order to guarantee a proper application of the VCW, the VCW team had to consider several factors: follow VCW assumptions, respect each participant's needs, and overcome the challenge of geographical distance. Due to the geographical distance between the VCW Center based at the Universidade Nova de Lisboa, Portugal, and the place of implementation in Nampula, the decision was made to carry out the project in three phases: (1) preparation and launch (Lisbon, Portugal); (2) VCW adoption (Nampula, Mozambique); (3) evaluation and further actions (Lisbon/Nampula).

Preparation and Launch (Lisbon)
The definition of the project characteristics (while identifying target profile and needs) was done in Lisbon, both by Girl Move and the VCW Center team. During this phase, all the strategy to approach the group of participants and the materials to support the training and knowledge acquisition were developed through online discussion with the local support team in Nampula, who already knew each of the future participants. A strategy to involve the stakeholders in Mozambique (family, friends, and Girl Move tutors) was also drawn up, as well as materials to collect

---

[11]http://www.OpenVCW.com.

their input according to the VCW process. A set of KPIs was also established to measure the impact and success of the initiative. Finally, the material and VCW methodology to be used to collect information from the group of stakeholders were sent by email. This preparation phase lasted two months.

VCW Adoption Supported by the Use of Social Marketing Techniques

The second step of the VCW project was located in Nampula, where participants participated in a full-day training period to better understand the VCW process and apply it to their social entrepreneurship initiatives. The five VCW steps were followed.

In the first phase of the VCW, participants started by contacting their stakeholders. The goal was to collect information on each of the 23 participants about their soft and hard skills as well as their professional expectations. Market research was conducted via telephone using a closed questionnaire. The same questionnaire was also filled in by Girl Move tutors in order to better understand the VCW process. After the collection of this information, participants were once again confronted with the initial goal of identifying their soft and hard skills as well as their professional expectations, in order to consider possible revisions.

During the second phase of the VCW, participants were asked to list possible products/services to be offered to the market and to provide an extensive list of criteria to help them decide about the best solutions. At this stage, the main goal was for participants to generate as many ideas and filters as possible. There are no good or bad ideas/solutions or filters/criteria. In this way, while promoting co-creation initiatives, the VCW adopts a disruptive and creative approach to ensure valuable outcomes.

During the third phase, participants reflected on the value of the ideas generated and established a ranking of criteria/filters to support the decision-making process;

In the fourth phase, participants had to identify the best social entrepreneurship challenges, to make a final decision, and to conceptualize the respective business (23 projects were the best from a total of 40). Finally, in the fifth phase each participant developed a business model for the project as selected. A go-to-market strategy was drawn up, including the basic principles concerning target market, products/services, price policy, partnerships, communication/promotion, distribution, people and resources needs, and time-to-market perspective.

The program was completed with the presentation of the 23 initiatives to Girl Move, and the project evaluations were conducted. The Leadership Academy then followed each of the initiatives with customized support. This adoption phase was developed over three days and lasted for a total 24 hours.

Evaluation and Further Actions (Lisbon/Nampula)

The evaluation of the overall project occurred in Nampula considering the initial KPIs and the project goals. This evaluation phase was conducted in the month following the adoption phase. The results and future actions are described in the next sections.

Price Definition

Taking into consideration the field of action and the social relevance of the project, the price policy was aligned with common practices adopted by European standards associated with programs of the European Commission to support African countries' development. This endeavor was assured by the Girl Move Foundation, which mobilized their own resources and made the necessary efforts to ensure the capital needs.

Although VCW projects have a high perception of value (the level of participants' satisfaction is normally above 90%), while recognizing the social value and possible impact of this project, the VCW Center at Nova SBE accepted the conditions proposed by Girl Move, which called for a price that was 1/3 lower than the price prevailing in the private sector. In addition, the Girl Move Foundation covered the travel costs and local expenses.

Place of Implementation

The project was executed in Nampula, the third largest city in Mozambique, situated in the northeastern part of the country. It is the capital of the Nampula Province, with 6,102,000 inhabitants.[12]

The VCW training was held in a room on the Girl Move premises. Although not being the ideal size for such a large group, the characteristics of the facilities (e.g., access to a kitchen, clean toilets, and potable water) were very positive and helped to generate a comfortable environment that promoted positive energy within the group, which was evident in the enthusiasm and engagement of the participants in the activities.

Promotion Initiatives

The Girl Move Foundation announced the Leadership Academy Program through its digital means, i.e., their own site, Facebook page, and email marketing to their local partners and others (e.g., Lúrio University), as well as other (off-line) channels to promote the initiative. The VCW Center at Nova SBE conceived a document to describe the specificities of the VCW program (syllabus), which was sent to the Girl Move Foundation and later shared with all of the participants. This syllabus included a summary of the project, its goals, duration, content, the target group identification, the VCW team involved, evaluation procedures, and learning materials to be accessed before and during the adoption phase.

The promotion strategy for the Leadership Academy Program was a challenging process because Mozambique is a country with weak communication channels (e.g., concerning the use of internet), which presents several cultural obstacles (e.g.,

---

[12]http://bit.ly/2FZIU2c.

lower educational levels across the population, the perceived role of women in society versus the role of men). This puts pressure on the team to maintain constant communication throughout the entire year, use word-of-mouth, and use traditional media in order to assure that the value of this program is perceived by all of the Mozambican citizens who have contact with this innovative reality (Rogers, 2003).

VCW Project Evaluation

The evaluation was carried out simultaneously in Lisbon and Nampula with an emphasis on Mozambique. It was dedicated to analyzing the results, evaluating project outcomes, and measuring the impact of the VCW integration into the Girl Move Leadership Academy Program. Through the evaluation of the KPIs, outcomes of the project were analyzed at different levels, as well as the effect on the participants' lives and the impact for the organization. The KPIs were measured by a questionnaire directed to the participants.

All of the 23 participants developed a project to address a common challenge. These projects were developed across different fields. Some of them aimed at developing new products or services (e.g., provide support to help women to develop economic activities, marketing services for the area of agribusiness, work in restorative projects in degraded areas). On average, each participant generated 11.3 initial ideas/solutions (phase 2a) and 12.1 criteria/filters (phase 2b). In phase 3, they selected on average 6.9 ideas/solutions (phase 3a) and 9.0 criteria/filters (phase 3b). By the end of the Value Creation Funnel (phase 4a), a total of 40 potential projects were identified. A total of 23 projects (1 project per participant) were then developed in the following phases of the VCW (4b and 5).

Participants' Evaluation

The evaluation provided by the participants (beneficiaries) revealed that their expectations were met. They considered the program to be a constructive and enriching experience. They enjoyed learning the content and mentioned their intentions to apply it to their future career. One of the participants stated that other groups should also benefit from the VCW implementation, and that the duration of the action could be extended, so that the teachings would not be so condensed, and for each notion and concept to be explained, clarified, and experienced more deeply.

One participant had started the Leadership Academy the previous year, when the VCW was not yet part of the content, but could not complete the Academy due to becoming pregnant. She re-entered the program in 2016/2017 and went through the steps of the VCW implementation. In her final report, she expressed her satisfaction with the use of all the strategic tools and specified that the VCW had brought a huge added value to the Girl Move's project, in comparison to the previous year.

The overall evaluation was very positive, showing the vast level of benefits brought by the application of the VCW in the Girl Move's project. Despite the significant geographical and cultural distance between Portugal and Mozambique, the average grade given for the training was 4.3/5, and the average grade received by the project executive and trainer Carlos Reis-Marques was 4/5. The main strengths of the program were the high quality of the knowledge transfer, achieved through simple examples of management cases, reinforced by marketing and management concepts; the program structure, which allowed learning to use the VCW through discovery and entertainment; the efficiency of the VCW framework used to identify key factors in the choice of the right career options; and the competencies and professionalism of the project manager, who demonstrated wide knowledge and know-how, and adopted the adequate pedagogy adjusted to the needs of the local market.

Contractor's Evaluation

The evaluation done by the Girl Move Foundation (client/contractor) was very positive and exceeded the initial expectations for the first edition. Due to the success of the 2017 VCW project implementation and the positive evaluation reported by all of the participants, the VCW was invited to participate at the 2018 edition of the Girl Move Leadership Academy Program (GM-LAP). As suggested by participants, an extra day of training was added, leading to a total of 32 hours.

The organizers of GM-LAP requested all the participants to give feedback about the VCW training's ability to provide the intended goals.

First, about the GM-LAP's goal to guarantee that participants would develop a set of personal and entrepreneurial skills that would support them as future leaders, comments included:

- The application of the VCW as a problem-solving tool was incredible as it made us think with no-box and understand that in order to compete in the market we should have a value proposition which will differentiate us from others.
- I've learned that the application of filters helps us to define clearly and precisely what we desire in the future.
- Through the application of the VCW, I've learned to filter my ideas and spend my energy in something concrete with high demand in the global market. This gives me a lot of pleasure and helps me to unite the useful with the pleasant.

Second, concerning GM-LAP's goal to support personal development both at the personal and professional levels, in the words of some participants:

- The VCW provided paths (...) to explore our potential and find opportunities both at the personal and professional levels.
- I've learned to listen and consider what the others think about me (...) and to identify several of my capabilities.

- I've learned to apply filters to my choices and not making choices simply because they are easy.

Finally, the GM-LAP was much concerned with the social impact in the region and in the world. Comments include:

- The VCW helped us to forecast what we can do and add to the world on an individual basis.
- The training was very important because it helped me to reflect about which values and innovations I can offer, the different fields where I can work, while giving me the opportunity to select the type of impact I want to have in the world.

As a result of the impact of the VCW workshops held in 2017 and 2018 editions, the GM-LAP invited the VCW once again for a third edition to be held in 2019, this time for 40 hours (5 days). Overall, in addition to the use of the VCW for addressing personal challenges (myVCW), during the last three years, the VCW had a positive impact on the development and change of the Leadership Academy (socialVCW).

Discussion and Lessons Learned

Among the benefits brought by the VCW project, we should consider the use of the VCW for personal value creation (i.e., myVCW), namely the development of leadership skills, discovery of a vocation, and personal value proposition, as well as the improvement of the participants' self-esteem and self-awareness. While developing their individual market approach, the participants were required to go through a deep analysis of their strengths and resources at the personal, academic, professional, and financial levels. It was a fruitful process because it allowed them to transform themselves and discover their own value as young, educated women entering the job market. Furthermore, they faced the need to analyze their external environment (both societal and professional aspects) to find the solution that would be most appropriate. This work provided them with a more accurate overview of the various opportunities they could explore. During the "VCW17 Conference on Innovation and Science for Social Impact" (Lisbon, 9 October 2017), the Executive Director of Girl Move Foundation mentioned:

The implementation of the VCW methodology, beyond being simple, and culturally adaptable, which was one of the doubts that we initially had, had a fundamental importance because every girl, for many reasons, was primarily able to recognize her own competencies, and on the other hand, the collection of several people's feedback, close to them, in regard to the opportunities that they can have to transform the world, but most importantly a concept, to dream about what they can become in the future, in order to change their country. We introduced decision-making criteria, the filters that allow the ranking of several opportunities, and the ideas that were born, but also, working on an individual value proposition. Basically, this instrument allowed us to reinforce all these components, but also the initial value proposition... Therefore, in this subject area of career development, the impact was quite big, in addition to being useful...beyond being a very interesting problem-solving methodology which has multiple purposes in the African context, where women's empowerment and leadership face many obstacles, and we intend to do exactly that.

The extra day of the VCW training included in the most recent 2018 edition (duration of a total of 32 h), helped to go deeper in defining the value proposition, in the conceptualization of each project, and in the design of the associated business model. For the future, some other improvements must be discussed, namely referring to the quality of the information collected from stakeholders (family and friends of the participants) and possible interactions to establish links among projects with synergies and/or complementary services.

Conclusion

Thanks to the VCW, the participants could define precise objectives, design a solution to answer the project challenges, and build an action plan to implement the solution(s). Compared to the previous year's project, the added value was increased by the VCW integration to the program and participants' satisfaction level was quite high. Therefore, Alexandra decided to keep the VCW as a tool to realize Girl Move's project for a third edition to be held in 2019 (five days' training).

Since no solution is perfect by itself, the VCW has been developed as a meta-framework, capable of being integrated, integrating and complementing other projects, frameworks, models, tools, and/or theories across different fields. It allows systematizing the innovation process, while supporting coordination, co-creation, and partnership with any organization or individual.

Although the VCW might have some similarities with other creativity and/or problem-solving tools that are transversal across problems and industries and are inspired by co-creation and creativity, it has major differences:

It is a meta-framework that can incorporate a wide range of solutions and/or frameworks from different fields. The VCW does not impose its own frameworks, tools, or filters.

It is stakeholder-centric (rather than user-centric).

It combines structure with agility, creativity with skepticism, and bottom-up with top-down approaches. It allows the use of "Yes & No", "And" and "But".

The VCW addresses only REAL problems/challenges, and solutions are expected to be REALLY implemented. As a consequence, the Key Decision Makers must: (a) launch those problems/challenges to be solved, (b) select ideas and then select and rank the "must have" and "nice to have" filters, and (c) be directly involved in the implementation.

Over the last two decades, the VCW has been growing following values of co-creation, collaboration, collective wisdom, cooperation, equal opportunities, open-network, partnership, and sharing, supported by principles of innovation, leadership, problem-solving, and global value creation. These years of collaborative research and open-projects led to the robustness of the VCW and its current stage of development. The VCW has also proven during this period that it is a process that can help organizations solve social problems and challenges in the most diverse areas while involving different stakeholders. The VCW is now finding key decision makers really interested in supporting its implementation to solve social problems across different fronts (e.g., refugees, children's rights, hunger, health, terrorism). It is here that NGOs and organizations with social concerns, through a partnership with VCW, can play an important role.

Discussion Questions

Group 1: While building on this case study, please answer the following questions:

1.1. What are the challenges faced when applying the VCW to a non-profit and/or social organization's project? How can they be overcome?
1.2. How important is the establishment of KPIs for social projects? Which KPIs would you propose to assess this VCW project in Mozambique?
1.3. A major challenge for leaders has to do with managing confidential issues and simultaneously benefiting from co-creation inputs that lead to creative ideas/solutions. Which recommendations would you provide to address this challenge?
1.4. Following the VCW application, which concrete actions should the participants take to meet the objectives defined during the project?
1.5. How can the project be replicated and expanded domestically or in other countries?

Group 2: While building on the VCW videos available on www.OpenVCW.com (VCW YouTube channel) and www.ValueCreationWheel.com, present examples and discuss the impact of:

2.1. VCW projects for social impact around the world.
2.2. VCW projects to address personal challenges around the world.
2.3. VCW projects in organizations and consultancy firms around the world.
2.4. VCW projects in academia and education around the world.

References

Andreasen, A. R. (1994). Social marketing: Its definition and domain. *Journal of Public Policy & Marketing, 13*(1), 108–114.

Berman, S. L., Wicks, A. C., Kotha, S., & Jones, T. M. (1999). Does stakeholder orientation matter? The relationship between stakeholder management models and firm financial performance. *Academy of Management Journal, 42*(5), 488–506.

Bocquenet, G., Chaiban, T., Cook, S., Escudero, P., Franco, A., Romo, C. G., et al. (2016). *The state of the world's children 2016: A fair chance for every child*. New York: UNICEF.

Brown, M. E., Treviño, L. K., & Harrison, D. A. (2005). Ethical leadership: A social learning perspective for construct development and testing. *Organizational Behavior and Human Decision Processes, 97*(2), 117–134.

European Commission. (2013). Guide to social innovation. *European Commission*, (February), 71.

Fonseca, V., Lages, L. F., & Kim, P. (2018). *Deimos: Expanding to a new market using the value creation wheel. Case-study BAB370-PDF-ENG*. Harvard Business Publishing.

Gabarro, J. J., & Kotter, J. P. (1980). Managing your boss. *Harvard Business Review*.

Goleman, D. (2017). *Leadership that gets results (harvard business review classics)*. Harvard Business Press.

Hoyer, W. D., Chandy, R., Dorotic, M., Krafft, M., & Singh, S. S. (2010). Consumer cocreation in new product development. *Journal of Service Research, 13*(3), 283–296.

INE. (2013). *Inquérito Demográfico e de Saúde 2011*. Calverton, Maryland, USA: MISAU, INE, and ICFI.

Jahanmir, S. F., & Lages, L. F. (2015). The lag-user method: Using laggards as a source of innovative ideas. *Journal of Engineering and Technology Management, 37*, 65–77.

Jones, T. M., Donaldson, T., Freeman, R. E., Harrison, J. S., Leana, C. R., Mahoney, J. T., et al. (2016). Management theory and social welfare: Contributions and challenges. *Academy of Management Review, 41*(2), 216–228.

Kotler, P., & Keller, K. L. (2012). *Marketing management* (14th ed.). UK: Pearson Education.

Kotler, P., & Zaltman, G. (1971). Social marketing: An approach to planned social change. *Journal of Marketing, 35*, 3–12.

Lages, L. F. (2016). VCW—Value Creation Wheel: Innovation, technology, business, and society. *Journal of Business Research, 69*(11), 4849–4855.

Lages, L. F., Fonseca, V., & Paulino, M. (2018). The VCW—Value Creation Wheel: A framework for market selection and global growth. In *Advances in global marketing* (pp. 253–279). Cham: Springer.

Lages, L. F., Jap, S. D., & Griffith, D. A. (2008). The role of past performance in export ventures: A short-term reactive approach. *Journal of International Business Studies, 39*(2), 304–325.

Payne, A. F., Storbacka, K., & Frow, P. (2008). Managing the co-creation of value. *Journal of the Academy of Marketing Science, 36*(1), 83–96.

Payne, A., Storbacka, K., Frow, P., & Knox, S. (2009). Co-creating brands: Diagnosing and designing the relationship experience. *Journal of Business Research, 62*(3), 379–389.

Prahalad, C. K., & Ramaswamy, V. (2004). Co-creation experiences: The next practice in value creation. *Journal of Interactive Marketing, 18*(3), 5–14.

Ranjan, K. R., & Read, S. (2016). Value co-creation: Concept and measurement. *Journal of the Academy of Marketing Science, 44*(3), 290–315.

Reis-Marques, C., & Popovic, A. (2016). Managing digitally enabled innovation: A conceptual framework. In *10th European conference on information systems management* (pp. 313–316). Évora: Academic Conferences and Publishing International Limited.

Rogers, E. M. (2003). *Diffusion of innovations* (5th ed.). New York: Free Press.

Scott, S. G., & Bruce, R. A. (1995). Decision making style: The development and assessment of a new measure. *Educational and Psychological Measurement, 55*(5), 818–831.

Service, D. (2016). Where do killer ideas come from? Value loops and UX design strategy. Retrieved March 11, 2018 from https://www.uxmatters.com/mt/archives/2016/11/where-do-killer-ideas-come-from-value-loops-and-ux-design-strategy.php#comments.

Windsor, D. (2017). Value creation theory: Literature review and theory assessment. In *Stakeholder management* (pp. 75–100). Emerald Publishing Limited.

Other Sources

Advanced Program for Leadership and Social Entrepreneurship: http://www.girlmove.org/eng/academy.html.

How VCW helped to find volunteers for a social organization (socialVCW): https://youtu.be/7j3TOQbFBjc.

How VCW helped to reinvent a professional career (myVCW): https://youtu.be/FUzfCfNTSV4.

Value Creation Wheel website: http://www.valuecreationwheel.com/.

Value Creation Wheel YouTube channel: http://www.openvcw.com.

VCW Career: How VCW helped an unemployed person to find a job: https://youtu.be/Ze2E7zP5S-8.

Operation Red Nose: Providing a Safe Holiday Ride and Raising Money for Charity Through Social Marketing

10

University of Lethbridge Pronghorns' Operation Red Nose Campaign

Katherine C. Lafreniere and Katharine Howie

Chapter Overview

One of the most important steps in developing a successful social marketing campaign is to identify and address the barriers of the targeted behavior (McKenzie-Mohr, 2000). In other words, marketers need to know what prevents the public from engaging in the activity they hope to promote. Most often, multiple barriers exist—both internal and external to the individual— for any given activity, and these barriers are specific to the activity (e.g., McKenzie-Mohr et al., 1995). For example, what prevents someone from donating blood may differ from what prevents him or her from recycling. Unfortunately, research suggests that there is a significant pressure for social marketers to skip this step, leading to failed campaigns that do not change behavior (McKenzie-Mohr, 2000). This case study demonstrates how the University of Lethbridge Athletics Department reduced impaired driving in their community by reducing the barriers and increasing the benefits of hiring a chauffeur service. In doing so, they created a win-win social marketing campaign that not only helps the community but also raises funds for their athletics program.

K. C. Lafreniere (✉)
Alberta School of Business, University of Alberta, Edmonton, Canada
e-mail: klafreni@ualberta.ca

K. Howie
Dhillon School of Business, University of Lethbridge, Calgary, Canada
e-mail: Katherine.howie@uleth.ca

© Springer Nature Switzerland AG 2019
D. Z. Basil et al. (eds.), *Social Marketing in Action*,
Springer Texts in Business and Economics,
https://doi.org/10.1007/978-3-030-13020-6_10

163

Campaign Background and Environment

The University of Lethbridge Pronghorns Athletics Department has found tremendous success pursuing sports excellence in basketball, soccer, rugby, hockey, swimming, and track. Yet in 1995, the department was facing budget cuts. Their directors were faced with the arduous tasks of increasing their ticket sales and finding new sources of income. It became clear that the ideal solution would be a single program that could generate revenue while simultaneously strengthening the Pronghorns brand in the community.

At the same time, Operation Red Nose, a national road safety campaign (hereinafter referred to as ORN) was looking to enter into new partnerships and expand its service to new parts of the country. The benefits of ORN are threefold:

1. ORN organizes volunteers to provide safe and sober rides to the community. The program operates by sending two drivers to each call, so they can pick up the individual and drive that individual's car home, along with a following car. This allows people in the community to have a designated driver and the convenience of having their car at home.
2. Since the drivers of the program are volunteers from a specific organization (in this case the Pronghorns Athletic Department), the volunteer organization receives both increased visibility and positive sentiment from the community for their charitable actions.
3. Although the service is free, the organization receives revenue from donations made by users of the ride service.

ORN had recently partnered with swim clubs and a couple of universities but believed that a variety of nonprofit organizations and sports programs could benefit from the fundraiser. In 1995, ORN had yet to offer their services in Southern Alberta. Each year ORN generates over $1,200,000 CAD in revenue to nonprofit organizations who participate in the program (Operation Red Nose, 2018). This case study explores how the University of Lethbridge Athletics Department partnered with ORN to offer a vital community service, raise money for the Pronghorns sports teams, and generate positive visibility for the Pronghorns in the community. The program used social marketing messages that included both a promotion and a prevention focus. This theory is explained in more detail later in the case.

ORN Mission

The mission of ORN is to encourage responsible behavior (in a non-judgmental manner) regarding impaired driving by enabling communities to provide a free and confidential chauffeur service to their members, and the financial benefits of which are redistributed to local organizations dedicated to youth or amateur sports.

SWOT Analysis (Strengths, Weaknesses, Opportunities, Threats)

Strengths

All Pronghorns athletes and staff represent a strong pool of potential volunteers. The Athletics Department staff can manage the campaign.

The University of Lethbridge Pronghorns is a well-known brand in the community.

The University of Lethbridge Athletics Department has available infrastructure and resources to handle such a program.

The University of Lethbridge has a good relationship with local media outlets.

Weaknesses

Pronghorns athletes may be reluctant to dedicate their free time, particularly on the weekends, to the campaign.

The size of each Pronghorns team is limited, so they may need to recruit additional volunteers.

The program runs over the holiday season, which is when many students, including Pronghorns athletes, leave the city to return home.

Opportunities

Community members want to meet the athletes.

Potential revenue as donations from an ORN campaign would go directly to the Pronghorns.

ORN programs are a valuable public relations tool. The program could help the Pronghorns give back to the community and be role models.

Lethbridge is a small city with light traffic and close city limits.

Threats

Many people do not like to admit they drank too much and need a ride home. There may be a perception of inconvenience in using a ride service.

Underage drinkers may be concerned they will get in trouble for drinking illegally.

Past and Similar Efforts

Before the athletics department partnered with ORN, its directors researched other ORN campaigns across Alberta. They found a swim team in Calgary, a city near Lethbridge that was operating an ORN program with a similar model. The swim team hired an employee to manage the campaign rather than recruit volunteers to manage the program. Likewise, the athletic department planned on assigning managerial responsibilities to their current employees. The advantage of the swim club's model is that the campaign would not have to rely on volunteers to organize such a complicated event in their spare time. The U of L directors met with the swim team's ORN manager to learn more about the logistics, challenges, and expectations of the fundraiser.

The swim team's ORN manager indicated that their two greatest challenges were recruiting sufficient volunteers and servicing the entire city. Regarding volunteer recruitment, the manager found that the swim team's parents preferred to donate their money to the campaign rather than their time because many of their parents were financially well off. Furthermore, the swimmers were too young to volunteer as drivers. As well, the sheer size of Calgary caused additional problems. Efficiency was greatly impacted by the distance between pickup and drop-off locations. Driving clients across the city significantly reduced the number of rides that could be completed each night and increased fuel costs. The manager tried to mitigate these problems by dividing the work with another sports team, wherein the swim team would service one side of Calgary and their partnering team would service the other. While this partnership increased the number of volunteers, it did not adequately reduce the average time and distance it took to complete a ride. Clients continued to ask drivers for a ride across the city. In the end, the swim team moved away from the traditional ORN service and began to exclusively contract their services to Christmas parties.

The athletics department knew that an ORN service in Lethbridge would face many of the same challenges and potential new ones. However, unlike the swim team, Pronghorns athletes and staff are old enough to volunteer for the campaign, which provides a solid base of volunteers (although the campaign will require additional volunteers as the client base expands). Furthermore, Lethbridge is one-tenth the size of Calgary, and therefore more manageable in terms of estimating the time required to complete a ride. Over time, though, this advantage may diminish as the city grows larger and expands its city limits.

Target Audience

The program's primary target audience consists of motorists living in Lethbridge who are not fit to drive. The target audience is not exclusive to motorists who have been drinking; it also includes those who do not feel fit to drive because of fatigue or medication, for example. Furthermore, the target audience does not exclude those who should not be drinking, such as residents under the legal drinking age of 18 years.

Campaign Objectives

Behavior Objectives

For the target audience, the program's overarching behavior goal was to reduce the number of impaired drivers during the holiday season. The specific behavior objective was to have target audience members call ORN when they are unfit to drive to secure a safe ride to their next destination. Given the significant increase of impaired drivers during winter holidays, the time frame for achieving this goal was limited to the month of December each year.

Knowledge Objectives

The knowledge objective for the target audience was to promote access-related facts and information about the service, including when and how clients can access the safe ride service. One key point the target audience should know is that the service is free but donations are accepted and encouraged. One hundred percent of all client donations are given to Pronghorns sports teams. This objective was important for motivating prospective clients to use the safe ride service while also making the program beneficial to the Pronghorns.

Belief Objectives

The athletics department in conjunction with ORN wanted their target audience to believe the following:

The service is confidential and free of judgment. Anyone who is not fit, or is unable, to drive can use this service.
One can call ORN more than once during the course of an evening, either to get from one location to another or simply to get home safely.
Driving while impaired is a very real risk to oneself and to others.

Other Important Objectives

As stated in ORN's mission statement, another important objective is that the program generates revenue for the nonprofit organization. However, this objective cannot be allowed to hinder ORN's main objective of providing a community service. That is why there is no charge for the service, but donations are accepted.

Factors Influencing Behavior

Motivators

Perceived benefits for using the safe ride service include the following:

Clients do not have to leave their vehicle behind.
The service is potentially cheaper than calling a taxi. Those who choose to donate over $30 will receive a tax receipt.
Pronghorns fans get to meet the athletes.
Clients do not have to risk the safety of themselves or others by driving while impaired.

Barriers

Formative research was conducted to identify potential barriers to using the service. Through interviewing prospective clients, the program identified the following barriers among the target audience:

Concern that the ORN Pronghorns drivers might feel their drinking is inappropriate (e.g., underage or pregnancy), and they may be negatively judged if they call for a ride home.
Some people may feel uncomfortable with someone else driving their vehicle. Likewise, some clients do not like the escort driver having 100% control of the vehicle and will insist that they shift gears instead of the driver.
Some people value having a high alcohol tolerance and therefore do not want to admit when alcohol has impaired their judgment.
Some people will not wait for the service if volunteers cannot pick them up immediately.
Some people value risk seeking and therefore see impaired driving as a thrill or badge of honor.
Some people are just reluctant to use the service because impaired driving was a social norm. Interestingly, older target beneficiaries were more reluctant to use the service than younger beneficiaries. Such a discrepancy may be attributed to the emerging road safety curriculums in high schools and universities.

Competing Behaviors

The chief competing behavior for the program is impaired driving. This dangerous behavior can result in several negative financial, mental, and health-related consequences. However, impaired driving is the most convenient behavior option. People do not have to wait for a driver or feel obligated to pay for the service.

From a fundraising perspective, other competing behaviors include the target audience using a taxi service, designated driver, or public transportation. However, ORN and their partners do not view these behaviors as true competing behaviors because they still allow the unfit motorist to safely arrive at their next location, which is the program's primary concern. Interestingly, taxi drivers in Lethbridge embraced ORN's service because (1) taxi companies within the city had trouble responding to all service requests during the winter holidays, (2) ORN made the roads safer for taxi drivers by reducing the number of drunk drivers on the road, (3) if someone without a vehicle phoned ORN, then ORN would call a taxi for them, and (4) ORN also responded to potentially difficult clients (e.g., drunks), alleviating some of the risk for taxi drivers.

Campaign Strategies

Product Strategies

ORN is a unique holiday program that allows individuals who have been drinking, or who otherwise do not feel fit or are unable to drive their own vehicle home, to summon a team of volunteers who will pick them up and drive their vehicle to their homes. A no-fee service, ORN accepts donations in support of Pronghorn Athletics. The program is designed to reduce the inconvenience of getting a ride home because motorists do not have to leave their vehicle somewhere and worry about picking it up in the morning.

Given that people tend to consume more alcohol during the winter holidays, the program starts on the last week of November and ends on the morning of New Year's Day. To meet demand, the athletics department runs the program primarily on the weekend starting at 9:30 p.m. but notes that other programs across the country will run every night in December. The athletics department will often have different volunteers each night, so, before the service begins, coordinators will provide a brief orientation and go over a script to clients' frequently asked questions. For example, if someone inquires about the cost, volunteers are taught to say, "ORN is a free service, but we do accept donations in support of Pronghorns Athletics. Our average tip is $20." To ensure smooth operations, the department will have at least four operators in the office; two operators will answer incoming calls and the other two will dispatch the road teams. The remaining volunteers will be assigned to a road team.

Each road team consists of three volunteers, including the escort driver, the volunteer driver, and the navigator. The escort driver uses his or her personal vehicle to drive the team to the location where the client is waiting. Upon arrival, the volunteer driver will drive the client in the client's vehicle. The navigator rides along with the volunteer driver and the client to make sure that everything goes well. He or she will also act as the team secretary by filling out the transportation form and preparing a receipt for any donation received. The escort driver will follow the volunteer driver to the client's destination to pick up his or her team-mates at the end of the transaction. Once the client has reached his or her destination, the navigator will give the client a receipt and hang a flyer on the client's rearview mirror, encouraging the client to fill out a short online survey for a chance to win a trip. The escort driver will then phone dispatch to receive instructions about the next ride or head back to the headquarters. At the end of the night, the navigator is responsible for handing in all the paperwork, donations, and uniforms (which are vests).

Pricing Strategies

ORN's pricing strategy is to decrease the monetary and non-monetary costs for the desired behavior. Before ORN, the non-monetary costs for people who need a safe ride home were inconvenience and worry, particularly about leaving their car overnight or picking it up the next day. Alternatively, the price for those choosing to drive impaired was the risk of being in an accident or receiving an impaired driving ticket, possibly resulting in the loss of their driver's license. The monetary cost was typically the cost of a taxi. ORN's safe ride service reduced these costs by offering a free ride home for the client and their vehicle.

Using ORN does present several costs to riders. Although the service is free, tips are generally given. Clients must call for a ride, then wait for the ORN team to arrive, which represents a time cost. Additionally, there may be an emotional cost, if clients are worried about having an ORN team member drive their vehicle. Finally, there may be apprehension about riding with a stranger.

Place Strategies

The place strategy is to make it as convenient and pleasant as possible to receive the safe ride service by reducing access-related and time-related barriers. Given that the target audience is geographically spread across Lethbridge's city limits, road teams cannot be at every possible pickup location. Furthermore, it is not efficient to merely wait outside of businesses for prospective clients, particularly if that business is not centrally located. Instead, the athletics department set up a single telephone number for clients to call when they need a ride, similar to that of a taxi service. Clients call the number and the operator dispatches a road team on their behalf. Although this phone service is not as convenient as having a road team already waiting outside (e.g., taxis waiting at the airport), it is more convenient than having clients wait outside to flag down a road team that may or may not drive by.

To reduce time-related barriers, the athletics department offers the safe ride service when clients are most likely in need of safe transportation. Most businesses in Lethbridge have their Christmas party in the evening on a weekend. As such, the service is available from 9:30 pm to 3:00 am on Thursdays, Fridays, and Saturdays. The program starts on the last weekend of November and runs until New Year's Eve. The service is available on New Year's Eve even if that holiday does not fall on a weekend.

Promotion Strategies

Promotional material is designed by ORN's national office with additional space for the charity to add any pertinent information (Fig. 10.1). However, organizations that want to add additional messages need approval from the national office. The primary message that ORN and the athletics department want to communicate to their target audience is to use the safe ride service when you feel unfit to drive. This message is typically presented in a tagline. In the past, ORN applied a rhyming technique to make the message easy to remember. The tagline read, "Planning some holiday cheer? Call a reindeer." They have since revised their tagline to read "This season, hand the reins over to us." This tagline better communicates the campaign's objectives by connecting the service to the entire season rather than a specific event. It also removes the idea that the service is only for motorists who have been drinking. Communication channels that can only support a brief message, such as posters or small print ads, typically include the tagline, ORN logo, and the nonprofit organization's service information (e.g., phone number and hours of operation). For communication channels that permit additional information, such as radio ads or

Fig. 10.1 2017 advertising campaign. *Photograph* http://operationrednose.com/advertisements

press releases, the creative strategy will also include what the service entails and statistics on how the service benefits the community. These statistics usually include how many people used the service, how many people volunteered, and how much money was raised for the organization, Pronghorns athletics in this case.

The athletics department attributes much of the campaign's success to word-of-mouth communications. Clients are so pleased with the convenience of the service that they are eager to recommend it to friends. Local media personalities embraced the campaign as a feel-good story about the community. In fact, audience feedback was so positive that radio stations which were not identified as a main sponsor eventually started covering the event and requesting interviews. Accordingly, the athletics department issued a public service announcement to the media each Monday while the campaign was running to offer updates on how many people used the service or volunteered the previous weekend.

The communication for the program used a mixture of promotion- and prevention-framed messages. Within the marketing literature, there is a wealth of research on how messages are framed and the implications of these differences. Individuals differ regarding whether they focus more on the positive aspects of a behavior or the negative aspects (Higgins, 2002). Messages that are framed positively, a promotion focus, can work well for people who are motivated to pursue good outcomes. For example, marketing ORN as supporting Pronghorn Athletes would resonate with this group of people. Conversely, other individuals are more concerned with avoiding negative outcomes, a prevention focus. For this group of people marketing messages about avoiding drunken driving crashes or tickets would be more effective. Both approaches were used in order to appeal to both promotion and prevention orientations within the target audience.

Other Important Strategies

Corporate Sponsors

The athletics department recognized that corporate sponsors were essential to gain reliable volunteers and reduce operating expenses. Businesses perceived the campaign as an interesting community service activity for their staff. Some businesses would even give their staff the afternoon off with pay so they could rest before their volunteer shift. Businesses have also been very generous covering various operational costs. Gas King, for example, provided gas gift cards to volunteers driving their own car. The City of Lethbridge provided a facility for volunteers and a telephone system to handle incoming calls. Other businesses covered other operational costs, such as food, beverages, or additional cellphones. The support has been so tremendous that the athletics department has never incurred more than $5000 in expenses.

Athlete Volunteers

The majority of the campaign's volunteers are Pronghorns athletes. Each athlete is required to work at least one shift each season, but many athletes volunteer multiple times. The amount of money donated to each Pronghorns team depends on how many volunteers the team provided that season, creating an incentive to volunteer more often. The athletics department noted two added bonuses to using athlete volunteers. First, they found that many clients were really interested in meeting the athletes and this connection encouraged clients to later attend Pronghorns games. Second, the campaign also seemed to encourage their athletes, most of them between 18 and 24 years of age, to make responsible decisions. The Department found that a lot of athletes took pride in being the responsible driver and were more willing to use the program themselves.

Concluding Remarks

Operation Red Nose is the quintessential win-win scenario, providing much-needed financial support for the university's sports program, along with a valuable community service that helps cut down on potentially impaired drivers. By taking the time to identify and address the barriers of a chauffeur service, the safe ride service offered by Pronghorns Athletics is one of the most successful ORN campaigns to date. Locally, more than $550,000 has been raised in support of Pronghorn Athletics over the past 19 years. Last season, the campaign provided almost 1300 safe rides with the help of 640 volunteers and raised over $40,000 in 12 days. Despite these impressive figures, the Department coordinators maintain that if a nonprofit organization was to only consider the safe ride service as a source of income, then the campaign would have little value. A nonprofit could probably make the same amount of money from a casino fundraiser or some other event in two days. The real value of the safe ride service is its effect on the Pronghorns brand. The campaign suggests that Pronghorns Athletics is dedicated to exceeding community expectations by developing not only athletes but also community leaders. It also reinforces the idea that Pronghorns Athletics is a vital program that deserves community support.

Discussion Questions

1. It is possible that this service does not reduce the number of impaired drivers if they are only attracting clients who would have otherwise called a taxi or designated driver. The service could merely be another alternative for people who are already making safe choices. How can campaign managers measure ORN's success in reducing the number of drunk drivers?
2. How valuable is publicity in this case? How valuable is publicity for social marketing in general?

3. The organization Operation Red Nose has the challenge of getting numerous stakeholders involved to grow their organization. Imagine that you are a marketing manager for the Operation Red Nose and are trying to enter a new community. What stakeholders do you need buy-in from for this expansion to be successful? What barriers is each stakeholder potentially facing?
4. This case study explained the differences between promotion- and prevention-focused messages. Find an example of social marketers using each type of framing, and explain why it fits into that category.
5. Many liquor companies donate money to programs that encourage the responsible use of their products. Do you think this is an ethical obligation of the company? Why or why not?

References

Higgins, E. T. (2002). How self-regulation creates distinct values: The case of promotion and prevention decision making. *Journal of Consumer Psychology, 12*(3), 177–191. https://doi.org/10.1207/S15327663JCP1203_01.

McKenzie-Mohr, D. (2000). Fostering sustainable behavior through community-based social marketing. *American Psychologist, 55*(5), 531–537. https://doi.org/10.1037/0003-066X.55.5.531.

McKenzie-Mohr, D., Nemiroff, L. S., Beers, L., & Desmarais, S. (1995). Determinants of responsible environmental behavior. *Journal of Social Issues, 51*(4), 139–156. https://doi.org/10.1111/j.1540-4560.1995.tb01352.x.

Operation Red Nose. (2018). *History*. Retrieved from http://operationrednose.com/history.

Social Marketing for the Reduction of Tax Evasion: The Case of Electronic Invoicing in Portugal

11

Beatriz Casais, Marisa R. Ferreira and João F. Proença

Chapter Overview
This case study is on a social marketing campaign to decrease tax evasion in Portugal. The main campaign goal was to promote wider general use of invoices with the customer's tax number. The social marketing campaign is based on marketing incentives to issue an invoice. The incentives involve tax deductions, an invoice lottery (with tax numbers) every month, direct marketing actions, and advertising. The process of generating invoices by traders became mandatory and simplified with certified systems. Customers can show a bar code which can be easily scanned to introduce their tax number in invoices. This process has become culturally accepted and part of the normal sales process. The social marketing intervention decreased VAT tax evasion in priority sectors and is creating a social norm of generating invoices with

B. Casais (✉)
School of Economics and Management, University of Minho, Braga, Portugal
e-mail: bcasais@eeg.uminho.pt

B. Casais
Polytechnic Institute of Cavado and Ave, Barcelos, Portugal

B. Casais
IPAM Porto, Porto, Portugal

M. R. Ferreira
School of Technology and Management, CIICESI, Polytechnic Institute of Porto, Porto, Portugal
e-mail: mferreira@estg.ipp.pt

J. F. Proença
Faculty of Economics and Management, University of Porto, Porto, Portugal
e-mail: jproenca@fep.up.pt

J. F. Proença
ADVANCE/CSG, University of Lisbon, Lisbon, Portugal

© Springer Nature Switzerland AG 2019
D. Z. Basil et al. (eds.), *Social Marketing in Action*,
Springer Texts in Business and Economics,
https://doi.org/10.1007/978-3-030-13020-6_11

tax numbers, through tax deduction incentives and an invoice lottery. In the long term, tax evasion as a social norm should be re-evaluated in order to control social marketing effectiveness.

Campaign Background

The non-declared shadow economy in Portugal was quite substantial at the end of the first decade of the millennium, with a VAT gap of 15% in 2012 (European Commission, 2015). Tax evasion has been highly researched in terms of its dimension, evidence, and causes. In Portugal, the non-registered economy in 2012 was estimated at 26.74% of Gross Domestic Product (GDP) (Afonso, 2014).

In January 2013, a new invoicing system was introduced in Portugal to fight against the underground economy and tax evasion. This system had several requirements and incentives: (a) all business firms had to issue an invoice on all transactions, even if not requested; (b) they had to make monthly reports of all invoices to the central system; and (c) consumers received a tax benefit of 15% of VAT in car and motorcycle maintenance and repair, accommodation and food services, hairdressing and other beauty treatments if the invoice had the customer's tax number (Cunha, 2015). Since January 2015, taxpayers who request invoices can benefit from a set of deductions. In 2013, Portugal incorporated a campaign with an extra tax deduction. Consumers initially received a tax benefit of 5% rising six months later to 15% of supported VAT (in four sectors) with a limit of 250 € per person. In order to have access to this reward, it was mandatory to insert the individual tax number in invoices. In 2015, a tax reform replicated the model for general expenditures, considering deductions of 35% income tax, with a maximum of 250 € per person, related to invoices with the tax number. Supporting all these changes, the authorities created a website that helps individuals and companies to register and track their tax situation. At the same time, several technical recommendations have been produced in terms of tax system reformulation and communication for behavior change. Promotional publicity encouraging citizens to ask for an invoice in all transactions was developed and broadcast on TV but lacked impact due to the absence of any associated reward.

To encourage voluntary compliance with requesting an invoice with the tax ID number, exchange theory in social marketing states it is important to demonstrate that the benefits outweigh the opportunity costs (Maibach, 1993; Peattie and Peattie, 2003). The use of incentives in social marketing is part of the benefit/price elements (Lefebvre, 2011) and a conscious form of exchange based on a positive reward—an exchange form called "hugging" (French, 2011). For that reason, a set of deductions was defined and integrated into the state budget as a reward system for those who request an invoice with tax number (Autoridade Tributária e Aduaneira, 2012). This situation led to the creation of an integrative social marketing campaign based on rewards as an incentive to effect behavior change, through highly persuasive communication using direct marketing with a positive/pleasure narrative to attract citizens to the social cause. Also, a national lottery was implemented using the generated invoices as coupons for citizens to participate in winning prizes.

Social norms theory holds that the perception of our peer group values determines our own behaviors (Kenny and Hastings, 2011). Thus, the phenomena of tax evasion can be connected as a social norm, based on the misperception of community members' acceptance of such attitudes and behaviors (Wenzel, 2005). In Portugal, tax evasion was misunderstood as a social norm commonly assumed by individuals, with serious implications in public budgets and fair competition between companies. It became a political priority for the European commission and its member states for the purpose of (a) recapturing lost revenues; (b) preventing administrative intervention in the promotion of voluntary payment systems; and (c) promoting a fair tax system and including it as a citizenship value, with non-compliance risks perceived in terms of punishment and negative effects on economic growth. Social marketing is considered to be an effective tool for changing attitudes in regard to misunderstanding social norms (Kenny and Hastings, 2011).

SWOT Analysis (Strengths, Weaknesses, Opportunities, Threats)

The following SWOT analysis is related to the Portuguese government tax authority (TA).

Strengths

The Portuguese government has implemented an electronic finances website. The website has a user-friendly layout, an email alert system for individual deadlines, and almost all tax services are available online, with some taxpayers having no other option but to use this service (e.g., electronic self-employed receipts) (Cunha, 2015).

In 2013, the Portuguese government created a mandatory licensed billing system for businesses. That system requires merchants to register all invoices, with or without the tax number of the client.

The Portuguese government intensified their role and intervention in supervising economic activities, with a special focus on the punishments for tax evasion.

Weaknesses

Lack of knowledge of companies and of their businesses and activities.
Lack of proximity with companies and other taxpayers.
Lack of communication with the target audience for the negative consequences of tax evasion.
Insufficient resources, namely inspection resources.

Opportunities

The general adherence to the electronic tax services in the official website offers an opportunity to create a system for taxpayer relationship management.

Rewards or tax reductions were well accepted by taxpayers, due to the high amount of extra tax levied at the time of financial crisis and the external support for public budgetary readjustment in Portugal.

Threats

The national commission for data protection declared that personal tax information should be an option (e.g., to get a reward) but not a mandatory step to get general tax deductions on income. Data protection is still an unresolved issue in this campaign, since authorities can track all personal purchases that citizens make.

There is a generalized culture of tax evasion as a social norm.

An "Invoice Culture" between taxpayers is difficult to implement due to the popularity of informal community markets, and transactions in the country.

The popular perception of exaggerated taxation and revenue misuse.

An historically "bad" relationship between the TA and individuals and business firms.

The high rate of VAT applied by the government to the majority of goods and services (23%) is a high cost for tax compliance.

Target Audience

All Portuguese citizens with a tax number were targeted by the campaign. It was necessary to change mentalities, attitudes, and behaviors of citizens in regard to the social norms of tax evasion. The campaign aimed to promote voluntary invoice requisition in all transactions. This goal is very difficult to reach, but consumers are responding positively. The Portuguese government considered restaurants and accommodation service providers and clients to be priority targets, along with hairdressers, beauty clinics, and vehicle repair garages. These services were the sectors of most concern in the parallel economy (Secetaria de Estado dos Assuntos Fiscais, 2015). To expand this campaign, later legislation specified other tax benefits related to general family expenses, health and education expenditures, and housing charges.

Individuals and business firms that buy and sell goods or services are also a target, since they must issue invoices on all transactions even if not requested, and they should communicate the essential elements of all invoices monthly to Tax Administration (Cunha, 2015). Traders are targeted through specific legislation and benefits, such as the possibility of reducing some of the current bureaucratic requirements and the simplification of some reporting obligations.

Campaign Objectives

Social marketing interventions may be effective in establishing social norms that determine tax compliance intentions (Bobek, Roberts and Sweeney, 2007; Kenny and Hastings, 2011). The Portuguese government developed an e-invoice social marketing campaign for the purpose of fighting fraud and tax evasion. With a dedicated website for electronic submission and validation of invoices by merchants and citizens, the campaign calls for voluntary compliance, giving tax incentives in exchange for the opportunity cost of tax evasion. The incentive is commonly part of social marketing interventions as a reward for a desired behavior (Lefebvre, 2011). The social marketing campaign follows the hugging model of exchange, which involves getting a reward from making a desired attitude and behavior change (French, 2011).

The main objectives focused on raising public awareness, recognition, and action: awareness of the problems related to fraud and tax evasion; recognition that asking for invoices is a simple and basic social norm which has a potential impact in fighting against tax evasion; action means that asking for invoices can bring benefits to citizens, and that this can propel/impact the desired changes.

Benefits, Barriers, and Competition

Citizens can feel they are fighting tax evasion and getting a tax benefit at the same time. Consumers are granted a 15% tax benefit on the VAT of acquisitions in the previously mentioned priority areas, as well as participation in a Lucky Invoice Lottery. Another important benefit is related to the access of information; because consumers can check if their invoices are correct on the Tax Administration (TA) website and add any invoices that have not been registered, if need be.

In terms of barriers, there is a sense of a lack of privacy since all the information about consumers' transactions is available on the website and accessible to different authorities, and the dominant economic model was supported by social norms that justified an underground economy and tax evasion.

In terms of benefits for traders, the system was created and designed in a way that should lead companies to face no significant additional costs; intentionally using existing accounting systems and in the medium/long term it was expected that companies would progressively have less bureaucratic issues (Cunha, 2015). Although, there are some constraints that adversely affect firms. First, it was necessary to have a computerized accounting system; second, there was a potential lack of appropriate tax management, coupled with previous experience of tax evasion; third, the perception that extra technical support would be needed and, finally, as previously mentioned, for citizens the dominant economic model was supported by values that justified an underground economy and tax evasion.

In terms of competition, we note the previous norm of consumers not asking for an invoice because of the fear of data loss and control of personal financial activity by the government, or because of the extra time it takes in the purchasing process; for companies, not issuing an invoice to avoid high VAT or informal activity which is not suitable for issuing invoices. This required a major behavioral change and had to overcome the risk aversion inherent to change, as well as the belief that tax evasion is more advantageous.

Positioning

The social marketing role of this campaign was to effect attitudes and behavioral change in the declaration of transactions. This is an important step to improving the economy in a spirit of fairness, with all the citizens fulfilling their tax obligations (Faizal and Palil, 2015). In brief, at a moment of high tax increases the campaign emphasized the importance of the collective contribution of citizens to creating a fair economy, because when everyone pays their obligations each individual pays less. So, we can say the marketing focus was on promoting fairness and equity (Faizal and Palil, 2015).

Marketing Strategy

Product

The campaign included a reward to promote the desired behavior change in terms of extra tax benefits, following the "hugging" form of exchange proposed by French (2011). Besides raising social consciousness on the need to declare income, the tax deduction is an incentive to a direct behavior response. The reward had a maximum amount, and invoice collection could be stopped after that amount. However, the campaign aimed for routine compliance through offering an extra reward in the monthly invoice lottery. The campaign also created higher merchant supervision, with penalties for tax evasion, and the creation of mandatory invoice systems certified by the authorities. It is not clear if the incentive strategy can be maintained, but we plan to monitor the campaign in a long-term period in order to evaluate the social marketing effectiveness in terms of change in social norms (Kenny and Hastings, 2011).

Price

Following the exchange theory in social marketing, the cost-benefit analysis is done by the audience and motivates behavior change. In the first stage of the campaign,

Fig. 11.1 e-Invoice Digital
Card available at https://
faturas.portaldasfinancas.gov.
pt/painelAdquirente.action;
accessed 09/01/2018

the reward was not giving commensurate value for the tax evasion alternative. This
meant that adopting the behavior change mediated the cost of the alternative
opportunity for tax evasion, which tended to be a higher amount. After six months,
the government decided to increase the reward to reduce the value of associated
opportunity. Based on this routine, citizens had to ask for an invoice with the tax
number in all transactions. This means repeating that number in daily routine
activities and the oral transmission of that number several times per day, in
supermarkets, at restaurants and shops, taking more time for payment and repeated
attempts to verbally convey personal information in very noisy environments.
To overcome that inconvenience, authorities created a digital card with the tax
number that citizens can show on their mobile phone or print for a bar code scan
(Fig. 11.1). The card offers a convenient way of including the tax number in
invoices, thereby reducing lost time and avoiding the need to memorize the number
and communicate it orally.

The psychological discomfort of asking for an invoice from retailers with whom
a customer has a long-time relationship could initially be a constraint, but with
reward incentives general adherence to asking for an invoice with tax number
quickly became the social norm, and the process was adopted by traders because it
was obligatory, with or without a tax number.

Place

The placement of the social marketing campaign is anywhere that consumers make
a commercial transaction. To access the tax benefits, all the invoices with a tax
number were automatically included in the e-invoice website. This means that the
taxpayers did not have to keep the paper invoices because a digital version is
automatically included in the tax services website. However, by the end of the year,
the taxpayer must validate each invoice and can also add any invoices not registered
by merchants. The mandatory equipment for generating bills and invoices by all
merchants allows easy access to the behavior change. Due to the high impact of the
campaign and the frequency of consumers asking for an invoice, this step started to

be included in the process of transactions. In fact, the merchant usually asks first if an invoice is required to avoid requests for invoices after the payment, which are not possible to generate. Also, some informal activities related to sectors with higher rewards tend to formalize an invoice system, such as transportation services, car parks, and canteens in companies and schools where citizens started to ask for an invoice with tax number.

Promotion

The campaign was communicated with persuasive public announcements in mass media—radio, television, and newspapers. In addition to promoting the social benefits of fighting tax evasion and the tax deduction rewards, a *Lucky Invoice Lottery* was also created. All invoices with a tax number are converted into lottery coupons. In the first stage, the monthly lottery was associated with a luxury car. Later, the number of lotteries was changed to 4/5 per month and the car was replaced by a money prize in the form of a treasury certificate. By the end of 2017, this special lottery had been won by 216 taxpayers. The *Lucky Invoice Lottery* is broadcast on television and has a mobile app so that taxpayers can verify the number of coupons they have, based on the number of invoices with their tax number.

As part of the direct marketing, authorities send e-mails and sms messages to remind people of the importance of asking for an invoice in all transactions. The positive narrative of these e-mails for contributing to the cause is personalized and signed by a responsible for tax services. The information includes the number of invoices collected by all citizens since the beginning of the year, the impact on the economy, and the number of coupons each person has for the next lottery. The e-invoice website also immediately calculates the amount of benefits in tax deductions for each citizen.

People

The campaign includes asking for (individuals) and issuing (companies) invoices, so on both sides we have people whose attitude and skills have an important role, not only in the service delivery but also in reaching the campaign objectives. The disposition and attitude of all actors and the way in which questions are handled can make the difference between retaining or losing another follower/adopter of the program or improving or ruining the reputation of the program.

Process

The process of the campaign should be as friendly and intuitive as possible. Consumers should ask for an invoice in all purchases, the invoices will appear on the website and consumers have the possibility of entering invoice elements into the website if they see some information is missing; traders must submit all invoices to the AT webpage. The process is easier for the consumers than for traders, so the process requires designing software solutions, an interface with the economic agents and the implementation of the reform (Cunha, 2015).

Program Evaluation

It is important to track and evaluate the program. The public budget records show an increase in the global tax revenues directly connected with e-invoice actions (Secetaria de Estado dos Assuntos Fiscais, 2015). The Portuguese VAT gap calculated by European Commission decreased to 12% in 2014. Figure 11.2 shows the evolution of invoices generated in Portugal between 2013 and 2016.

In 2013, more than 2 million taxpayers deducted the incentive, the total value of the incentive was €25.4 million and about 8.5 million Portuguese have invoices issued in their names and participate in the Lucky Invoice Lottery draw weekly (Cunha, 2015). However, some families tend to organize the invoice requisition based on the amount of reward associated, which means that by the end of the year individuals may not ask for invoices with the same frequency, when the maximum reward has passed. For that reason, the Lucky Invoice Lottery is an extra reward to counter that eventual reaction, but this implies that the behavior change may not be sustainable and may not work without the incentives, although there has not been any study on those who have won prizes and their continued compliance. We know that five years after the introduction of the e-invoice campaign the number of invoices increased, and issuing invoices is still a casual act in many shops. However, social norms theory requires a long-term social marketing intervention (Kenny

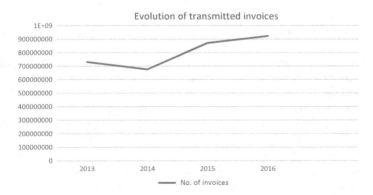

Fig. 11.2 Evolution of invoices generated in Portugal. *Source* Portuguese Tax and Customs Authority accessed at https://faturas.portaldasfinancas.gov.pt/ on 09/01/2018

and Hastings, 2011). A long-term evaluation of the campaign for some changes in social norms, especially with generational transformations, may provide evidence of the social marketing effectiveness.

Discussion and Lessons Learned

Giving information to taxpayers about the seriousness of the non-declared economy, its risks, and ways to be part of the solution is essential, since taxpayers may estimate others' practice of tax evasion as greater than their own (Wenzel, 2005). Different promotional mechanisms (e.g., e-mails, sms messages, tv advertisements) are an integral part of the e-invoice program outreach efforts to help improve the awareness and recognition of the program. These promotional mechanisms give information on topics related to tax benefits and deductions. Through clear and informed involvement, the website community members can learn more about fiscal taxes and incentives, the importance of making more transparent choices (asking for invoices in all economic operations) and be active on a regular basis.

The program has attained some level of respect and success, although the evolution and transformation of some aspects may not have yet been fully realized. Firstly, the typology of tax deductions has expanded, increasing tax benefits and making it possible to get them in a wide diversity of areas. However, the fact that the reward is conditioned by a maximum amount of expenses/invoices may decrease the behavior change after reaching the stipulated maximum value. This means that the campaign has not affected an attitude change, but just a behavioral change connected to a reward. So, the behavior may not be sustainable and may not work without the incentives, probably meaning that the self-interest value for prizes and incentives outweigh the collective and mutual value, underlining the importance of personal norms, i.e., one's own self-based standards or expectations of appropriate behavior (Cialdini and Trost, 1998; Bobek, Roberts and Sweeney, 2007). It is expected, however, that social norms may change regarding the culture of tax evasion in the long term, and new generations will consider tax compliance as the social norm.

Secondly, the website is the central pillar of the program and has undergone several changes to be more user-friendly, and nowadays most users find it very intuitive and easy to use.

To make the program more popular and call the taxpayers' attention, there are prizes/rewards for the website users. These prizes were offered through lotteries that were made and announced regularly. Initially, the awards were luxury cars, and 74 cars were offered in 2014 and 2015. The fact that the prize is a luxury car (with a value between 30,000 and 50,000 € and always from the same brand) is an easily criticized aspect, since it may be considered that the motivation to fight against non-declared economy is intimately linked with a luxury car, thus it may not lead to a sustainable behavior change. In 2016, with a different government, the prize was changed to an amount of money in treasury certificates (of equivalent value). There are regular prizes every week (35,000 €) and extraordinary prizes, two per year (50,000 €). We can identify some advantages in this new prize, since it encourages family savings through the promotion of a state-saving financial product.

Discussion Questions

1. Are the promotional mechanics adequate and enough to create awareness in the target audience?
2. What are the weaknesses of this program?
3. Do you have suggestions for improving the program's promotional efforts?
4. Are the fiscal benefits suitable and sufficient for increasing the problem recognition?
5. Are the rewards for website users adequate for increasing the problem recognition?
6. Are there ways of moving the self-interested values to the recognition that the total declaration of taxes can bring advantages to individuals and society?
7. Are there other target incentives that should be approached?
8. Are there opportunities to improve the program (for taxpayers)?
9. Are there some ethical considerations about data protection?

Acknowledgements João F. Proença gratefully acknowledges financial support from FCT-Fundação para a Ciência e Tecnologia (Portugal), national funding through research grant UID/SOC/04521/2019.

References

Afonso, Ó. (2014). *Economia não-registada em Portugal, observatório de economia e gestão de fraude - estudos*. Porto. Available at: http://www.gestaodefraude.eu/wordpress/?p=14339. Accessed January 10, 2018.
Autoridade Tributária e Aduaneira (2012) *Decreto-Lei n.º 198/2012, de 24 de Agosto*.
Bobek, D. D., Roberts, R. W., & Sweeney, J. T. (2007). The social norms of tax compliance: Evidence from Australia, Singapore, and the United States. *Journal of Business Ethics, 74*(1), 49–64. https://doi.org/10.1007/s10551-006-9219-x.
Cialdini, R. B., & Trost, M. R. (1998). Social influence: Social norms, conformity and compliance. In S. T. Gilbert & G. L. Fiske (Eds.), *The handbook of social psychology* (pp. 151–192). New York: McGraw-Hill.
Cunha, I. (2015). *'Portugal | The new billing e-invoice system'*. Ministry of Finance—Tax and Customs Authority.

European Commission. (2015). *Study to quantify and analyse the VAT gap in the EU member states, report for DG taxation and customs union,* .... The Netherlands. Retrieved from: http://scholar.google.com/scholar?hl=en&btnG=Search&q=intitle:Study+to+quantify+and+analyse+the+VAT+gap+in+the+EU-25+Member+States#0. Accessed January 10, 2018.

Faizal, S. M., & Palil, M. R. (2015). Study on fairness and individual tax compliance in Malaysia: Preliminary findings *International Journal of Business, Economics and Law, 8*(1), 74–79. Retrieved from: http://ijbel.com/wp-content/uploads/2016/01/Acc-35.pdf.

French, J. (2011). Why nudging is not enough. *Journal of Social Marketing. Emerald, 1*(2), 154–162. https://doi.org/10.1108/20426761111141896.

Kenny, P., & Hastings, G. (2011). Understanding social sorms: Upstream and downstream applications for social marketers. In G. Hastings, K. Angus, & Bryant, C. (Eds.), *The SAGE handbook of social marketing* (pp. 61–79). London: SAGE Publications Ltd. https://doi.org/10.4135/9781446201008.

Lefebvre, R. C. (2011). An integrative model for social marketing. *Journal of Social Marketing. Emerald, 1*(1), 54–72. https://doi.org/10.1108/20426761111104437.

Maibach, E. (1993). Social marketing for the environment: Using information campaigns to promote environmental awareness and behavior change. *Health Promotion International, 8*(3), 209–224. Retrieved from: http://dx.doi.org/10.1093/heapro/8.3.209.

Peattie, S., & Peattie, K. (2003). Ready to fly solo? Reducing social marketing's dependence on commercial marketing theory'. *Marketing Theory, 3*(3), 365–385. https://doi.org/10.1177/147059310333006.

Secetaria de Estado dos Assuntos Fiscais. (2015). *Plano estratégico de combate à fraude e evasão fiscais e aduaneiras 2015-2017, Portugal - gabinete do secretário de estado dos assuntos fiscais.* Retrieved from: http://info.portaldasfinancas.gov.pt/nr/rdonlyres/e245bdae-d856-4186-a950-f0be649869df/0/plano_estrategico_combate_fraude_fiscal_aduaneira_2015_2017.pdf. Accessed January 10, 2018.

Wenzel, M. (2005). Misperceptions of social norms about tax compliance: From theory to intervention. *Journal of Economic Psychology, 26*(6), 862–883. https://doi.org/10.1016/j.joep.2005.02.002.

Worn Wear: Better than New—How Patagonia's Social Marketing Campaign Enhances Consumers' Responsible Behavior

Nina Bürklin

Chapter Overview

With its *Worn Wear: Better Than New* campaign, outdoor manufacturer Patagonia challenges the boundaries between social and commercial marketing and succeeds in its attempt to induce behavioral change among their customers. Despite the apparel industry being highly competitive, the campaign propagates a more conscious use of clothing instead of simply disposing of used items and purchasing new ones. Thus, it provides a telling example of how to use corporate activities in inspiring and implementing solutions to the environmental crisis. Following the company's mission to build on the principle of social norms, the campaign introduces practical ways for embodying a lifestyle of voluntary simplicity. Thus, it enhances environmental protection, as well as personal well-being. Seeking to inspire, educate, and take action, the campaign includes different elements for inducing behavioral change regarding the repair, recycling, and disposal behavior of Patagonia's customers. Among other things, the corresponding activities include physical repair centers for clothing and gear, either permanently or temporarily installed. Moreover, on their website, the outdoor manufacturer communicates personal stories of customers who successfully participated in the campaign, and it offers more than 40 freely downloadable repair guides. Finally, the company has established an online shop for used clothing to implement a practical alternative to current practices of mere consumerism. This case study illustrates how social marketing is applied in a commercial context and illustrates how one far-reaching campaign can thereby induce behavioral change among customers and, in doing so, contribute to the greater good and quality of life.

N. Bürklin (✉)
Ludwig-Maximilians-University, Munich, Germany
e-mail: buerklin@bwl.lmu.de

© Springer Nature Switzerland AG 2019
D. Z. Basil et al. (eds.), *Social Marketing in Action*,
Springer Texts in Business and Economics,
https://doi.org/10.1007/978-3-030-13020-6_12

Campaign Background[1]

In 2013, the outdoor manufacturer *Patagonia* launched its campaign *Worn Wear: Better Than New* to encourage consumers to use and care for their outer wear responsibly. A national initiative throughout the USA marked the starting point of the campaign to help consumers get their clothes repaired in local workshops, instead of simply disposing of them. The campaign aimed to bring about behavioral change from merely consumerist to a conscious lifestyle that includes environmental protection, resembling the idea of voluntary simplicity (Leonard-Barten, 1981). Further, the goals of *Worn Wear* comprise the repair and reuse of used gear, which opposes the simple, yet environmentally costly behavior of quick disposal. Now, five years later, the social marketing campaign has reached a new level with over 40 free downloadable repair guides on the Patagonia website, and a complete online shop for used clothing only. Although empirical research to investigate the effectiveness of the campaign is still lacking, the sports manufacturer's marketing approach through the *Worn Wear* campaign provides a valuable learning opportunity.

The Company—Between Environmental Protection and Business Success

Patagonia, a California-based manufacturer of upmarket outdoor clothing, was founded by climbing enthusiast Yvon Chouinard, after long years of experience in the production of climbing gear. Inspired by a rugby shirt from Scotland a few years earlier, the company introduced brightly colored, functional clothing to the outdoor apparel market in North America. At the beginning, it served merely to support the marginally profitable hardware business for climbing gear. Soon, however, the company expanded its product portfolio to other types of outdoor wear, and targeted different kinds of sport such as surfing or hiking. In 1973, having grown from another small company that made tools for climbers, Patagonia was officially founded. They focused on soft goods like clothing for sports such as skiing, paddling, and trail-running, but also developed products like backpacks and sleeping bags. Right up to the present, alpinism is at the core of this global business that considers itself to be an "activist company." While many conventional apparel producers strive solely to maximize their profits year upon year, Patagonia commits 1% of their total sales or 10% of their profit to hundreds of environmental groups. Despite their already high standards, the company introduced even higher norms for the use of natural animal materials after regularly being attacked by various not-for-profit organizations (NPOs). The company's values echo those of passionate outdoor lovers like climbers or surfers who live and promote a minimalist

---

[1]This case has been written on the basis of published sources only. The interpretation and perspectives presented here are not necessarily those of the company in question, nor of any of its employees.

lifestyle. Patagonia's approach is also reflected in their designs which demonstrate simplicity and utility. Since the company's inception, the manufacturer has invested significant amounts in research and design not only to improve and innovate their materials and designs, but also to enhance their sustainability actions. The company focuses on socially responsible investment as a positive impetus for change. They do this by adhering to new indices that measure sustainability and potential improvement throughout the value chain (Chouinard, Ellison, & Ridgeway, 2011). Currently, with more than 1000 employees and an estimated revenue of $209 million (for 2017), the sportswear manufacturer is regarded as one of the industry leaders.

"Better Than New"—Social Marketing to Enhance Consumers' Voluntary Simplicity

Since its foundation, Patagonia has followed a business ethos holding strong ethical values on which the *Worn Wear: Better Than New* campaign could be founded. Although the outdoor manufacturer strove to adhere to the highest social and environmental standards during all production processes, it admits honestly that even its own products consume natural resources that cannot be replaced immediately or ever. Their *Worn Wear* campaign seeks to put something back by offering practical advice to support consumers in treating their clothing and gear responsibly, e.g., providing free guides on how to repair gear instead of discarding it. The campaign aims to affirm a minimalist lifestyle that embraces aspects of sustainability, such as environmental protection, reusing resources, and consciously making purchasing decisions. Thus, it reflects the idea of voluntary simplicity, a concept that captures choosing an alternative consumption style rather than mere consumerism (Shaw & Newholm, 2002). Underlying this pursuit, is the awareness that growing numbers of consumers reject the conventional notion of a capitalist economy based on consumerism, rather consciously striving for a lifestyle with less possessions, that will lead to a higher quality of life and greater personal well-being.

Although not scientifically analyzed and proven, the *Worn Wear* campaign vigorously picks up the concept of voluntary simplicity and tries to empower its customers toward a lifestyle consciously following this concept. From a social marketing perspective, the campaign aims to initiate behavioral change from strong consumerism to more responsible purchasing, using, and disposing of clothing. Part of what this campaign provides is one of the biggest garment repair centers in North America, where 45 employees take care of broken gear that customers send for mending. The *Worn Wear* campaign followed this approach of repairing and reusing, in conjunction with retail partners, and aimed particularly at repairing used items instead of discarding them. Additionally, it included a road show that travelled across North America using remodeled, biodiesel-fueled campers with integrated workshops to repair worn items. The campaign was successful to the extent that its approach to repairing used Patagonia products for free was confirmed, thus preventing them from ending up in the landfill and being replaced by newly produced materials.

The *Worn Wear: Better Than New* campaign makes use of the principles that underpin social norms as they are known from social impact and environmental psychology (Schultz, Nolan, Cialdini, Goldstein, & Griskevicius, 2007). Generally, social norms serve as guidelines for "correct" behavior, to support social change efforts, as in fostering responsible alcohol drinking behavior. These norms depend on the idea that relevant social others, e.g., friends and family or opinion leaders, function as role models that other individuals strive to imitate. The *Worn Wear* campaign uses this psychological concept in integrating sensitive and responsibly acting customers in their social marketing efforts. Specifically, in its *Worn Wear* campaign, the sports manufacturer identifies role models that are portrayed on the company's website, detailing their environmentally responsible behavior. Using the slogan "repair, care, and share," they invited customers to share stories of gear they repaired, as well as of experiences using and wearing their Patagonia products. The campaign succeeds by means of a form of communication that presents role models that shape social norms and simultaneously inspire other customers. Thus, the intended behavioral change is fostered through technological means (the website and the system for returning used clothes), as well as through the social norms disseminated in communities of sport and outdoor lovers. Positive effects are that people gain greater awareness of how they treat clothing and sports gear in general, as well as increase their contribution to environmental protection by reduced consumption of valuable resources over time.

SWOT Analysis (Strengths, Weaknesses, Opportunities, Threats)

Strengths

One of the key strengths of the *Worn Wear* campaign lies in that it engages directly with customers. Instead of focusing on social marketing advertisements in print magazines or in outdoor media, the campaign succeeds in building personal relationships with their customers. On the one hand, diverse activities reach out to customers in engaging ways that can potentially overcome barriers like the exorbitant effort in getting things repaired. For example, the *Worn Wear* road show with workshops in refurbished trucks offers customers a unique experience to get an instant free repair and at the same time to learn more about the campaign's goals. Further, these experiences demonstrate how much fun this kind of responsible behavior can be. On the other hand, the campaign showcases experienced customers who serve as credible and authentic role models for a conscious lifestyle. Another strength of the campaign lies in Patagonia's corporate philosophy that provides a stamp of credibility to its environmental goals and, thus, also to the campaign. The company's clear mission to "[b]uild the best product, cause no unnecessary harm, use business to inspire and implement solutions to the environmental crisis", emphasizes how the campaign's overall objectives are strongly supported by its overarching business ethos. This assures that consumers conceive of the campaign not as mere commercial marketing, but as a sincere effort to increase environmental protection and induce a behavior change toward the greater good among their customers. Lastly, the manufacturer's loyal and supportive customer base is a strength. Their passion for outdoor sports and nature, and their preference for a simplistic lifestyle show that they share the same values and therefore support the campaign through their contribution. For example, many customers voluntarily share their personal stories of how they have repaired their gear and, in doing so, serve as role models. Personal recommendation behavior is pervasive in the campaign. Customers initiate conversations about their own (reduced) consumption behavior, thus strengthening the strategy of telling stories about people, not products.

Weaknesses

Nevertheless, despite its stable customer base and strong value system, the *Worn Wear* campaign also has weaknesses, such as the skepticism of other customers, especially those new to their products. Over the past few years, sustainability has emerged internationally as a key social trend, so that many companies in the apparel sector have been caught out on "greenwashing." This causes increased customer insecurity regarding who to trust and what to believe, which carries over to the campaign. Further, the *Worn Wear* campaign with its different activities such as the road show, the repair centers, and a state-of-the-art website requires high financial investment. These pay into the social marketing approach that Patagonia follows in order to create behavioral change and, hence, cannot be used in the company's traditional marketing. This could be considered a double-edged sword from a commercial and social marketing perspective, respectively.

Opportunities

One of the most important opportunities of the *Worn Wear* campaign lies in the development of a new customer mindset toward more sustainability and, ultimately, a higher quality of life. This resonates well with the idea of voluntary simplicity, a lifestyle that strives to reduce conventional consumerism and instead to focus more on experience and personal well-being (Shaw & Newholm, 2002). Sustainability through simplicity mirrors the company's ethical values and puts relevant social norms in place for its customers. Especially, members of the younger generation, e.g., millennials, possess different personal values to those before them, also engaging themselves in various socially relevant causes in their free time. Mostly, they prefer experiences with friends or out in nature to consumerist activities like purchasing. Another opportunity for *Worn Wear* is constituted in current digitization and the Internet-based advancements, such as mobile applications, through which customers are globally connected and can join forces worldwide. In this way, the *Worn Wear* campaign and its overarching goals can be disseminated more quickly and at lower costs than before. Additionally, through the rise of the sharing economy, sharing and reusing (otherwise idle) resources—an idea underpinned by the concept of repairing and/or returning used clothes—is more readily accepted. The principles of sharing resonate strongly with the campaign's aim to encourage people's care for their own clothing through repairs on the one hand, and accepting used clothes instead of new ones on the other hand. Patagonia's approach to repair and reuse resources through the *Worn Wear* campaign can therefore potentially bring growth in their loyal customer base. By contrastive, high expectations and demands from ecological grassroots initiatives that constantly challenge and question the company's sincere intentions toward greater sustainability, could turn the company's strength into a possible weakness.

Threats

Patagonia and Worn Wear experience threats in the growing market of sustainable outdoor gear and the subsequent increase in communication means. While the *Worn Wear* campaign's development in itself can be considered to be a positive one, it brings a challenge of higher competition in the sports industry. A range of sustainability-centered clothing companies have similar genuine aims of improving their production processes; however, a least the same number of companies will abuse the trend toward sustainability merely to maximize their own profit. In the future, the *Worn Wear* campaign needs to be extended into even more countries to stabilize the company's market position as an industry leader. Yet another threat lies in the overall size of the market. While the outdoor-wear market is worth $4 billion in the USA alone, sustainable clothing represents a niche market only. Despite so many tendencies toward increased environmental consciousness, the majority of potential customers worldwide have not transformed their positive attitudes into specific resonating actions, yet.

Target Audience

Over time, Patagonia realized that the largest market group is not sport professionals, but rather young urban customers wearing the gear during daily activities. Thus, the *Worn Wear* campaign needed to target this customer segment. Still, the majority in this segment love the outdoors and engage in activities like surfing, hiking, skiing, or trail-running. It is beneficial that most of them share similar values regarding the preservation of natural resources, as well as a minimalist lifestyle that harmonizes with the concept of voluntary simplicity the campaign communicates. Thus, these customers stand to gain from support for their lifestyle and confirmation of their adherence to current social norms. Further, these customers gladly provide and share their stories with and through Patagonia's network, thus inspiring even more people to follow a similar lifestyle. Additionally, positively associating their name with environmentalism can potentially attract new customers in the near future and, hence, increase the impact of the *Worn Wear* campaign. Despite the perception of only limited effectiveness on an individual level, Patagonia's social marketing approach based on the *Worn Wear* campaign has helped outdoor lovers to form the basis of a global movement. A possible barrier to achieving behavioral change within this customer group is the seemingly high effort required to repair and/or recycle clothing. As simply disposing of old clothes and buying new ones at relatively low prices has become normalized, the *Worn Wear* campaign must focus especially on the benefits of increased environmental protection, of belonging to a like-minded group, and of a fashionable minimalist lifestyle. Due to Patagonia's premium price for outdoor gear is sometimes perceived to be comparatively high, competitors could derail behavioral change with low prices and high accessibility.

To do justice to the campaign's social marketing approach, the campaign should target new groups by applying a holistic stakeholder perspective (Sachs & Rühli, 2011). Although the company's stakeholder network is rather complex and entangled, two illustrative examples will be given here. First, retail partners who make up another relevant audience of the *Worn Wear* campaign, by collaborating with the sportswear manufacturer during the pre- and post-purchase phases. This partnership includes communication at the retailer's point of sale, as well as the after-sales service regarding repairs or even setting up workshops in their stores. The campaign proposes that clothing be reused rather than new clothing being purchased, as this is considered environmentally favorable, even if potentially threatening to the retailers. Competitors with lower prices could prevent retailers looking for quick revenue increases from cooperating in the campaign. The challenge for Patagonia is to develop a trusting relationship that enables retailers to cooperate with the *Worn Wear* campaign. Key to these partnerships is a similar value base that includes concern for sustainability and a positive societal impact. Second, environmental grassroots initiatives are an important stakeholder group of the outdoor apparel company. As the *Worn Wear* campaign has been initiated in order to provide and implement specific solutions to environmental problems, it is important for the company to stay close to sustainability activists. On the one hand, these groups can directly benefit from financial support by Patagonia. Nevertheless, at times they could be overly critical in their perspective on business activity in this field, and condemn the campaign as greenwashing. On the other hand, NPOs can assist the campaign's approach toward inspiring more and more people to take action when they contribute to raising public awareness.

Campaign Objectives and Goals: Inspire, Educate, Take Action

As Patagonia's idea of sustainability goes far beyond a single social marketing campaign, the general objectives of its *Worn Wear* campaign are threefold: the campaign seeks to inspire people to buy consciously, to educate on the cause of environmental protection, and to offer specific opportunities for repair or recycling. First, as an outdoor clothing manufacturer it seeks to draw attention to the widely distributed attitude of excessive consumption through its nation-wide *Worn Wear* road show in the USA. This initiative, which uses refurbished campers on its round trips, has already been extended to a number of other countries across the globe. Since its inception, resourcefulness, and sustainability have been in this company's DNA. On their website, they provide all information related to their social marketing campaign, including the stories people tell of their outdoor gear and how they either repaired their clothes or bought used clothes from the online shop.

Second, the *Worn Wear* campaign aims at educating its customers through providing information through different communication channels. On its website, it follows its goal by giving details on why recycling (instead of disposing) is highly advantageous to environmental protection and, thus, can be considered a radical and fundamentally new intellectual approach in a time of mass consumerism. Through partnerships with retailers, it raises awareness at the point of sale and in temporary workshops installed to provide advice and concrete support in repairing items. In some of their own retail spaces, small repair centers are set up permanently, to substantiate the company's values and inform its customers. Moreover, free guides are published on the website, providing information and valuable advice on how customers can repair items by themselves, e.g., explaining how to fix a zipper or patch a down jacket. The guides include tips on all types of sport gear, ranging from outerwear, bottoms, and tops to fasteners and luggage.

Third, the *Worn Wear* campaign seeks to induce behavioral change in a large audience by complementing their bids to repair, reuse, and recycle with specific opportunities for customers to act on them. Through the campaign, customers are offered free gear repairs in either temporary workshops, or through their repair center. Customers are further incentivized to return used items that they no longer wear, as these are redeemed with merchandise credit and then resold on Patagonia's *Worn Wear* website. Additionally, the company asks customers to return the gear they regard as beyond repair so that the company can recycle the fibers and, thus, contribute to a closed system in the sense of a circular economy.

Evident barriers to the campaign's success lie in the limited attention from people who are not yet inclined to a lifestyle of voluntary simplicity. Stemming from a strong consumerist attitude, many customers like to purchase new items, simply wanting, for example new colors, innovative materials, or the sheer joy of a new acquisition, but they are not willing to make the effort to change this behavior. When all is said and done, there will still be individuals who do not care about the campaign's environmental mission, but prefer to lead a materialistic lifestyle.

Behavioral change toward more conscious consumption behavior appears to be rather improbable for this group of people. The benefits of the *Worn Wear* campaign are manifold, yet two aspects are specifically strong. First, this social marketing campaign has increased public awareness of current complex environmental challenges. Through direct interaction with customers and integrating them into the campaign, a growing community is engaged who have become aware of the sustainability problems and can spread the word. Second, with each item that, instead of being disposed of, is repaired or resold on the *Worn Wear* website, the negative environmental impact is reduced. Thus, the campaign's benefits are manifested in specific contributions to secure our natural environment.

Positioning

Despite the highly competitive environment of the apparel industry, Patagonia chose a drastic social marketing approach with its *Worn Wear* campaign to reach its corporate goals. Although the past few years have seen the industry as a whole advance considerably toward more sustainable practices, negative media attention on ethical and environmental issues, such as poor working conditions or the use of toxic dyes, has highlighted unsustainable behavior in a way that overshadows the positive contributions from the fashion sector. This publicity is driven by both production and consumption practices, which are explicitly addressed in one of the United Nations sustainable development goals, namely in the 12th goal aimed at ensuring sustainable consumption and production. The industry's relevance in the context of sustainability becomes pertinent considering that currently it is one of the most polluting industries in the world. This is enhanced by consumers' habits of extravagantly buying and using clothing, which then lead to environmentally and socially harmful forms of production. Further, although post-consumer textile waste often could be reused or recycled, mostly it is simply discarded in landfills. The *Worn Wear* campaign responds to such waste by offering concrete opportunities to induce suitable behavioral change.

Patagonia applies social marketing strategies toward behavioral change by providing their customers with repairing and recycling possibilities. In doing so, the company tries to reverse the decline in the overall environmental well-being of planet earth. With the *Worn Wear* campaign, it seeks to attract attention and differentiate itself from competitors through more directly associating with environmentalism. In contrast to relevant NPOs in this field, such as animal protection groups, mountain conservation groups, or national park funds, the outdoor manufacturer can make use of its industry leading position, using its global recognition to disseminate the company's social marketing messages worldwide. So far, the *Worn Wear* campaign has spread to half a dozen countries outside the USA. Compared to one of its biggest competitors, North Face, Patagonia's *Worn Wear* campaign, with its special efforts to increase consumer responsibility, displays a unique effort. Although North Face has also introduced a recycling approach to used clothes and gear that is incentivized by a bonus system, it does not apply a coherent social marketing approach. So far, it fails as a competitive contender with a holistic approach toward greater sustainability similar to the *Worn Wear* campaign.

Marketing Strategy

For the *Worn Wear* campaign, Patagonia refers to its core *products*, namely to merchandise for outdoor activities and sports, such as climbing, snowboarding, or surfing. In terms of materials, the company relies on natural resources or recycled materials, such as organic cotton or recycled PET. This resonates well with the campaign's goal of contributing to behavioral change regarding the preservation of natural resources through reuse and recycling. The *Worn Wear* campaign has increased Patagonia's service portfolio by offering free repairs. On the one hand, this is a permanent offer operationalized in its big repair center. On the other hand, the campaign's road show provides repair services on a temporary basis throughout the whole country.

Place

The *Worn Wear* campaign was initiated close to the company's roots in North America. To date, the campaign's activities are spread out across the country with retail partners in their shops, as well as through special events with Patagonia's road show. As the outdoor manufacturer has developed into an international player, the campaign's efforts were expanded widely beyond North American borders, especially toward Europe where many are embracing a lifestyle of simplicity similar to the one in North America. So far, events of the *Worn Wear* campaign have taken place in six different European countries, namely Germany, France, Switzerland, Italy, Austria, and Scotland. Important elements such as the free repair guides and the personal stories are already globally accessible on the website. With retail shops in eighteen countries and online access via the Internet, this corporate development will enable further expansion of the social marketing campaign in the near future.

Promotion

The promotion strategy of the *Worn Wear* campaign relies on an integrated marketing approach. The campaign started out with a cross-country road show using reclaimed wood campers that accommodated temporary repair workshops. These efforts were enhanced in the expansion to Europe, as well by establishing collaborations with retail partners to include repair stations permanently. Further, instead of only promoting the products, the company lets customers speak for them, inviting them to report their stories of experiences with and in Patagonia's gear.

This approach of using stories has proven to be very successful in the context of social marketing as it confirms authenticity and thereby creates trust in current and future customers. Then, through the campaign's communicative means, social norms were successfully used and disseminated. On its website, *Worn Wear* explicitly asks customers to "share your story." The narratives are then integrated into the corporate blog. Since the values of Patagonia's customers and the corporate strategy with an environmentalist mission are aligned, the *Worn Wear* communications approach appears to be coherent and credible.

Pricing

Considering themselves an "activist company," pricing plays an important part in the overall goals of Patagonia's *Worn Wear* campaign. This needs to be reflected upon from two perspectives. On the one hand, pricing is traditionally linked to the specific cost of products that internalize costs of more ethical and environmental production processes and the cost of complying with the high labor standards postulated in the campaign's objectives. Thus, the manufacturer can charge a price premium that offsets the loss of more regular repeat sales. Keeping in mind the products' lifelong guarantee, as well as the free value-add services of the campaign, such as repairing gear, a pricing strategy that considers real costs seems reasonable. On the other hand, in the context of the social marketing campaign, pricing can be considered differently, reflecting the perceived cost charged for behavioral change. In this sense, pricing would include the cost of time and effort that customers need to invest in repairing or recycling their used clothing. While this has no negative effect on expenditure in terms of financial means, customers have to invest their time, skills, and effort to reach the goal. In the long run, this could actually save them money, while also increasing their personal well-being through a more conscious lifestyle. Thus, the positive outcome of this second type of cost needs to be clearly addressed as part of the *Worn Wear* campaign.

People

Being part of the natural environment, people are at the core of Patagonia's business strategy and therefore an important part of the *Worn Wear* campaign. It is important that the company attracts individuals who share the same values as itself. Thus, the social marketing campaign focuses on values like consciousness, environmental protection, experience as opposed to consumption, and deep connection to nature. This reflects its aim toward behavioral change of the customers, so that they invest more in repairs and recycling than in quick disposal of used items and/or purchasing new items. Further, the *Worn Wear* campaign directly integrates people into their efforts by letting them tell stories about their own experiences on its website. This reflects a human-centered approach that makes individual persons, not products, the center of attention. While there is no doubt that this approach pays off economically as well, an important feature is that it mirrors the social marketing campaign's goal to accomplish change on an individual level today, in the hope that it will develop into an international movement in the future.

Purpose

The *Worn Wear* campaign is based on the purpose of the outdoor manufacturer to enhance behavioral change toward a more conscious lifestyle among its consumers. While the company was founded merely as a producer of outdoor clothing, its success of the past few decades can be ascribed to its deeper purpose to use business to inspire and implement environmentally oriented solutions. The social marketing campaign has played a big role in this development, as it created and contained specific opportunities for customers to support this vision.

Organization and Campaign Evaluation/Campaign Objectives and Goals: Inspire, Educate, Take Action

To raise awareness for environmental protection and the customers' opportunities to contribute to these issues, the *Worn Wear* campaign was spread widely beyond the US borders. That way, it inspired thousands of customers to participate in the environmental efforts. In 2016 alone, the campaign took place in seven European countries and over 2000 repairs, such as fixing zip fasteners, buttons, or torn fabrics, were done at their "Worn Wear Stations." Best-practice examples of people who successfully repaired their items are displayed on the company's website which, in turn, inspire more customers to take action. Today, this part of the campaign contains dozens of personal success stories, often combined with private photographs or videos of the authors wearing their Patagonia gear. Regarding the campaign goal to educate people, the manufacturer has continued to publish free repair guides as part of the campaign. To date, over 40 guides that give advice on how to repair gear, e.g., to replace a jean's button or wash a waterproof jacket, can be downloaded for free. Intending to induce behavioral change, Patagonia established the *Worn Wear* online shop for trading used clothing only. While the Worn Wear campaign's social marketing approach aims at changing customers' behavior, it continues to take action in its own realm as well. Since April 2017, merchandise can now be returned for new merchandise credits. The company then cleans and repairs the used goods to be sold on their *Worn Wear* website. In addition, they sell used Patagonia clothing at the Portland retail store through an innovative trade-in program. Customers are asked to return products that are beyond repair to one of the stores for recycling. Since 2005, Patagonia has recycled over 82 tons of clothing through this program. Nevertheless, considering that the company recycles only a minor portion of its annual sales, it is clear that not all customers follow the company's encouragement to recycle.

Overall, Patagonia has established an image of being a retail inventor that can still be regarded as an outstanding example of a socially driven enterprise. Their *Worn Wear* campaign has contributed significantly to the environmentalist reputation of the company and stabilized its customer base without compromising their corporate ethics. In 2016, the company had sales of $800 million, which was double the amount of 2010. Currently, it has 29 standalone stores in the USA and 23 in Japan. By keeping the company as a privately owned business, the founder, Chouinard, has been able to continue running it while staying true to his values (Chouinard, 2016). Moreover, Patagonia became a recognized *B-Corporation* in 2012, namely a for-profit company with official certification for its social and environmental commitment. Further, its innovative social marketing approach continues to increase awareness for environmental protection and induces behavioral change in customers. As early as 1986, Patagonia committed to donating 10% of its annual profit to these groups in the areas of climate, food, land, pollution, water, and wildlife. All along, they have kept to this commitment to what they call "1% For the Planet" by donating either 1% of their sales or 10% of their profit—whichever one is greater. From the start until 2015, the ongoing program already raised more than $70 million in donations. Regarding repairs, in the same year, they estimated to have repaired more than 40,000 items.

Discussion and Lessons Learned

In a highly competitive environment, Patagonia has often developed innovative, yet risky, approaches such as the *Worn Wear* campaign to redefine the outdoor clothing market. To date, no systematic research has been conducted to investigate this campaign's effectiveness. In spite of anecdotal evidence suggesting success regarding recycling of clothing items, gear being repaired and, hence, increased environmental protection, a thorough study of the campaign and what it has achieved, is still necessary. An analysis to determine the social campaign's success factors from which we can learn with a view to the future would require detailed data, specifically on number of various items, namely items repaired, items returned for reuse or resale on the website, items returned for correct disposal by extraction of fibers for further industrial use, and items sold. Also important would be data on the number of customer's stories shared on the website, and revenue of the *Worn Wear* online shop. Further, in-depth interviews should be conducted with engaged customers to find out more about the campaign's influence on an individual's lifestyle according to the principle of voluntary simplicity. Moreover, capturing retail partners' opinions on the *Worn Wear* campaign to discover potential risks, but especially also success factors of Patagonia's social marketing approach should be worthwhile.

Despite a financial crisis in the 1990s, Patagonia has always made commitments in favor of their ecological or social commitments. The business ethos is manifested in their very strong corporate mission. What was implemented as the essence of what Patagonia stands for more than four decades ago, is not only relevant today, but more than ever crucial to the goal of environmental protection. Further, as their certification as *B-Corporation* recognizes, the outdoor apparel company provides a good example of the idea that profit and social concern need not be mutually exclusive. This type of company is rated by an independent agency that applies rigorous standards of environmental and social performance, as well as accountability and transparency. Patagonia, through the *Worn Wear* campaign, so far has shown that when social, environmental, and corporate goals are aligned from the start, they can serve the greater good and society at large.

Discussion Questions

1. What are the potential benefits and risks of the *Worn Wear* communication strategy, especially regarding the social and environmental commitment of the company?
2. How was the principle of social norms adapted in the *Worn Wear* campaign? In how far do you think it was successful?
3. What are potential opportunities and downfalls of combining social and commercial marketing? In how far can business activities support the social change?
4. Stakeholders: Who are the stakeholders of the *Worn Wear* campaign and what can be learned from it for other social marketing approaches? In class, identify all relevant stakeholder groups and their roles. Next, form groups of three to four people who each represent one stakeholder group and discuss its stake as well as its goals. [in class activity]
5. Persona: Who is the target customer of the social marketing campaign? What is their need and what's important to this customer regarding environmental sustainability? Develop a target persona that reflects personality, goals behavior and lifestyle. [out of class activity]

References

Chouinard, Y. (2016). *Let my people go surfing—The education of a reluctant businessman*. New York: Penguin.
Chouinard, Y., Ellison, J., & Ridgeway, R. (2011). The sustainable economy. *Harvard Business Review, 89*(10), 52–62.
Leonard-Barton, D. (1981). Voluntary simplicity lifestyles and energy conservation. *Journal of Consumer Research, 8*(3), 243–252.
Sachs, S., & Rühli, E. (2011). *Stakeholders matter: A new paradigm for strategy in society*. Cambridge: Cambridge University Press.

Schultz, P. W., Nolan, J. M., Cialdini, R. B., Goldstein, N. J., & Griskevicius, V. (2007). The constructive, destructive, and reconstructive power of social norms. *Psychological Science, 18* (5), 429–434.

Shaw, D., & Newholm, T. (2002). Voluntary simplicity and the ethics of consumption. *Psychology & Marketing, 19*(2), 167–185.

Inculcating the Handwashing Habit Through Social Marketing Among Poor Children in India

13

Dinesh Kumar and Punam Gupta

Chapter Overview
This case describes a campaign run by the Rotary Club in Chandigarh, India, to introduce the habit of handwashing among poor children living in slum areas in a city in India. Several studies have pointed to the fact that inculcating the simple habit of handwashing among children can reduce disease and improve mortality rates. However, due to various constraints and beliefs, it is difficult to develop long-term habits. Through this project, an effective attempt was made to apply marketing principles to this social cause and to build excitement around the activity to affect long-term behavior change. The authors were part of this project. This case is the result of direct experience in the project together with a theoretical background.

Introduction

The legitimate aim of companies is to sell products and services to make a profit. However, it is increasingly being felt that they should benefit society as well. While some companies give donations to social organizations and others start social projects, many others depend on corporate social responsibility (CSR) activities. This paper shows that great benefits can be achieved if management and marketing principles are applied to CSR activities to bring about behavioral changes among

D. Kumar (✉)
Jagran Lakecity University, Bhopal, India
e-mail: mmindchd@gmail.com

P. Gupta
Dev Samaj College for Women, Chandigarh, India
e-mail: punam.devsamaj@gmail.com

© Springer Nature Switzerland AG 2019
D. Z. Basil et al. (eds.), *Social Marketing in Action*,
Springer Texts in Business and Economics,
https://doi.org/10.1007/978-3-030-13020-6_13

people. Indeed, social organizations have a lot to learn from the marketing discipline to bring about the lasting changes that they seek.

Since marketing is concerned with identifying and fulfilling consumer needs, social organizations too must identify the needs of the target audience before embarking on their programs. This case study describes how marketing principles were used successfully to inculcate the habit of handwashing among poor children in India.

Campaign Background and Environment

The target audience was identified as children and their mothers. But they were not receptive to direct messages about public health. Thus, introducing elements of marketing and branding helped make a success of an otherwise boring hygiene message. The paper shows how marketing activities can be devised in ways that will be relevant to the target audience and generate interest. It has great applicability for social organizations who wish to market similar messages for affecting long-term change in habits.

Theoretical Background

Many theories of social learning have been proposed. The Health Belief Model (HBM) explains and predicts health behaviors and takes into account the attitudes and beliefs of individuals. It was developed by Hochbaum, Rosenstock, and Kegels and has been used and adapted to explore health behaviors (Rosenstock et al., 1998). The HBM predicts people's "readiness to act," which, together with cues, stimulates behavior. In other words, attitudes and beliefs have to be addressed to induce health-related behavior.

Another theory that is relevant here is the Extended Parallel Process Model (EPPM), which analyzes the use of fear appeals to motivate people to change their behavior. The EPPM attempts to answer how and why fear appeals succeed (Witte, 1992). Fear appeals are often used in hygiene-related interventions and the fear of illness usually causes people to adopt better habits and behavior. Unfortunately, fear appeals have been overused by health professionals. They can be ineffective among very poor people, because they feel they have nothing to lose.

We also draw upon reports that describe similar work across the world. Diarrhea is reportedly a common cause of morbidity and a leading cause of death among children aged less than five years, particularly in low- and middle-income countries, according to the *Hand washing for Preventing Diarrhoea Review* (Ejemot, 2008). Interventions such as inculcating the habit of handwashing interrupt the transmission of diarrhea-causing pathogens; studies have shown that strategies to encourage handwashing with soap can reduce the incidence of diarrhea by about one-third, and in young children by as much as 48%.

Though it is an easy way to prevent diseases, and despite its low cost and proven benefits, rates of handwashing with soap are very low throughout the developing world (*The World Bank*, 2005). Both knowledge of the practice and availability of water and soap are the basic requirements. Mere washing with water is not enough; soap helps in removing pathogens and also chemically kills contaminating and colonizing flora making handwashing more effective.

Studies by the World Bank of handwashing habits in Peru and Vietnam show that campaigns relying on mass media and limited community intervention often fail. A study of a large-scale handwashing campaign in Vietnam in 2010 (Galiani et al., 2012) shows that there was no difference between the treatment in the experimental and control groups, with no impact on health or productivity. "These results suggest that even under seemingly optimal conditions, where knowledge and access to soap and water are not main constraints, behavior change campaigns that take place on a large-scale face trade-offs in terms of intensity and effectiveness," says the report. The World Bank evaluation of a large-scale intervention in Peru also shows limited results (*The World Bank Policy Research Paper 6257*). It found that the mass media intervention alone had no significant effect on handwashing knowledge or handwashing behavior among the target audience.

Most campaigns to encourage handwashing place emphasis on the threat of disease to get people to change their behavior and educating people about transmission of disease. Mass media is also shown to be an ineffective method for such campaigns. The failure of these campaigns suggests that focusing on disease prevention or using mass media is not very effective. The need is to change the habits and motivations of the target audience. Behavior change campaigns thus have to be devised that yield trade-offs in terms of effectiveness. This is what we set out to do.

We decided to change habits by using the "five levers of change" used by Unilever (Weed, 2015), which consists of cementing habits by (a) making it understood, (b) make it easy, (c) make it desirable, (d) make it rewarding, and (e) build it into a habit. We also decided to approach the problem by applying marketing principles to building habits just as we would sell a consumer product.

The Clean Hands Project

The Rotary Club, which is active in social projects, took up the task of inculcating the habit of handwashing among poor children in the slum areas of Chandigarh. It used marketing principles and elements of branding and promotion to identify the target population, communicate to them, get them involved, and thereby inculcate the habit of washing hands after using the toilet or before eating meals. The aim of the project was to prevent disease and to improve general hygiene.

An initial study was undertaken to understand the target market and its motivations. While talking to a sample of the population, we found that people in the slums near a city were subject to several awareness campaigns taken up by government and non-government organizations regarding the importance of education, hygiene, environmental protection, and so on, but there was little implementation and practically no follow-up. The net result was that the efforts of do-gooders had in fact turned away people rather than educating them. Nor did people want to be lectured on their lifestyles.

We also learnt that organizations rarely went beyond generating awareness. They came and lectured but did not involve the people. As a result, there was skepticism about the efforts of these organizations. We therefore discovered that a campaign or even a workshop on washing hands would generate little interest among the people. We had to approach the problem in a new, creative way.

Target Audience

Chandigarh is a planned and modern city in India. It is home to a large number of well-to-do people, which is evident from the fact that it has the highest density of vehicles in the country. Though it ranks among the highest per capita income cities of India, studies show that 21.8% of the population lives below the poverty line. Of its population, 29% lives in unauthorized colonies or slums (*Indian Express*, 2013). A large number of slums dot the city, which have grown over a period of time. Despite government efforts and rehabilitation schemes, the city continues to live with its slums.

The target market was identified as children living in these slums. Parents of these children often lack access or ability to send their children to schools. It was also realized that the role of parents—and especially the mothers—was important if long-term behavior change was sought for. Thus, the target market was expanded to include mothers as well.

This was important, because we had to choose a message that would appeal both to children and their parents. Timing was also important; to ensure that parents accompanied their children, Sundays were chosen for the activity.

Target Audience Barriers and Benefits

We had to overcome several beliefs among the target market. The most important one was how to generate interest among the audience. As mentioned earlier, there was a fatigue for social messages among people, who felt that many well-intentioned people came to their locality, but hardly went beyond words. "We are more than aware about cleaning our environment, hygiene and even sending children to school. But nobody shows us how to do all this practically," a mother told us. We could understand that this perception had resulted because many social campaigns rarely went beyond the awareness objectives and thus could be classified as "all talk and no action."

Another problem was to get people interested in an otherwise boring message of health and hygiene, while another barrier was how to develop long-term habits.

The benefits that would be gained among the target audience were lower diseases and stomach infections, and also improvement in children mortality rates.

Barriers, Benefits, and Competition

There were several barriers that we faced. The first was that of communication. We faced the problem of how to get the message across and frame it in such a way that it would be acceptable to the audience. This case study describes how the communication barrier was broken. The second barrier was the cost of soap. But the most important barrier was habits. People believed that their hands were clean and did not require washing. A major barrier was changing this belief.

Another barrier related to the non-availability of water. Tap water was only available for a few hours each day, so washing hands was a problem. We had to educate people to store water in their homes and make it available for handwashing for both adults and children.

The benefits that were expected among the target audience included better health and hygiene. An unexpected benefit that we had not anticipated was the children's showing off the pleasant smell that their hands had after washing with soap. For mothers, the benefits were immense in terms of illnesses that could be avoided by better hygiene.

The competing behaviors that we had to get over (a) that hands "appeared clean," (b) the belief that handwashing was a waste of time, and (c) non-availability of water. Volunteers were employed to help families get over these competing behaviors.

SWOT Analysis (Strengths, Weaknesses, Opportunities, Threats)

Strengths

The Rotary Club has credibility and a great reputation for social causes.
It has a strong and committed volunteer base.
It has the ability to mobilize medical experts and specialists.
It could attract sponsors and partners for the activity.

Weaknesses

The costs of buying materials such as soap and supplying it to poor households were prohibitive.

We also needed doctors and medicines to support people who had contracted diseases.

We had to get over the resistance of people to social projects and awareness campaigns.

Opportunities

We had to create a campaign that would be interesting and exciting to the target audience.

We could be part of an activity that could actually save lives or at least prevent diseases.

We could be involved in inculcating safe, hygienic habits among poor people.

It would provide an opportunity for people to actually get involved in giving time or doing something for the poor.

There could be an opportunity to involve partners and young people as volunteers.

It could generate goodwill for the organizations involved in the project.

Threats

Resistance to the message by the target audience as awareness campaigns had been conducted in the past.

There was a danger that people would not attend these activities, and even if they did, would not translate them into long-term action.

Inculcating habits was not an easy task.

Limited availability of water.

Past and Similar Efforts

There have been many efforts to encourage handwashing in the past by social and commercial organizations. One notable campaign was by the Unilever brand, Lifebuoy. The brand campaigned at the Kumbh Mela in India, to raise awareness about good handwashing habits, partnering with more than 100 restaurants and cafés at the festival. The Kumbh Mela is one of the largest gatherings of people on the banks of the Ganges, so it was the ideal place to propagate a social message. For every food order placed, the first *roti* carried the branded message "*Lifebuoy se haath dhoye kya?*" ("Did you wash your hands with Lifebuoy?"). The words were heat stamped onto the baked *roti* to draw attention at the time when handwashing is critical (Lifebuoy, 2013). More than 2.5 million branded *rotis* were consumed during the month-long campaign. Lifebuoy also placed soap in the toilets of each of the eateries to enable people to wash their hands with soap before eating.

Through this campaign, the company used its knowledge of how people use products and reminded them of washing hands when it was most important. If a person is reminded to do something at a particular time, it would hopefully result in a habit as the cue gets associated with a trigger. This was in line with the World Bank studies, which had showed that only awareness interventions do not result in long-term behavior change.

Campaign Objectives and Goals

Behavior Objectives

The event organizers were seeking behavior change among poor children. The idea was that they should develop the habit of washing hands properly before meals and after using the toilet.

Knowledge Objectives

Awareness about diseases and how they spread was to be generated, with habits that would halt their spread.

Belief Objectives

People did not understand the importance of clean hands. They believed that their hands were usually clean, and if they felt the need to wash them, they would simply wipe them or wash them with water. It was important to impart the belief that even if hands looked clean, they still needed to be washed with soap and water.

Campaign Strategies

Product Strategies

The Global Handwashing Handbook describes a marketing approach and says that the only way to change long-held habits related to handwashing is to understand the factors that drive and facilitate handwashing among the target consumers. The marketing approach focuses on the needs of the target audience and determines the nature and scope of the promotional activities based on perspective of the target audience. Changing behavior requires the following three issues to be addressed:

Lowering Environmental and Cultural Barriers

Barriers in the environment include access to water, the high cost of soap, lack of handwashing facilities, and strong cultural prohibitions against washing on certain days in parts of Africa and Asia. These barriers had to be addressed while changing habits.

Transforming Old Habits

The aim of handwashing promotion is not to achieve a single event, but to instill a new habit that is followed automatically after every contaminating event. Essentially, new habits have to be installed replacing old ones.

Finding Motives and Drivers

Drivers are innate modules in the brain that motivate particular behaviors. They come in the form of emotions and the feelings. Discovering drivers and motivators help in successfully promoting the handwashing habit.

To add tangibility, a medical camp was also organized to attract people. Qualified doctors were invited to inspect patients and medicines were dispensed on the spot. This was an added attraction for people, who otherwise had little access to medical facilities.

Place Strategies

The events were conducted in a local school, which was quite near the slum area. The venue was chosen to provide easy access for children and their parents on the appointed days.

Promotion Strategies

Communication often becomes a problem in poverty-stricken areas as they are "media dark" in the sense that newspapers or mass media does not reach them. Innovative and direct methods have to be devised to reach the targeted population. Instead of using media or printed posters, we decided to hire a person who went around the locality on a bicycle announcing the message through a loudspeaker, so that it reached each and every home. Small leaflets showing a magician's picture were also distributed.

Positioning

A lot of thought went into the positioning of the campaign. It is known that washing hands before eating prevents many diseases, but many people, especially the poor, do not have this habit. The campaign positioning had to be done in a way that it would appeal to the audience. That is, the problem had to be seen from the prism of the audience, not the organizers.

Most campaigns are designed from the point of view of organizations. The underlying logic is, "the poor must be taught." Thus, many programs are launched to increase awareness but they do not contribute to social objectives. The World Bank studies clearly show resistance of the target audience to such efforts. So, the problem has to be seen from the point of view of the people. This is where social campaigns go wrong, as the efforts of the campaigners are often not seen in a similar light by the audience.

The campaign positioning that evolved after our initial study thus did not consist of mere lecturing but as fun events. While developing the positioning statement, we asked ourselves many questions, including:

What does the target audience expect from us?
Why should they listen to us?
What message will appeal to them?

By answering these questions, we came on a positioning statement that defined the problem from the consumers' point of view. The answer to the first two questions showed that the positioning should be "fun" and not "education." The messages were then designed accordingly; that appealed directly to children and their parents—the message did not give even a hint of the handwashing activity. It just invited people to come for a magic show and spend a day of fun.

Message Design

We realized that the activity could not be sold as a "handwashing workshop" or a teaching experience, which tends to put off the target audience. Instead, it was important to involve the people and to build excitement around the activity. It was thus marketed as a fun and excitement filled magic show in which people could also win prizes (Fig. 13.1). No social message was sought to be imparted and there was no hint of handwashing in the advertising message. This was one of the chief reasons that a large crowd gathered on the day of the event.

A screen showed movies with social ads. One ad "*Haath, muh aur bums*" (Hands, mouth, and bums) by Unilever was shown, which generated excitement among the children. It communicated the handwashing habit effectively.

Fig. 13.1 A magician shows tricks to local children. The handwashing theme was built in

Other Important Strategies

Volunteer Engagement
Volunteers were essential to demonstrate handwashing, to manage crowds, and to manage the clinics that were part of the medical camps. Volunteers from the Rotaract Club, which is a youth wing of the Rotary Club, signed up for the various activities. Children and families of Rotary Club members also pitched in.

Strategic Third-Party Sponsors
Sponsors to provide soap for cleaning hands, candies for the participants, and medicines for the medical camp were required.

Soap
A distributor of a company manufacturing soaps sponsored us by providing small soap packs.

Medicines
Medicines for the medical camps were obtained from sponsoring companies. While medicines for common ailments were distributed by doctors, patients were referred to hospitals for less common diseases.

Gifts
Participants were given small gifts such as candies and chocolates once they pledged to adopt the handwashing habit. The organizers achieved tangibility by

Fig. 13.2   A volunteer demonstrates the proper way of washing hands to children

offering prizes to participants. Children who participated in the event would also get a free soap and a candy if they promised that they would wash hands with it before meals and after using the toilet. The promise of a freebie associated with the event generated anticipation and excitement around the event. The Rotary Club gave demonstrations to motivate children to develop the habit of washing their hands. Another tangible element was added by volunteers who cut the overgrown nails of children, showing the dirt trapped in them that was likely to be ingested (Figs. 13.2 and 13.3).

On the appointed day, a magician enthralled the audience with magic tricks. Children loved it. After every few tricks, he would invite children from the audience who thought they had clean hands. Then, he would show the real "magic"— their hands under an ultraviolet light and magnifying glass, which showed that the hands were not clean as they thought. "All this will go in your stomach when you eat," he would say, drawing sighs from the audience. Washing of hands with plain water was not enough, he showed, adding that soap was needed. He would then distribute soap to them and ask them to wash their hands. Volunteers helped the

Fig. 13.3 A volunteer cuts the nails of children, adding to the tangibility of the message

children wash their hands and demonstrated how the hands and nails could be cleaned (Figs. 13.2 and 13.3). After the washing, the magician again showed their hands in ultraviolet light, and they were clean.

Volunteers showed how hands were to be cleaned properly. Then, the children were asked to promise that they would use soap and water every time they washed their hands.

The activity was a success each time it was conducted. It helped in building excitement in an otherwise simple message, and also in collecting crowds for the event and succeeded in teaching people the importance of handwashing. The "aha moments" were introduced in the form of ultraviolet light and magnifying glasses, which showed the dirt embedded in hands.

The integrated approach helped in affecting long-term changes in the target audience. The message was formulated that not only generated excitement but fulfilled the need of the audience to get entertained. It was executed in a manner that was at once acceptable to the people, without sermonizing or teaching. Mothers were also involved, who would serve to remind their children to wash hands, so the chances of success of habit formation were quite high.

Evaluation

Evaluation of the project was carried out on the following objectives: (i) change in behavior, (ii) long-term habit formation, and (iii) incidence of water-borne diseases.

Through follow-up visits, mothers and children were asked questions relating to the above. We found considerable behavior change among the respondents. Mothers reported that the children were initially excited about washing their hands and cleaned their nails too. They also reported that children were talking about their experiences and had showed learning about invisible germs and the dangers they posed.

Mothers also reported a positive response regarding long-term habit formation. They said that children would wash their hands without being reminded. Children also insisted that soap be bought by their families. These were positive outcomes.

Regarding the third objective, the response was confused as mothers could not specify why children fell ill. They said that some children were more prone to fall ill than others. Even the data from local clinics was not reliable so no conclusions could be drawn.

However, one recurrent response from mothers was that they appreciated efforts made the volunteers in trying to improve their lives. They said that they were motivated by the message to attend the programs being organized by us and appreciated the fact that we had involved their children. A recurrent remark was, "In other social programs they just go to collect freebies, but in this one they came back with some actual learning."

Lessons Learned and Future Direction

Social organizations operate within their specified areas, often using a direct approach toward problems. This is often seen as sermonizing and talking down to people, turning them away.

What we learned from this initiative was that messages must be devised that appeal directly to the target audience and that delivering an experience was very effective in influencing people. We had to go beyond the confines of generating awareness to bring about actual changes. Marketing uses BTL campaigns, and we had to provide a memorable experience so that habit change could be initiated. By providing such an experience, we ensured better receptivity of the message.

Using marketing principles thus helped us in achieving our social objectives. We feel that social organizations can learn a lot from marketing and communication techniques. Since the direct approach of teaching and counseling has limited gains, messages have to be framed that fit in the lives of the target population, fulfilling their needs. Excitement must be built around the message, in the manner of branding. Learning, providing cues and triggers, and promise of rewards are elements that generate curiosity. Surprising the audience by introducing "aha moments" also helps in building successful campaigns. The handwashing project showed that such elements worked well in social change efforts.

Our experience showed that there is a need for a professional marketing approach in social organizations. They have to think "outside the box" and create programs that find quick acceptability among the target audience. This will help not only social organizations but the people as well.

Discussion Questions

1. Changing habits calls for innovative approaches. This case study describes some methods that were used to introduce the handwashing habit. Can you suggest other methods that can be used to change habits for the long term?
2. A key feature of such social campaigns is getting sponsors. How can organizers generate interest in sponsors where the profit motive is not primary?
3. Habit changing campaigns have not been very successful in many countries, as described in the case. Do you think the strategy used in the above case can be applied elsewhere? What changes would you suggest so that this program can be replicated in other areas or countries?
4. A problem that is faced in such campaigns is that of overcoming resistance to change. How can this problem be tackled?
5. Do you agree that application of marketing and management principles in the handwashing campaign helped it become more acceptable? Describe the principles used and their effectiveness in the above campaign.
6. Were the elements of marketing strategy used effectively in the handwashing campaign? What improvements would you have used?

References

Brands. (n.d.). Retrieved from http://www.unilever.com/brands-in-action/detail/Lifebuoy-creates-innovative-roti-reminder/346332/.

Claire, C., & Do, Q. T. (2012). *Handwashing behavior change at scale: Evidence from a randomized evaluation in Vietnam*. The World Bank Policy Research Working Paper 6207. Retrieved from http://documents.worldbank.org/curated/en/734571468125692904/Handwashing-behavior-change-at-scale-evidence-from-a-randomized-evaluation-in-Vietnam.

Ejemot, R. I., Ehiri, J. E., Meremikwu, M. M., Critchley, J. A. (2008). Hand washing for preventing diarrhoea. *Cochrane Database of Systematic Reviews*, (1), CD004265. https://doi.org/10.1002/14651858.

Galiani, S., Gertler, P., Orsola-Vidal, A. (2012). *Promoting handwashing behavior in Peru: The effect of large-scale mass-media and community level interventions*. The World Bank Policy Research Working Paper 6257. Retrieved from https://openknowledge.worldbank.org/handle/10986/19928.

Indian Express. (2013, August 2). 21% of Chandigarh population living below poverty line. Retrieved from http://archive.indianexpress.com/news/21–of-chandigarh-population-living-below-poverty-line/1150157/.

Lifebuoy. (2013, February 21) Lifebuoy hand washing roti reminder. Retrieved from http://www.youtube.com/watch?v=e_2tQekUDy8.

Rosenstock, I. M., Strecher, V. J., & Becker, M. H. (1998). Social learning theory and the health belief model. *Health Education Quarterly, 15*(2), 175–183.

The Global handwashing partnership. (n.d.). Retrieved from http://globalhandwashing.org/resources.

The World Bank. (2005). *The Handwashing Handbook*. Available at: https://siteresources.worldbank.org/INTWSS/Publications/20389151/HandwashingHandbook.pdf.

Weed, K. (2015, June 16). Change consumer behavior with these five levers. Retrieved from http://blogs.hbr.org/cs/2012/11/change_consumer_behavior_with.html.

Witte, K. (1992). Putting the fear back into fear appeals: The extended parallel process model. *Communication Monographs, 59,* 329–349. https://doi.org/10.1080/03637759209376276.

Social Marketing Campaigns for Healthier Eating Habits in France: VIF and "LES BONNES PORTIONS" (The Right Portions) Campaign Against Childhood Obesity

14

Patricia Gurviez and Sandrine Raffin

Chapter Overview

"Les Bonnes Portions" campaign, meaning "the Right Portions," addresses children's eating patterns as a whole and is part of the program «Vivons en forme» (meaning: "let's be fit and healthy!") or VIF®. This program is driven by FLVS, a non-profit organization which for more than 10 years has proposed preventive health programs targeting French children, following the former EPODE program.

This campaign has a specific focus on the portion sizes theme: which portion for which child, regarding his/her age? And which portions of the different ingredients of a diet? Its main behavioral objectives are:

For the school-meal staff: to help them give the right portion in accordance with nutritional recommendation linked to the child's age.
For the children of elementary school: to raise their good practices regarding treats such as candies, sugary drinks, and chips, however adding also emotional and sensory enjoyment experiences, and offering mindful eating apprenticeship.
For children and their families: to adopt servings to the child's needs—especially on meat, fries—and including all kinds of treats.

P. Gurviez (✉)
UMR Ingénierie, Procédés Aliments, AgroParisTech, INRA,
Université Paris-Saclay, Massy, 91300 Paris, France
e-mail: patricia.gurviez@agroparistech.fr

S. Raffin
LinkUp Factory, 92300 Levallois-Perret, France
e-mail: sandrine.raffin@linkup-conseil.fr

© Springer Nature Switzerland AG 2019
D. Z. Basil et al. (eds.), *Social Marketing in Action*,
Springer Texts in Business and Economics,
https://doi.org/10.1007/978-3-030-13020-6_14

It consists in forming professional actors (canteen staff and extracurricular staff) at a local level to support changing the behaviors of canteen staff, children, and families regarding food portion sizes and treats. The campaign is still ongoing, but some positive partial results are provided, such as the food waste in school canteens in Saint André-Lez-Lille, one of the first towns to adopt the campaign, which has halved, suggesting that children are receiving servings that are more adapted to their needs.

Campaign Background

A 2015 survey on 8124 French 5th grade students revealed that 18% of them were overweight and almost 4% obese (DREES, 2015). However, the proportion largely depends on the children's social origins: Working-class children are overweight or obese (22 and 6% respectively) significantly more often than those of management-level employees (13 and 1% respectively). Moreover, children from higher-income households develop life habits that are more conducive to a healthy life. Forty-two percent of them say they eat vegetables every day (27% among working-class children), and 15% say they consume sugar-sweetened beverages (26% among working-class children). Almost 8 out of 10 engage in a sporting activity, against only 67% of working-class children. Fewer children of management-level employees spend more than 2 h in front of screens on school days (8% compared to 16%).

These dramatic social differences go hand in hand with geographical specificities. From 2007 to 2013, national surveys on students in different grades (kindergarten, 5th grade, and 9th grade) showed that the prevalence of overweight and obese children is higher in northern and eastern France (DREES, 2015). These are former mining areas with an outdated steel industry and high rates of low-income households and unemployment.

"Vivons en forme" or VIF® ("Let's live healthily") is a non-profit organization (NPO) which for more than 10 years has proposed preventive health programs targeting French children. Its main objective is to promote health and well-being by focusing (1) on the prevention of childhood obesity and overweight and (2) on social inequalities regarding food intake and physical activities. VIF has designed a unique methodology with the active involvement of a now national network of 252 towns. It promotes better eating and physical activity among children and families through various campaigns and tools targeting local communities and needs. Each campaign aims to provide concrete solutions to towns and facilitate the commitment of local stakeholders. When a partner town decides to join the campaign, a local VIF manager is put in charge of meeting locals to tailor the planned actions to the community's needs. All VIF interventions and tools are developed with the help of a partner, LinkUp, an independent French company specialized in social marketing and public health campaigns. Since 2016, VIF has delivered the

"LES BONNES PORTIONS" campaign to address the issue of portions served to children at home and in school canteens, which all too often fail to take the children's actual needs into account. Research has suggested that portion sizes have an effect on food intake (Ebeling et al., 2002; Robinson et al., 2016), especially for children over 5 (Rolls, Roe, Kral, Meengs, & Wall, 2004). The WHO recommends limiting portion sizes to reduce the risk of children becoming overweight or obese (WHO, 2014).

SWOT Analysis (Strengths, Weaknesses, Opportunities, and Threats)

Strengths

– VIF is currently active in 252 French towns, mainly in poor areas. 97% of VIF towns are situated in zones with high obesity and social inequalities regarding health.

VIF has already affected 4 million people, mainly families and children.
VIF is now an experienced partner (more than 10 years).
VIF and LinkUp base their campaigns on strong and lasting principles.

– Non-stigmatization of people, behavior, or food.
– Targeting the most vulnerable families to avoid their withdrawal from their local communities.
– Taking into account the "modern way of eating": convenience and quick meal preparation and cooking.
– A positive, progressive, and tangible approach focused on the emotional pleasure of eating, physical activity, and sharing.
– Strengthening social links and sharing to promote sustainable health.

Every new VIF program includes a living laboratory phase to improve and validate the chosen approach and tool content.
VIF has achieved encouraging figures showing a specific impact on more deprived families.
The network of towns is still on board after 10 years, developing a unique step-by-step strategy.

Weaknesses

In France, social marketing is very underdeveloped and VIF has to convince new partner towns of the appeal of tacking local issues related to children's health.
Methodological difficulties in setting up a recognized scientific assessment of the VIF program's efficiency.

Due to its local embeddedness, VIF has to gather ongoing assessment data for greater recognition as a major stakeholder in preventive actions against childhood overweight and obesity in France.

Opportunities

VIF is attracting growing interest from local and national public authorities.
Knowledge about healthy diets has increased, even though there has been little behavioral change.
Although a general knowledge about healthy diets has increased, probably thanks to public information campaigns, only little behavioral changes have been observed, especially in deprived areas.
There is a new vision at the French Health Ministry to consider social marketing as a valuable tool to change behavior.
The obesity epidemic is (sadly) worsening among children in lower socioeconomic classes.
Enrollment of youths as a lever to change families' eating habits.

Threats

Private partnership may be criticized in French culture, although public grants are decreasing. This can lead to a lack of credibility among academics and public decision makers, even though public–private partnerships (PPPs) are governed by a strict charter made public.
Resistance to change from certain parts of the population, especially economically and culturally disadvantaged people.
Difficulties identifying legitimate local supporters (called "ambassadors" by VIF).
Difficulties financing the process needed to define the right messages to support behavioral change.
Development of local social marketing programs is dependent on partnerships with towns and public subsidies.

Past and Similar Efforts

At a national level, since 2001, the French National Nutrition and Health Program (PNNS) has issued recommendations to increase healthier eating. Specific recommendations were made for children, although most campaigns have been generic and educational such as the French version of the "5 a Day" campaign ("manger 5 fruits et legumes par jour"). A significant general improvement has not yet been observed in terms of decreasing childhood overweight and obesity, even though there is increasing awareness of the PNNS recommendations.

Taking into account the dramatic data on social inequalities regarding childhood overweight and obesity, VIF's objectives focus on deploying local actions with a decisive impact on the habits of disadvantaged population segments. Since expanding knowledge of food guidelines has not been sufficient to change eating behavior, VIF and LinkUp decided to design and implement community-based actions. The first step was to investigate the lifestyles and motivations which cause certain disadvantaged families to adopt the usual behaviors that lead to childhood overweight and obesity. For example, VIF has already developed the following action themes to foster healthy eating literacy and sports activities: 60 min of extracurricular physical activity "BOUGE AVEC LES ZACTIFS" (keep busy and active), using fun to tackle low levels of activity among the most vulnerable children; and "UN FRUIT POUR LA RECRE" (fruit at recess) to encourage every child to enjoy a piece of fruit during the break at school, a change in the habits of the poorest children. In 2016, VIF designed its next campaign, "LES BONNES PORTIONS" ("the right portions"), to address the issue of serving portion sizes that are adapted to children's needs.

LES BONNES PORTIONS Target Audience

The social ecological model (Bronfenbrenner, 1977, 1979; Stokols, 1996) provides a framework to analyze four types of nested environmental systems of influence: (1) immediate environments such as home, school, or peers; (2) the systems connecting these immediate environments; (3) external environmental settings with indirect influences; and (4) the wider cultural context. A key element of VIF is to target not only children but also their immediate environments such as the people who care for them, which includes families as a whole, canteen staff, and extracurricular facilitators. In France, breakfast and dinner are usually eaten as a family, and children's plates are served by an adult who can control the portion size. Pupils who have their lunch every day in a canteen eat a complete meal including 4 compulsory courses (starter and main course, dairy product or cheese, and dessert) 5 times a week. School canteen staff (generally women often called "canteen aunties") belong to the same community as children and parents and share their motivations and values regarding the food served to children.

VIF first conducted qualitative research (interviews and focus groups with adults from immediate environments) to understand food habits and motivations and barriers to changing them. The data collected were consistent with the 2015 national study by DREES: Poor children were eating fewer vegetables than other children, had poor levels of physical activity, and spent a lot of time in front of screens. A gap in portion sizes was also observed, with the usual serving in deprived families often bigger than in more affluent households. Indeed, most disadvantaged parents displayed a lack of knowledge about the right portion sizes and food types to serve to their children. This confusion was connected with the gap observed between "5 a day" recommendations and the food habits of families: Big portions of

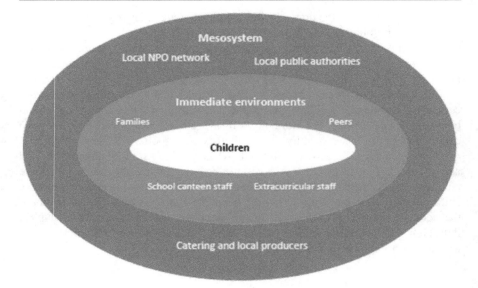

Fig. 14.1 VIF's social ecological model of community-based campaigns in the most deprived areas

minced meat, nuggets, French fries, and unchecked treats are served by parents keen to ensure their children are fed and satisfied. Some parents were found to be intent on ensuring their children eat enough food to compensate for the other more expensive purchases which they must limit due to their low income levels. Moreover, working-class families perpetuate a cultural tradition of high-density meals needed for demanding physical jobs, even when they face unemployment. Combined, these factors lead to confusion, with a lot of parents calling for help to assess whether their children ate well, too much, or not enough.

The "canteen aunties" revealed the same lack of knowledge when it came to adapting children's portion sizes to their specific needs. In addition, the research showed that children registered at an after-school center, which is often the case in low-income families, spend 20 h per week with staff members in these facilities. Extracurricular facilitators and canteen staff ultimately control the child's physical environment, including their activity levels and what they eat. It is important to involve them in the campaign (Fig. 14.1).

After analyzing the data, the targets of the "LES BONNES PORTIONS" campaign can be defined on two levels:

Immediate environmental actors, such as staff in canteens and after-school centers, are VIF's primary target to make them active partners in delivering the right message to children and their families and adopting new habits in relation to portion sizes.

Children and their families are the final target, with the objective of promoting healthier food habits. In order not to stigmatize disadvantaged families, all children attending elementary school (6–11 years old) are targeted, including those who already get the right portions at home.

On a wider level, the mesosystem which includes other local influential stakeholders (network of NPOs, catering, local producers, and local public authorities) was involved to support the project, although this part of the campaign will not be described in this chapter.

Campaign Objectives

To be as efficient as possible, VIF adopted a "small paces" approach, and its partner towns chose to be involved in annual thematic initiatives such as "LES BONNES PORTIONS." Each campaign has a specific objective.

LES BONNES PORTIONS campaign focuses on portion sizes: (1) serve suitable portions for every child and (2) serve balanced portions of the different ingredients that make up their diet.

Behavioral Objectives

For canteen staff: Serve the right portions in accordance with nutritional recommendations linked to each child's age.

For extracurricular facilitators: Adopt new behavioral norms when giving sweets to the children and use the kit tools that provide emotional and sensory enjoyment while adding an educational approach.

For children and their families: Adapt servings to the child's needs, including treats.

Belief and Knowledge Objectives

Social cognitive theory (Bandura, 1977, 1986) holds that the perception of our self-efficacy is crucial and determines how we feel and think about ourselves and how we behave. According to Bandura, people's self-beliefs are more likely to influence what they do than their actual skills and competencies. Indeed, the qualitative field data suggest low levels of self-belief among canteen employees. They are not at all considered—and do not consider themselves—as skilled individuals. The campaign aims to strengthen their self-efficacy regarding food portions as they become aware of the importance of this issue and feel they have the skills to address it. Parents feel these staff members can act as partners rather than unqualified waiters, as professionals who can enjoy the knowledge that they are serving children the right portions. Facilitators often serve as role models for children. Providing appropriate cues on when to treat children helps them feel confident and benevolent. They can introduce new social norms on treats by helping children to choose their own portion sizes.

Some parents have asked for easy guidance to indicate whether they are serving proper meals to their children. Raising awareness of new norms on portions of various food types which are adapted to the child's age is not simply an educational aim. The ultimate objective is to give parents helpful references and improve their food literacy in order to increase feelings of self-efficacy, a crucial factor in effecting behavioral change. As for children, the objectives underpinning fun food initiatives and sensory games are to help them feel more autonomous and actively reflect on their choices and to increase their food literacy.

Barriers, Benefits, and Competition

Both targets and local stakeholders were included in a participative process designed to identify barriers and motivations for change. Barriers have already been discussed above: The psychological need of parents and school staff to ensure children are eating enough suffers from a lack of knowledge about portions that are adapted to each child's age. Cultural and geographical habits reinforce these barriers, especially among disadvantaged people.

Benefits are mainly psychological in the short term (higher perceived self-efficacy) because without raising the self-efficacy of stakeholders, the behavioral benefits cannot be attained. The health benefits for children are strongly connected to healthier food and adapted portions, although research has shown that health is not a core value for impoverished people (Reckinger and Régnier, 2017), which can be a strong barrier to behavioral change.

Competition is really hard considering that eating habits are often mindless activities and embedded in social, psychological, and cultural factors. This is why VIF interventions seek to influence environmental triggers and behavioral prompts rather than behaviors themselves, as recommended by French and Gordon (2015). Giving children excessive portions of meat, French fries, or candy is an indulgent way to feel generous with long-term negative consequences for their health. Campaigns must also challenge the appeal for children of fatty and sweet treats by helping them to feel more autonomous and actively reflect on their food choices, albeit within the limitations inherent in each child's development stage. Eventually, it is important to change the social norm for the right portion sizes for caregivers and children.

Positioning

VIF seeks to be considered by the primary target (canteen staff and extracurricular facilitators) as a long-term local partner rather than as an outside agency interfering in their habits and judging them negatively. The relationship between local VIF managers and locally identified ambassadors is thus paramount. When VIF is seen as a partner by the professionals, they feel more confident and have a growing sense of self-efficacy, which allows for the stigma-free spread of new norms to the final targets: the most vulnerable children and families. Primary and final targets really need to feel nudged by VIF as a local partner that is close to their community, without any negative or formative judgement.

Research

When developing the campaign approach, VIF and LinkUp always start with a research phase that includes a systematic literature review involving academics and qualitative research to determine their target audiences with greater efficiency. Both targets and local stakeholders are included in a participative process aimed at identifying barriers and motivations for change. This process involves the joint creation of the next campaign, in order to involve everyone in achieving the campaign objectives. Next, the living laboratory process is a decisive step for real-world testing, thereby making it possible to optimize the set of tools, the efficiency of the training sessions, and the experiences on offer. An assessment device measures the capacity of the proposed tools to mobilize and involve local stakeholders, who then become campaign "ambassadors," and to reach out to the final target. This is an essential step in ensuring the relevance of the campaign and the overall design.

Marketing Strategy

Product

Training workshops are first proposed by the local VIF manager to the primary targets in order to give them an understanding of appropriate servings and the correct behaviors when treating children with candy or other kinds of treats. The "local ambassadors," i.e., local stakeholders who work closely with the local population and can support the preventive campaign, are identified through these workshops and then sign on for long-term communication efforts involving key messages after the training period. Facilitators are invited to use the kit tools to raise awareness and children's autonomy, and then to distribute educational flyers to bring home to their parents, with easy and funny guidance on adapted and balanced portion sizes. None of these actions can really be monitored, so VIF has to help its targets to adopt the desired behaviors.

Price

The campaign must challenge indulgence and the habit of serving excessive and unchecked portions with tangible, fun, and helpful techniques that can easily be implemented to make healthier portions a norm that is shared in the children's immediate environments.

Place Strategies

A key place strategy is to establish regular, high exposure for the recommended portion practices. It is therefore essential to be present with posters in school canteens when meals are being served, and to remind staff what they learned during the training workshops. Extracurricular activities (in France, these last between 3 and 5 h every day) are also a key opportunity to reach children collectively (within peer groups) in an enjoyable and dynamic way.

Promotion Strategies

VIF and its communication agency designed specific leaflets aimed at reaching out to the primary and final targets. These offer practical and easy solutions to cope with perceived difficulties.

For canteen staff, wall posters act as reminders of the importance of serving age-adapted portions (Fig. 14.2). Two examples are given, one for a preschool meal and the other for an elementary school meal, since canteens often provide meals to both groups. Both show a regular meal for children (burger and French fries) rather than an "ideal" meal which could hinder its acceptance by the staff.

Posters targeting children are also designed for after-school centers to help them adopt healthier attitudes toward fatty and sweet food and counter its appeal. The

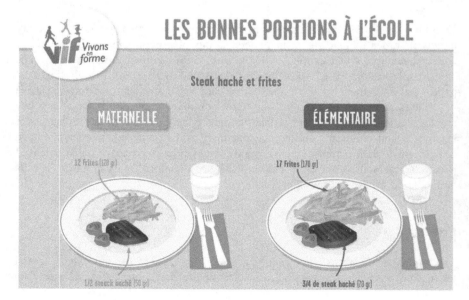

Fig. 14.2 Poster for canteen staff. *Courtesy* of VIF and LinkUp

Fig. 14.3 Poster for children at an after-school center. *Courtesy* Of VIF and LinkUp

message is very easy to understand, does not generate guilt, and is a light-hearted way to evaluate the right quantity by using the child's own hand. It helps children feel more autonomous (Fig. 14.3).

"For me, candy, chocolate, sweets, and salty treats.

Once in a while. Examples of suitable occasions are given, such as on Wednesday afternoon (free afternoon for kids), at a birthday party, or after physical activity.

Preferably during the afternoon snack to avoid eating between meals.

In small quantities. The poster suggests an easy and fun way to measure portion sizes: You can eat treats the size of your closed fist.

With mindfulness. To savor the treat, rather than eat it while doing something else, such as playing video games, will give you more pleasure."

Leaflets can also be distributed to families through their children to reassure parents about the proper portions.

The leaflets are easy to understand, address situations that parents encounter and have to deal with (portions of chips, chocolate, or soft drinks), and explain why they need to be careful about quantities and frequency. These are key elements for improving parents' food literacy and self-efficacy (Fig. 14.4).

Program Evaluation

No specific scientific evaluation of the EATING PATTERNS campaign has yet been made available since it started in 2016, and not all of the towns involved began at the same time. However, the food waste in school canteens in Saint André-lez-Lille, one of the first towns to become involved in the campaign, has halved, suggesting that children are receiving food portions that are more adapted to their needs.

Overall figures are available for VIF's preventive actions.

Growth of the network of towns involved (Fig. 14.5).

Assessment of the quality of the involvement of participating towns: 48% say they are highly committed to VIF's actions.

600–700 initiatives are implemented each year throughout the network of towns, reaching a total of 78,000 children aged 3–12.

Significant results on obesity and overweight prevalence, including in more deprived areas (figures for children aged 6–11 in six towns with deprived neighborhoods):

Saint André-lez-Lille	−40.5% in 7 years
Saint Quentin	−6.6% in 8 years
Vitré	−17% in 11 years
Meyzieu	−48% in 11 years
Royan	−40% in 10 years
Douchy-les-Mines	−13% in 8 years

Fig. 14.4 Leaflets for parents. "Does my child eat well, too much, or not enough?" This is a question shared by many parents. *Courtesy* of VIF and LinkUp

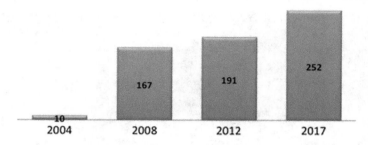

Fig. 14.5 Number of VIF's partner towns from 2004 to 2017

These measures have been selected because of the quality of the process—led at school by school nurses—and because of its integrity throughout the periods concerned. Many other towns have assessed the impact on childhood obesity, but the measures have not been selected so far because of lack of coherence in age or the numbers of children being weighed and measured.

Discussion and Lessons Learned

The living laboratory—which tested the key messages, training sessions, and tools in real life in two pilot towns—showed that facilitators found the first kit tools too complicated and informational. They did not want to become experts on nutrition and were afraid to redesign the after-school period as a teaching period focused on balanced diet. New kit tools were therefore developed as a more entertaining and interactive way to meet their expectations. The test also revealed the importance of taking into account the kinds of dishes actually served such as minced meat and French fries and not only broccoli and carrots. The living laboratory real-world testing, although time-consuming and very demanding in terms of organization and budget, has, over time revealed the weakness of the designed roadmaps and tools, making it possible to address the failures and fine-tune the empowerment strategy. Where implemented, the ongoing campaign is very much welcomed by local canteen and after-school staff. "LES BONNES PORTIONS" is capitalizing on the role that local immediate environments such as people in canteens and after-school centers can play to change food habits. Peer-group dynamics, tangible nudges, and appealing reminder devices are based on the specification of behavioral and psychological sources of value. They provide opportunities for value creation with primary and final targets and the empowerment of local communities, in order to target the most vulnerable families within their social network. The growing demand of towns to join the VIF network shows that it is meeting communities' expectations in the fight against childhood overweight and obesity. It would nevertheless be interesting to examine the long-lasting efficacy of the campaign in terms of developing a new social norm on the right portion sizes for children.

Discussion Questions

1. Do you have suggestions to strengthen the preventive actions aimed at the primary and final targets?
2. What other factors might affect obesity and food choice?
3. How else might food portions and food choice be targeted?
4. How can the influential environments be analyzed using a social ecological approach? How can it be adapted to your local scale?
5. What other health problems related to poverty and the social environment of children can VIF address in its next annual thematic campaign? In line with exchange theory, how can value be jointly created to change the behaviors that lead to negative health outcomes?

References

Bandura, A. (1977). Self-efficacy: Toward a unifying theory of behavioral change. *Psychological Review, 84*(2), 191.

Bandura, A. (1986). The explanatory and predictive scope of self-efficacy theory. *Journal of Social and Clinical Psychology, 4*(3), 359.

Bronfenbrenner, U. (1977). Toward an experimental ecology of human development. *American Psychologist, 32*(7), 513.

Bronfenbrenner, U. (1979). *The ecology of human development Cambridge*. MA: Harvard.

DREES Direction de la recherche, des études, de l'évaluation et des statistiques. (2015). L'état de la santé de la population en France, Rapport 2015. *Collection Etudes Statistiques*.

Ebbeling, C. B., Pawlak, D. B., & Ludwig, D. S. (2002). Childhood obesity: Public-health crisis, common sense cure. *The Lancet, 360*(9331), 473–482.

French, J., & Gordon, R. (2015). *Strategic social marketing*. California: Sage.

Reckinger, R., & Régnier, F. (2017). Diet and public health campaigns: Implementation and appropriation of nutritional recommendations in France and Luxembourg. *Appetite, 112*, 249–259.

Robinson, E., Oldham, M., Cuckson, I., Brunstrom, J. M., Rogers, P. J., & Hardman, C. A. (2016). Visual exposure to large and small portion sizes and perceptions of portion size normality: Three experimental studies. *Appetite, 98*, 28–34.

Rolls, B. J., Roe, L. S., Kral, T. V., Meengs, J. S., & Wall, D. E. (2004). Increasing the portion size of a packaged snack increases energy intake in men and women. *Appetite, 42*(1), 63–69.

Stokols, D. (1996). Translating social ecological theory into guidelines for community health promotion. *American Journal of Health Promotion, 10*(4), 282–298. https://doi.org/10.4278/0890-1171-10.4.282.

WHO. (2014). Limiting portion sizes to reduce the risk of childhood overweight and obesity. Biological, behavioral and contextual rational. *E-Library Evid Nutr Actions (eLENA).* http://www.who.int/elena/bbc/portion_childhood_obesity/en/.

Smile Train India: A Social Marketer Targeting Cleft Lip/Palate as a Socio-Medical Issue

15

Sivakumar Alur

Chapter Overview

Smile Train India is the Indian arm of the US-based Smile Train that works to provide free cleft surgeries in India. India is one of the major operating countries of this social marketing organization. The key focus of this organization has been to increase awareness about cleft among all stakeholders and help poor families with cleft-afflicted children with funding to undertake surgery for cleft correction.

Campaign Background

In India, an estimated 28,000–35,000 children are born with cleft lip or palate every year. Only about one-sixth of these children undergo corrective surgery by a trained surgeon (https://www.smiletrainindia.org/media/press/smile-train-completes-16000-free-cleft-surgeries-orissa). Others endure cleft lip and palate, if they survive until adulthood, due to illiteracy and poverty. Vitamin deficiency, high exposure to tobacco and alcohol, viral infections, and specific medications during a mother's pregnancy raise cleft risk for the child. Genetic causes like gene mutation and cleft incidence in the family could also be the reasons for cleft lip. An exact diagnosis of the cause of cleft is difficult.

Cleft lip and cleft palate are two different facial deformities that affect children for multiple reasons. While doctors can detect cleft lip during pregnancy using scans, cleft palate is difficult to detect. When doctors detect cleft lip, they advise parents to seek surgical correction within 6 months of childbirth. Poor reading of

S. Alur (✉)
VIT Business School, Vellore, Tamil Nadu, India
e-mail: sivakumar.a@vit.ac.in

© Springer Nature Switzerland AG 2019
D. Z. Basil et al. (eds.), *Social Marketing in Action*,
Springer Texts in Business and Economics,
https://doi.org/10.1007/978-3-030-13020-6_15

237

scans and untrained sonologists and doctors can miss cleft lip detection during pregnancy.

In many cases, parents of cleft children do not seek surgery due to several reasons. Parents lack access to health care facilities and surgeons that require specialized training for surgery and post-operative care. Some parents are superstitious (Naram et al., 2013). They consider cleft not as a treatable medical condition but as God's curse (http://www.asianage.com/india/over-10-lakh-kids-india-live-cleft-lips-055). A few local cultures blame the mother for various unscientific reasons like (a) using a knife during an eclipse or (b) having committed adultery, for the child's cleft lip. Some families cite previous instances of miscarriage or cleft lip as a condition in the family as the reason. Poor parents cannot afford tertiary health care where a specialist team of doctors and paramedical staff need to work. In very complicated cases, multiple surgeries over time and sensitive post-operative care entail additional expenses (https://yourstory.com/2017/03/smile-train-india-cleft-surgeries/). Parents due to fear and religious reasons do not undertake corrective surgery for cleft treatment.

Cleft lip results in the baby or an adult to suffer several difficulties. A disfigured face leading to social ostracism is a common problem. Schoolmates and various society members ridicule and denigrate cleft patients due to disfigured faces. Cleft also results in life threatening conditions like difficulty in breathing, drinking milk or liquids in children, and intake of food. This can lead to inadequate nutrition and stunted growth. Many cleft patients end up with a sonorous voice as they grow up due to the gap in the lip and palate (http://www.thehindu.com/features/magazine/Cleft-no-more/article12086004.ece). In addition, cleft creates ear and nose infection, as the ear, nose, and throat are related organs. Infection spreads from one of these organs to another easily. Smile Train India is the Indian arm of the US-based Smile Train that works to provide free cleft surgeries in India. India is one of the major operating countries of this social marketing organization. The key focus of this organization has been to increase awareness about cleft among all stakeholders and help poor families with cleft-afflicted children with funding to undertake surgery for cleft correction. Smile Train USA started in 1999 and the activities in India started in 2000.

Social marketers usually follow a phased implementation of their programs, namely policy advocacy followed by engaging community leaders, and then targeting the primary audience. This would mean the strategy of regulate, educate, and facilitate. However, Smile Train follows the strategy of educating the community on cleft and facilitating cleft surgeries simultaneously.

SWOT Analysis

Strength

The biggest strengths of Smile Train are the various stakeholders (namely partner hospitals and doctors/clinics [http://zeenews.india.com/sports/tennis/wimbledon-

2013/smiling-pinki-flips-coin-at-wimbledon_764772.html]), the target population (namely parents of cleft-afflicted children), and adults and donors who contribute to this cause. The dedicated staffs and their smaller number compared to similar social marketing organizations is another key strength. The partnership and networking model facilitates working with a small staff. Partner hospitals not only facilitate cleft surgeries but undertake comprehensive cleft care. These hospitals offer either cleft surgeries and/or comprehensive cleft care free due to their service for the cause or because Smile Train covers their costs due to their partnership. The parents of affected children and cleft-affected adults after treatment turn into voluntary ambassadors for the cause. Being an international charity helps Smile Train benefit from its global network and its US-based parent organization.

A key strength of Smile Train is that it operates as a local organization. It partners local hospitals and clinics and its spare capacity for cleft surgeries and cleft care. Such partnerships help poor cleft patients too, as they facilitate easy access to affordable care. Smile Train's sustainable financial model is another major strength (http://www.afaqs.com/news/story/46992_Cleft-patient-Jyothi-smiles-for-the-first-time-with-Himalaya-Lip-Care). It follows a combination of pro-bono surgeons and other healthcare staff, corporate and individual donors, and funding through government schemes to sustain its organization.

Smile Train India employs information technology and Internet efficiently for its activities and processes. It has an updated Web site that provides useful information for various stakeholders. Cleft surgeons are their key stakeholders. A free web-based virtual surgical simulator helps cleft surgeons to practice cleft surgery. Cleft specialists among researchers have access to Smile Train's largest web-based global cleft database. In addition, its specialist review panel ensures that the cleft surgery adheres to quality parameters.

Smile Train started as US-based charity in 1999. Its vast global experience has added to its learning and reputation across different communities.

Weaknesses

The greatest weakness of Smile Train is its operational model. Its operational model involves activities that encompass awareness building to comprehensive cleft care. However, it focuses mainly on acting as a facilitator between donors and corrective surgery patients. If the network of donors, hospitals, and doctors shift from Smile Train to competitors, it can hardly stop this shift.

Smile Train focuses on cleft corrective surgeries. This entails work on cleft after it has set in as a medical condition in an individual. However, prevention is another way of working on this condition. Thus, while the focus is on cure, lesser focus on prevention is a weakness.

Opportunity

Smile Train operates globally, especially in populous countries like India where cleft prevalence is high. However, tertiary health care required for cleft surgeries are mostly available in urban areas. As rural patients have lesser access to tertiary care, expanding cleft care services to remote rural areas is an opportunity. India's rural poverty and illiteracy are greater than urban areas. Opportunity exists to, therefore, spread awareness and fund surgeries in rural areas to advance Smile Train's mission.

Another opportunity available is to work with different social organizations. This would help Smile Train to serve several patients and foster behavioral change. Smile Train can work with governments to bring in legislation to facilitate better lives for cleft-affected. This effort can include cleft specialist certification for doctors and other paramedical staff and sensitization programs for employers about cleft as a medical condition.

Threats

Health insurance is under penetrated in India. Currently, Smile Train India connects funding from donors to hospitals that perform cleft corrective surgery on poor patients. This model works in India as most health care costs are borne as direct private payment. However, increased coverage of employer or government provided health insurance could make cleft surgery funding slowly redundant. In addition, better access to low-cost tertiary government health care can reduce private health care dependence.

Greater health literacy can help reduce the need for cleft surgeries. More information and awareness on causes of cleft among prospective mothers act to prevent clefts among newborns significantly. Greater monitoring of the expecting mothers during pregnancy can reduce cleft childbirths. This monitoring could involve providing adequate nutrition and vitamins. It could also entail advising pregnant mothers to avoid tobacco and alcohol as it would increase the risk of a cleft child being born.

Target Audience

The target audience is the cleft patients and their parents who need the medical and financial help. Cleft patients are mainly children who are not earning members. They need to get help from their parents. However, these parents are usually from a poor economic background. They need education about cleft corrective surgery and money to perform their children's surgery. Donors are another target audience who need to be convinced about donating for cleft corrective surgery compared to other social causes.

The secondary target audience also includes specialist doctors (e.g., cleft surgeon), paramedical staff (e.g., nurses), hospitals, schools, and the community that need to be aware and act in reducing cleft incidence.

Campaign Initiatives and Objectives

Smile Train's overall campaign objective is to ensure comprehensive cleft care for children of economically weak parents. The main campaign initiatives are to raise the awareness among children, adults, and parents that (a) cleft is a curable condition; (b) cleft care requires a multi-pronged approach involving the medical and social intervention; and (c) economically poor parents can seek Smile Train's help in cleft corrective surgery. The other important objectives are (a) raising public and doctors' awareness about economic and social issues surrounding cleft and (b) increasing donors' awareness about donating for cleft care and its positive social implications. Smile Train India's key objectives are to provide free corrective cleft surgery to each one of the estimated 35,000 newborns with cleft, training Indian doctors to conduct cleft surgeries, and providing Indian hospital funding for the procedures.

Barriers, Benefits, and Competition

The key barriers to cleft prevention and treatment are (a) lack of awareness, (b) financial- and access-related difficulties in taking steps to prevent or treat, (c) superstitious beliefs that one cannot prevent cleft and it is God's curse or one should not change a cleft lip or palate, (d) paucity of time to go through comprehensive cleft post-operative care, and (e) misinformation that cleft is not treatable or may take too much time, effort, and money.

The key benefits for the target audience in cleft are (a) better quality of life as a whole, (b) reduction in ear, nose, and throat infection, (c) better physical growth due to better nutrition and food intake, (d) greater societal acceptance due to the change in face disfigurement, (e) higher job opportunities due to better voice and lesser physical deformity, and (f) reduction in spending on quacks and superstitious rituals that would not have any effect on cleft.

Adults can use cleft-afflicted children to garner sympathy and gain monetary benefits. For example, some may use abandoned children with cleft as beggars. Disability benefits in government and private sector may prompt some not to take any cleft remedies. Fear and fatalism are other reasons for no change in behavior. In addition, absence of financial resources, time, and the tendency to avoid any effort at changing the status quo are other compelling reasons. Moreover, the target audience may also face prospects of very low accessibility to tertiary healthcare facilities required for comprehensive cleft care.

Other organizations worldwide that compete in the same space include Mission Smile, Transforming Faces, Re Surge International, and Smile Network International.

Positioning

Smile Train positions itself as a social marketer that provides free cleft surgery for poor patients. It funds poor newborn cleft children and adults for corrective surgery. In positioning itself as a funding provider, it needs to attract donors. However, raising awareness about cleft, screening and detection of cleft, and selecting deserving poor patients are also key activities of Smile Train.

It concentrates on (a) financial help for comprehensive cleft care so that cleft-afflicted integrate into society well, (b) train Indian doctors on cleft care rather than employ foreign specialist doctors, and (c) use the local hospital infrastructure for screening, diagnosing, surgeries, and comprehensive cleft care.

Research

The major theories that underpin most efforts in social marketing are Theory of Reason Action/Planned Behavior (Ajzen, 1991), Extended parallel processing (Witte, 1992), social learning (Ghazi et al., 2018), and diffusion of innovation. All these theories concentrate on three major actions, namely identification of motives of action, message strategies, and target audiences. In the case of Smile Train, these have been well understood in relating to the strategy that targets all stakeholders with different messages addressing each of their motives. The key Stakeholders are parents, partner hospitals and doctors, and donors. In addition, stage theories of behavior change (Weinstein, Rothman, & Sutton, 1998) help explain how different audiences react and thus define the segments.

Several studies have analyzed different aspects of cleft as a condition. In addition, Smile Train and its activities in India have also done studies. The published papers dealing with cleft are mostly in the medical area. These papers focus on the various descriptions of the medical condition and the related complications, diagnosis, and effectiveness of different interventions for treatment. The papers related to Smile Train and its activities in cleft care have, however, focused on the socio-economic dimensions of the problem. Moreover, the effect of different communication methods targeted at different members in the cleft ecosystem, i.e., patients, parents, etc.

Marketing Strategy

Product

Smile Train offers complete cleft care as a service for cleft patients (https://timesofindia.indiatimes.com/city/ahmedabad/Smile-Train-completes-10000-free-cleft-surgeries-in-Gujarat/articleshow/49335803.cms). It focuses on funding the poor for corrective surgery. It collaborates with doctors and hospitals to achieve its goal. Moreover, Smile Train helps in (a) spreading awareness about causes and detection of cleft, (b) removing superstitions surrounding cleft, and (c) helping educational institutions, employers, and public about cleft being a treatable condition.

Place

Globally, Smile Train has a presence in more than 100 countries. In India, it has a presence through its partner doctors and hospitals across more than 100 towns and cities. In addition, sharing of cleft correction success stories through media like radio, television, and Internet has helped in achieving greater reach. The Smile Train partnership provides an opportunity for the doctors, clinics, and hospitals to highlight indirectly their activities to the prospective clients. To ensure consistent and reliable surgical outcomes across locations, Smile Train facilitates surgeons and paramedical staff training with both volunteers and a virtual surgical simulator available online. In addition, a medical review board monitors the treatment quality. Another big contribution to the medical practitioners and researchers is that all the cleft patient data (identifier data masked) are available in the Smile Train database online for research and scrutiny.

Price

Smile Train seeks funding from donors to provide for a single cleft surgery. In addition, Smile Grants (http://www.livemint.com/Leisure/yqIL1Q5hGXNob7lTkj940N/Freedom-to-smile–Satish-Kalra.html) ensure that poor cleft patient families receive money (a) to reach hospitals, (b) to compensate for lost work in treatment, and (c) children school fees. The cleft-afflicted families incur costs, when they decide to treat their children. These costs include the visit to a doctor, consultation, surgery, post-operative care, loss of wages due to care giving, and the cost of the child getting back to school. Thus, the huge costs associated with cleft are the price poor children and adults pay. In addition, psychological costs are high due to social embarrassment and religious beliefs.

Promotion

Smile Train uses several programs like Cleft Week and different media like Internet to raise cleft awareness and promote giving for cleft surgery. Cleft Week is a week dedicated to promoting doctor training on cleft and fun-filled activities for children at partner hospitals to raise cleft awareness. Smile Train uses partner doctors and hospitals to conduct cleft screening camps. It specifically targets schools for creating awareness that cleft is a treatable condition. It sensitizes normal school children to the ill-effects of socially ostracizing cleft-afflicted children. Smile Train uses days like the World Plastic Surgery day to create cleft awareness among doctors and the community.

It roped in a lip care marketer to create a special campaign of a cleft-affected girl getting over social ostracism after surgery. This multimedia (TV & Internet) campaign helped create greater cleft awareness among the public. Celebrities and ambassadors like Aishwarya Rai (https://www.mumbailive.com/en/bollywood/aishwarya-rai-bachchan-announces-her-father-krishnaraj-rai-birthday-as-day-of-smiles-supports-smile-train-india-17566), a popular Bollywood actor, in association with Smile Train, create greater cleft awareness. Internationally, Megan Mylan's 2009 Academy Award-winning documentary has helped raise awareness and funds for cleft corrective surgery for poor children. Smile Pinki (http://zeenews.india.com/sports/tennis/wimbledon-2013/smiling-pinki-flips-coin-at-wimbledon_764772.html) the documentary film dealt with an Indian girl's struggle with cleft and getting over it through surgery.

People

Smile Train has a small administrative setup managing the Indian operations. The key people, however, are the partner doctors and hospitals. They help in cleft corrective surgeries and pre- and post-operative care. Moreover, paramedical staff like audiologists and speech therapists also play a crucial role. Cleft care requires a team of medical and paramedical staff for successful treatment. Celebrities, volunteers, members of community organizations, and donors are people who facilitate cleft awareness through Smile Train.

Physical Evidence

In tertiary health care services, infrastructure plays an important role. A cleft surgery requires a team of specialist doctors and staff and a safe/hygienic environment. Since cleft surgery affects ear, nose, and throat, sterile conditions need maintenance for effective surgery. Therefore, Smile Train selects partner hospitals based on an exhaustive survey.

Process

Smile Train helps cleft patients undergo surgery in partner hospitals. It has to process two different screenings simultaneously. The first screening is to identify financially needy cleft patients. An economic background check ensures eligibility for corrective surgery funding. The second simultaneous screening is for the prospective doctors and hospitals. Smile Train needs to screen doctor, staff, and hospital infrastructure. In addition, funding organizations or individual donors need to be vetted before associating as partners.

Program Evaluation

Smile Train India has helped perform more than 475,000 surgeries in 170 partner hospitals through 300 surgeons across more than 100 cities. This has been possible with only eight full-time employees on its rolls. Collaborations with CSR activities of large corporates (e.g., Bajaj Group), foundations (e.g., India Bulls Foundation), and charitable trusts (e.g., TATA Trusts) have helped it further its activities (https://yourstory.com/2016/10/the-smile-train/). Government is a contributor to betterment of its citizens' health. A key program metric is the success in partnering with the Government of India. Several missions like National Health Missions and programs under these missions like Rashtriya Bal Kalyan Karyakram (National Child Welfare Program, http://www.dailypioneer.com/state-editions/bhubaneswar/35k-kids-are-born-with-cleft-lip-palate-a-year-in-india.html) have helped Smile Train in its social marketing efforts.

Discussion and Lessons Learned

Poor cleft patients face a serious challenge in getting over their health condition. They are unaware that it is a treatable condition and have constraints in accessing and affording corrective surgery. In view of this, they continue to suffer and face social ostracism due to their disfigured face. Smile Train India is a social marketing organization that targets awareness creation, screening and cleft detection, and funding of corrective cleft surgery. Smile Train achieves it through a unique design of partnership with doctors/hospitals and donors. It thus helps in social acceptance of cleft-affected, post-surgery, and contributes to developing healthy working individuals. Its networking model is helping the local community to gain and develop local expertise. Community involvement and local commitment help scale up and sustain efforts in social marketing. A social marketer as an enabler can spread a social message faster than a controlling organization. Another lesson from Smile Train's success is the power of demonstration (through success stories) in media. This has resulted in greater awareness of cleft as a treatable condition. Awareness leads to the breaking of superstitious beliefs.

Discussion Questions

1. What behavior change is Smile Train addressing? Does it involve all types of behavior change?
2. What place strategies would you suggest for Smile Train?
3. How does the concept of exchange work in Smile Train's case?
4. How do you distinguish between non-profit marketing and social marketing in Smile Train's efforts?

References

Ajzen, I. (1991). The theory of planned behavior. *Organizational Behavior and Human Decision Processes, 50*(2), 179–211.

Ghazi, C., Nyland, J., Whaley, R., Rogers, T., Wera, J., & Henzman, C. (2018). Social cognitive or learning theory use to improve self-efficacy in musculoskeletal rehabilitation: A systematic review and meta-analysis. *Physiotherapy Theory and Practice*, 1–10.

Naram, A., Makhijani, S. N., Naram, D., Reddy, S. G., Reddy, R. R., Lalikos, J. F., et al. (2013). Perceptions of family members of children with cleft lip and palate in Hyderabad, India, and its rural outskirts regarding craniofacial anomalies: A pilot study. *The Cleft Palate-Craniofacial Journal, 50*(3), 41–46.

Weinstein, N. D., Rothman, A. J., & Sutton, S. R. (1998). Stage theories of health behavior: Conceptual and methodological issues. *Health Psychology, 17*(3), 290.

Witte, K. (1992). Putting the fear back into fear appeals: The extended parallel process model. *Communications Monographs, 59*(4), 329–349.

Enhancing Existing Communication Channels for Large-Scale Health Interventions: Making Every Contact Count in the United Kingdom

16

Katherine C. Lafreniere and Andy McArthur

Chapter Overview

This case investigates a large-scale health intervention developed by Social Marketing Gateway in the City of Salford, UK. The Making Every Contact Count (MECC) program indirectly encourages Salford residents to make healthier lifestyle choices by training frontline staff, particularly those in the health industry, to have conversations with clients about their health and wellbeing. The training program covered interpersonal and communication skills, basic behavior change theories, issues related to wellbeing, and local services. By using communication channels that already exist, MECC was able to increase the efficiency of health guidance without exhausting limited resources.

Campaign Environment and Background

The 220,000 residents of Salford, UK, face significant health inequalities. A woman born in Salford can expect to live almost 3 years less than the national average and a man from Salford can expect to live 4 years less than the national average. The health issues underlying these inequalities place a huge financial burden on local service providers at a time when they are under increasing pressure to cut staff and deliver services. Local health and other public sector agencies therefore set out to

K. C. Lafreniere
Alberta School of Business, University of Alberta, Edmonton, Canada
e-mail: klafreni@ualberta.ca

A. McArthur (✉)
Social Marketing Gateway, Glasgow, Scotland, UK
e-mail: andy@socialmarketinggateway.co.uk

© Springer Nature Switzerland AG 2019
D. Z. Basil et al. (eds.), *Social Marketing in Action*,
Springer Texts in Business and Economics,
https://doi.org/10.1007/978-3-030-13020-6_16

tackle the arduous task of increasing the efficiency of health guidance without additional resources.

Following a visit from the Department of Health (UK) Health Inequalities National Support Team, local agencies decided to create an early interventions program, where public sector staff would be trained to provide public health guidance to their clients. The Department of Health speculated that such a program, if delivered systematically and on a large enough scale, could significantly impact the health and well-being of Salford residents. Building the assets of local people would reduce the burden on local services and, in turn, allow service providers to target resources to where they are needed. Also, raising awareness among the frontline staff of other services and supports, and improving the levels of quality referral and signposting that they can deliver, will both improve coordination between services and more effectively connect people with the services they need.

A core arguement for the Making Every Contact Count (MECC) program is that millions of health practioners and other staff from a diverse range of professions talk to members of the public every day. These frontline service staff, if properly trained, have the potential to influence the behaviors of the wider public and help people stay well. MECC, therefore, seeks to achieve behavior change at two levels: first the behavior of frontline service delivery staff working within service delivery organizations, and second the lifestyle behaviors of citizens who are the customers of public services.

MECC aims to teach the local workforce how to carry out conversations with residents about their health and well-being in order to encourage healthier lifestyle choices. This aim is based on the idea of *whole systems* working, a broad, holistic, and multi-agency approach where health is everybody's business. If frontline staff across the full range of public services can have helpful and consistent conversations with their customers and clients, then a major impact can be made on population health and well-being.

MECC adopted an asset-based approach to achieve organizational change and improved population health and well-being. An asset-based approach assumes a community development philosophy that seeks to build on the skills of local people and the supportive functions of local institutions. MECC does this by seeking to change the culture and practice of service delivery organizations, encouraging and supporting their frontline staff to work in new ways to build stronger, healthier, and more sustainable local communities for the future.

Governance of the MECC programme was through a MECC Program Board that fed into the local Health and Wellbeing Board for the area. The Health and Wellbeing Boards are a new governance level established across the local government sector in England in 2013 in response to the new public health responsibilities given to local government. A MECC delivery team was formed in Salford to focus on the nuts and bolts of implementation, and a stakeholder group also came together to provide regular input from the perspective of the key organizations participating.

In Salford, the rollout of the MECC training began early in 2012, with a number of courses scheduled on a monthly basis. The courses were delivered in community venues or in the premises of some of the participating organizations (e.g., local hospital or community centre). The number of staff participating in individual training courses varied but averaged around 15 people per session.

SWOT Analysis (Strengths, Weaknesses, Opportunities, Threats)

Strengths

Health Services is already a well-recognized health resource for the public.

The Local Government's Health and Wellbeing Board is firmly behind MECC, as are senior leaders from the other main service delivery organizations.

MECC was introduced as a central part of the local health service's strategic commissioning plan in 2010. Since then, heavy investment has been made in developing a program that will meet the recommendations of the National Support Team for Health Inequalities to "industrialize" the health gain conversations of the local workforce.

The delivery team organized a group of stakeholders to offer additional input.

Weaknesses

At the time, MECC was a new effort with a new delivery team. Although the delivery team members had experience of implementing other projects, none had worked on a project quite like MECC.

Opportunities

The UK has a huge healthcare workforce which, along with the many thousands of other public- and third-sector workers, represents a very significant asset that can be mobilized to support behavior change at the population level.

Frontline staff members are in a position to ask, advise, assist and prompt the people they interact with on a daily basis to think about and act to take care of their own well-being.

Threats

The causes of ill health and health inequalities are complex and usually cannot be dealt with by one service or organization acting alone.

Staff may not be interested in the program or changing how they do their job.

Work, housing, and income variables act as competition to behavior change among Salford residents.

Target Audience

The MECC program targeted frontline staff, particularly those in the health industry and other industries who have a direct or indirect role in helping their clients or customers change their health-related knowledge, attitudes, and behavior. This target audience was ideal because they regularly interacted with numerous clientele, therefore providing an extensive communication channel to a large proportion of Salford residents. In Salford, there are over 15,000 frontline staff members and volunteers that represent the target audience.

Barriers to Adopting MECC

Staff may not be experts in all factors influencing health and well-being, particularly those factors that are outside of their specific service area.

Some staff members would have more time to chat with clients than other members.

Staff may be reluctant to move beyond the comfort zone of *doing their job in the way they have always done it.*

Campaign Objectives and Goals

The MECC program aims to change the behaviors of both frontline service staff who interact with the local population and of the local population itself. The focus is on workers within public services and on encouraging them to have short, opportunistic conversations ("healthy chats") with members of the public that they interact with on a daily basis. The intention is that all frontline staff have a role to play, not only health and social care workers, but also other staff members who meet the public on a daily basis; they can all help improve local health and well-being by "making every contact count." In turn, it is expected that, as a result of these conversations, the public would start to take better care of their health and access a range of local services that support well-being. Thus, the main objective was to initiate another route to encourage healthy behaviors by using a communications system that was already in place: frontline staff. The overall goal is to raise the level of population health and well-being and reduce the rising cost of health services at a time when the public-sector expenditure in the UK is under severe strain.

Behavioral Goals

The behavioral goal was to increase the number of healthy chats, in the form of brief advice or interventions that frontline staff and volunteers held with Salford residents. This goal was established through the creation of MECC competencies. These competencies are segmented to reflect the fact that some staff involved in MECC would deliver only *brief advice*, while others would deliver both *brief advice* and *brief interventions*. While brief advice was seen as being a very short chat, possibly leading on to the client being steered in the direction of an appropriate service, a brief intervention would involve a slightly longer, and possibly more complex, structured conversation that looked to build the client's motivation to change an unhealthy behavior and could conclude with a planned course of action that would support the behavior change identified.

To reach this goal, staff members need to be able to quickly assess a person's need and motivation to change and to be confident enough to encourage people to act and take small steps along the change journey. Staff would either be strengthening a person's ability to self-care, delivering brief advice or a brief intervention, signposting to other sources of help, or making a quality referral. The principle of engaging with people and opening up a conversation is a simple one, but is also potentially a difficult one to implement in the context where many staff are reluctant to move beyond the comfort zone of *doing their job in the way they have always done it*. But to do MECC and to do it well, staff would need to understand that they were being asked to do things differently.

Campaign Strategies

Product Strategy

The MECC training program was developed around the distinction of brief advice versus brief interventions and involved two levels of training (Level 1 and Level 2). The competencies developed for MECC covered interpersonal and communication skills, basic behavior change theories, issues related to well-being, and local services. Level-1 training prepared staff to engage with the public, encourage self-care, and signpost people to appropriate sources of support. Level-2 training went further, ensuring that the staff knew the range of factors that could influence well-being and were prepared to deliver brief interventions.

Three courses were developed with a range of interactive elements. Two half-day courses were prepared for Level 1, and one full-day course was organized for Level 2. To lay the foundations for long-term sustainability, a separate *Train the Trainers* course was also developed to establish a pool of internal trainers that would ensure that staff could continue to gain the necessary competencies when they needed them. The program designer (Social Marketing Gateway), incorporated extant behavioral theory to show how staff members might be able to help others in a short space of time. For example, staff members were taught about incentivizing and removing barriers in order to encourage behavior change (McKenzie-Mohr, 2000). Other theories that were particularly useful for the program were the Stages of Change Theory and Exchange Theory.

Stages of Change Theory (i.e., Transtheoretical Model; Prochaska & Velicer, 1997) demonstrates that needs vary in terms of information, motivation, and support, depending on the client's stage. So, frontline staff had to learn how to identify the client's stage in order to provide appropriate guidance. For example, action-oriented guidance is only useful for clients in the action stage, and such guidance would be counterproductive for clients in earlier stages (Prochaska & Velicer, 1997). A basic appreciation of the theory allowed staff members to assess how ready a person was to change and to decide how (if at all) to help.

Exchange Theory (Houston & Gassenheimer, 1987) suggests that successful health interventions require a voluntary exchange of resources (e.g., money, time, effort) for perceived benefits. To encourage a client to participate in an exchange, the client must believe that the benefits of adopting a healthy behavior outweigh the costs of purchase/adoption. It is important to note that clients may not be willing to exchange certain resources at all, but incentives can be offered to ensure benefits outweigh the costs (Alcalay & Bell, 2000). Frontline staff were therefore taught to acknowledge the costs and benefits of healthy behavior in order to minimize costs and maximize benefits.

In general, staff working directly with the public needed to appreciate that a range of factors (lifestyle and other) can influence a person's health and well-being. As such, staff members working in one area of service delivery (e.g., giving financial advice, delivering a smoking cessation service, working as a receptionist in a library, and so on) needed to be sensitive to factors outside of their specific service area that contributed to a client's situation. They did not need to be experts in these other service areas. Rather, a basic understanding of the main factors affecting well-being and the key services available would help staff members be in a better position to spot a person's needs, engage them in conversation, and encourage them to take even a small step in the right direction. Ten key factors that influence the well-being of the local population were identified: housing, employment, welfare benefits and tax credits, money and debts, smoking, weight management, substance misuse (including alcohol), physical activity, emotional health and well-being, and sexual health.

Initially, staff members aspiring to deliver brief interventions (Level 2) needed to first demonstrate that they met the competencies for delivering brief advice (Level 1). This led to some staff needing to complete multiple self-assessments and courses. The system was therefore revised, such that both brief advice and brief interventions were covered by one self-assessment and, if required, one training course. Staff members also used a technique called "MECC Touch Point Mapping" to identify intervention opportunities that existed in their day-to-day work environment. By rooting the training firmly in the "working realities" of staff members, it was easier to highlight the range of factors that influenced well-being and the importance of a more holistic approach between different services.

Rollout of the MECC training courses began early in 2012, with a number of courses scheduled on a monthly basis. The courses were delivered in community venues or in the premises of some of the participating organizations (e.g., the local hospital or community center). The number of staff participating in individual training courses varied but averaged around 15 people per session.

Augmented Products

An online self-assessment tool (SAT) in multiple-choice format was developed to assess whether or not staff members met the required MECC competencies. For example, SAT asked staff about (1) their confidence in starting a conversation with clients, (2) the factors influencing health and well-being, (3) their understanding of the Stages of Change model, (4) confidentiality and safeguarding issues, (5) their knowledge of key local services, and (5) how and when to refer people to other services. The implementation of SAT brought significant negative feedback from the target audience. Many were critical of the questions and viewed the self-assessment as an onerous *test* rather than a supportive tool. Revisions were made to improve the clarity of the questions, but criticism and resistance from staff did not completely disappear. Consequently, SAT was abandoned in favor of a new MECC Induction Session wherein staff members decide for themselves what, if any, further help they need from MECC. Additional augmented products included the following:

- A Web site offering training and supplementary resources
- Drop-in classes and workshops for staff members who continued to struggle with delivering brief interventions after attending the training courses
- Action Learning Sets and forums in which staff members could share experiences and problem solve real-life interventions.

Pricing Strategies

MECC's price strategy is to decrease the monetary costs for frontline staff to participate in the program. In order to offer the training courses at no cost to staff members, the local public sector organisations covered the cost of the training program for all users. However, employers were responsible for paying any additional tangible or intangible costs (such as inconvenience, reallocating staff duties).

Place Strategies

The place strategy is to make attending the courses as convenient and accessible as possible for frontline staff members. As such, the courses took place in a variety of local venues in the City of Salford. Venues were selected by the employers of the staff members in order to ensure that the venues were locally accessible. In many cases, the courses were taught right in the staff's place of work (e.g., a hospital environment).

Promotion Strategies

MECC focused on promoting the program to public and third-sector employers in Salford. Employers have the authority to not only schedule a time during work hours for their staff members to complete the course, but also ensure that staff members held brief chats with their clients (e.g., by adding this duty to their job description). MECC primarily recruited employers through direct, face-to-face marketing. In their sales pitch, organisations promoting MECC focused on how easy it is for frontline staff to make real changes to the health and well-being of Salford residents. A comment from the local Director of Public Health carries a key advertising message: *"The great thing about MECC is its simplicity. A frontline worker having a quick chat with people about their well-being is all that is required. That's going to feel a normal part of the job for people that work in public service. And when you add that chat to the conversations that thousands of other workers will have, we'll really see some benefits for the people of Salford."* Once employers committed to the training program, the MECC delivery team worked directly with managers to launch the event. To help managers sell the program to staff members, the MECC delivery team also offered an interactive website, posters, handouts, and introductory videos.

Evaluation Techniques

At the end of each MECC training course, evaluation sheets were filled out by participants and returned to the instructors. Post-training evaluation sheets requested specific feedback on the perceived value and applicability of the course content. The evaluations, coupled with the registration data, provided the basis of a monthly report to the commissioning organisation. Additionally, an independent review was commissioned after the first year to assess whether or not the original objectives of Salford MECC had been achieved and to identify areas for improvement. The review employed a mixed methods design, using information from the self-assessment tool, post-training evaluation, semi-structured interviews, focus groups, online questionnaires, and consultation with key stakeholders and the commissioning group.

Lessons Learned and Future Direction

The MECC approach has grown across the UK's public sector. In 2012, there were 17 examples of MECC in practice and that number has grown steadily since. Currently, the Salford program still represents the largest and most ambitious MECC health gain program yet implemented in the UK. After its first year of delivery (March 2013), 1509 staff members from 36 organizations had successfully completed the program. Furthermore, results from the one-year review indicated that frontline staff and volunteers felt better equipped to carry out brief conversations and brief interventions with their clients. MECC's strength lies in their ability to acquire feedback and willingness to revise the plan. While many challenges were addressed within the first year, MECC identified new challenges for the program to overcome in the future.

First, the one-year review highlighted differences in motivation among frontline staff and management. Compared to managers, frontline staff members were more willing to participate, less skeptical about MECC's impact on the general population, and more optimistic about the sustainability of MECC in the future. The above findings highlighted a major challenge for the MECC program: the strength of buy-in and the engagement of senior and management staff. Consequently, some organizations have been slow to include MECC into their appraisal, monitoring, and core training processes. The sustainability of MECC therefore depends on program acceptance by these key stakeholders. One solution is to offer tailored communications to different stakeholders. To assist stakeholder buy-in, a communications toolkit with specific sections for each staff group was added to the MECC website.

Second, the review indicated a difference in satisfaction among staff members participating in the Level-1 course and Level-2 course. Specifically, staff members who completed the Level-1 course, compared to those who completed the Level-2 course, had more knowledge of and confidence to carry out health chats. Furthermore, staff members who completed the Level-1 course were more likely to incorporate MECC in their day-to-day work. These findings suggested a need to improve the Level-2 course offer. To increase the value of the Level-2 course, instructors were therefore advised to go in-depth on key topics, such as *asking the difficult question, dealing with resistance,* and *withdrawing from a difficult situation.*

Finally, it remains to be seen how the MECC program affects the health and well-being of Salford residents. This unknown is a key limitation to the evaluative evidence to date. Better monitoring and evaluation mechanisms are needed to show stakeholders the impact of MECC on the health and well-being of local residents. This intelligence will make it easier for advocates of MECC to sell the program to new organizations and markets.

Discussion Questions

1. What can MECC do to further increase the number of healthy chats?
2. The MECC program assumes that frontline service staff, if properly trained, have the potential to influence the health behaviors of the wider public. How might they monitor and evaluate this causal relationship?
3. How might MECC promote the program to senior management?
4. What can MECC advocates do to expand the program into other cities?

References

Alcalay, R., & Bell, R. A. (2000). *Promoting nutrition and physical activity through social marketing: Current practices and recommendations*. Sacramento, CA: California Department of Health Services.

Houston, F. S., & Gassenheimer, J. B. (1987). Marketing and exchange. *Journal of Marketing, 51* (4), 3–18.

McKenzie-Mohr, D. (2000). Fostering sustainable behavior through community-based social marketing. *American Psychologist, 55*(5), 531–537.

Prochaska, J. O., & Velicer, W. F. (1997). The transtheoretical model of health behavior change. *American Journal of Health Promotion, 12*(1), 38–48.

Saving Lives Through Lifebuoy's "Help a Child Reach 5" Social Marketing Campaign

17

Sonal Kureshi and Sujo Thomas

Chapter Overview

"Saving Lives through Lifebuoy's 'Help a Child Reach 5' Campaign" describes the launch and effect of this campaign. It discusses a social marketing initiative by Hindustan Unilever conceived to fight the grave issue of child. They identified a cost-effective way to deal with the problem through the simple task of hand washing. The company partnered with several global bodies as well as village communities to achieve its goal. The campaign model was structured to benefit Lifebuoy through building an image of a socially conscious brand, as well strengthening its positioning of health soap, while ensuring the healthy lives of millions of people. First, the case focuses on the reasons which prompted the company to launch this initiative and further to create, promote, and manage a brand over time. Second, the case focuses on the barriers and competitions that the company had to face to achieve its objectives. The case further examines the outcome of the campaign and the lessons learnt.

This case has been prepared with the help of published sources and does not portray the viewpoint of Hindustan Unilever Limited. The case is not designed to demonstrate either correct or incorrect handling of managerial problems.

S. Kureshi (✉)
Indian Institute of Management Ahmedabad, Ahmedabad, India
e-mail: sonalk@iima.ac.in

S. Thomas
Marketing Department, Ahmedabad University, Ahmedabad, India
e-mail: sujo.thomas@ahduni.edu.in

© Springer Nature Switzerland AG 2019
D. Z. Basil et al. (eds.), *Social Marketing in Action*,
Springer Texts in Business and Economics,
https://doi.org/10.1007/978-3-030-13020-6_17

Campaign Background and Environment

Lifebuoy soap was launched in the year 1895 with the goal to prevent cholera in the Victorian England. It has been working toward better health and hygiene across several countries. Marketed as a health soap brand, Lifebuoy, along with its partners, ran several hygiene-related promotional social initiatives. It had impacted the lives of nearly 183 million people in 16 countries (Unilever, 2014). The vision was "to make 5 billion people across the world, feel safe and secure by meeting the personal care hygiene and health needs" through their hand washing programs (HUL Brand Lifebuoy, n.d.). This social marketing vision was integrated in the commercial marketing strategies of the Lifebuoy business. The message of protection from germs and hygiene education was carried by all their communication and innovation activities like: product development, advertising, point of sale, and consumer activations. The mission was to ensure behavioral and attitudinal change of the target audience, which in turn would benefit them as well as the society in which they live (Andreasen, 1994). Based on the understanding of behavioral science, Lifebuoy had developed a 5-point model, as explained below, to achieve its mission (Unilever, n.d.).

1. Make it understood. The first step was to create awareness and acceptance about the necessity of hand washing with soap using evidence that only water is not enough.
2. Make it easy. The second step was to create convenience to do what is right and feel confident about the same.
3. Make it desirable. The third step was to fit the new behavior with self and society.
4. Make it rewarding. The fourth step was about the reward for the behavior, which includes the payoff.
5. Make it habit. This was the final step which was about the continuity of the activity through reinforcements and reminders.

This model was developed around the "Theory of Planned Behavior" (Fishbein & Ajzen, 2011) where individuals made cognitive decisions to engage in behaviors by processing and analyzing the information available to them. Here, the outcome was determined by the individual's perception about the value it added and the ease with which it could be performed. The Lifebuoy model works toward providing mechanisms to evaluate information and to facilitate the ease of hand washing behavior by projecting the value this behavior can add to their mundane lives. The goal was to bring about a social transformation in villages through hand washing with soap by identifying and mobilizing relevant influencers like mothers, teachers, and community leaders.

A large number of people, especially in rural India, lacked access to proper sanitation and safe drinking water which led to bad hygiene practices. India had the highest number (380,000) of annual child (<5 years) deaths occurring due to diarrhea. It translated to nearly 1000 deaths per day (Unilever, n.d.). Tackling this problem was critical to reduce mortality from diseases originating from poor hygiene habits. Hand washing with soap before meals (11%) and after defecation (1%) by mothers in India was extremely low (APAC Effie Awards & Tenasia Group Pvt. Ltd., 2015). Hindustan Unilever (HUL) over the years, through its brands Lifebuoy, Pureit, and Domex has addressed a lot of hygiene issues prevailing in India.

The WHO (2017) report revealed that diarrhea was one of the major causes of death among children under five years of age. India accounted for 21% of the under five child mortality rate. One of the ways to reduce these deaths was following a regular hand washing habit with soap which also proved to be a cost-effective mechanism. The goal of Lifebuoy through its various initiatives was to increase awareness and change attitude toward hand washing with soap, ultimately leading to a lifesaving behavioral transformation.

"Help a Child Reach 5" Campaign

In partnership with Tropical Medicine and International Health (United Kingdom), HUL conducted an intervention experiment with 70 low-income communities in Mumbai (India) for 41 weeks. Households with children around 5 years studying in a municipal school were selected. They were provided free Lifebuoy soap along with other marketing activities to create awareness, educate, motivate, and reward. Enlisting the support of mothers through "Good Mums Club," meetings, and reminder wall hangings, as well as small gifts like toys and coins were also used as a part of the behavioral change principles (Claessen, Bates, Sherlock, Seeparsand, & Wright, 2008). The results showed 25.3% reduction in diarrhea in case of 5-year-olds and 30.7% for whole families (Nicholson et al., 2014). Encouraged by these findings, Lifebuoy formalized its hand washing program and launched the first "Help a Child Reach 5" initiative. These findings motivated them to also think about public–private partnerships to achieve their goal of reduction in child mortality.

Lifebuoy had launched its new campaign in India called "Help a Child Reach 5" in the year 2012. The campaign was launched in the Indian village of Thesgora, in the state of Madhya Pradesh, which had the highest rate of child diarrhea. In partnership with global bodies (USAID,[1] WSUP,[2] and PSI[3]) and non-government organizations at the village community level, the company attempted to take this campaign to the remote districts of India. The company engaged their employees and trained professionals to visit homes, health centers, and schools to create awareness regarding proper hand washing. Lifebuoy had designed a unique social campaign to generate awareness about how the simple task of hand washing could help save several lives every year. Reaching the age of five for a child in some parts of India was difficult due to diseases like diarrhea. An emotional real-life story advertisement and later a video of the same were aired on television as well as YouTube. The response to this video encouraged the company to extend this

[1]United States Agency for International Development.
[2]Water and Sanitation for the Urban Poor.
[3]Population Service International.

campaign to the other villages in India. Along with the Children's Investment Fund Foundation and Bihar State Government India, the next phase was launched in the year 2013. It also included new mothers and midwives as their target market by giving them visit at home and at health care centers to create awareness and encourage hand washing with soap (Unilever, n.d.). Moreover, they also carried out several other activities in other states of India to promote the hand washing habit.

Lifebuoy adopted communication mediums like television, mobile, and digital platforms over direct contact to penetrate faster. These platforms were interactive with respect to sharing stories and experiences by consumers, which in due course proved to be meaningful and far reaching (Unilever, n.d.).

SWOT Analysis

Strengths

- This campaign was based on clinical research data.
- The village where this initiative was operating showed reduced child mortality.
- Managed to create awareness about hand washing among mothers and children.
- Sensitized urban population toward rural health problems.
- The red color of Lifebuoy soap had a strong brand association.
- The carbolic smell was strongly linked to Lifebuoy soap.
- Lifebuoy soap was associated with hygiene and germ protection since its inception.
- Lifebuoy had extensive distribution ranging to more than 5 million outlets.

Weaknesses

- India being a large country makes it difficult to cover all regions.
- Public–private partnership has operational limitations.
- The initial positioning was as a masculine brand.
- Hygiene positioning made competing on the beauty platform challenging.
- Appeal was more rural than urban.

Opportunities

- Ample opportunity to associate the brand with social initiatives.
- Prospect of partnering with government and other non-profit organizations.
- Global associations could be further leveraged to strengthen the brand image.

Threats

- Hygiene platform was getting crowded with other competitor brands.
- Other competitors were introducing similar social campaigns.
- Balancing between hygiene low-priced versus beauty high-end soaps was tough.

Target Audience

Lifebuoy's "Help a Child Reach 5" was a campaign under the overall global initiative of sustainable living. This campaign included all stakeholders as their target audience including residents of the village, rural school authorities and teachers, and local health community members. HUL employees who were involved in the initiative formed an important part of the target audience.

Parents were considered to be the target as they could identify with loss of child and in turn help to spread the message. Mothers were their prime target as they were identified as key agents of change both at home and school. The fathers' involvement was sought through community activities (Unilever, n.d.). They also actively included new mothers as the first 28 days were critical for survival of the infant. Another crucial target audience was school teachers without whose support this activity could not be carried out. Involvement of local representatives was also sought to leverage the collective effort toward social change. Their secondary audience was the general public in India. Everyone involved was required to reinforce hand washing activity at critical points like before eating, after defecating, playing, working in the fields, etc.

Campaign Objectives

Lifebuoy brands global objective was to bring about a transformation in the hygiene behavior of one billion consumers in Asia, Africa, and Latin America (APAC Effie Awards & Tenasia Group Pvt. Ltd., 2015). There were three main objectives of this campaign: creating awareness, influencing attitude, and changing behavior. This was to strengthen the image of being a socially concerned brand.

Creating Awareness

Several activities were undertaken to create awareness about hand washing and its impact on child mortality. This was done at two levels, first with the rural population who were directly affected by lack of this habit and second with the urban population to sensitize them toward the problem of child deaths due to avoidable diseases. Different modes of communication were used to create awareness. They leveraged the power and penetration of social media by making emotional appeals through video clips on YouTube to involve the urban Indian population to make these invisible deaths visible. They requested the people to make a pledge on Facebook and Twitter to ensure that every child celebrates their fifth birthday.

Influencing Attitude

The next step was to influence the attitude toward hand washing itself and share this message. The influencers in case of children were the teachers and parents, while in case of new mothers, it was the doctors and midwives. They were approached with repetitive messages about hand washing evidence materials and reminders.

Changing Behavior

This was the ultimate objective of the company for which all the stakeholders had to be targeted. Their main objective was to drive hand washing behavior and make it a permanent habit. Different campaign activities were focused on one single problem "not washing hands at critical times." HUL employees were assigned to schools and villages in remote parts of India to educate about hand washing habits. Songs that would attract and remind children were used to inculcate the hand washing behavior. The objective was to present the solution in a manner that would lead to a lasting behavioral change.

Barriers, Benefits, and Competition

The main hurdle that faced the target audience was the attitude and in turn the behavior toward hand washing with soap. It was ignorance and indifference toward this habit and this rigid mentality which was Lifebuoy's toughest competitor. Further, only 1% of the people in rural India were found to wash hands regularly before eating and after defecating despite having access to soap (HUL, 2012). Availability of running water and basic infrastructure at schools was another obstacle ahead of the company.

The main benefit was reduction in mortality arising from these diseases for children as well as neonatal. The child remained healthier which in turn led to less days lost at school. The household members benefited economically, mentally, and socially. The habit could further benefit the community when the evidence was visible and would lead to proper hand washing habits for even adults.

In rural India, soap was often replaced with ash which was easily available from their cooking stove (coal/wood) for washing hands and utensils. At times simple wiping of hands on clothes was considered an option instead of washing with soap. All these methods were faster, cheaper, and easily available options that prevented use of soap for hand washing. This was also a result of lack of education and awareness that what appears clean is not always so.

Positioning

Initially, Lifebuoy had very little competition when it was first introduced in India in the year 1895. Since 1933, it was positioned as a hygiene and germ protection hand and body wash soap. It maintained this position in the mind of the consumers for decades. Its catchy advertisement and jingle in the Hindi language was clearly communicating this first on the radio and then with visuals on television.

After independence, the red soap in a red, rough wrapper started losing its appeal in the urban markets with competing brands being positioned on the beauty platform. Over the years, Lifebuoy, after several product line extensions and packaging modifications, had variants for both rural and urban consumers. However, it retained the hygiene and germ protection arena in the soap market. In order to achieve this objective, the brand had followed the global positioning strategy and had launched several campaigns in India to support the brand communication.

Social campaigns by other competing soap companies addressing the need for hand washing with soap were initiated by Dettol Soap in the year 2015 which was the closest competitor to Lifebuoy in the Indian market. The brand was competing with Lifebuoy on the health positioning and in the year 2015, it launched a social marketing campaign called "Dettol Banega Swachh India." They had partnered with Media Company NDTV and Facebook for this campaign along with endorsement by Mr. Amitabh Bachchan, the well-known Indian celebrity. The objective of this campaign was to address the hygiene and sanitation needs in India (Dettol, n.d.). One part of their campaign was a "School Hand Wash Program" and "Young Mothers Program." The other part was toward improving sanitation facilities. Their main target was the pilgrimage city of Varanasi and the religious fairs at Rishikesh and Ujjain in India. They undertook installation of incinerators, sanitary-pad disposal machines, mirrors, exhaust fans, and soaps for hand washing in one of the girls' schools in Varanasi. The fair sites had volunteers providing water sprayers and sanitizers at critical locations like food stalls, bathing areas, and toilets to ensure proper hand washing (The Economic Times, 2016a). They also planned to build sanitation facilities in two other states of India—Maharashtra and Bihar. They had enrolled the support of 500 village community leaders, 500 natural and faith-based leaders, 500 accredited social health activists, child care workers, and mothers for this initiative (The Economic Times, 2016b). To involve children and turn them into spokespersons at home, a series of modules and game toolkits were created to educate them about regular hygiene practices. The goal was to carry this message to first, second, and third grade students every year through 15 sessions. They had made a few schools to incorporate an e-curriculum for the same purpose (The Economic Times, 2016c).

Another close competitor brand to Lifebuoy was Savlon brand, owned by Johnson & Johnson, which had launched the campaign "Savlon Swasth India Mission" in the year 2016. Under this initiative, the brand had carried out interactive programs for adults and children through storytelling and visual engagement to create awareness about hygiene practices. Training about water, sanitation, and hygiene practices were imparted to students and teachers. In order to motivate the students, they themselves were made responsible to ensure that healthy habits were observed by forming student representative committees (ET Brand Equity, 2016).

A school engagement program was launched for students to discover the motivation to hand wash with soap at lunch breaks and created chalk sticks which doubled up as soap when hands were washed with water. Since rural Indians were using slate and chalk for school work, it was decided to distribute it to several schools across the country. The goal was to distribute and to reach around 1 million children across 2000 schools (Law, 2017). The objective behind this campaign was to bring about behavioral change toward hand washing with soap.

The latest activity in furtherance of the same program had been initiated in three metro cities in India—Delhi, Mumbai, and Kolkata. This initiative created awareness about the necessity of cleaning hands for street food vendors. Consumers were encouraged to ring a bell which was placed at some stalls to remind the vendor to wash hands before touching the food. Besides placing the bell, free Savlon sachets were provided to the vendor (CSR Vision, n.d.).

Campaign Strategies

Product Strategies

The red Lifebuoy logo was used to run many social marketing campaigns in India. "Help a Child Reach 5" was one such campaign linked to this brand. The visual of the logo was used since it communicated the core value of cleanliness and protection from germs to the rural population. The campaign was associated with the brand name Lifebuoy without specifying any product in particular. They had launched a small Rs. 5/- mini 18 g soap bar to make soap affordable for the low-income segment. This would last for 13 days for one person to wash their hands at critical times of the day.

Pricing Strategies

Since several variants of the Lifebuoy were available at different price points, the campaign could attract a larger consumer base by associating itself with the whole range of Lifebuoy soaps. The affordable soap bar could appeal to rural consumers while the other premium variants could appeal to the urban consumer base.

Place Strategies

The campaign was initiated in the most affected village of Thesgora in central India in the year 2012. Later in the year, several other villages in the Indian states of Madhya Pradesh and Bihar were covered under this campaign. These states account for more than 50% of child deaths before the age of 5 years. At the ground level, Lifebuoy trained health promoters, who during the initial weeks visited rural primary schools in these villages to demonstrate proper hand washing techniques, made home visits, and visited health centers.

Promotion Strategies

In order to ensure the success of the campaign, the company at the onset identified the villages that had to be targeted and other critical support partners. Those villages that had a high rate of child diarrhea were selected for this program. As for the partners, government, local bodies, and leaders were involved from the beginning for assistance. The implementation was carried out by an expert team along with local support to ensure better communication as well as understanding of ground reality (Unilever, n.d.).

Several activities were undertaken as a part of this campaign. A team of employees visited the villages along with trained health promoters. House visits were conducted to explain the importance of hand washing using pictorial guides. Mothers were given monitoring sheets to ensure that they washed hands before touching the new born baby. Government run child care centers and school teachers were educated about hand washing. Charts were given to children to record daily hand washing. School teachers were requested to promote hand washing habits in the class room. Wall danglers were placed at several places as a reminder for hand washing. Hand washing was made fun through a variety of activities like songs and games. Flipcharts and posters were placed at hand washing places. A novel fun hand water pump in the shape of a horse was created.

Besides that, advertisements and long-format digital films based on real-life stories were created and uploaded on YouTube, the Facebook brand page, and Web site. Anyone could share as well as donate to the cause. Lifebuoy donated Rs. 1/- for each share. The first long-format digital film was about "Gondappa" who walked on his hands to the deity when his child reached five years of age. The next film was about a lady who had lost her child and had affection toward a tree. The third film showed the unborn daughter of a pregnant women talking to her about hygiene practices. They also provided a link for Facebook and a hashtag for Twitter where people could go and pledge their support to the initiative.

A lifesaver volunteer program was started in the year 2014 to promote this campaign in the various cities. Initially, a hundred student volunteers from colleges were enrolled and trained. They were required to visit schools and also their own communities. As an extension of this, around 1000 Guide and Scout leaders in the states of Maharashtra and Madhya Pradesh were trained under the four-week global program called "School of 5" which made the mundane task of hand washing into fun-filled activities with games and rewards. The leadership skills of these children were used to impart education to their communities and further to at least 10 other children (WAGGGS, 2017).

Other Important Strategies

Roti[4] Reminder: Another innovative activity undertaken by Lifebuoy was stamping of its hand washing message onto millions of rotis at a large religious fair held in India. More than 100 restaurants and cafés were included as partners to help promote hand washing awareness. The rotis on top carried the message "Lifebuoy se haath dhoye kya?" which was meant to be a reminder to wash hands with Lifebuoy soap.

Jump-Pumps: Joining hands with the Government mid-day meal scheme in two states of India, Lifebuoy discovered the reason for inertia about hand washing: the old rusted hand pump was the only source of water at the schools. The Lifebuoy team replaced this with a crafted rocking horse using a simple mechanism.

Program Evaluation

Evaluating the impact of the campaign, the following facts could be observed:

- It generated awareness of the campaign leading to interest, as seen from the response to the videos on YouTube. More than 3.5 million views and 2 million likes along with several thousand pledges on Facebook and Twitter were recorded (Social Samosa, 2013).
- 356,093 children were reached as a result of sharing the film and Lifebuoy donating Rs. 1/- per share.
- They received 20 million rupees as a donation for this activity from global citizens.
- Results from a survey by Nielsen of 579 households in Thesgora that overall the health of the community had improved (Unilever, n.d.).
- Further based on mothers' assessments, there was a reduction in occurrence of diarrhea from 36 to 5%.

---

[4]Roti is an Indian flat bread.

- Higher percentages of mothers (33%) and children (26%) were using soap to wash hands.
- Nearly 600,000 children were educated about the importance of proper hand washing by the year 2015 (Unilever, n.d.).
- The results of this campaign in India had led to implementation of this program in other states of India and further to other countries across the world.
- During the second phase where the focus was on the neonatal period, the ad film received 14 million views and was the most viewed advertisement in the year 2015 (Unilever, n.d.).
- This initiative led to its adoption in other villages across 14 countries in Asia and Africa (APAC Effie Awards & Tenasia Group Pvt. Ltd., 2015).

Discussions and Lessons Learned

HUL had adopted its global strategy in case of Lifebuoy and had integrated its promotional approach with their sustainable living vision. Over the years, Lifebuoy had been creating awareness about the importance of hand washing through several campaigns in India. "Help a Child Reach 5" was another promotional activity that further associated Lifebuoy with its hygiene and germ-free platform. What began in a small village in India was now a campaign which had been scaled up to reach several other villages not just in India but in several countries across the world.

They identified a cost-effective and easy way to deal with a serious issue like child mortality through a simple task of hand washing. Hand washing message with soap at five critical times in a day was disseminated. Besides creating awareness about this, reminders about the same were ensured. This was done for at least 21 days as research indicated that 21–50 days were needed for behavior to become habit and eventually become permanent practice. They attempted to remove the barriers to hand washing with soap by using a variety of creative promotional tools like banners, posters, games, and ad-films to appeal to different target audiences. Lifebuoy had gained market acceptance as a socially trusted brand.

It was a planned and systematic approach by the company in connecting the problem with the solution and further adopting it to promote the brand. The first lesson was the significance of identifying the appropriate target audience, powerful influencers, and decision makers. They had identified the influencers and decision makers who needed to be engaged to achieve the positive results. The importance of implementing the campaign at ground level was another lesson. Moreover, it was not possible to achieve the objective unless the company joined hands with partners like the government of various states in India plus big and small non-government organizations. They also collaborated with celebrity spokespersons to help promote the program and leveraged an emotional connection with the consumers. The consistent message disseminated by the brand over the years and its association as a hygiene platform through several of its campaigns certainly led to a strong brand positioning.

Discussion Questions

1. Evaluate the campaign in light of the objectives of the company.
2. Should this social marketing campaign be continued and extended? If yes, please justify and suggest suitable changes.
3. Do you think the promotional activities are effective for the given target audience?
4. Suggest if any other target audience could be approached by the company for better results?
5. What are the changes, if any, that you recommend in the message strategy keeping in mind the campaign objective and the overall marketing objective?

References

Andreasen, A. R. (1994). Social marketing: Its definition and domain. *Journal of Public Policy and Marketing, 13*(1), 108–114.

APAC Effie Awards & Tenasia Group Pvt. Ltd. (2015). *2015 APAC Effie awards gold.* Retrieved from http://www.apaceffie.com/docs/default-source/resource-library/ae2015-gold–help-a-child-reach-5.pdf?sfvrsn=2 as on February 24, 2018.

Claessen, J. -P., Bates, S., Sherlock, K., Seeparsand, F., & Wright, R. (2008). Designing interventions to improve tooth brushing. *International Dental Journal, 58*, 307–320.

CSR Vision. (n.d.). SAVLON swasth India embarks on a unique initiative this world hand hygiene day. *CSR India.* Retrieved from http://www.csrvision.in/savlon-swasth-india-embarks-on-a-unique-initiative-this-world-hand-hygiene-day/.

Dettol. (n.d.). *About banega swachh India.* Retrieved from http://www.dettol.co.in/en/banega-swachh-india/about-banega-swachh-india/.

ET Brand Equity. (2016, November). *Savlon flags off new brand activation campaign, swasth India mission.* Retrieved from https://brandequity.economictimes.indiatimes.com/news/advertising/savlon-flags-off-new-brand-activation-campaign-swasth-india-mission/55413246.

Fishbein, M., & Ajzen, I. (2011). *Predicting and changing behavior: The reasoned action approach.* Taylor & Francis.

HUL. (2012, October). *Lifebuoy leads pledge to help children reach their fifth birthday.* Retrieved from https://www.hul.co.in/Images/lifebuoy-leads-pledge-to-help-children-reach-their-fifth-birthday_tcm1255-463910_en.pdf.

HUL Brand Lifebuoy. (n.d.). Retrieved from https://www.hul.co.in/brands/our-brands/lifebuoy.html.

Law, A. (2017, July). ITC campaign for Savlon mission bags Cannes award. *Hindu Business Line.* Retrieved from http://www.thehindubusinessline.com/companies/itc-campaign-for-savlon-mission-bags-cannes-award/article9744777.ece.

Nicholson, J. A., Naeeni, M., Hoptroff, M., Matheson, J. R., Roberts, A. J., Taylor, D., … Wright, R. L. (2014). An investigation of the effects of a hand washing intervention on health outcomes and school absence using a randomized trial in Indian urban communities. *Tropical Medicine & International Health, 19*(3), 284–292.

Social Samosa. (2013, March). *Social media campaign review: Help a child reach 5 by lifebuoy.* Retrieved from https://www.socialsamosa.com/2013/03/social-media-campaign-review-lifebuoy/.

The Economic Times. (2016a, December). Improved sanitation facility. *CSR Compendium Touching Lives 2016.* Retrieved from https://economictimes.indiatimes.com/csr-compendium-touching-lives-2016/initiative/improved-sanitation-facility/articleshow/56137465.cms.

The Economic Times. (2016b, December). Creating sanitation change leaders at community level. *CSR Compendium Touching Lives 2016.* Retrieved from https://economictimes.indiatimes.com/csr-compendium-touching-lives-2016/initiative/creating-sanitation-change-leaders-at-communitylevel/articleshow/56137361.cms.

The Economic Times. (2016c, December). Driving change through Dettol school modules. *CSR Compendium Touching Lives 2016.* Retrieved from https://economictimes.indiatimes.com/csr-compendium-touching-lives-2016/initiative/driving-change-through-dettol-school-modules/articleshow/56136613.cms.

Unilever. (2014, September). Unilever appeals to first ladies to help a child reach 5. *Unilever News.* Retrieved from https://www.unilever.com/news/Press-releases/2014/14-09-24-Unilever-appeals-to-First-Ladies-to-Help-A-Child-Reach-5.html.

Unilever. (n.d.). *Towards universal hand washing with soap* (Social Mission Report 2015). Retrieved from https://www.unilever.com/Images/lifebuoy-way-of-life-2015_tcm244-418692_en.pdf as on February 24, 2018.

Unilever. (n.d.). Retrieved from https://www.unilever.com/brands/our-brands/lifebuoy.html.

Unilever. (n.d.) *Unilever sustainable living plan: India progress 2015.* Retrieved from https://www.hul.co.in/Images/unilever-sustainable-living-plan-india-2015-progress-report_tcm1255-483536_en.pdf as on February 24, 2018.

WAGGGS. (2017, October). *WAGGGS partners with lifebuoy to drive handwashing with soap in India.* Retrieved from https://www.wagggs.org/es/news/wagggs-partners-lifebuoy-drive-handwashing-soap-india/.

WHO. (2017). *Newborns: Reducing mortality factsheet.* Retrieved from http://www.who.int/mediacentre/factsheets/fs333/en/ as on February 24, 2018.

Behavior Change and Nutrition Education for Teenagers: Nestlé Social Marketing "Healthy Kids Programme" in India

18

Andrei Tiganas, Anamaria Boghean and José Luis Vázquez

Chapter Overview

This study tackles a campaign carried out by Nestlé, a famous international company that also rules the national food Industry of India. The Nestlé Healthy Kids Program is a campaign that aims to determine major behavior changes in terms of nutrition and lifestyle by educating teenagers to set a balanced and healthy diet together with an active lifestyle. The campaign seeks to foster good nutritional behaviors in order to meet the major challenges of India regarding malnutrition. The paper emphasizes the strengths of the campaign along with its limitations in terms of branding, communication, and image challenges encountered so far by the company.

Campaign Background

India has been growing economically over the past years (Bajpai, 2017).

The country currently ranks sixth in the world by nominal GDP and the third by purchasing power parity (PPP) (Bajpai, 2017). As a consequence, the purchasing power of consumers is expected to be more than $1 trillion by 2021 (NDTV, 2012).

A. Tiganas (✉) · A. Boghean
International Advertising Association of Young Professionals
Cluj-Napoca—IAA Young Professionals Cluj, Cluj-Napoca, Romania
e-mail: contact@andreitiganas.ro

A. Boghean
e-mail: anamaria.boghean@gmail.com

J. L. Vázquez
University of León, Leon, Spain
e-mail: jose-luis.vazquez@unileon.es

© Springer Nature Switzerland AG 2019
D. Z. Basil et al. (eds.), *Social Marketing in Action*,
Springer Texts in Business and Economics,
https://doi.org/10.1007/978-3-030-13020-6_18

Nevertheless, the country has been struggling over the past years with social challenges, such as malnutrition, one of the major public health issues.

According to the World Bank, almost 50% of children in India, nearly 60 million, are underweight, 75% are anaemic, and 57% struggle with deficiency of Vitamin A (World Bank, 2013). Only 10% of children are getting nourished properly (Sheonyi, 2018).

The rate of nutrition-related diseases like diabetes and obesity is growing in India, considering that half of undernourished children in the world are based in this country.

Moreover, according to the Global Nutrition report 2017, "more than 51 percent of women of reproductive age suffer from anemia and more than 22 percent of adult women are obese or overweight" (The Health Site, 2017).

Nestlé is one of the major players in the food industry in India. The company has been running business operations in India for more than one hundred years.

As a major player in the national food industry, Nestlé seeks to capitalize on several market opportunities such as the growing purchasing power, the increasing interest in healthy lifestyle along with the increasing number of females in the workforce (Mitra, 2017).

Therefore, the company launched several programs aimed at meeting the country's challenges in terms of nutrition.

The current study will tackle the Nestlé Healthy Kids Program (HKP), a project started by the company in 2009.

The aim of HKP is to determine new public behaviors related to nutrition. As a long-term expectation, HKP is aimed at changing beliefs and social norms of young people regarding food and lifestyle.

The case study will also emphasize the way that Nestlé struggles to change the false perception of teenagers that junk food and toxic beverages are "cool."

SWOT Analysis (Strengths, Weaknesses, Opportunities, Threats)

Strengths

The activities run through the Healthy Kids Program are a major strength of HKP. Activities such as "Art on The Plate," for instance, are well organized, well communicated, and the message delivered is sound.

Weaknesses

The naming and the logo of the campaign: "Healthy Kids Program." As we will emphasize in the next section, the "target audience" the campaign seeks is an audience that consists mainly of students aged 13–17. Nevertheless, the name "kids" and the "childish" logo might not fit the teenagers.

Opportunities

The qualified human resource involved in the campaign consisting of very well-prepared trainers and teachers.

Nestlé Healthy Kids Program is part of a global undertaking initiated by the company.

Support from the Government: The campaign is highly promoted by the Government and other institutions as the Minister for Rural Development and representatives of Government of Rajasthan.

Accessibility, since the training material is published and communicated in six local languages: English, Hindi, Bangla, Sinhalese, Kannada, and Punjabi.

The partnership with Magic Bus Foundation—an NGO focusing on behavior change. The cooperation involves over 9000 youth mentors across 22 states and 58 districts in India.

Nestlé's reputation as a leading company in nutrition, health, and wellness.

The growing competitive advantage of Nestlé as a responsible company, committed to supporting local communities.

Threats

Similar campaigns run by major competitors such as the Community Nutrition and Welfare Program by Kraft Heinz.

Public authorities have limited capacity to decrease the number of children who struggle with malnutrition and nutrition-related diseases. That can create a serious problem of efficacy in the long run.

Target Audience

The target audience of this campaign consists of students aged 13–17 based around Nestlé's eight factory locations including Bangladesh and Sri Lanka (Nestlé, 2018).

A segment of this audience consists of teenage girls. In most of rural India, a girl often gets less food than a boy. As they become young women, their need for good-quality food increases because they start doing physical work, they get pregnant, or have to breastfeed. If a woman is malnourished she risks suffering from anemia, weakness, or exhaustion and also to have complications at childbirth (Hesperian Health Guides, 2018). Most of them are future mothers as well and this will have a strong influence on their children's eating habits.

A secondary target consists of parents and teachers who are parents as well. They might not have had access to education on a healthy lifestyle before. Parents and teachers should get more information on this topic, since they can control/influence children's eating habits.

Competition

The food processing industry is one of the largest industries in India (IBEF—India Brand Equity Foundation, 2018). Some of Nestlé's competitors in India are running campaigns like the HKP, that aim to have a positive impact in the society and improve the diet of Indian people.

For example, the Indian *LT Foods*, leading processor of rice, launched in 2017 the rice-based premium snacks brand "Kari Kari" which supports farmers in cultivate ing organic rice (LT Foods, 2018).

The French *Danone,* first company in the world in the fresh dairy industry, has an important presence across India. Nutrition is a major focus in their portfolio and they run various CSR programs in this field. One example is "GCP Connections," an education project where health care professionals learn and share the latest insights on maternal and child health (Danone India, 2018).

The American *Kraft Heinz* is another competitor that is worth attention. Under their Community Nutrition and Welfare Program, the enterprise deals with delivering fortified meals in schools, orphanages, or shelter homes. The company has created The Heinz Nutrition Foundation (India). The organization offers free consultation on nutrition to people in Chennai and Delhi, workshops for the public bodies (such as the Directorate of Public Health and Preventive Medicine), and research funding for hospitals (Kraft Heinz India, 2018).

All the major players in the food industry run nutrition-related CSR programs in order to increase their brand equity and contribute to a healthier society.

Campaign Objectives

The aim of Nestlé Healthy Kids Program is to "create and raise awareness on good nutritional practices, healthy lifestyles and greater physical activity" among teenagers in India and in the proximity regions of Bangladesh and Sri Lanka (Nestlé, 2018).

The campaign also aims to meet the increased nutritional demands of teenage girls and offer education related to a healthy and active lifestyle.

The expected long-term behavior of the target audience is to influence in the future their own families to adopt a healthy diet.

Therefore, Nestlé's Healthy Kids Program aims to determine major behavior changes in terms of nutrition and lifestyle by educating teenagers to set a balanced and healthy diet together with an active lifestyle.

Positioning

As an educational program that aims to change behaviors among teenagers through a balanced diet and a healthier lifestyle, HKP positions itself as student-friendly undertaking.

The tone of voice used within the communication strategy is warm and friendly overall.

One of the activities carried out within the campaign, "Art on the Plate," embodies very well the positioning of HKP. "Art on the Plate" is a typical student-friendly activity that encourages *children to turn healthy recipes into edible works of art that were fun to make and healthy to eat* (Nestlé Professional, 2017).

Activities carried out through HKP are mainly based on interactivity, entertainment, and *coolness*.

Nevertheless, as stated in the SWOT analysis, the naming and the logo seem to be more focused on children, although the core target audience consists of teenagers.

This discrepancy can create in the long run a barrier of communication between Nestlé and the target audience.

As a long-term consequence, teenagers may think that attending the activities of HKP is a waste of time, something that matches children aged under age 12.

Marketing Strategy

Product

Nestlé Healthy Kids Program (HKP) runs several activities carried out jointly by the company and six partner universities.

The activities run through HKP, such as creating edible artwork, sports, music lessons, or workshops, are entertaining, flexible, and easy to match with the curriculum and the specific needs of each school targeted by the HKP.

The most representative activities of HKP are "Art on the Plate" and "Sports for development" (Figs. 18.1 and 18.2).

Price

Each student targeted by the campaign has to fulfill at least 12 h of training activities for a period of 6 weeks. That means that over 429,000 h of training are completed in each region during a session of one month and a half.

Fig. 18.1 "Art on the Plate" is a workshop that consists basically of cooking sessions and plating presentations. The activity encourages children to be creative with food and discover new dishes they may otherwise avoid (Nestlé UK, 2017)

Fig. 18.2 "Sports for development" (S4D) is a specific activity that promotes the importance of nutrition and healthy habits through playground fun activities. Thus, students are challenged to practice open air activities and questioned about the importance of what goes into the physical well-being (Shifa Merchant, 2016)

Therefore, the commitment of time is the main price to be paid either by the target audience or by the human resources involved in the project. The students have to spend hours attending the courses organized through the HKP.

The pretty low interest of the target audience justifies the need of Nestlé to approach the theory of diffusion of innovations (Rogers, 2010). As a way to implement this scientific approach, Nestlé should foster its effort to raise awareness among teenagers and make them understand that changing behaviors in terms of nutrition is a prior condition for their health in the long run.

Teachers also have little time to get involved in HKP. Most of them are overwhelmed by various extracurricular activities and might not be keen to allow time to a healthy nutrition program.

On the other hand, the parents seem to be more motivated to encourage students to attend nutrition-based courses and seminars although these kind of activities affects their "family time."

Place

In terms of accessibility, the program is delivered in schools, high schools, and universities in India, but also in Bangladesh and Sri Lanka.

HKP deals with several channels that help the campaign to reach the target audience:

- Local partner NGOs such as the Magic Bus Foundation;
- Local government representatives in charge of public health care or education institutions representatives;
- Committees of parents.

Trainers as well are requested to master experiential learning techniques and nutrition knowledge in order to be allowed to teach and facilitate educational activities.

The activities ran by Nestlé are delivered in classrooms, schoolyards, or restaurant kitchens.

Promotion

The main promotion channels used for this campaign are the company website, the YouTube channel (4332 views as of March 14, 2018), and social media (Fig. 18.3).

Therefore, Nestlé provides relevant know-how in terms of social marketing due to its consistent experience related to social marketing campaigns carried out worldwide. However, the online visibility of the program still needs a massive increase.

The lack of online visibility and engagement is counterbalanced by offline influencers that bring awareness and credibility for the whole undertaking.

Nestlé ✓ added **24 new photos.**
October 20, 2015 at 3:24pm · ❂

On the occasion of World Chefs Day, Nestlé India
organized a cooking workshop on healthy eating
habits for adolescents. Through this initiative,
students who are a part of the Nestlé Healthy Kids
Progr...

👍 62

2 Comments 4 Shares

Fig. 18.3 Example of a promotional tweet on Twitter

For instance, national and local administrations in charge of implementing programs in health care and education have a major potential to spread the message of the campaign to the target audience.

Moreover, Nestlé uses below the line (BTL) approaches in terms of promotion. A relevant example in this respect is the International Chef's Day. In 2017, the company organized cooking workshops for teenagers from several marginalized communities in Mumbai, Delhi, Kolkata, and Chennai (FMT, 2017). Thus, over 250 teenagers who were part of the Nestlé HKP interacted with chefs in order to learn about the benefits of a variety of foods and create healthy recipes (ibidem).

Publics

Policymakers and gatekeepers are important subgroups of the target audience. Their aim is to facilitate or diminish the link between the campaign and the target audience.

Approval teams from Nestlé and partner universities are also part of the target audience.

Partnership

Nestlé runs a wide range of partnerships consisting of over 311 partners from 84 countries (as of December 2016).

The major Indian partners of Nestlé in charge of developing the curriculum are:

1. College of Home Science, Punjab Agricultural University
2. College of Home Science, Govind Ballabh Pant University of Agriculture and Technology, Pantnagar
3. Goa College of Home Science, Goa University
4. College of Home Science, CSK Himachal Pradesh Agricultural University, Palampur

5. National Dairy Research Institute, Karnal
6. Rajiv Gandhi University of Health Science, Karnataka (Bangalore)

In 2012 Nestlé also collaborated with the Embassy of Switzerland in order to organize nutrition workshops in Delhi.

Nestlé currently partners with the Magic Bus Foundation India in five metros: Delhi, Bangalore, Mumbai, Hyderabad, and Chennai. This NGO created the curriculum and facilitated the access to government schools for the workshop delivery.

Policy

Policymakers are essential partners for the implementation process of such a campaign.

The Indian Government carries out various programs on child and maternal health care and also runs a public institution dedicated to this topic: The National Health Mission.

The policies run by the Government are a proof that the Nestlé Healthy Kids Program has a clear public utility.

Purse Strings

HKP is a Nestlé-sponsored program (Nestlé Creating Shared Value Update 2010 Report).

Program Evaluation

Nestlé developed a global monitoring and evaluation (M&E) framework, based on the company's experience in 81 countries. The undertaking enrolls over 14.4 million children (Nesté, 2017). M&E is validated by scientific experts and based on five goals: "balanced meals, portion control, and drinking water, being active and maintaining good hygiene habits." (ibidem).

According to M&E, the reach of the program is of more than 41,000 students in India, Bangladesh and Sri Lanka. As we have stated within the marketing strategy, each student attended approximately twelve hours of workshops on nutrition awareness during six weeks. Therefore, the program provided more than 492,000 h of training.

Several evaluation procedures were run in order to measure the impact in terms of behavior change and knowledge achievement. The results were used to see how effective the implementation was and if the learning goals were reached. To assure the highest accuracy, the assessment was run at the local level, by external bodies. Like most of the company's programs, this campaign is evaluated by national academic organizations and scientific institutions.

There is no evidence on the impact of the campaign in India, but studies carried out across the other countries targeted by the HKP show a clear change in children's behavior:

In *Japan*, evaluations run by the Child Health Council of the Japan Society of Nutrition Circle showed that children acquired a "sound knowledge on good nutrition and were more aware about how physical exercise positively impacts on their well-being."

In *France*, the pilot program was run in northern France, in partnership with University of Lille that led the data analysis as well. The evaluation included measuring the body mass index (BMI) of participating children every two years. Findings showed a decrease in childhood obesity since 2005, compared to other areas in France.

In *Greece,* the three-year module of the pilot program started in 2013. Results showed that "over 80% of children were able to identify foods from the fruits and vegetables group, in comparison to 74% at the start. More than 40% were able to distinguish the grains group, compared to 27% at the beginning of the program."

Nestlé presumes that the program led to an increased enrollment and attendance in school and improved learning outcomes. These outcomes were not initially intended goals, but the company is considering ways to measure this impact in its evaluation framework.

Magic Bus, Nestlé's partner in India created a collection of case studies, showing the impact of the program on teenagers (Fig. 18.4).

Baljeet Singh PRINCIPAL

"The best thing about the Nestlé Healthy Kids Programme is how easily it changes the way children think – which is the most difficult thing to do. As adolescents, they are most vulnerable to being pulled into different directions. At this critical stage, these simple sport-for-development sessions and life lessons productively engage their minds and bodies. Not only has this helped minimize drug abuse among older children but has also almost eliminated caste-based discrimination, which was previously a problem here."

Fig. 18.4 Principal of a school states the benefits of the HKP

In May 2018, Nestlé was ranked first in the 2018 Access to Nutrition Index (ATNI) for its overall results in its nutrition-related initiatives. This confirms the company's contribution in matching global challenges of undernutrition and obesity. HKP worldwide program is definitely concerned, so HKP in India as well.

Discussion and Lessons Learned

In order to get more success, HKP needs to adapt locally the global concept of the campaign by involving the community in design and implementation.

A lot of different partners are involved in the planning, implementation, and evaluation of the campaign: education institutions, research institutes, NGOs, government bodies, and even foreign governments (i.e., Embassy of Switzerland).

Behavior change is a long-term goal and in order to be sustainable, it has to be correlated with other (public) policies on education and healthcare.

Discussion Questions
In order to go deeper in this case study learning objectives, some questions can be raised:

1. What are the benefits of the campaign for the target audience (including the sub groups)?
2. What is the expected long-term impact of the program and how can it be monitored?
3. How can the workshop facilitators make the sessions appealing for teenagers, in order to attract them and make them adopt a positive behavior?
4. Time is the highest cost for the students and also for their families. Since this is a threat for the program, how can Nestlé cope with that?
5. Which is the public utility of the program?
6. "Over the next 10 years, Nestlé will slowly move from packaged food, to focus on health and nutrition products" (Mitra, 2017). Is such a decision sustainable in the long run?
7. Will the company give up less healthy products, in order to position itself as the leader in the nutrition in India?
8. How will the company reconcile its "responsible" image with proof of its unethical activities?

References

Bajpai. (2017). *The world's top 10 economies*. Retrieved from: https://www.investopedia.com/articles/investing/022415/worlds-top-10-economies.asp. Accessed at 11/03/2018.

Business Maps of India. (2018). *Top food brands in India*. Retrieved from: https://business.mapsofindia.com/top-brands-india/food-products.html. Accessed at 03/06/2018.

Danone India. (2018). Company website. Retrieved from: https://www.danone.in/initiatives/hcp-connections/. Accessed at 03/06/2018.

Fry, E. (2016). *Nestlé's half-billion-dollar noodle debacle in India*. Retrieved from: http://fortune.com/nestle-maggi-noodle-crisis/. Accessed at 10/03/2018.

Hesperian Health Guides. (2018). *Women are more at risk for disease and poor health*. Retrieved from: http://en.hesperian.org/hhg/Where_Women_Have_No_Doctor:Women_Are_More_at_Risk_for_Disease_and_Poor_Health. Accessed at 03/06/2018.

Kraft Heinz India. (2018). Company website. Retrieved from: http://www.heinz.co.in/csr. Accessed at 03/06/2018.

LT Group. (2018). Company website. Retrieved from: http://ltgroup.in/. Accessed at 03/06/2018.

Magic Bus, Stories of Change—Case Studies. Retrieved from: https://issuu.com/magic-bus/docs/magic_bus_case_stories.

NDTV. (2012). *Spending power of Indian consumers to touch $1 trln by 2021*. Retrieved from: https://www.ndtv.com/business/spending-power-of-indian-consumers-to-touch-1-trln-by-2021-296686. Accessed at 8/02/2018.

Nestlé. (2017). Full report "Nestrlé in society Creating Shared Value and meeting our commitments". Retrieved from: https://www.nestle.com/asset-library/documents/library/documents/corporate_social_responsibility/nestle-csv-full-report-2017-en.pdf.

Nestlé. (2018). *Nestlé food safety institute India*. Retrieved from: https://www.nestle.in/aboutus/researchanddevelopment/nestle-food-safety-institute-India. Accessed at 11/01/2018.

Rogers, E. M. (2010). *Diffusion of innovations*. Simon and Schuster.

Sheonyi. (2018). *India loses 4% of GDP to malnutrition; ASSOCHAM-EY paper to Jaitley in run up to budget*. Retrieved from: https://timesofindia.indiatimes.com/business/india-business/india-loses-4-of-gdp-to-malnutrition-assocham-ey-paper-to-jaitley-in-run-up-to-budget/articleshow/62590523.cms. Accessed at 04/03/2018.

Shifa Merchant. (2016). *Nestle healthy kids programme towards a better future*. Retrieved from: http://www.sassyshifsays.in/nestle-healthy-kids-programme/. Accessed at 06/06/2018.

The Health Site. (2017). *Malnutrition, anemia pose huge health challenge to India—Global nutrition report 2017*. Retrieved from: http://www.thehealthsite.com/news/malnutrition-anaemia-pose-huge-health-challenge-to-india-global-nutrition-report-2017-ag1117/. Accessed at 01/03/2018.

World Bank. (2013). *Helping India combat persistently high rates of malnutrition*. Retrieved from: http://www.worldbank.org/en/news/feature/2013/05/13/helping-india-combat-persistently-high-rates-of-malnutrition. Accessed at 11/03/2018.

Using Social Marketing to Promote Handwashing with Soap for a Healthier Vietnam

19

Hoang Minh Doan and Van Dao Truong

Chapter Overview
Diseases such as diarrhea, hepatitis, helminthic infections, and other infectious diseases resulting from poor personal hygiene remain prevalent worldwide. This chapter reports on Vietnam's *Wash Your Hands with Soap* campaign that encouraged young children and their mothers to wash their hands with soap. A number of challenges were identified, including the poor sanitary conditions in local schools, the misperception of the efficacy of water-only handwashing, the consideration of communication as the key tool of intervention, and health officials' red-tape practices. Yet, there were opportunities such as governmental agencies' coordination, international donors' financial support, and Unilever's substantial resources, and marketing skills. Informed by the exchange theory and social learning theory, free soap was distributed to local households and public areas in targeted regions by the Clean Hands Task Force. The Clean Hands Toolkits were also developed, and the Clean Hands Squad Game offered. The campaign raised the awareness of and engaged with not only the target audience but also the wider public in the promotion of handwashing with soap. Its scope of implementation was expanded from 18 provinces to 50, reaching 26 million people. The proportion of population who reported washing hands with soap rose from 14.6 to 66.5% in targeted areas.

H. M. Doan (✉)
Department of Marketing, National Economics University, Hanoi, Vietnam
e-mail: dhminhmkt@gmail.com

V. Dao Truong
School of Tourism and Hotel Management, North-West University,
Potchefstroom, South Africa
e-mail: vabdao83@yahoo.co.uk

© Springer Nature Switzerland AG 2019
D. Z. Basil et al. (eds.), *Social Marketing in Action*,
Springer Texts in Business and Economics,
https://doi.org/10.1007/978-3-030-13020-6_19

Introduction and Background to the Campaign

Diseases—such as diarrhea, hepatitis, helminthic infections, and other infectious diseases related to personal hygiene, a lack of clean water, and poor sanitation—that affect the digestive and respiratory systems remain prevalent in many parts of the world. These diseases are responsible for the death of millions of children in less developed countries (World Health Organization (WHO) 2017), as many people do not have good sanitation habits in general and hand hygiene in particular. According to WHO (2017), diarrhea and pneumonia are among the five leading causes of death of children under five years. Handwashing with soap has long been considered as an important preventive measure against gastrointestinal diseases as well as hepatitis A and E, and hand, foot and, mouth disease (HFMD). This preventative measure has thus attracted increased attention from international institutions, development agencies, and governmental organizations.

In Vietnam, many problems persist with respect to awareness and practice of hand hygiene behavior, particularly the low awareness of the importance of hand cleaning with soap for the prevention of disease. A Ministry of Health study (MOH, 2016) found that between 1 and 10% of malnutrition cases in children under five could be reduced if parents regularly washed their hands with soap. According to a national hygiene survey conducted by the MOH and UNICEF (2007), just 12% of the rural populations wash their hands with soap before eating and 16% after using the toilet. Overall, 98% of rural residents are unaware that handwashing with soap and clean water is essential for preventing infectious diseases (UNICEF, 2007).

In October 2008, the first *Global Handwashing Day* was launched by UNICEF, the World Bank, and some development organizations from both the private and public sectors (World Bank, 2008). It has since become an annual campaign with the goal of raising public awareness of personal hygiene, environmental sanitation, and healthy living, as well as promoting handwashing with soap as an effective, low-cost, and easy way to prevent diseases. Although this seems a simple behavior that everyone can adopt, in Vietnam, the practice of handwashing is not engaged in as a comprehensive and self-motivated behavior among the population at large, including in medical and healthcare organizations (Curtis, 2005).

Over the period 2012–2016, the *Wash Your Hands with Soap for a Healthier Vietnam* campaign was implemented by the MOH, Ministry of Education and Training, and the Unilever Vietnam Foundation. Targeting high-risk groups such as young children and their mothers, the campaign aimed to change the handwashing behavior of these target groups and save 25 million children from contracting diseases caused by viruses and bacteria by 2020 (Unilever, 2012, 2013). The campaign encouraged people to wash their hands with soap at five critical times: after using the toilet, before breakfast, before lunch, before dinner, and while bathing. The campaign received Vietnamese Dong (VND) 50 billion (about US $2.2 million) in grants from Unilever Vietnam, over the specified period (Unilever, 2012; Lifebuoy Vietnam, 2013a).

SWOT (Strengths, Weaknesses, Opportunities, Threats) Analysis

In a project to evaluate the effectiveness of the above-mentioned *Wash Your Hands with Soap for a Healthier Vietnam* campaign, the authors conducted a SWOT analysis identifying a number of opportunities and challenges that might have undermined/strengthened its effectiveness. The results of the SWOT analysis appear in summary form Fig. 19.1. The challenges included the poor sanitary conditions and unsafe hygiene practices in local schools; the misperception of the effectiveness of water-only handwashing; and the consideration of communication as the key tool for promoting handwashing, regardless of significant barriers to behavior change. On the other hand, there were opportunities such as the commitment and coordinated efforts from governmental agencies, and the support and financial aid from international donors. In addition, the substantial resources and marketing skills employed by Unilever Company, which has a long history of running hygiene promotion campaigns worldwide and has established collaboration with international and national organizations, were significant advantages for the campaign to be successfully implemented in Vietnam. However, the red-tape practices often observed in Vietnamese society could have been potential obstacles preventing the joint effort from achieving its goals.

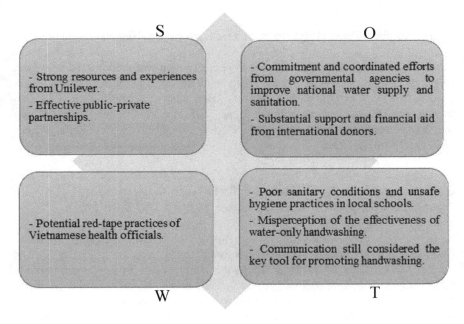

Fig. 19.1   SWOT analysis of the campaign

Strong Resources and Experiences from Unilever

Lifebuoy soap is one of Unilever's fastest-growing brands and considered the world's number one antibacterial soap brand. Thanks to its large-scale handwashing projects worldwide (29 countries with 379 million people reached over the period 2010–2016), the brand has gained substantial social marketing skills and knowledge, which allows it to deliver the opportunity for effective handwashing behavior change at a low cost. The brand's international experience (as mentioned) in running joint public–private programs was also an important asset for this campaign to be implemented effectively in Vietnam.

Effective Public–Private Partnerships

Through its extensive hand hygiene promotions in different countries, Unilever has achieved acceptance by—and the cooperation of—international and national health institutions, such as the Royal Society of Public Health and the London School of Hygiene and Tropical Medicine (Unilever, 2016). Governmental health organizations, having experience in public communication and favorable access to remote communities, coupled with the marketing expertise of a private partner, significantly enhanced the campaign's effectiveness.

Potential Red-Tape Behaviors of Local Health Officials

The Vietnamese administrative system is generally known for its bureaucracy, and its public health sector still exhibits many limitations, difficulties, and challenges (Puffer, 2015). Social marketing projects, especially those that involve public–private partnerships in the health sector, are still rare. Vietnamese health officials who have insufficient social marketing experience might hinder the campaign from realizing its full potential.

Commitment and Coordinated Efforts from Governmental Agencies to Improve National Water Supply and Sanitation

In 1998, Vietnam released a rural water supply and sanitation strategy, while the National Target Program on Rural Water Supply and Sanitation had been in place for years (UNICEF, 2007). In addition, the Rural Water Supply and Sanitation Partnership, made up of relevant ministries and nearly 20 international organizations, has been active since 2006 to strengthen the coordination of efforts to improve the national water and sanitation situation in Vietnam (UNICEF, 2007).

Substantial Support and Financial Aid from International Donors

A number of donors, including UNICEF, WHO, and the World Bank, strengthened their support for sanitation, hygiene, and water supply improvements in Vietnam. This included technical and managerial assistance for policy making as well as capacity building at the local level. Investment in Vietnam's water and sanitation was estimated at about US$10 million per year, including government and external sources. The key financial partners also included the Asian Development Bank, the French AFD, Danida, AusAID, JICA, and Finida (UNICEF, 2008).

Poor Sanitary Conditions and Unsafe Hygiene Practices in Local Schools

The sanitary conditions in rural Vietnamese schools were poor. UNICEF's (2007) national survey on sanitation and hygiene showed that the quality of sanitary facilities in households, schools, and public areas and the lack of safe hygienic behaviors remained issues of great concern. About 88% of schools in rural regions did not possess adequate toilet facilities, and more than a quarter did not have toilets. As a result, students had to relieve themselves in forests, gardens, fields, or on riverbanks (UNICEF, 2007). Although personal hygiene education was included in school curricula, the survey showed that just 36% of schools had handwashing areas, while a mere 5% had soap available for handwashing (UNICEF, 2007). Research suggests that the availability of a water supply and the condition of household sanitary facilities greatly influence handwashing behavior. Thus, difficult living conditions may limit people's response to sanitation interventions (Rheinländer et al., 2010).

Misperception of the Effectiveness of Water-Only Handwashing, Making Behavior Change Difficult

Some misconceptions were identified among the target audience as critical obstacles to campaign interventions, including their belief and behavior with respect to hand rinsing using just water, low awareness of the importance of using soap for handwashing, high rates of forgetting to wash hands before and after contact with feces (Nguyen et al., 2011). For example, while 92% of mothers reported rinsing hands at critical times, 60% of those who rinsed their hands with water did not feel that soap was important or necessary and many mothers stated that "soap was too expensive" (Nguyen et al., 2011).

Communication Remains the Key Tool for Promoting Handwashing

Although the local government has employed a range of state propaganda instruments and mass media to promote hygienic behaviors, the achieved results seem stronger in terms of awareness than in actual behavior change (PSI Vietnam, 2016). This also holds true with foreign-funded campaigns aimed at promoting handwashing with soap. For example, the *Vietnam Handwashing Initiative* (HWI), launched by the MOH and funded by the Danish Embassy in Vietnam, combined mass media with interpersonal communications to disseminate information about the threat of diseases associated with water-only handwashing (Nguyen et al., 2011).

Target Audience

The campaign targeted elementary school children and their parents countrywide. It found that the audience's belief that washing hands with water alone was sufficient was a major barrier to behavior change (Curtis, 2005). Indochina Research's (2007) survey indicated that both the children and their parents perceived cleaning hands with soap as time-consuming; that in some rural areas, the cost of buying soap was reported as a reason for not using it when washing hands; that parents also perceived the time required to teach their children how to wash their hands properly as an additional cost; that children of this age are vulnerable to infectious viruses, but are not aware of the risk of diseases related to unhygienic behaviors; and that they tend to be hasty and hence reluctant to wash their hands, and if they do, it is just with water.

Campaign Objectives

The campaign's objective was that, over the specified period (2012–2016), the target audience understand the importance of personal hygienic behaviors for disease prevention and practice handwashing with soap at five critical times, as noted: after using the toilet, before breakfast, before lunch, before dinner, and while bathing (Unilever, 2012, 2013, 2014, 2015, 2016).

Positioning

The campaign positioned itself as being among the few in Vietnam that focused exclusively on young children and their parents. Handwashing with soap was positioned as a fun and easy behavior that helped prevent diseases and in this way contributed to building a healthier Vietnam. Since children like to become heroes, the act of handwashing with soap was associated with a brave man fighting against bad enemies (harmful infectious germs) to save the Earth.

The campaign also approached handwashing behavior change by emphasizing five core principles of all Lifebuoy-sponsored campaigns in other countries: disgust (germ contamination), nurture (mother and child interaction), affiliation (group of heroes fighting against bad enemies), habit (mothers and children to repeat proper handwashing until they stick), and pledging (mothers and children taking pledges publicly).

4Ps and Implementation

The design and implementation of the campaign interventions were based on the exchange theory from commercial marketing and the social learning theory from behavior psychology. The 4Ps (product, price, place, and promotion) are summarized in Table 19.1.

Table 19.1 Summary of 4Ps

Product	Price	Place	Promotion
Soap	Free	<1600 communities in 18 provinces	Members of the Clean Hands Task Force distributed free soap to local households and at public areas; 5-min films are made as reality shows and broadcasted on HTV3 channel; fun music videos demonstrated handwashing with soap behavior
Clean Hands Toolkits consisting of Lifebuoy disinfectant, a handwashing comic handbook, a 3D ruler, and a pledge bracelet	VND45,000 (about US $2)	A Web site (http://biet-doi-tay-sach.muare.vn/) was created so that the toolkits could be purchased	Members of the Clean Hands Task Force travelled to schools nationwide to raise school children's awareness of handwashing with soap and the toolkits in particular
Clean Hands Squad Game	Free registration and participation	Schools in different provinces nationwide	Annual *Global Handwashing Day*

The Clean Hands Task Force in Action Reality Shows

A key driver of the campaign, the Clean Hands Task Force (Fig. 19.2) whose members included candidates of *The Voice Kids Vietnam 2013* was formed. From December 2013 to May 2014, the said Task Force travelled to more than 1600 communes in 18 provinces nationwide to promote handwashing with soap and daily cleaning among children, establish the habit of hand hygiene, and urge people to join the team to communicate the message to the wider public. Free soap was distributed to local households and provided at public places, which helped encourage people to practice handwashing with soap at home (i.e., free soap in exchange for handwashing behavior). At each of the Task Force's destinations, a five-minute film was recorded and developed as a reality show. A total of ten films were broadcast in Sunday primetime on the HTV3 television channel. Fun music videos also demonstrated the five critical times and six proper steps of handwashing with soap to assist schoolteachers and parents in teaching children (Lifebuoy Vietnam, 2013b). The Task Force organization not only helped to disseminate the campaign message to the target audience (children) and made them more responsible for protecting their health (by washing hands with soap) but also allowed local parents to learn from practical experience and act as role models for their children. In addition, the sending of the Task Force to local destinations suggests the importance of establishing rapport and partnership with community members in disseminating the message and encouraging handwashing behavior.

Fig. 19.2 Members of the Clean Hands Task Force. *Source* Photograph from trailer Clean Hands Task Force, Lifebuoy Vietnam YouTube Channel, 2013

The Clean Hands Toolkit

The Clean Hands Toolkit (Fig. 19.3) consisted of Lifebuoy disinfectant, a hand-washing comic handbook, a 3D ruler, and a pledge bracelet. Released in October 2014, the toolkit was intended to make handwashing more enjoyable for children and also to support parents in teaching hand hygiene to their children (Unilever, 2014). Every step of handwashing was associated with an interesting adventure. Through each "challenge," children discovered new things without being aware that they were learning. Finally, like "adults," the children were asked to sign a commitment to wash their hands properly. The toolkits were available for purchase at http://biet-doi-tay-sach.muare.vn/, at VND45,000 each (about US$2). Members of the Clean Hands Task Force travelled to local schools nationwide to raise school children's awareness of the importance of handwashing with soap as well as of the toolkits in particular. For each toolkit sold, Lifebuoy donated two soap bars to the Young People's Charity Journey in support of medical treatment and housing for children in remote areas. The objective was to distribute 200,000 soap bars to rural children and communicate proper handwashing practices to over 100,000 people in 50 provinces and cities (Muare, 2014).

The Clean Hands Squad Game

In October 2015, the fun and exciting Clean Hands Squad Game (Fig. 19.4) was released, which attracted substantial attention among young children and their parents countrywide. The game was promoted in schools throughout the country on the occasion of the annual *Global Handwashing Day*, where registration for participation was free. In this game, children played the role of space heroes of the

Fig. 19.3 Clean Hands Toolkit. *Source* Muare (2014)

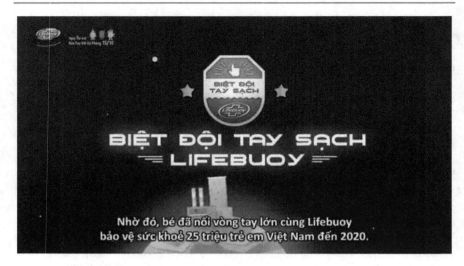

Fig. 19.4 Clean Hands Squad Game. *Source* Photograph from trailer Clean Hands Squad Game, Lifebuoy Vietnam YouTube Channel, 2015

Clean Hands Squads, who fought against and killed ten harmful bacteria from enemy planets in the galaxy, helping the lifeboat land safely in Vietnam on a journey to protect the health of 25 million children by 2020. In each round, children learned about common pathogens that cause infections such as the flu as well as red eyes and boils and got to understand the importance of washing their hands and body with antibacterial soap. Designed to be simple and fun with useful content, this game served to assist parents in teaching their children how to protect themselves. For every successful registration in the game, Lifebuoy donated five health toolkits to children in rural and remote areas (Giadinhvatreem, 2015).

Campaign Evaluation

The campaign's progress was tracked annually over the five-year period. Its scope of implementation was expanded from 1600 communes in 18 provinces at the beginning, as indicated, to reach six million people by 2014 and 26 million in 2015 (Unilever, 2015). The campaign not only engaged its target audience (i.e., children and parents) but also members of private and public sectors (e.g., members of the Youth Union and government organizations) as well as the wider public in the promotion of handwashing with soap behavior, as evidenced by their participation in campaign activities organized. The Unilever Vietnam Foundation provided funding for the organization of the annual *Global Handwashing Day*. PSI Vietnam's (2016) survey of 1200 rural households in Tien Giang and Dong Thap provinces indicated that 74.5% reported handwashing with soap and about 84% of rural residents were aware that handwashing with soap is important after defecating, compared to 68% of those who stated that this practice is important after eating. Overall, the proportion of population who reported washing hands with soap rose from 14.6 to 66.5% in targeted areas (Unilever, 2015). Details of specific behavioral change outcomes are not available, given that Unilever Vietnam has not released its campaign reports. As part of its Sustainable Development Plan, Unilever Vietnam is committed to helping improve the health and well-being of more than one million people, in which handwashing with soap remains a critical component that will not only be sustained in previously targeted areas but also expanded to cover many others countrywide (Unilever, 2018).

Lessons Learned

A number of lessons were learned from this campaign. Firstly, the campaign had targeted regions with high levels of digestive infections and poor hygienic conditions, particularly rural and remote ones. Embracing both elementary school children and their parents helped address the targeted behavior change more comprehensively. Secondly, a five-year roadmap with a specific focus for each period made the changes and outcomes significant enough to sustain. Thirdly, the campaign had created a range of tools and activities for children that were enjoyable and easy to understand. Fourthly, well-organized and managed partnerships from two governmental agencies (MOH and Ministry of Education and Training) and a corporate entity (Unilever's Lifebuoy) secured the necessary resources and facilities to implement the campaign effectively. Fifth, although the product element was well developed, with a variety of tools and activities (reality shows, fun music videos, a game, and Clean Hands Toolkits), some products might not be easily accessible to those in rural areas, such as computer games. Finally, it was not possible to compare behavioral change in the target audience before and after the campaign, given that information about the campaign's formative research and outcome measurement was not available (Unilever, 2012, 2013, 2014, 2015, 2016).

Discussion Questions

1. Evaluate the campaign's targeting and positioning strategy.
2. How were the barriers to behavior change in the target audience addressed? How do you evaluate the effectiveness of the price element in this campaign?
3. What would you recommend to enhance the campaign's effectiveness?

References

Brand Vietnam. (2013). *Clean hands task force in action*. Retrieved from: http://www. brandsvietnam.com/3282-Lifebuoy-Viet-Nam-Biet-Doi-Tay-Sach-Hanh-Dong, February 6, 2018.

Curtis, V. (2005). *Hygiene and sanitation in Vietnam*. Retrieved from: http://siteresources. worldbank.org/INTTOPSANHYG/Resources/1923125-1166719802892/SWAT_Vietnam_ hygieneandsanitation_0505.pdf, January 15, 2018.

Giadinhvatreem. (2015). *Clean hands squad: Useful playground for kids*. Retrieved from: http://m. giadinhvatreem.vn/xem-tin_biet-doi-tay-sach-%E2%80%93-san-choi-bo-ich-cho-tre_572_4254. html, February 24, 2018.

Indochina Research. (2007). *Vietnam national handwashing initiative consumer research baseline survey final report*. Hanoi: World Bank.

Lifebuoy Vietnam. (2013a). *Wash your hands at 5 critical times with Lifebuoy*. Retrieved from: https://www.youtube.com/watch?v=WFi-cxr1R10, February 25, 2018.

Lifebuoy Vietnam. (2013b). *Clean hands task force in action*. Retrieved from: https://www. youtube.com/watch?v=n8eI1Tr5mfQ&list=PLfeG706MynWcqFSZuIkNCITHTkrZ8vOZu, February 25, 2018.

Lifebuoy Vietnam. (2015). *Clean hands squads game*. Retrieved from: https://www.youtube.com/ watch?v=IKZ2zD3kDy0. August 12, 2018.

Ministry of Health (MOH). (2016). *The ministry of health launches the campaign "10 million clean hands journey"*. Retrieved from: http://moh.gov.vn/news/Pages/TinHoatDongV2.aspx? ItemID=1732, February 23, 2018.

Muare. (2014). *Lifebuoy clean hands team toolkit global handwashing day*. Retrieved from: https://muare.vn/posts/lifebuoy-bi-kip-biet-doi-tay-sach-ngay-the-gioi-rua-tay-voi-xa-phong. 3357640, February 23, 2018.

Nguyen, N., Paynter, N., & Nguyen, M. H. T. (2011). *Vietnam: A handwashing behavior change journey*. Retrieved from: https://www.wsp.org/sites/wsp.org/files/publications/WSP-FA-Viet nam-LN-HWWS-lowres-DEC-2011.pdf, February 10, 2018.

PSI Vietnam. (2016). *2016 Rural sanitation and hygiene behavioral study Vietnam*. Retrieved from: http://www.psi.org/wp-content/uploads/2017/10/Final-Sanitation-Behavioral-Study-2016-Report-PSI-VN-September-2017.pdf, February 25, 2018.

Puffer, S. M. (2015). *International management: Insights from fiction and practice*. London: Routledge.

Rheinländer, T., Samuelsen, H., Dalsgaard, A., & Konradsen, F. (2010). Hygiene and sanitation among ethnic minorities in Northern Vietnam: Does government promotion match community priorities? *Social Science and Medicine, 71*(5), 994–1001.

UNICEF. (2007). *A summary of national baseline survey on environmental sanitation and hygiene situation in Vietnam*. Hanoi: UNICEF.

UNICEF. (2008). *Poor sanitation putting children at risk in rural Vietnam*. Hanoi: UNICEF.

Unilever (2012). *Lifebuoy: Global handwashing with soap day*. Retrieved from: https://www. unilever.com.vn/news/press-releases/2012/ngay-the-gioi-rua-tay-voi-xa-phong-chung-tay-vi-tuong-lai-vietnam.html, February 6, 2018.

Unilever. (2013). *Handwashing with soap for effective prevention of diseases*. Retrieved from: https://www.unilever.com.vn/news/press-releases/2013/rua-tay-voi-xa-phong-huu-hieu-de-phong-benh.html, February 15, 2018.

Unilever. (2014). *For a healthier Vietnam with Lifebuoy*. Retrieved from: https://www.unilever. com.vn/news/news-and-features/2014/vi-mot-viet-nam-khoe-manh-cung-voi-lifebuoy.html, February 23, 2018.

Unilever. (2015). *Lifebuoy way of life, towards universal handwashing with soap*. Retrieved from: https://www.unilever.com/Images/lifebuoy-way-of-life-2015_tcm244-418692_en.pdf, February 25, 2018.

Unilever. (2016). *Changing handwashing habits for better health.* Retrieved from: https://www.unilever.com/sustainable-living/improving-health-and-well-being/health-and-hygiene/changing-handwashing-habits-for-better-health, February 25, 2018.

Unilever. (2018). *Sustainable development for a brighter future.* Retrieved from: https://www.unilever.com.vn/sustainable-living/, March 25, 2018.

World Bank. (2008). *SOAPBOX: The public-private partnership for handwashing newsletter.* Retrieved from: http://documents.worldbank.org/curated/en/677411468162258540/text/483690NEWS0Soa10Box338903B01PUBLIC1.txt, February 24, 2018.

World Health Organization. (WHO). (2017). *Children: Reducing mortality.* Retrieved from: http://www.who.int/mediacentre/factsheets/fs178/en/.10, February 20, 2017.

Using Social Marketing to Increase Bicycle Ridership to Major Events in Vancouver, Canada

20

Better Environmentally Sound Transportation's Bicycle Valet

Katherine C. Lafreniere and Debra Z. Basil

Chapter Overview
This case examines the social marketing efforts of Better Environmentally Sound Transportation (BEST) in Vancouver, Canada. BEST encourages bicyclists to ride to major local entertainment events by providing convenient and secure bicycle parking at these events. The goal of BEST is to increase bicycle ridership to major events in order to reduce traffic congestion at events, with the secondary goal of encouraging bicycling more generally. BEST works with event planners to offer secure, professionally attended bicycle corrals at major events where cyclists can store their bikes and their bicycling gear. This can increase bicyclists' self-efficacy toward cycling to major events. By offering a useful service, making the service free for cyclists, conveniently locating bike corrals, and promoting their service in locations that cyclists frequent such as bike shops, BEST has developed a successful social marketing campaign to reduce event traffic congestion and encourage bicycling.

This case is based on an interview with a Better Environmentally Sustainable Transportation manager, follow-up information provided by email from a BEST representative, and the organization's project reports presented to their donors.

K. C. Lafreniere (✉)
Alberta School of Business, University of Alberta, Edmonton, Canada
e-mail: klafreni@ualberta.ca

D. Z. Basil
Dhillon School of Business, University of Lethbridge, Lethbridge, Canada
e-mail: debra.basil@uleth.ca

© Springer Nature Switzerland AG 2019
D. Z. Basil et al. (eds.), *Social Marketing in Action*,
Springer Texts in Business and Economics,
https://doi.org/10.1007/978-3-030-13020-6_20

Introduction

This case study examines how Better Environmentally Sound Transportation (BEST) made sustainable transportation easier for local residents of Vancouver, British Columbia, Canada. Their efforts facilitated the use of sustainable transportation to attend major events in the area, thus reducing traffic congestion at events and encouraging cycling behavior. By reducing concerns of safety for their bicycles, the BEST program enhances self-efficacy for cyclists wishing to ride to events.

Bandura's (1989) Social cognitive theory describes how people's self-efficacy (i.e., one's belief in their ability to succeed at a task) influences their level of motivation. The more a person believes in their own capabilities, the more likely they are to complete a desired behavior (e.g., riding a bike to work). Naturally, those with low self-efficacy often abandon the behavior when they are faced with difficulties, opting for easier alternatives (e.g., driving a car). In these instances of self-doubt, social marketers have two options to encourage perseverance: (1) they can reassure their target audience of their own competency and the positive feelings associated with completing the action (which may or may not be successful given that ordinary social realities are full of setbacks, failures, and inequities; Bandura, 1989), or (2) they can simply make the desired behavior easier to complete.

Campaign Background and Environment

BEST has been a leader in promoting sustainable transportation in the Lower Mainland of British Columbia (BC) since 1991. With support from the City of Vancouver and other generous donors, BEST has implemented social marketing programs to make sustainable transportation easier. BEST also aids land use planning in order to support pedestrian, cycling, and transit-oriented neighborhoods.

With over 1.2 million licensed vehicles, the Lower Mainland of BC faces several challenges from automobile transportation. In the early 2000s, the Vancouver Sun published a poll showing that 47% of Lower Mainland citizens felt that transportation was the most important issue facing local residents, well ahead of crime (17%), health care (12%), and education (12%). The transportation problem in the region was fueled by vehicle levies and transportation taxes, a long transit strike, cuts to transit services, and the political difficulties facing TransLink (the region's transportation authority). To meet growing demand from predicted increases in economic activity, population growth, and environmental needs, innovative mechanisms were needed to increase the motivation of local residents to use sustainable transportation.

Bicycling is typically the fastest mode of transportation for trips less than 5 km. Since around 50% of all trips made in Metro Vancouver are less than 5 km, cycling is a time-competitive alternative to the automobile for about half of all trips made in the region (TransLink, 2011). Secure bicycle parking plays an important role in increasing self-efficacy beliefs toward cycling. More people will ride their bicycle knowing they have a safe place to park. The bicycle valet (BV) is intended to provide secure bicycle parking at a variety of events in and around Metro Vancouver. Bikes are neatly organized in a custom-made, fenced corral, instead of having bikes locked up at every available pole.

The Bicycle Valet in Vancouver

BEST has run an annual Bike Month campaign promoting sustainable transportation in Metro Vancouver since 1996. After running Bike Month for ten years, BEST staff felt enough ground had been covered and moved from building awareness to making sustainable choices easier. In 2006, with the continued support of the City of Vancouver and TransLink, BEST launched a pilot program to increase motivation for cycling to local events and festivals. Because of the limited and unsecure bicycle parking at festivals at the time, the strategy was to provide a free "coat check" style parking service at community events for individuals using active transportation. BEST staff and volunteers would tag incoming bicycles and provide the user with a claim stub. Users would then bring back the claim stub when they want their bicycles returned. Users were also permitted to leave their helmets, panniers, trailers, and other accessories securely attached to their bicycle in the valet.

SWOT Analysis (Strengths, Weaknesses, Opportunities, Threats)

Strengths

BEST has a great reputation and brand recognition in the cycling community.
BEST has a strong volunteer base that could be trained to run the valet.
BEST has the ability to customize the service to meet the needs of specific events.

Weaknesses

The start-up costs to build a bicycle valet are expensive and require grant support. The operational costs to run the valet at an event would require financial support from event organizers or sponsors.
BEST staff had no experience providing a well-executed valet service.

Opportunities

Users would feel like they're part of something exciting.
There was a high demand for a well-executed valet service from event patrons and organizers.

More people will ride their bikes knowing they have a safe place to park, and more people will attend an event that is easy to get to.

There are a substantial number of green consumers in the region.

A bicycle valet service at high traffic community events would create a unique marketing opportunity for businesses and event organizers to promote "green goodwill." Since the valet would be the first point of contact at an event, the valet is a highly visual indicator that an event supports a local, sustainable initiative. BEST could enter into strategic partnerships with potential sponsors. Furthermore, BEST would be able to negotiate premium locations with event organizers who value "green goodwill."

Consumers expect and value socially responsible efforts on the part of companies (Cone, 2015). Sponsors can use their support of BEST to demonstrate their commitment to social responsibility, which could increase companies' willingness to sponsor.

Threats

Other non-profit organizations may enter the bicycle valet market.

Any bicycle theft from the valet could reduce the users' confidence in the service.

The accessibility of the valet depends on the location and space provided by the event organizers.

The success of the valet at each event would depend on the event organizer's commitment to promoting the service in their promotional material and on their website.

If users perceive that the service takes too long to use (slow check-in and check-out process), they may be unwilling to check their bikes at future events.

Past and Similar Efforts

BEST's bicycle valet service was the first of its kind in the Lower Mainland of BC. Their research on similar efforts in other areas was the foundation of their operations. They learned how to provide good service in terms of speed and consistency from event organizers in San Francisco, California. The city of San Francisco has a bylaw that requires events of a certain size to offer a bicycle valet, so their event organizers had a lot of experience providing efficient service. However, BEST needed their equipment to be more customizable than that in San Francisco in order to accommodate events that varied in terms of size and space. Their equipment also had to be light and compact in order to reduce the burden on staff and volunteers moving and setting up the equipment in different locations. After carefully researching portable valet services, BEST concluded that they needed to fabricate custom-built racks and fencing. Their custom equipment allows them to fit enough racks and equipment to park 1000 bikes into one cargo van.

Target Audience

BEST chose two target audiences for their efforts. The program's primary target audience is the event organizers in the region. This program focused on event organizers for two reasons. First, event organizers are the decision makers that choose how their event will be accessible to their patrons. In order to run a bicycle valet, event organizers have to book the service and allocate enough space for equipment and racks. Second, event patrons use the event's communications materials for information about traveling to the event. Event patrons were not targeted by demographics, but rather by lifestyle. Individuals who ride bicycles were the target. This group tends to lead an active lifestyle. Event organizers are the messengers that deliver the valet's communication strategy to potential users.

Each event organizer, such as small community organizers, corporate clients, or event management companies, has different goals and challenges for each event that need to be targeted with a personalized marketing strategy. However, event organizers do have some mutual values that BEST needs to address for every event. These values are that:

BEST operates effectively in the background.
Clientele are treated well and are happy.
The valet facilitates cross-promotion.
The valet operates professionally.
The valet is a practical solution for traffic management.

The program's secondary target audience consisted of men and women in the region committed to living a healthy lifestyle. In view of the high demand for a well-executed valet service, many event patrons want to use the service, but still need information about its availability and accessibility. For that reason, it was essential to build their knowledge of the valet prior to each event.

Target markets can be understood according to their proximity to and role in the ultimately desired behavior change. Lee and Kotler (2016, pp. 142–143) discuss downstream, midstream, and upstream targets. A downstream target is the group sought to actually adopt the behavior. In this case, these are the event patrons who valet their bicycles. Midstream targets are those who have close and influential relationships with the downstream group. In this case, no midstream groups were targeted, but a hypothetical example might be if employers in the local area had been targeted to encourage their employees to bike to the event and valet park with BEST, rather than driving cars, to reduce traffic congestion. Upstream targets facilitate adoption of the core desired behavior by creating infrastructure and environments that promote the desired behavior change. In that sense, event organizers can be seen as an upstream group targeted by BEST. In this case, it is actually the event organizers who compose the focal target group, because without adoption of the services of BEST, the infrastructure which makes it convenient to bicycle to events would be lacking.

Target Audience Barriers and Benefits

Through a market analysis, BEST identified that the main barrier preventing event organizers from offering the valet service was cost. Event organizers were uneasy about the idea of paying for a service that competed with one of their sources of revenue—motor transportation was often a source of revenue because they could employ a pay and park service. However, organizers also recognized that some patrons may avoid events if parking is perceived to be difficult. The valet service would enhance the attractiveness of bicycling as an alternative transportation mode for patrons, thus increasing potential event attendance.

Motor transportation was seen as a competing behavior for event patrons because of its convenience. However, parking at events around the city is often limited and costly. Patrons would be more likely to ride their bikes if they knew that parking their car was going to be a hassle. The valet service would provide a safe place to keep their bicycle, making bicycling an attractive option.

Positioning

The bicycle valet is positioned as an environmentally friendly alternative to driving and parking, for events in the Vancouver area. The service is positioned as offering-enhanced transportation convenience for those attending events, which appeals to both event patrons and event organizers. Since concern over traffic can discourage people from attending events, the valet service is positioned as a way for organizers to increase event attendance while being environmentally responsible.

Campaign Objectives and Goals

Behavior Objectives

For the event organizers, the program's overarching behavior goal was to provide not only the valet service at all main events held during the bike season, but also place the service in a visible location near the event's entrance. Event organizers had to understand that if they want the valet to run successfully, then they have to make it a priority in terms of location.

For event patrons, the behavior goal was first of course to bicycle to the event (rather than taking another mode of transportation) and to use their bicycle valet service. Beyond that, the goal for patrons was to encourage their cooperation to facilitate quick service by valet workers. Specifically, patrons must remove their helmet and other biking accessories before they get to the front of the line in order to minimize processing time.

Knowledge Objectives

BEST sought to increase knowledge of the following key facts among event organizers:

The valet invites repeat exposure: 44% of patrons said they used the valet more than once; 37% use the valet service regularly.

The valet adds value to the event: 99% of patrons said it contributes to a positive experience at the event.

The valet connects event organizers directly to their patrons: 66% of patrons said they used the resources provided at the valet's booth.

For event patrons, BEST wanted them to know that the valet was free and safe. They also wanted event patrons to know that they can leave all their gear, including bike accessories and trailers, with their bike in the valet.

Belief Objectives

The belief objective for event organizers was to promote the idea that the value of providing the valet at their event would be worth the cost. Specifically, organizers should believe that the valet is in high demand from event patrons, reduces traffic congestion at the event, and adds value to the overall event experience and brand. An additional belief objective for event organizers was to promote the idea that the bicycle valet was hassle free. BEST sets up the valet, provides the service, and then takes down the valet without leaving a mess. They are also flexible on how sponsors are seen and interacted with.

Campaign Strategies

Product Strategies

Since 2006, the bicycle valet has been providing professional, secure, coat-check style bicycle parking at a variety of events in and around Metro Vancouver. With over 80,000 bicycles (and counting) returned safely to happy owners, BEST is confident that their product strategy meets the needs of both event organizers and patrons. Given the varying attendance rates for each event, BEST made sure that valet staff could easily change the size of the valet corral to fit the needs of the event. A key product strategy was to make the valet highly efficient to set up and take down. This ensures that the valet is extremely mobile, with set up taking less than an hour. The valet is so efficient that they are able to compact a valet with a 1000 bike capacity into one van. The valet's efficiency also ensures that no permanent damage results from their service—parking lots look the same after the valet leaves an event with no permanent damage.

For patrons, the product is safe and convenient bike storage during major events. This allows them to bicycle to events, thus avoiding traffic and the hassle and cost of parking.

Pricing Strategies

In order to offer the valet service free of charge to event patrons, event organizers are responsible for paying for the valet. BEST does not charge a fixed price for each event. Pricing depends on service factors, such as the bike capacity required, the length of the event, expected turnover rates, and staffing requirements. However, event organizers can mitigate the cost of the valet by partnering with third-party sponsors and selling ad space.

In addition to the actual charge for BEST services that event organizers must pay, there is the potential of losing revenue that would have otherwise flowed into their parking services. BEST encourages event organizers to recognize that this loss is offset by additional patrons drawn to the event through the promise of the convenience offered by bicycling rather than facing the hassle of driving and parking.

For patrons, the service should be a net benefit, by eliminating the hassle of driving and parking at a crowded event. However, if they are not confident in the service, they may be faced with concern for the safety of their bike and riding equipment. Additionally, they may be anxious about the potential inconvenience and wait time for checking in and checking out.

Place Strategies

A key place strategy was to establish a regular, high-exposure location for the bicycle valet at each event venue. It was therefore essential that BEST managers developed relationships with venue managers and event organizers. One way they managed these relationships was to provide preferred supplier agreements with key venues. Such agreements ensured that BEST has a regular and accessible location at many venues, thereby significantly increasing the valet's exposure to all forms of traffic.

Promotion Strategies

Given that event patrons often use the event's website for transportation options, it was important that BEST got the event organizers on board in promoting the service. BEST developed a promotional information guide to help event organizers promote the valet prior to their event. The guide gives advice on how to promote nearby bike routes and how to link the location to online maps so patrons can map their own routes. The guide further explains that patrons need to know where the bike racks will be located and how they can be accessed. It was also important for the organizers to negatively frame motor parking by notifying patrons that parking is limited and comes at a cost.

BEST maintains an online presence on social networking sites, such as Facebook and Twitter, in order to promote their exact location, encourage event attendees to ride their bikes, and provide a forum for feedback. BEST provides updates on their website and in their newsletter with a short description of all events that are offering the valet service in the coming weeks. Online presence is also a factor in attracting event organizers, as it allows patrons to request the service to event organizers who might not be aware of the service or have decided not to offer it. Personal recommendations from bloggers have also attracted new patrons.

Message Design

At each event, clear signage is critical to promote the valet service and its benefits. BEST wanted patrons to know that valet service was "free and safe bicycle parking." Therefore, they created banners promoting this message that could be easily attached to their fencing for maximum exposure (Fig. 20.1). The banners also doubled as advertising for third-party sponsors. A clear and concise logo was created to brand the service in all their promotional material (Fig. 20.2).

Fig. 20.1 Bicycle valet at Sunset Beach.   Courtesy of Better Environmentally Sound Transportation

Fig. 20.2 Bicycle valet logo

Other Important Strategies

Volunteer Engagement

Reliable volunteers are essential for smooth operations of The Bicycle Valet. In 2012, over 115 volunteers signed up for shifts at various events throughout the season. An increased reliance on volunteers is necessary, particularly as the bicycle valet became more popular at events and its operations became increasingly labor-intensive. In order to develop volunteer engagement and recognition, BEST focused on incentives such as volunteer parties, free entry to ticketed events, flexible scheduling, onsite training, discounts at local bike shops, and a complimentary T-shirt.

Strategic Third-Party Sponsors

In order to offset the costs of the valet, BEST sought out strategic partnerships with travel companies, such as TravelSmart, in the form of a cause-related marketing campaign. Companies, such as Lululemon, could financially sponsor the service at high-profile events like the UBC Grand Prix. Sponsors also increased the valet's marketing reach by ensuring that the service could be offered at events that could not afford it otherwise. To attract potential partners, BEST hired a branding professional to revise sponsorship documents, sales scripts, and language surrounding the service. Presenting sponsors were awarded a strong presence at the valet during the event. Promotion included the sponsor's banner on valet fencing, their logo on valet ticket stubs and tags—patrons often left their tags on their bicycles after the event—and their logo on flags ushering patrons through the valet line. Sponsors were also featured in monthly and special newsletters (which had over 7000 subscribers in 2013), on BEST's social networking pages, and on the valet's website. BEST was also flexible about taking on other promotional opportunities for sponsors on a case-by-case basis. For example, volunteers handed out TransLink transit maps as well as information cards promoting a sponsor's product or service.

Evaluation

Given the tremendous growth of cycling and the rampant theft of bicycles in Vancouver, the bicycle valet is in a great position to continually increase its popularity, while providing a valuable service for events and a highly visible, feel-good story for sponsors.

Performance and Growth Measure

BEST keeps track of the number of events attended and the number of riders using their valet service. Annual growth in these measurements is one way to evaluate their success. Using figures provided for 2013 and 2017, we are able to compare their performance over a five-year span. These figures show positive growth for the organization.

In 2013, the vicycle valet was present at 130 events from March to October, parking over 22,000 bikes. In 2017, the number of events was quite a bit lower, at 89, reflecting a decline of 32% in number of events. Despite attending fewer events, the overall number of bikes parked in 2017 increased by 33%, to 29,150.

Volunteer Engagement Measures

BEST kept track of active volunteers, and their number of hours logged each year. In 2013, there were 140 volunteers and staff, and volunteers logged in over 1000 hours. By 2017, BEST had 442 volunteers, who logged a total of 2267 hours. This reflects an increase in volunteer hours of about 127%.

Other Performance Highlights

The bicycle valet has parked a total of 182,310 bicycles as of April 2018, since their inception in 2006. BEST regularly receives inquiries for advice on starting and operating bicycle valets from other organizations in Canadian and international communities, some even as far away as Australia. In 2017, they received 849 Instagram "likes."

Lessons Learned and Future Direction

With the growing success of the valet service, BEST is looking to expand its service into other regions by investing in a second set of valet equipment and transportation. Feedback from users and event organizers also suggests that BEST would benefit by expanding their range of products in order to serve people that would not benefit from a full valet service. Some potential products include rental racks, pop-up valets, or perhaps in some conditions, a fee-for-service operation.

By providing a safe and free bicycle valet service, BEST increased self-efficacy beliefs associated with cycling to community events and motivated event patrons to keep their cars at home. Segmenting and targeting event organizers ensured that BEST provided the depth of communication necessary for debunking myths regarding the valet's cost/benefit ratio for event organizers, its demand by event patrons, and its ease of operations. Similarly, promotional material at each event, in the form of clear and visible banners that the valet was free and safe, encouraged event patrons to frequently use the valet and to request the service from event organizers that did not offer it. The bicycle valet's winning marketing and operations strategy has attracted international admiration, with organizations all over the world now approaching BEST for start-up tips and advice.

Discussion Questions

1. What can BEST do to further increase the number of patrons using the valet service at each event?
2. What are some other ways for BEST to benefit third-party sponsors?
3. Where might a similar valet service be successful or unsuccessful?
4. What types of events should BEST target?

References

Bandura, A. (1989). Human agency in social cognitive theory. *American Psychologist, 44*(9), 1175–1184.
Cone Communications/Ebiquity (2015). *Global CSR study*. Retrieved from http://www.conecomm.com/research-blog/2015-cone-communications-ebiquity-global-csr-study
Lee, N., & Kotler, P. (2016). *Social marketing: Changing behaviors for good* (5th ed.). Los Angeles: Sage.
TransLink. (2011). *Cycling for everyone: A regional cycling strategy for Metro Vancouver.* Retrieved from http://www.translink.ca/ ~ /media/Documents/cycling/regional_cycling_strategy/Cycling%20for%20Everyone.ashx.

Akureyri on the Verge: Carbon Neutral and Beyond Through Targeted Social Marketing

21

G. Scott Erickson

Chapter Overview

Akureyri, Iceland, possesses a lot of natural advantages when seeking carbon neutrality. Even so, at a time when many municipalities, regions, or even states and nations are looking at becoming carbon neutral by the middle of the century, at best, Akureyri is already on the verge. And this is not easy. Carbon neutrality is achieved when carbon emissions (usually energy generation) are matched or exceeded by carbon removal (e.g., sequestration, planting trees). Looking more closely at this exemplar city allows us to study a question that will face every sustainability campaign at some point, how does the community go the last mile? What happens after mass campaigns are generally successful? Success will create an environment calling for different approaches, and the experiences of those first crossing this threshold can be instructive for others. More specific to social marketing, what happens when you move from a successful mass market approach to one more targeted at remaining micro-segments or even individual entities needing tailored solutions?

SWOT Analysis (Strengths, Weaknesses, Opportunities, and Threats)

Strengths

Akureyri is relatively small (19,000) but is the largest city in Iceland outside of the Reykjavik area.

G. Scott Erickson (✉)
School of Business, Ithaca College, Ithaca, USA
e-mail: gerickson@ithaca.edu

© Springer Nature Switzerland AG 2019
D. Z. Basil et al. (eds.), *Social Marketing in Action*,
Springer Texts in Business and Economics,
https://doi.org/10.1007/978-3-030-13020-6_21

The "capital of the north" is a major regional economic, political, and educational center, relatively cosmopolitan and with important industries such as fishing, tourism, and consumables (meat, beer, coffee).

Even so, Akureyri is still small enough to maintain a sense of community. Personal relationships abound among key decision makers.

The city has been receptive to previous sustainability initiatives including recycling stations and curbside pickup of household compost.

Awareness and understanding of sustainability issues are high.

A number of prominent non-governmental organizations are key players in the commercial and sustainability communities.

Weaknesses

The remaining sustainability issues are in key industries that drive the local and regional economy. Costs may be substantial and directly borne by a few firms or individuals though with a wider economic impact.

There is a lack of infrastructure for transportation initiatives, especially electric recharging facilities (Fig. 21.1).

Opportunities

Iceland has tremendous clean energy capabilities in geothermal (electricity, heating) and hydropower (electricity). Electricity needs (100%) and hot water and heat (87%) are provided by these sources (exceptions are often on outlying islands off the main grid) (Fig. 21.2).

Fig. 21.1 Recharging spots at Akureyri University

Fig. 21.2 Household geothermal hot water/heating system

Although numerous political parties exist and have a presence in government, they are not traditional right/left parties as we see in the USA and similar countries. There is political cohesiveness around the topic of sustainability, present across the political spectrum.

Individuals are very knowledgeable about climate change issues and very thoughtful about their personal choices. In considering electric cars, for example, many also consider the environmental costs of building the new car and disposing of a perfectly workable old car. This attitude is in line with a sense of anti-consumerism, also quite apparent.

Threats

As a small, isolated island, the economy is susceptible to shocks. During the US/EU financial crisis of 2008, for example, the entire economy declined sharply and took years to recover. Some similar occurrence would likely delay any further sustainability actions requiring a substantial investment.

Geographic isolation also requires Iceland to import a lot of goods since either the climate would not support their production (agriculture) or the market is too small to justify domestic manufacturing. Imported goods are expensive and generally require less-sustainable transportation options.

Disposing of waste is also an issue.

Segmentation and Targeting

One of the key tools in the social marketer's playbook is effective segmentation and targeting. Along with the marketing mix, segmentation is the area in which a good decision can be critical to the success of the campaign (Kotler & Zaltman, 1971; Lee & Kotler, 2015). Conceptually, we know that segmentation can help with understanding the needs and wants of segment members, allowing us to target those most receptive to an offering. Moreover, the marketing mix of offerings can then be adapted to each segment, allowing customized products, distribution, pricing, and communications. In the case of social marketing, better understanding the perceived benefits, costs, and barriers of a segment allows construction of an exchange coaxing behavior change out of the targets.

Describing target segments in Akureyri can be done most effectively by referring to the *Six Americas* studies on climate change attitudes in the USA. *Six Americas* is based on research from the Yale Project on Climate Change Communication and George Mason University, repeated on an annual basis over most of the last decade (Maibach, Roser-Renouf, & Leiserowitz, 2009; Roser-Renouf, Maibach, Leiserowitz, & Rosenthal, 2016). Based on self-reported attitudes and behaviors (or intended behaviors), US respondents are segmented into six categories, with associated population percentages:

Alarmed (17%): high interest, high belief, takes individual action
Concerned (28%): pays attention, probable belief, convenient actions
Cautious (27%): notices discussion, notices evidence, not ready for action
Disengaged (7%): little interest, low belief, too busy otherwise to take action
Doubtful (11%): little interest, uncertainty, unwilling to take action
Dismissive (10%): interest, disbelief, individual action in other direction.

Although this segmentation scheme recognizes dramatic differences in the US population, including that climate change as a political concern drops off sharply once we move beyond the "Alarmed" segment, very few sustainability initiatives actually address the differences. Even when social marketing is employed, it often treats the entire population similarly and discussions about sustainability often focus only on the two extreme segments—the true believers and the climate change deniers--with no middle ground. In fact, the vast majority of the public lies in the middle.

Conducting effective segmentation and actually adjusting the social marketing exchange, as appropriate, for different targets can be a key to a successful campaign. Segments can differ by the attitudes and behaviors, perceived barriers or costs, desired benefits, responsiveness to different parts of the marketing mix, and other aspects. Continued success in reducing smoking rates, for example, can be traced to identifying and addressing the how the youth market, in particular, differs from other segments. When rebellion against authority is a major benefit to smoking, stop smoking messages from authority figures lose their power and can actually be counterproductive (Hicks, 2001). Even more recent efforts, such as identifying micro-segments of smokers referred to as "hipsters" show the power of effective segmentation by creating social marketing exchanges aimed at the hardest of the hard-core smoking segments (Ling et al., 2014).

Similarly, Rare Pride has made a name for itself in social marketing circles through its habitat preservation interventions around the world. Although the template remains similar (branding by iconic species, local leadership, person-to-person communications), the social marketing initiatives work because they are adapted to each location, essentially a customized solution to the special circumstances of the community (Boss, 2008).

Akureyri not only does not have the full range of climate change attitudes seen in the USA, but the three that are apparent are clustered at the alarmed/concerned end of the spectrum. The respondents classified themselves as belonging to one of those segments or pointedly asked to be put somewhere in between (not alarmed but more than concerned). This added segment does believe in global warming and takes some individual actions but is not "panicked." Even with a more truncated range of segments, differences in belief were apparent, such as whether warmer temperatures were necessarily a bad thing for Iceland (especially among farmers), whether to buy an electric car (when also adding in recognizable manufacturing costs and disposal costs of quite adequate existing cars), whether capital expenditures in businesses still dependent on carbon-based fuels were justified, and so forth. Discussions with Akureyri residents revealed a deep, sophisticated knowledge and understanding of the issues, both pro-sustainability and con-sustainability that was much more nuanced than what is generally seen in the USA. The segments, based on depth interviews with over 50 key respondents, can be described as:

Alarmed, strong concern about climate change even if it might not affect them directly (e.g., dislocation or even war in other parts of the world). Already taking personal actions beyond the community expectation such as biking to work, electric vehicle, reduced consumption and etc.
Alarmed/concerned, also strong concern about climate change but less immediate. Intentions to take personal action such as electric vehicle but waiting for barriers such as few charging stations to be reduced.
Concerned, understand issues and believe action should be taken, just not yet. Often more considerable barriers exist, related to commercial interests (replacing a fleet of boats or cars, turning over part of a farm to reforestation).

Other segments, identifiable in the USA, were not apparent in Akureyri: Cautious, Disengaged, Doubtful, or Dismissive. There were rumors of a few old farmers who may fit one of these designations, but none were encountered during interviews.

Much of the successful work to date on carbon neutrality has targeted the entire municipality on a mass market basis. This has worked, but community leaders clearly do understand that differences exist in those they target for further behavior change. In moving from the mass market to more personalized, even one-to-one efforts, understanding the existing segments will become more important.

Objectives, benefits/barriers in an exchange context, and the marketing mix to address the exchange do differ between segments, micro-segments, and even individuals. More customized marketing is dependent on fully understanding the targets and their differences.

One key aspect to note is more precise differences between the reconfigured segments. The alarmed segment, in particular, is identified by its actions, so a word about consumer response is probably in order. A general marketing framework for obtaining positive target behavior is the consumer response hierarchy: cognitive, affective, and behavioral responses. Lavidge and Steiner (1961) originally proposed this hierarchy of effects model, progressively moving from awareness through knowledge, liking, preference, conviction, and finally purchase. Cognitive, affective, and behavioral (conative) is simply the shorter version of the same process. From a marketing standpoint, we want to interact with the consumer, usually through communications, to move through the stages. So advertising might create awareness, while brand activation achieves stronger affect, moving an individual from liking to preference. More specifically, individuals pass from unaware to aware and knowledgeable (cognitive response), on to increasing degrees of feeling toward a brand including preference (affective), finally engendering enough motivation to drive purchase (behavior). The alarmed segment is motivated enough to act. The concerned/alarmed and concerned segments have awareness/knowledge and some degree of motivation but not yet enough to obtain action. Any reconfiguration of the social marketing exchange must increase motivation enough to drive behavior, moving the target to take that final step on the hierarchy.

Campaign Objectives

Many of the initiatives in Akureyri are driven by the local utility, Nordurorka (electric, hot water, cold water, sewage) and affiliated units Vistorka (alternative energy), Orkusetur (energy efficiency), and Eimur (energy innovation), though the municipal government also plays a key role as do some other entities. Current projects include (Sigurdarson, 2016):

• Recycling (mostly at the source but converting to curbside pickup)
• Composting (curbside pickup)
• Free local bus service
• Walking and bike paths
• Reforestation (a national program but pursued aggressively around Akureyri)
• Methane capture from the local landfill, processing, and refilling stations (biogas)
• Biodiesel from cooking oil recapture, processing, and use (mainly on city buses)
• Agricultural plastic recycling
• Electric vehicle recharging stations (Fig. 21.3).

As noted earlier, the original objective was carbon neutrality, so reducing carbon-producing activities while increasing carbon neutral or carbon reduction ones. As also noted, this has generally been achieved, with results tracked as shown

Fig. 21.3   Nordurorka headquarters; Akureyri (with charging station and trees)

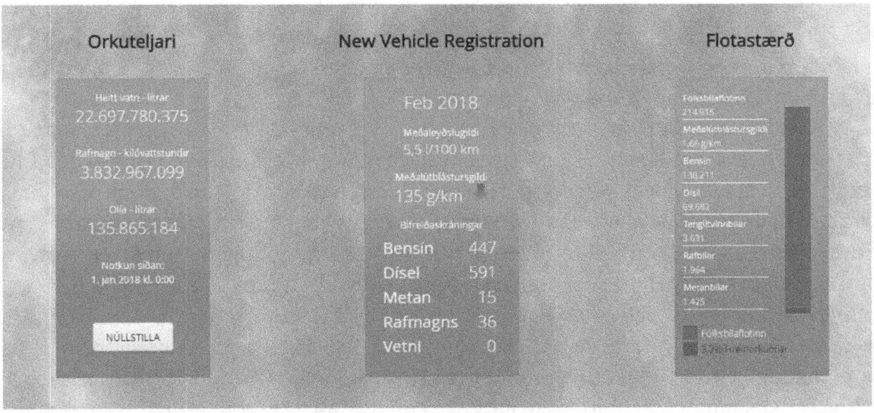

Fig. 21.4   Tracking key performance indicators (Orkusetur.is)

on the Orkasetur Web site. These include energy use by source, new vehicle purchases by type, and fleet makeup (Fig. 21.4).

Post-neutrality, the general initiative changes but objectives become more specific. Akureyri calls its plan for moving forward "carbon integrity," continuing to make further progress beyond carbon neutrality. Further improvements call for more person-by-person successes as those aware but not yet fully motivated to act (the alarmed/concerned and, especially, the concerned segments) are convinced by a more attractive proposition. Consequently, and as is somewhat illustrated by the Orkasetur tracking, each additional non-carbon vehicle purchased, each farmer agreeing to plant trees, and each business making a change in assets or procedures is its own initiative and success. That moves beyond the mass market to a more individualized approach and calls for different marketing tools.

Barriers, Benefits, and Competition

With the alarmed segment, a motivated and action-oriented group already exists. The onus is on community leaders to remove barriers (e.g., few recharging stations locally or on the ring road around the country), and then, action will happen. Segment members are already convinced of the benefits of behavior change and have no attachment to competitive behaviors. Remaining barriers will be removed, and it is only a matter of time.

With the alarmed/concerned group, the personal intentions are similar but even less immediate. So, while an intention may exist to buy an electric or methane vehicle, the individuals already own a perfectly good car and a strong anti-consumption attitude drives many not to discard usable items in favor of something new, at least not until necessary. But when the new behavior makes sense (car purchase, participating in curbside recycling), this segment will also willingly discard competitive behaviors as they are also already convinced of the benefits of change. Removing remaining barriers, finding ways to enhance benefits, and adopting more persuasive ways to communicate the attractive exchange should again gain change on a case-by-case basis.

Those in the concerned group are tougher. Though convinced climate change is real and expressing some concerns about it, they are less convinced of the need for immediate personal action. As a number of individuals in this group also have commercial interests, the benefits/barriers assessment is also somewhat different. Similar personal benefits accrue from participating in behaviors aimed at slowing climate change, but this segment has higher barriers, including the cost of retro-fitting fishing boats with new engines, replacing a fleet of rental cars, committing scarce farmland to reforestation, or paying grocery employees to unwrap food for composting. The current competitive behavior (not invest in new capital assets, use labor for sustainable activities) would be seen as more attractive than is the case in other segments, even if each individual understands that the changes will need to be made eventually. The more the barriers can be removed and benefits realized closer to the present time, and the more that persuasive techniques can again be employed, the more quickly these sometime more impactful case-by-case changes will happen.

Positioning/Research

Consequently, we can capture the positioning approach similarly for each segment: Move more quickly. The details vary by segment as the alarmed and alarmed/concerned segments are waiting for barrier removal, while the concerned will need more convincing on the benefits (or that barriers/costs are not as high as perceived). But the message from community leaders is that sooner is better. The community is convinced, so let us get this done sooner rather than later.

As the effort moves to a more personalized approach, the individual relationships between community members become a key. Broad-based research efforts, much like mass marketing, would not be effective. Much like the Rare Pride case cited earlier, each intervention depends on the knowledge of a local community leader and team, customized solutions, and a more grassroots level marketing approach. Extensive interviews supporting this case analysis established not only the range of climate change attitudes but also identified the structure of the social network/relationships behind sustainability activities. Personal knowledge of the targets, personal relationships, and customized approaches characterize the carbon integrity emphasis.

Marketing Mix

Product/Offering

As noted earlier in this case, much of the hard work to get to carbon neutrality has already been accomplished. Offerings providing non-carbon energy alternatives nationwide were developed in the 1970s (and are tailor-made for an electric car infrastructure as electricity is cheap), and more recent initiatives such as recycling and composting have also been largely adopted by the entire community (Fig. 21.5). Consequently, this discussion focuses on the more recent challenges and responses, taking the last steps to carbon neutrality and going beyond, to "carbon integrity."

A further discussion of the concept of exchange can help in understanding how the offering can be adjusted to better appeal to the target. Rothschild (1999) stressed the importance of understanding the exchange from the target's perspective, to see what they perceive as the barriers/costs of changing behavior as they evaluate whether the potentially accrued benefits are worth it. He also noted how benefits and costs in standard marketing are often a good/service exchanged for a monetary price. But in social marketing, the broader range of benefits (psychological, social) and costs (time, entrenched behaviors, entrenched attitudes) are potentially just as powerful options for encouraging change. His example of a drunk driving prevention program, where individuals knew their behavior was wrong but continued to do it because of inconveniences such as not having their car for work the next day (if left at the bar) or because perceived punishments were seen as unlikely, highlighted both the insights to be drawn and how creative solutions can effectively alter the benefit/cost evaluation (Rothschild, Masten, & Miller, 2006). In this case, it was a low-cost limo/taxi service.

The product/offering part of the social marketing plan is all about creating something delivering more benefits or removing more barriers than the status quo.

Fig. 21.5 Household compost/trash bin

One potentially effective aspect to add to the exchange is social acceptance/rejection, captured by the concept of social norming.

Social norming (Schultz, Nolan, Cialdini, Goldstein, & Griskevicius, 2007) has to do with expected attitudes and behaviors within a group. Pressure exists for members of the group to conform to those expectations with associated rewards (social acceptance) or costs (social rejection). It can be quite effective in social marketing, and important studies in the field have linked social expectations with increasing recycling or decreasing dangerous health behaviors (smoking, drug usage, unsafe sex). If the community is together and individuals behave outside of expected norms, the pressure to conform can be considerable. So, an added benefit to the exchange is social acceptance of the new behavior, and the individual now feels more a part of the community.

During the Fulbright—NSF Arctic research project conducted in Akureyri, social networks were explored, asking respondents for personal contacts who influenced their attitudes toward climate change. At the heart of such research is social network analysis (SNA), assessing the number and strength of connections between social network participants (Scott, 2017). One of the key objectives of SNA is identifying key influencers in the networks (centroids) and those who provide a connection across different parts of the networks (border spanners). With such information in hand, social maps can be constructed, determining the important connections within subnetworks, how subnetworks (segments) intersect, if at all, and what key individuals employed to influence others in the network. In the case of SNA for knowledge exchange (Liebowitz, 2005), the method is used to identify from whom individuals obtain knowledge. We can use the technique, as he did, to identify the key sources of information or knowledge (here, on climate change), and how they diffuse through the social network. With that understanding, key relationships can be identified and employed to improve community knowledge and establish social norms. In Akureyri, the network is cohesive; there are some slight but noticeable distinctions between the government, academic, and commercial networks; and the centroids and boundary spanners are readily apparent.

What is interesting, however, is that the centroids and border spanners are actually the same individuals and revolve around Nordurorka (the regional utility). Such non-governmental (NGO) agencies play a particularly important role in the social network surrounding sustainability efforts in Akureyri. At the center, with the most connections are several executives from the Nordurorka group and spouses in a prominent role at the university and heading the local consumer affairs agency. During the interviews, numerous parties pointed toward them as key leaders. They were also the links to the commercial entities. What that adds up to is a cohesive social network with a narrow range of climate change attitudes. Slight differences exist in perceptions of acceptable behaviors to address climate change (though, as noted earlier, those differences are more about readiness for action). So social norming has the potential to be a very powerful driver of continued changes in behavior, especially when the social pressure is applied by personal acquaintances known to be highly respected in the community.

Relating the social network/norming back to the targeted segments, the presence of cohesive social pressure to change behavior will enhance the appeals to the alarmed and alarmed/concerned segments. But the real impact is seen in the concerned segment, especially with the commercial interests. It is very clear to individuals in this segment what the community attitude is toward conforming behaviors, especially when personally delivered by highly respected individuals within the social network (who lead sizable organizations themselves). Moreover, the personalization of the appeals allows the exchange to be tailored to the individual. The customized benefits, barriers, and competitive behaviors that frame the proposed exchange have the potential to better drive behavior change. Moreover, community leaders have given themselves options.

The area of transportation, for example, is still dependent on carbon-based fuels, in general. Though intentions are good (almost 100% of respondents said their next personal car would be electric), electric cars are still rare. The fishing fleet uses considerable carbon-based fuel as do the tourism providers (rental cars, tour companies, whale watching). But as changeovers are made, there are options, including not just electric but methane/biogas and biodiesel (at present, there may actually be more methane stations available and Orkusetur claims it to be better performing and less costly) (Fig. 21.6). So as the fishing fleet considers new ships, the rental car agency new cars, or even individual consumers look at changing vehicles, there are options as to which best fits their needs and budget. Options may also confer different, additional benefits such as enabling waste disposal (methane/biogas and biodiesel). These are the sorts of customizable details best explored through one-on-one conversations.

Similarly, community leaders can consider the target and not just offer multiple options but use their expertise to craft an offering specifically for that individual's circumstances. We already discussed how the exchange will be different for a fishing

Fig. 21.6 Methane/biogas refilling station

Fig. 21.7 Farm with tree line beneath a steep slope

company as opposed to a car rental agency. But outside of transportation, solutions are even more varied. The farm agency (RML) and the forestry service (Sko-graektin), for example, work with individual farmers to identify specific parcels for carbon-friendly solutions such as planting trees. There is an obvious community benefit, but the benefit to the farmer is enhanced if a tree line can help provide mudslides down some of the steep slopes towering over many landholdings. The exact suggestion depends on the circumstances of that farm and what the experts can recommend in terms of the best possible solution for that installation (Fig. 21.7).

Place/Distribution

For the alarmed and alarmed/concerned segments, Akureyri has been following the traditional social marketing playbook in getting to carbon neutral. Generally, behaviors have been made convenient. Compost is picked up curbside, and dedicated compost bagging and containers have been provided. The free local bus service has convenient stops and frequent runs. Walking paths are often more direct than driving.

In other circumstances, there is still more work to do but planners are moving in the direction of improved distribution. Most residents take recycling to centralized locations (usually the grocery stores where purchased). Curbside pickup of recycling bins has just been introduced, but residents must pay for the service. One would imagine that is likely to change. But the key for moving toward carbon integrity will be more convenient refill options for transportation, help with planting trees, and so forth, resulting in easy-to-adopt personalized solutions.

Price

Some of the price aspect has already been considered in the barriers/competitive behaviors section. But the pure financial cost is a factor for all segments. While operating costs in transportation are clearly cheaper with electric or methane vehicles, boat engines, and such, there are capital costs in purchasing new vehicles. Similarly, farmers taking productive land offline lose whatever crops might have been grown there. And operating costs can be a factor, as in the case of composting at groceries and their required additional labor. A balance exists between costs, savings, and more intangible benefits, and the balance has clearly not swung far enough to the savings/benefits side, especially for the commercial interests in the concerned segment.

One clear advantage to a more customized, person-to-person approach to the concerned segment, however, is the ability to reframe the pricing issue. Choosing from multiple options can help if there are differences in the financial and social costs. But more interesting is the capability of being able to frame the discussion as shared sacrifice. As noted in the discussion concerning social networks and norms, there are key, identifiable individuals using personal relationships to drive behavior change. These and other community leaders have set up the organizations and the financing for several of the more innovative initiatives (biogas, biodiesel, agricultural plastic recycling), putting their personal funds, and those of numerous other social network members, at risk. The willingness to bear financial loss provides some moral authority in one-on-one discussions with others that may have some hesitation in making major investments in sustainable options.

Promotion/Integrated Marketing Communications

It is not unusual for social marketing initiatives to eschew expensive mass media communication techniques and instead pursue more low-cost guerilla or social media methods. Akureyri is no different, utilizing digital and local media as well as branding opportunities such as sides of busses, recharging/refilling stations, and other high-visibility locations.

But what is really innovative about this approach is its reliance on person-to-person communication, particularly for the more challenging concerned segment. In many ways, it is about personal selling, even though the participants probably would not call it that. Certain unique characteristics enable this approach. Targets are relatively few and individually identifiable. We know that one-to-one communications are highly persuasive and so could be particularly effective in moving the aware and partially motivated toward action. One-to-one is also more flexible, with options to discuss customized solutions. Person-to-person communication also reinforces the social network of the community and associated social norms. Explicit attention to personal selling as part of the marketing communications mix makes strategic sense in this case.

Program Evaluation

Campaign objectives continue to be monitored through Orkusetur, as detailed earlier. The move to carbon neutrality has been tracked and reported. Individual successes are celebrated as they occur. Every non-carbon car sold, every switch made by a commercial operation, and other moves toward carbon integrity can be recognized and counted individually.

Lessons Learned

The Akureyri case illustrates a unique situation, one in which a standard social marketing approach has been a great success, with carbon neutrality imminent. Much was due to special circumstances such as massive alternative fuel capacity built decades ago and a population already holding positive attitudes toward sustainability activities. But there was still work to be done, and community leaders provided the right mass market approaches to get the community this far.

Continuing further will take some changes. In the case of the alarmed and alarmed/concerned segments, the mass market approaches can continue, perhaps speeding up behavior change. Individuals are already committed, and much of the work will be removing barriers to change and reminding the community of the social norms of taking such actions.

The unique learning to pull from the Akureyri example, however, is the move to a more customized approach to the concerned segment. With a range of offerings to satisfy different circumstances, a powerful social network with clear social norms, influential self-sacrificing leadership, and a willingness to take the time to communicate person-to-person, the approach makes for a strategically solid approach to cleaning up remaining loose ends. Objectives and results can be evaluated on a one-on-one basis.

Discussion Questions

1. The segments/social networks in Akureyri are not that dissimilar to one another. How might this type of approach need to change in an environment with markedly different segments? What do you think needs to be done in the USA, given the *Six Americas* results?
2. Why would a wider range of solutions be attractive as an offering? A particular target can only choose one, so why does diversity matter?
3. What other social marketing applications might be ripe for a social norming approach?
4. How would a sense of self-sacrifice enhance an individual's standing in a social network? How would it impact their standing and persuasiveness with others in the network?
5. Given what you know about different marketing communication approaches, why is one-to-one communication so effective in this kind of application?

Acknowledgements The author gratefully acknowledges the support of the Fulbright—National Science Foundation Arctic Research Program, particularly the Iceland Fulbright Commission.

References

Boss, S. (2008). The cultural touch. *Stanford Social Innovation Review, 6*(4), https://ssir.org/articles/entry/the_cultural_touch.
Hicks, J. J. (2001). The strategy behind Florida's "truth" campaign. *Tobacco Control, 10,* 3–5.
Kotler, P., & Zaltman, G. (1971). Social marketing: An approach to planned social change. *Journal of Marketing, 35,* 3–12.
Lavidge, R., & Steiner, G. (1961). A model of predictive measurements of advertising effectiveness. *Journal of Marketing, 25,* 59–62.
Lee, N. R., & Kotler, P. (2015). *Social marketing: Changing behaviors for good* (5th ed.). Thousand Oaks, CA: Sage.
Liebowitz, J. (2005). Linking social network analysis with the analytic hierarchy process for knowledge mapping in organizations. *Journal of Knowledge Management, 9*(1), 76–86.

Ling, P. M., Lee, Y. O., Hong, J., Neilands, T. B., Jordan, J. W., & Glantz, S. A. (2014). Social branding to decrease smoking among young adults at bars. *American Journal of Public Health, 104*(4), 751–760.

Maibach, E., Roser-Renouf, C., & Leiserowitz, A. (2009). *Global warming's six Americas 2009: An audience segmentation analysis.* Yale University and George Mason University, New Haven, CT: Yale Project on Climate Change Communication.

Roser-Renouf, C., Maibach, E., Leiserowitz, A., & Rosenthal, S. (2016). *Global warming's six Americas and the election, 2016.* Yale University and George Mason University, New Haven, CT: Yale Program on Climate Change Communication.

Rothschild, M. L. (1999). Carrots, sticks, and promises: A conceptual framework for the management of public health and social issue behaviors. *Journal of Marketing, 63,* 24–37.

Rothschild, M. L., Masten, B., & Miller, T. W. (2006). Reducing alcohol-impaired driving crashes through the use of social marketing. *Accident Analysis and Prevention, 38*(6), 1218–1230.

Schultz, P. W., Nolan, J. M., Cialdini, R. B., Goldstein, N. J., & Griskevicius, V. (2007). The constructive, deconstructive, and reconstructive power of social norms. *Psychological Science, 18*(5), 429–434.

Scott, J. (2017). *Social network analysis* (4th ed.). Thousand Oaks: Sage Publications.

Sigurdarson, G.H. (2016). "Local climate change adaptation," at http://eea.rec.org/uploads/documents/BilateralRelations/Balatonfured/10_Gudmundur_Ungverjaland-haust%202016.pdf.

Vancouver Aquarium and World Wildlife Foundation's Great Canadian Shoreline Cleanup: Increasing Volunteerism by Targeting Social Networks

22

Katherine C. Lafreniere and Michael D. Basil

Chapter Overview

Shoreline litter is one of the most widespread pollution problems today. Since shorelines represent very sensitive and large geographical areas, any organized cleanup event requires considerable manpower in order to be successful. This case study illustrates how Vancouver Aquarium and World Wildlife Foundation recruited, organized, and retained tens of thousands of volunteers in order to build a shoreline cleanup movement across Canada.

Introduction

By some accounts, the shoreline cleanup movement began in 1986 when a Texas resident was collecting garbage along a beach and realized how much of it kept washing ashore. Something had to be done. Since then, shoreline cleanup events eventually caught international attention, growing from 12 sites along the Texas coast to more than 6000 sites in more than 100 countries. Shoreline litter is one of the most widespread pollution problems today. It threatens not only water quality, but also wildlife population as a result of ingestion or entanglement. Birds often pick up shoreline litter, such as cigarette butts, and use it for their nests. Many think it is food and ingest it, which can result in poisoning, starvation, and even death. Other animals or plants become entangled with bits of shoreline litter, and this

K. C. Lafreniere (✉)
Alberta School of Business, University of Alberta, Edmonton, Canada
e-mail: klafreni@ualberta.ca

M. D. Basil
Dhillon School of Business, University of Lethbridge, Lethbridge, Canada
e-mail: michael.basil@uleth.ca

© Springer Nature Switzerland AG 2019
D. Z. Basil et al. (eds.), *Social Marketing in Action*,
Springer Texts in Business and Economics,
https://doi.org/10.1007/978-3-030-13020-6_22

327

hampers their mobility, often resulting in life-threatening consequences. Importantly, the threat of shoreline litter is largely preventable. This case examines an event that was originally initiated by the Ocean Conservancy and named the International Coastal Cleanup. This case study examines how Vancouver Aquarium and World Wildlife Foundation (WWF) successfully introduced the shoreline cleanup movement across Canada. Their Great Canadian Shoreline Cleanup is recognized as one of the largest direct-action conservation programs and as the most significant International Coastal Cleanup in Canada.

The Great Canadian Shoreline Cleanup

The Great Canadian Shoreline Cleanup (GCSC) began in 1994 when a small group of Vancouver Aquarium employees decided to participate in the International Coastal Cleanup by tackling a local shoreline near Stanley Park in Vancouver. At the time, VA employees were actively researching conservation stewardship and therefore joined the initiative in order to "walk the walk." This small event was such a success that the aquarium decided to invest some resources in order to grow the program. Within a few years, VA employees were organizing and recruiting site coordinators and volunteers to clean up initiatives across the province. By 1997, 400 volunteers were participating in 20 sites across British Columbia as part of the Great BC Beach Cleanup.

In 2002, the GCSC emerged as a national program, providing all Canadians with the opportunity to make a difference in their local communities. Cleanups started to appear in every province and territory, and by 2003, more than 20,000 volunteers were actively participating in the program. Over the years, the program continued to expand its reach and influence, aided by the support of sponsors, donors, and partners (such as WWF Canada, who became a full partner of the Shoreline Cleanup in 2010).

SWOT Analysis (Strengths, Weaknesses, Opportunities, Threats)

Strengths

The International Coastal Cleanup is a functioning nonprofit that has a positive reputation.

Vancouver Aquarium employees are knowledgeable and have positive attitudes toward environmental protection and stewardship.

The Vancouver Aquarium has good credibility in the greater Vancouver area, which can attract sponsors, donors, and partners.

Weaknesses

The Vancouver Aquarium is not widely recognized in other communities across Canada.

Resource limitations mean that the program requires volunteers to organize their cleanup in their own local community.

Opportunities

Shoreline cleanups can be very flexible and customizable. The geographical size can be tailored to fit the needs of each volunteer group. There is also no need for a minimum number of volunteers per shoreline. Volunteers could organize a private group cleanup or open it up to the general public to drop in.

The growing popularity of the Internet and social media makes it faster, cheaper, and more efficient to distribute information than traditional methods.

Group leaders can recruit their own friends, family, and colleagues in the program.

Shoreline cleanups instill a great sense of pride in the community.

By tracking the type of litter being collected, employees can identify which activities were responsible and can then develop targeted education and marketing campaigns for prevention.

Threats

The International Costal Cleanup limits the timeframe for cleanups to late September. This timeframe is particularly challenging for recruiting larger groups, like schools, who want to clean up in the spring or summer because of the nice weather. It is also challenging for groups in other regions where this is not the optimal season. It will be especially difficult to encourage participation in bad weather.

This initiative would benefit from a wide range of volunteers. As such, the target audience for this program would ideally be very broad.

Vancouver Aquarium's association with the ocean may make people think of coastal regions instead of other shorelines. Target audiences might not see the connection to other water.

Prospective volunteers may think that they lack the knowledge or skills needed to carry out a shoreline cleanup event.

If the shoreline cleanup were to grow to a national scale, it would be very costly to provide all the supplies that are required, such as garbage bags and gloves and result in a large carbon footprint.

Target Audiences

The GCSC recognized that tailoring their promotional campaign to specific target audiences would be a challenge because their target audience was very broad as many different types of people and groups could participate in the cleanup. Furthermore, the program needed volunteers to sign up as organizers in order to reduce overhead. For these reasons, the GCSC decided to target groups and especially group leaders. Targeting potential group leaders is particularly advantageous because these volunteers not only participate in the program themselves but also recruit volunteers, often friends and family, to join them in the cleanup. This form of multi-level marketing allows the GCSC to reach audiences that are often quite costly to reach using traditional marketing methods. However, unlike traditional multi-level marketing systems, leaders are merely providing an opportunity for camaraderie and community involvement, resulting in a win-win for both volunteers and the cause.

The advantage of targeting group leaders is evident in the social network literature. First, referrals from friends and family are more influential than traditional marketing methods. Research shows that strong interpersonal ties (e.g., friends) are more likely to influence decisions than weak ties (e.g., acquaintances; Brown & Reingen, 1987) because strong-tie sources are perceived to be more credible (Rogers, 1983). Groups with strong interpersonal ties also have more homogeneous preferences for a variety of goods and behaviors because such groups are more readily available to each other as sources of information and influence (Granovetter, 1982). As such, volunteer requests from strong-tie sources are more credible and accessible than the same request from traditional marketing campaigns. Second, groups of volunteers from various backgrounds can facilitate diffusion of information about the campaign (Granovetter, 1982). Each group will have members with weaker associations to other groups, thereby serving as a bridge between groups and allowing information to travel from one group to another. For example, if one group of colleagues decided to participate in the GCSC then other associated groups (e.g., suppliers, competitors, partners) also more likely to learn about the volunteer opportunity. Finally, participating as a group can add an element of fun.

To attract group leaders (and by extension, their social networks), GCSC first targeted the groups with a traditional leadership system in place, such as schools, youth groups, and companies. Almost one-third of the number of registrants each year comes from these groups, such as Girl Guides and Boy Scout chapters. GCSC has since expanded their recruitment strategy by also targeting a wider variety of group leaders.

Campaign Objectives

GCSC has the ambitious goal to engage every person within Canada through the program by either participating in the shoreline cleanup or understanding the effects of people's daily behavior on the shoreline. In practical terms, their goal is to increase the number of participants and the number of sites registered each year. It also hopes to allow year-round participation in the program. A continuous program would encourage volunteers to feel a greater sense of ownership of their environment and actions.

Behavioral Objectives

Shoreline visitors generally clean up after themselves when they visit the beach. GCSC employees found that it was not particularly hard to generate interest in cleaning up shorelines. The real challenge for this effort was getting people to sign up for the program and to complete the tally forms used to identify which items were most collected. The GCSC believed that they could increase compliance with these objectives through group leaders.

Knowledge Objectives

The phrase 'pack it in/pack it out' was already well established throughout the province. As a result, GCSC's knowledge objectives focused on making potential volunteers aware of the cleanup and increasing the attractiveness of the program to prospective volunteers. Specifically, GCSC employees wanted volunteers to know that (1) shoreline cleanup sites could be any size—there is no minimum size required—and (2) groups can choose whether or not they want to organize a private cleanup event or open their event to the general public.

Belief Objectives

GCSC established a belief objective that they hoped would reduce the barriers to signing up as a group leader. A central internal barrier preventing group leaders from joining the program is the fear that they lack the knowledge or skills needed to organize a successful cleanup event. Consequently, GCSC employees want prospective group leaders to believe that they will be given all the tools need to easily carry out a cleanup event.

In the hope of encouraging participation across Canada, GCSC employees wanted Canadians to believe that shorelines are anywhere that land meets water, including ponds, swamp land, drainage ditches, rivers, and sewers. One of the biggest challenges in the program has been to convince people who live inland that all the estuaries across Canada needed to be cleaned—not just the coastal areas. GCSC employees also wanted Canadians to believe that all our water is connected. For example, if litter goes into the river in Edmonton, it could flow through the North Saskatchewan River, across the prairies and into the Hudson's Bay, where it would end up in the Arctic Ocean.

Positioning

There are other small-scale cleanup programs, often the initiatives of cities or neighborhoods. However, judging from a quick online search of "Canada cleanup" the Great Canadian Shoreline Cleanup is probably the best known and best recognized. Further, the tie-in with the Ocean Conservancy's International Coastal Cleanup has helped to provide more awareness and status to the effort. As a result, the GCSC is likely positioned as the *market leader* in cleanup efforts across Canada, and other efforts, while they pose some threat, can be considered market followers.

Research

The foundational research for the GCSC and the Vancouver Aquarium's participation in the International effort was primarily the evidence on the amount of pollution and litter in the ocean and evidence of its threat to fish and wildlife. Volunteers are likely primarily affected by the esthetics of litter in their environment and secondarily the damage done to fish and wildlife. The Vancouver Aquarium staff are primarily responsible for knowledge of this damage and therefore could serve as experts for media stories on the damage done to the environment. By serving as a spokesperson, Olympian Andreanne Morin, having swam across the Atlantic Ocean, provided a compelling story of someone who was personally affected by ocean pollution and helped to popularize media stories on the topic.

Strategies

Product Strategies

To attract potential volunteers, GCSC employees designed a comprehensive website where users could reserve a cleanup site that suited their needs. (The GCSC website can be found at http://www.shorelinecleanup.ca/en.) More than 50,000 cleanup locations were presented on a map with a description so users could see where all the potential cleanup sites were located across Canada. The cleanup sites available were approximately one kilometer long. Each site then had varying levels of garbage. When group leaders sign up as a site coordinator, they are asked to estimate their group size and provide an event date, ensuring that (1) the site is not cleaned by another group right before their event date and (2) the site fits the group's needs. GCSC staff also offers one-on-one support to troubleshoot potential problems. For example, some shorelines might not have enough garbage for the size of group in the reservation. Group leaders are encouraged to call GCSC staff to help resolve these types of issues. Some solutions include adding another cleanup site that was nearby or finding another suitable cleanup location.

Augmented Products

When the program first started, GCSC provided a lot of supplies, such as garbage bags, gloves, waiver forms, and data cards, in a cleanup kit in order to attract volunteers. However, as the program grew, they were not able to maintain that. Some kits had enough gloves and bags to accommodate groups of 200 people. The staff realized that the kits were creating more garbage, particularly in terms of packaging, instead of eliminating it. Plus, group leaders were often reporting that they had their own supplies; it was quite easy for volunteers to get garbage bags, and many of them wanted to use their own gloves. As such, the transition away from cleanup kits was a natural progression. Now group leaders are only sent a welcome letter, a waiver form, a data card, and a return envelope. All the other, the paperwork, is made available online. After discontinuing the cleanup kits, GCSC staff has been able to devote more resources toward recruiting volunteers and promoting conservation messages.

However, new group leaders still need guidance on how to do their job effectively. Volunteers therefore have access to everything they need to organize and promote a shoreline cleanup in their area on the website. The website includes an interactive training program, curriculum guides, promotional materials (posters, banners, etc.), donation letters, award announcements, and various supplemental information (e.g., infographics) to reduce the burden of organizing a cleanup. GCSC employees also provide ongoing support and responses for frequently asked questions. For example, staff members know where volunteers can dispose of garbage or acquire supplies in each participating municipality.

GCSC also created an award program to recognize outstanding site coordinators. Various studies have shown that the target of flattery (i.e., the award winner) has better evaluations the flatterer (i.e., the organization) because humans have a basic desire to believe compliments about themselves (Chan & Sengupta, 2010; Gordon, 1996). As such, the Site Coordinator Achievement Award was designed to celebrate the dedication, effort, and commitment of site coordinators by honoring individuals who exemplify the spirit of volunteerism, both in their own community and during the shoreline cleanup. Nominations are made in one of two categories: new site coordinators and returning site coordinators. Award winners are then profiled on the website, given a gift package and certificate, and featured in a special section of final report. Anyone can easily nominate a site coordinator by submitting a form online or by mail.

To further motivate volunteers, GCSC employees organize a celebration event each year. At first, the event was used to kick-off the shoreline cleanup week. It has since evolved into a celebration of cleaner shorelines. The party gives volunteers the opportunity to participate in the larger markets that might not have enough shoreline or site coordinators. In 2013, GCSC held five different celebration events in different markets, attracting almost 1500 event patrons in total.

Pricing Strategies

In order to minimize barriers for participation, people could access GCSC services and participate in the shoreline cleanup at no cost. To reduce the cost of acquiring cleanup supplies, GCSC employees tried to identify common household items that could be used to aid a cleanup instead of requiring volunteers to purchasing their own supplies. They also tried to identify establishments in each municipality that provided the necessary supplies at minimal to no cost for volunteers.

Place Strategies

A key place strategy is to offer groups more options in terms of cleanup dates and sites. Up until about five years ago, GCSC had been organizing shoreline cleanups only in September. However, GCSC employees have started broadening the event dates in order to reach their goal of offering the program all year long. In 2010, they started to encourage groups, particularly schools, Boy Scouts, and Girl Guides, to participate in the spring. The following year, groups in Ontario were encouraged to join the program. In 2014, the GCSC program was open Canada-wide from April 1 until the end of July.

A more recent place strategy is to make cleanup sites more appealing. GCSC employees recognized that a lot of groups, particularly community and corporate groups, wanted to clean up nearby shorelines because they want to give back to their own community. Furthermore, many groups wanted to be responsible for a particular shoreline for the whole year so that they could adopt it and make it their own. Popular cleanup sites were booked so often that volunteer morale began to decline. Specifically, volunteers felt like they weren't making a difference because they did not have very much garbage to pick up. By automating the site reservation system on the website, GCSC could ensure that volunteers would feel like they are helping their community by allowing groups to reserve their desired shorelines at a time when the shoreline needed it most. GCSC recommends a minimum of four weeks between cleanup events.

Promotion Strategies

Promotion strategies focused on getting prospective group leaders to sign up for the program. Given that many prospective volunteers feared that they lacked the resources needed to carry out a successful cleanup event, GCSC primarily employed various direct recruitment strategies. For example, employees often set up booths at local festivals in order to get people interested and answer any questions in person. Through face-to-face interaction, they encouraged event patrons to check out their website and consider signing up as a group leader or as a participant. At these events, patrons were also encouraged to sign up for their newsletter in order to learn more about shoreline cleanups and receive practical conservation tips.

GCSC also appointed a staff member to lead the direct recruitment strategies. This job involved contacting various headquarters, municipalities, schools, and corporate head offices, with the goal of executing a top-down distribution strategy. For example, in order to recruit volunteers from schools, GCSC first offers a K-6 curriculum guide. Employees from both GCSC and WWF reach out to every single school board across Canada on a regular basis, promoting the curriculum and, by extension, the cleanup program. This strategy allows them to explain how easy it is for teachers to organize a cleanup and to engage their students.

To get GCSC's message out to the media, GCSC partners with spokespeople and dive groups to create attention-grabbing media stunts. For instance, they worked with the Ottawa Police Service's Marine, Dive, and Trails Unit to show what kind of garbage ends up the water. Police officers dived into the Ottawa River at the Rideau Canal and pulled out different items that they would find under the water. They pulled out bottles, wrappers, containers, bicycles and even oil tanks. GCSC also partnered with local spokespeople, such as the Olympian Andreanne Morin and other athletes who swam across the Atlantic Ocean.

Message Design

When GCSC transitioned into a national campaign, they had to update their communication materials (Fig. 22.1) to attract volunteers across Canada. In order to meet their belief objective that all the estuaries across Canada needed attention, GCSC had to minimize any affiliations with the western coastal region. The program was promoted as a joint conservation initiative that was separate from Vancouver Aquarium or WWF. Furthermore, the primary messengers to deliver their message became animals and aquatic creatures that all Canadians could relate to, such as ducks and turtles, instead of coastal creatures, such as crabs, sea lions, and whales. Finally, each advertisement included a call to action, which encouraged people to sign up as site coordinator or participant at a shoreline cleanup.

Fig. 22.1 Email footer advertisement. Photograph available at http://shorelinecleanup.ca

Another Important Strategy: Data Collection

Collecting information on the garbage picked up during a cleanup event is a critical aspect of the GCSC. Recognizing and recording litter items helps determine their origins and leads to creating solutions to reduce the amount of garbage that ends up on Canadian shorelines. Once data from each cleanup event was submitted online, GCSC employees summarized the data for each region across the country. The national results were then sent off to the International Coastal Cleanup to be compared globally. The reports were shared with policy makers, businesses, schools/colleges, and the general public to illustrate the problem of aquatic garbage and the importance of a clean environment. From analyzing these data, GCSC has begun to put together a campaign to discourage people from disposable water bottles and grocery bags but instead to carry reusable water bottles and grocery bags.

Program Evaluation

GCSC's primary goal was to increase the number of participants and cleanup sites each year. GCSC keeps track of the number of registrants in the program and at each site as well as an estimated number of people who actually participated in the program. These measures show which areas have the most growth and which areas require special attention. GCSC also keeps track of the number of sites that were cleaned across Canada. In 2013, 1950 sites were cleaned across Canada that covered 3035 km of shoreline. That is approximately the length of the Saint Lawrence River. The data showed that groups were often cleaning up areas greater than their registered one-kilometer site. However, these estimates only include cleanup events affiliated with the shoreline cleanup program. There are other cleanup programs that are not affiliated with GCSC which are not included in these measures. GCSC also keeps track of various secondary measures, such as the number of media hits and positive impressions from the media. They also record activity on their social media channels to ensure that these channels continue to grow and whether people are sharing their information.

Discussion, Lesson Learned, and Future Directions

In 2012, GCSC celebrated its nineteenth anniversary with more than 57,000 volunteers and expanded the cleanup event to include school groups in Ontario and British Columbia. Today, it is recognized as one of the largest direct-action conservation programs and the largest contributor to the International Coastal Cleanup in Canada.

GCSC provides a clear example of the advantage of analyzing the social marketing environment and identifying market benefits and barriers, to minimize threats and capitalize on opportunities. For example, GCSC identified and reduced the threat of the limited timeframe on volunteering opportunities by expanding the program into the spring and summer months. This solution further reduced the threat of competing for popular cleanup sites by making it possible for different groups to clean up the same areas of shoreline throughout the year. The emphasis on research to guide marketing strategies has allowed GCSC identify and test potential future campaigns. For instance, GCSC is currently testing a program to clean up microplastics (plastic beads, fibers, pellets, or other pieces generally less than 5 mm in size) from local shorelines in British Columbia. This test market will let them see whether or not it would be feasible to introduce this campaign at the national level.

Discussion Questions

1. What *exchange* is offered to participants?
2. How could recruitment be improved?
3. In some urban areas, there are more volunteers than shorelines that can be cleaned up. What sorts of opportunities could this provide for expanding the program?
4. How else would you suggest improving this social marketing effort?
5. What would the advantages and disadvantages be of extending the time frame for the program outside of the initial month of September?
6. What forms of evaluation would be helpful? How could these be done? Explain.

References

Brown, J. J., & Reingen, P. H. (1987). Social ties and word-of-mouth referral behavior. *Journal of Consumer Research, 14,* 350–362.

Chan, E., & Sengupta, J. (2010). Insincere flattery actually works: A dual attitudes perspective. *Journal of Marketing Research, 47*(1), 122–133.

Gordon, R. A. (1996). Impact of ingratiation on judgments and evaluations: A meta-analytic investigation. *Journal of Personality and Social Psychology, 71*(1), 54–70.

Granovetter, M. S. (1982). The strength of weak ties. *American Journal of Sociology, 78*(May), 1360–1380.

Rogers, E. M. (1983). *Diffusion of innovations.* New York: Free Press.

A Community-Based Social Marketing Anti-littering Campaign: Be the Street You Want to See

23

Mine Üçok Hughes, Will McConnell and Stephen Groner

Chapter Overview

The "Be the Street You Want to See" (BTS) is a regional litter abatement program developed by the Bay Area Stormwater Management Agencies Association (BASMAA) in California. The program primarily targeted 14–24-year-old San Francisco Bay Area youth who had been identified as a key polluting demographic. The case study in this chapter presents this campaign and how it used the CBSM approach to reduce the problem of littering.

The program, launched in 2012, applied community-based social marketing (CBSM) techniques to a well-defined audience to reduce pollution. It focused heavily on social media and innovative outreach strategies with the end goal of promoting peer-to-peer interactions regarding littering and raising awareness of its environmental impacts. Whenever possible, the program involved the target audience themselves and invited them to recast the messaging in their own words. In this way, the content remained fresh and relatable, and the target audience felt the program was talking "with them," not "at them."

The comparison of pre- and post-campaign survey results shows increased awareness of littering among the target audience, willingness to engage others to promote pro-environmental behaviors, willingness to become environ-

M. Üçok Hughes (✉)
Marketing Department, California State University, Los Angeles, CA, USA
e-mail: Mine.UcokHughes@calstatela.edu

W. McConnell
Interdisciplinary Studies, Woodbury University, Burbank, CA, USA
e-mail: Will.McConnell@woodbury.edu

S. Groner
Stephen Groner Associates, Long Beach, CA, USA
e-mail: SGroner@sga-inc.net

© Springer Nature Switzerland AG 2019
D. Z. Basil et al. (eds.), *Social Marketing in Action*,
Springer Texts in Business and Economics,
https://doi.org/10.1007/978-3-030-13020-6_23

mental stewards, and to pick up the litter of others. However, demonstrating behavior change through clear metrics remains a challenge for this approach.

Campaign Background

Litter has long been recognized as a national problem. "Litter clean-up costs the US more than $11.5 billion each year, with businesses paying $9.1 billion"; local and state governments, schools, and other organizations combined contribute the remaining cost (Keep America Beautiful, 2010). Litter also has increasing environmental consequences. Litter moved into gutters, lawns, and landscape areas by wind, traffic, and animals; litter gathered near storm drains; litter swept into local waterways—all non-point sources of pollution which cause serious environmental contamination. The problem of non-point sources of pollution is particularly acute in high-density habitation areas such as San Francisco—exacerbated by the sizable network of water flows in the San Francisco Bay area. A recent study by BASMAA has found that "Bay Area residents pollute San Francisco Bay every year with enough trash to fill 100,000 kitchen garbage bags" (Rogers, 2012).

Geoff Brosseau, executive director of BASMAA, noted that trash "is 100 percent preventable [...] If we can get people to modify their behavior, we'll make huge gains" (Rogers, 2012). To eliminate multiple sources of pollution, the city needed ambitious, outcomes-driven approaches to solving a wide range of issues—including messaging that contributes to changing from current to more sustainable forms of behavior. But San Francisco administrators faced a daunting problem: *How* to change human behavior that is a leading cause and contributor to the pollution in the San Francisco Bay area?

Studies show that information-based campaigns or approaches that promote economic self-interest do not foster sustainable behavior change in the long run (Costanzo, Archer, Aronson, & Pettigrew, 1986; McKenzie-Mohr & Smith, 1999). CBSM is proposed as an attractive alternative to these models (McKenzie-Mohr & Smith, 1999). CBSM aims at removing community-level barriers to an activity while enhancing that activity's benefits (McKenzie-Mohr, 1999).

SWOT Analysis (Strengths, Weaknesses, Opportunities, Threats)

Strengths

The campaign used CBSM as its central approach rather than a top-down, information-based one. The target audience took part in the design and dissemination of the message through various social media platforms. The social media campaign that was at the core of the program had high levels of engagement from the target community (see Appendix 2). It was effective in changing attitudes towards social norms about littering.

Weaknesses

It is challenging to affect behavior change in a short period of time. Longitudinal research is necessary to measure the long-term effects of this campaign. Post-campaign data were collected among a small group of self-selected participants. The results are more indicative of change in social norms than the present measurable results of actual behavior change in the long run.

Opportunities

The campaign relied heavily on social media, which still remains popular among the target audience. As new social media platforms develop and become popular among young audiences, new opportunities arise. Litter continues to be an environmental problem that needs to be tackled. As environmental issues are taking more center stage of news and political debates around the world, more attention to litter pollution (e.g., The Great Pacific Garbage Patch) is given by, and available to, larger audiences.

Threats

The novelty of campaigns that require audience participation can eventually wear off; audiences start losing interest in the topic, or their excitement diminishes. Social media platforms keep losing popularity among target audiences. The campaign needs to be updated regularly to keep it relevant for the target audience or new target audiences.

Target Audience

Research suggests younger people litter more (Schultz & Stein, 2009). Stephen Groner Associates, Inc.'s (SGA) 2009 KLAB Youth Litter Study identified youth profiles and the beliefs, motivations, and barriers associated with these profiles. The statistical work helped identify five important market segments. The goal was to provide a starting point for clustering the demographic and motivational bases associated with littering behavior among adolescents and young adults, with an eye toward designing effective strategies for consistent behavior change, ultimately, to reduce littering behaviors in the target audience.

The five subgroups comprising the larger youth population are "Apathetics," "Digitally Disengaged," "Acceptance Seekers," "New Adults," and "Green Crusaders" (see Fig. 23.1 for further information). As a result of this more nuanced categorizing of subpopulations, this campaign did not seek to engage the extremely hard-to-reach groups directly and instead focused energies on the other three subpopulations most likely to change. Therefore, the target populations for this campaign included the "Green Crusaders," "New Adults," and "Acceptance Seekers." Collectively, these three groups account for 56% of the target population and became a catalyst for reaching the other two. Identifying these target populations and their profiles was a key step in moving towards tangible behavior change.

"Green Crusaders," who were found across all age groups, were least likely to litter, they felt more guilty when they did, and they were less influenced by peers. They were also found to be less likely to smoke cigarettes, to watch less TV, to spend more time volunteering, less time in organized sports, and less time playing video games. They were also generally knowledgeable about what happens to litter on the ground. They widely perceived fewer reasons for not properly disposing of litter, and they were willing to overcome greater barriers to avoid littering. They were more likely to litter if an item being discarded is biodegradable.

"New Adults," whose average age was 22, were typically working and not attending school. They had a higher probability of smoking, spent fewer hours in sports, watching TV, and playing video games. They were likely to litter when no trash cans were nearby.

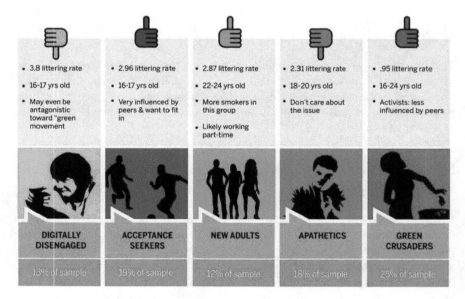

Fig. 23.1 Target market segments

Finally, "Acceptance Seekers," whose average age was 18 or younger, were typically in high school, cared about their academic performance, and were involved in sports and other organized activities. They were less likely to smoke and more likely to volunteer. They were less knowledgeable about what happens to litter on the ground and were likely to litter when there was already trash on the ground.

This strategy of approaching the definition of "audience"—one that will most likely not litter first hence easier to influence—resembles the Diffusion of Innovations Theory (Rogers, 2003). Rogers argues that innovation is communicated through certain channels over time among the members of a social system and different types of adopters accept an innovation at different points in time (Lee & Kotler, 2016). In that sense, the Green Crusaders, New Adults, and Acceptance Seekers could be likened to Innovators, Early Adopters, and Early Majority, while Apathetics and Digitally Disengaged are like the Late Majority and Laggards.

The "thumbs up" symbol represents audience subgroups that the campaign focused on reaching directly, while the "thumbs down" symbol represents audience groups that the program did not specifically reach out to but were affected through indirect interaction with the target audience groups.

Littering rates at the top of each column are based on a 10-point system calculated by three multiple regression analyses:

a. willingness to litter by various predictor variables (i.e., age, guilt about littering, concern about environmental problems),
b. willingness to litter by barrier and motivator variables (i.e., mood, being in a hurry, no trash can nearby),
c. willingness to litter and by hours of activity variables (i.e., watching TV, working).

Campaign Objectives

The overarching goal of the campaign was to develop a strategy to reduce littering via littering behavior change in its target audience. Thus, the campaign focused on delivering a set of targeted messages that not only increased the audience's awareness of trash as a pollutant but also actually reduced the audience's littering frequency. The campaign sought to walk the target audience up the path to behavior change by first raising awareness through a general advertising campaign, then producing engagement through various social media marketing strategies, and finally changing behaviors by delivering consistent and actionable messages.

Given that in the BASMAA study, 97% of respondents reported littering was a problem, the logical conclusion is that littering is already perceived to be a problem by the vast majority of the general public (Astone, 2007). This information provides a meaningful directive for developing potential messaging. The goal then should not be to convince the target audience that littering is a problem; rather, the messaging should impart that littering is a *more important and solvable* problem than this audience currently often perceived.

Positioning

"BTS" was carefully branded to connect with its target audience. The brand was developed to be youthful, vibrant, and engaged. The messaging encouraged youths to take ownership of the state of their community and actively shape their environment. In this campaign, the "street" was a reflection, for better or worse, of the youth who use it. Rather than passing the blame on to peers, adults, or others, BTS asked that individuals take action to clean up and invigorate their surroundings. The program was positioned as "a campaign by the people for the people." Whenever possible, the program involved the target audience in the campaign itself and invited individuals to recast the messaging of the campaign in their own words. The target audience felt the program was talking "with them," not "at them."

Marketing Strategy

This section provides a brief overview of the marketing strategy. (More detailed information is provided in the following section titled "Community-Based Social Marketing Campaign.")

Product

The goal of the anti-litter campaign was to reduce littering, promote peer-to-peer interaction regarding littering, and raise awareness of pollution related to the audience found to be most often littering, namely 14–24-year-olds. The benefit that the audience would gain was a clean environment, freedom from litter, and an element of pride in the community. By exploring and engaging problems and solutions to community and environmental issues, street-by-street, participants would be rewarded with the pride, and the fun, of having created the kind of "street" they have always wanted to live on.

Price

The cost of participating in the campaign and a key step in building behavior change is the time required for participants to create the videos and images for the video and meme contests. In the long run, the main cost is disposing of litter properly.

Place

The campaign's geographic location was the San Francisco Bay Area. The campaign took place mostly online at various social media platforms like Facebook, Instagram, and YouTube.

Promotion

The litter abatement program developed by the Bay Area Stormwater Management Agencies Association in California first attracted participants through Facebook ads. It relied heavily on social media, some being more successful than others. Initially, a web site was created, which later was replaced by the campaign's Facebook page. A YouTube video contest and Instagram meme contest were also created. See Appendix 2 for a complete list of promotional elements.

Community-Based Social Marketing Campaign

BTS was built upon the principles of CBSM. CBSM realizes that awareness of an issue is often not sufficient to initiate behavior change and more is required than simply providing people with information. CBSM is a framework that is specifically tailored to help researchers identify how to isolate attitudes and behaviors and to focus a campaign's strategies on changing behaviors. CBSM is positioned both as a contestation of information-based campaigns, which often drive the wider social marketing mix of strategies, and as an antidote to the assumption that increased knowledge and economically motivated forms of self-interest can, or often do, drive changes in behavior. McKenzie-Mohr (1999) identifies the central insight of the approach: "a variety of barriers can deter individuals from engaging" in behavior desired by society (and/or social marketers). A strategy that incorporates effective behavior modification will attempt to use specific tools to uncover, or discover, those barriers at the level of community-based field research. The approach then uses community-based feedback to create targeted outreach tactics and develop key messages likely to reach a specific, well-defined audience; that is, the audience itself participates in answering questions of how to overcome the barriers identified in the research process. Identifying an audience's barriers and motivators in encouraging certain types of behaviors is central to CBSM approaches.

Another hallmark of the CBSM is the introduction of multiple perspectives and methodologies from social psychology, behavioral theory, economics, and other social science-based research approaches. McKenzie-Mohr (2011) provides a 5-step guide for CBSM that includes "carefully selecting the behavior to be promoted; identifying the barriers and benefits associated with the selected behavior; designing a strategy that utilizes behavior change tools to address these barriers and benefits; piloting the strategy with a small segment of a community; and finally; evaluating the impact of the program once it has been implemented broadly" (p. 8).

Step 1: Selecting Behaviors

The first step starts with collecting information to determine which sector(s) merit targeting as well as identifying barriers and motivators (McKenzie-Mohr, 2011). The program began with an exhaustive study and literature review designed to discover who was littering and why they were doing it. Studies indicate that littering is both an individual and community-environment behavior (Schultz & Stein, 2009). At the individual level, age is predictive of littering; at the contextual level, perceived cleanliness of the community environment is a major factor in individuals' awareness of their own littering behaviors.

Across all age groups, the most powerful factor in understanding littering behaviors is the influence of perceived social norms—what is perceived as the "right" thing to do based on social norms, or "what everyone else is doing" (Schultz & Stein, 2009). Part of the difficulty of disaggregating contributing factors to individual behaviors is that a variety of perceptual and cognitive mechanisms contribute to behavior. One such mechanism is the perception of a social norm through the impact of human behavior on the environment in which individuals most often find themselves. For example, Keizer, Lindenberg, and Steg (2008) concluded that the very presence of disorderly items in an environment, whether or not they are examples of outright littering, implies that others are engaging in disorderly behavior, thus augmenting the likelihood of others littering. On the other hand, Bator (1997) found that social disapproval is a strong motivator of individuals' decisions not to litter, particularly when a visual cue in the environment is repeated in a public messaging campaign. Bator's findings are echoed in the 2007 BASMAA Public Opinion Survey, where 92% of those surveyed who do not litter cite the belief that littering is morally and socially wrong as their primary reason not to litter (Astone, 2007).

Step 2: Identifying Barriers and Benefits

The campaign began in spring 2012, with a short, pre-campaign online survey which assessed littering behavior, contextual factors related to littering, peer-to-peer interactions about littering, and willingness to participate in varied, proposed campaign activities. A total of 353 individuals out of the initial 416 who began the survey were eligible for inclusion in the sample population based on age (14–24 years) and residence (provided zip code within the BASMAA region). Recruitment for the survey included outreach to Bay Area high schools and colleges, and placement of an ad on the social networking website Facebook. The sample was 60% female, had a mean age of 17 years, and almost all respondents were in high school. The 5-min survey was available 24 h per day, 7 days per week, from January through March 2012. Some of the specific questions the survey included were as follows: what type of litter was most commonly and least commonly littered?; in what contexts were respondents relatively more likely to litter?; to what extent were respondents willing to participate in campaign activities?; and, what did participants perceive as barriers to avoiding littering?

Context, or one's social and physical environment, is one of the most significant factors in driving *and* curtailing littering behaviors. While general social and physical context remains a strong factor in CBSM approaches, often less visible factors such as individual preferences play a much larger role in youth littering behaviors. Precedents set by a friend or known peer's behavior may be indicative of an especially salient social norm (SGA, 2009). In SGA's youth littering study for KLAB, survey results revealed that the most impactful, non-situational factor in determining individuals' likelihood of littering was the littering habits of their friends. Moreover, in this demographic, friends' littering behaviors were found to be twice as impactful as the littering habits of their parents (Appendix 1).

In leveraging this discovery, a distinction should be made between a social norm and "peer pressure." In the 2007 BASMAA Public Opinion Survey, the least-cited cause for appropriate trash disposal behavior was "peer pressure" (Astone, 2007). The principal difference between peer pressure and perceived social norms is the concerted participation of separate parties in the attempt to influence certain behaviors—that is, peer pressure is defined as an individual or group of individuals that are actively trying to influence their peer's behaviors. Social norms are defined as those effects stemming from the perceived behavior of others by the individual; thus, social norms theory (Berkowitz, 2005) "describes situations in which individuals incorrectly perceive the attitudes and/or behaviors of peers and other community members to be different from their own, when in fact, they are not" (p. 193). It is important to make this distinction when identifying the social norms acting on the target population; equally important is understanding the difference to mobilize those norms to activate the desired behavior change.

Step 3: Developing Strategies

The overarching goal of the marketing campaign strategy was to encourage the target population to curb and eventually eliminate their littering behaviors. In promoting this behavior change, the campaign applied a series of strategies to encourage the viral spread of anti-littering messages through peer-to-peer networks of communication. This grassroots approach sought to incite action among the target youth audience, allowing for engagement and empowerment in the peer-to-peer distribution of campaign messages. By promoting these specific, action-oriented messages, the campaign was better equipped to mold the behaviors of the target population by attempting to influence the social norm.

Program leaders focused heavily on social media in an effort to promote peer-to-peer interactions to reduce littering and raise awareness of the link between the target population's behavior and the environmental impacts of those behaviors. The program began with raising awareness of the newly launched, youth-focused campaign. Targeted advertising via Facebook encouraged 14–24-year-old viewers to visit a website or enter a meme and/or short video contest. The ultimate goal of the advertising campaign was to involve this group in the program, either by joining a Facebook page, entering a contest, or contributing posts or photographs. Connecting with this target population through social media would allow marketers to continue engaging the participants throughout the life of the campaign.

The audience knew that littering was/is inappropriate behavior. This finding in the pre-campaign phase of the initiative provided a key insight into how to structure the campaign. Since the campaign goal was to change behavior, messaging tactics aimed at achieving a shift in attitudes about littering, in general, were avoided. Instead, the campaign strategy focused on the link between social mores and inclusivity: A grounding assumption was that any young adult expressing a lack of ownership of their environment was more likely to litter; and any communication perceived to be coming from the government, whether local or federal, would be met with suspicion. Surveys showed that the target audience would be disengaged by direct connections with government agencies; therefore, the brand created needed to provide programmatic credibility and consistency to this specific audience. BTS did this by avoiding direct "messaging" between the government and its target audience, and instead, encouraged members of the target group to create enough participatory messaging on their own to suggest that "not littering" was the norm among the target population.

The pre-campaign research was clear: The target population was likely to respond only to materials and communication coming from other teenagers and young adults. The communication strategy, then, was twofold: First, the tone of the entire campaign had to feel like it belonged to someone born during the Clinton administration; and second, the initiative had to mobilize crowdsourcing, a distinct interweaving of social media communication and activity organization, among the majority of members in the target audience.

Step 4: Piloting

A six-month-long pilot social media campaign using Facebook was conducted prior to the launch of the actual campaign. The main reason for conducting the pilot on social media was that these forms of communication and interaction could provide a solid base for data and a secure medium for gaining feedback through analytics. Messaging, tone, and motivators were tested by putting out different posts and tactics at events. Social media responses were tracked to gage engagement.

Step 5: Broad-Scale Implementation and Evaluation

BTS engaged with the target population primarily through social media to deliver inspirational and educational content. This content included a YouTube video contest with a live stream award show, interactive photo booths, a meme contest, and the development of a mobile app that gamified environmental awareness and sent users into the streets to complete challenges, win points, and get prizes.

The meme and video contests attracted the audience and encouraged individuals to develop materials that would be used in the advertisements. Memes are a critical means of communication for today's digital youth. Consisting of a picture and a caption (generally sarcastic in nature), memes are an easily shared, often socially critical material that becomes viral through social media. The audience was asked to make memes (Fig. 23.2) which would be used as advertising.

As with the meme contest, the audience was asked to produce 15–20 s videos as entries; perhaps, more importantly, friends of the audience were also asked to produce content—but by word-of-mouth, in person, and through social media. Winning entries would be used as paid advertising, which later appeared on Pandora, Spotify, and YouTube. Fifty-two entries were received, representing active participation from more than 700 kids and young adults. More than 5000 unique

Fig. 23.2 Sample meme

votes for best video and more than 40,000 YouTube views were received. All fifty-two can be seen on the BTS YouTube page (https://www.youtube.com/user/BetheStreet/videos).

The campaign developers were able to honor their voices and learn from their messages, while fostering actual behavior change. Thus, the campaign designed messaging not from a top-down, authoritarian position, but from networking or organic, evolutionary metaphor of message and behavior adoption and transmission. Both the meme and video contests drew participants through active, direct engagement in the production of positive messaging, rather than direct messaging that provided information or chided current behaviors by deploying a negative, declarative style for either denotative or connotative messaging among the target population.

At this point, the messaging in the meme and video contests turned into demonstrated behavior adoption; thus, each step of the campaign was an attempt to engage target populations not only at the level of ideas or conceptual reframing, but also at the level of encouraging increased participation in actual behavior change. This design in the campaign reflects the CBSM credo of creating and measuring behavior change itself—not merely exposure to messaging, or adoption of ideas devoid of behavior that could accompany "new thinking."

Program Evaluation

The data collected in the pre-campaign surveying served as a baseline against which follow-up survey data could be measured to help determine the overall impact of the BTS program. A follow-up survey was conducted during the summer of 2014 through Facebook and through traditional intercept outreach. The survey was designed to mirror the baseline survey to ensure data comparability. Only respondents who fit the target demographic of the program were included in the analysis. A total of 60 responses which fit these criteria were collected. Thus, this response rate is an issue in substantiating claims of the campaign's efficacy in changing behaviors in its target population.

> **Key Findings of Post-Campaign Survey**
> **Exposed are nearly 3X as likely to pick up litter.** 90% of exposed respondents reported that they were "very likely" or "likely" to pick up someone else's litter, while only 38% of unexposed respondents reported the same.
>
> **Exposed are nearly 2X as likely to disapprove of friends littering.** 94% of exposed respondents reported they "strongly disapprove" or "disapprove" of their friends littering, while only 52% of unexposed reported the same.

Exposed are nearly 1.5X as likely to voice that disapproval. 70% of exposed respondents reported that they were "very likely" or "likely" to voice disapproval when their friends litter, while only 48% of unexposed respondents reported the same.

Exposed are more than 2X as likely to disapprove of their own littering. 58% of exposed respondents reported the "strongly disapprove" or "disapprove" of their own behaviors when they have littered in the past, while only 29% of unexposed reported the same.

Unexposed are nearly 2X as likely to litter in the future. 19% of unexposed respondents reported that they were "very likely," "likely," or "somewhat likely" to litter in the next month, while only 10% of exposed respondents reported the same.

Unexposed litter more than 2X as often. 8% of unexposed respondents reported littering at least a few times a week, while only 4% of exposed respondents reported the same.

"Baseline" refers to the data collected in 2012 prior to the start of the BTS program. "Exposed" refers to respondents captured in the 2014 follow-up survey who reported being aware of the BTS program. "Unexposed" refers to respondents captured in the follow-up survey who reported being unfamiliar with the BTS program. The difference between unexposed and exposed demonstrates the impact of the program.

In addition to the statistical differences demonstrated in the box above, the BTS program had significant levels of engagement (Appendix 2). Thanks to content rooted in a somewhat sardonic teen style, with pop culture references or anchors for the campaign, and a focus on community empowerment, BTS's Facebook and Instagram pages became the most trafficked, most active social media outlets in the history of California municipal efforts at addressing the stormwater/pollution prevention efforts—more than 5500 fans and 11,000 interactions ("Likes," comments, and shares) in a period of about two years.

The campaign was deemed highly successful by its sponsor, BASMAA, in reaching its goal of reducing littering behaviors in the San Francisco Bay area and won the "Outstanding Regional Stormwater News, Information, Outreach and Media Award" given by The California Stormwater Quality Association (CASQA), which found it to be "extraordinary in both its levels of engagement and the innovative use of social media and breadth of technology used to cultivate a dedicated user base" (CWEA, 2014).

Discussion and Lessons Learned

The metrics by which the program has been evaluated suggest that, given youth's involvement in brand development, as well as their interest in social causes (Furlow, 2011), marketers could use multiple characteristics of the case study presented here in the design and implementation of environmental sustainability strategies as well as campaigns promoting the public good. In order to maximize success in social marketing campaigns, researchers and marketers should seek target communities to involve directly in both the design and implementation of a behavior change program. Such a tactic not only increases the community's ownership over the campaign's outcome but also a shared commitment to the cause driving the need for behavior change.

It should be noted that numbers show the social norm, not the behavior change. Demonstrating behavior change remains a challenge. The target audience was eager and willing to engage on social media, lend their name and voice to the movement, and click buttons. They were reluctant, however, to take the very substantial next step and document themselves undertaking the desired behavior. During community events where the audience interacted with staff, they were less reluctant to take that additional step and document their actions. The fact that this part of the campaign was not successful does not suggest that a causal connection can be made between "documenting new behaviors" and experiencing a behavior change. To address closing the loop on the link between a study of this nature and the behavior change it produces, future campaigns designed along CBSM principles should not seek to achieve documented behavior change through social media platforms. Rather, additional studies should consider what types of behavior changes can reasonably be expected to create success in soliciting evidence of a campaign's success. Community events should be utilized to achieve documented behavior changes.

As Schuster, Kubacki, and Rundle-Thiele (2016) note, "increasing the visibility of the [targeted] behavior in the community ensures that the social norms of an appropriate reference group, the community in which the target audience resides," can be among the most significant of actions promoted (p. 6). The BTS follow-up survey indicates that the *visibility* of behaviors, desirable and undesirable, was pronounced and was perhaps the most successful component of the campaign; however, the BTS campaign's steps do not allow for a clear demarcation between shifts in attitudes and shifts in (observed) behaviors. Accurately measured differences in both attitude and behavior remained difficult to isolate in the campaign, and more complex designs of steps 4 and 5 in the CBSM model are necessary. This conundrum, closing the gap between "attitudes" and "behaviors," is the key to environmental sustainability—arguably the most complex set of phenomena targeted for behavior change. The metric for establishing a causal link between the campaign and result in the community is difficult to establish due in part to the complexity of understanding distinctions between the individual and the larger social and physical environment. Simply put, these are difficult to isolate from one another. Social marketing researchers must take this reality into account in order to develop more effective strategies.

One significant limitation of the BTS campaign is, simply, that littering behaviors often appear to be "upstream"—that is, behaviors that surface as littering at point-of-origin often have their origins in assumptions about the limitlessness of earth's processes. These attitudinal adhesions are difficult to isolate in social science research paradigms and account for the difficulty of using campaigns limited to providing "information" to target audiences. As Lynes, Whitney, and Murray (2014) observe, the application of social marketing principles—even when understood through the CBSM lens—"is relatively new" (p. 112). Bates (2010) expresses a more pointed critique, as well as articulates a limitation that is embedded in the BTS approach: He notes the "paucity of empirical studies that examine social marketing campaigns for sustainability and inconsistencies in program design and implementation that inhibit empirical evaluation" (Bates, 2010). For example, in the summer of 2014, there was only one post-campaign survey to document the impact of the campaign on the target audience's behavior; similarly, this part of the campaign reached a very small audience—sixty direct participants—a response rate that contributes little to the call to end the "paucity" of empirically based studies. In part, this limitation of the BTS campaign illustrates the difficulty of integrated approaches to step five of CBSM approaches when researchers attempt to study the efficacy of changing behavior in environmental sustainability contexts. Although the campaign attempted to measure changes in behavior at different stages of the implementation phase, and thereby eliminated some strategies to focus on others (i.e., elimination of the development of a website and a re-focusing of the campaign on Facebook), the small response rate to the follow-up survey suggests empirically based decision-making presented problems for the campaign at varying stages in its implementation. The two-year cycle of feedback begs the question: How much time passes before behaviors can be "proven" to have changed in the long-term?

Lynes et al. (2014) have also recognized that the "application of social marketing models in environmental sustainability is still in its infancy in comparison to other contexts such as public health and safety" (p. 130). Thus, campaigns that target the adoption of sustainable behaviors (and the reduction or elimination of un-sustainable behaviors and attitudes) are hampered by both the complexity of the links between wider social contexts beyond individuals' control and the relative lack of similar campaigns upon which to build.

Another limitation of the 2014 follow-up survey: Respondents self-reported the changes they themselves were observing in both their attitudes and behaviors; however, the veracity of self-reporting on attitudinal changes is difficult to isolate in respondents' answers, in part due to the wording of questions in the survey instrument. The prevalence of single-method data collection (predominantly self-reported surveys) and lack of multiple method formative research studies in social marketing has been a noted issue (Carins et al., 2016). While "using a single method during formative research […], or combining methods that emerge from a single perspective […], may provide valuable insights *from an audience's perspective*, [it] may not provide the required depth of understanding needed to create strategies that initiate and foster sustainable behavior change" (Carins et al., 2016, p. 1084).

Conclusion

This case study has presented a campaign that would allow marketers to envision campaigns that can take advantage of regional social norm differences. As a regional outreach program, the target audience was of a sufficient size that critical mass of participants could be achieved. Through social media, the "likes" of thousands of similarly situated youth vouched for the program and helped it spread. Further studies can and should address the issue of measuring behavior change, but despite the limitations in measurable, quantifiable results in the main goal of the campaign, the results of this ground-breaking effort suggest a powerful approach for engaging not simply a target population's ideas of itself and its surroundings, but also its behaviors for producing, and changing, that environment.

Discussion Questions

1. Find other anti-littering campaigns. Analyze what type of approach they use. Do they use an informational approach to educate people? Do they use fun approach to entertain to change behavior? In your opinion, which approach is more effective? Why?
2. It has been several years since the BTS campaign was launched. It relied primarily on Facebook and YouTube to reach to its target audience of Gen Y. Evaluate how effective these social media platforms would be in today's digital environment. Suggest other apps for today's Gen Y and Gen Z who were born between 1995 and 2012.
3. One of the challenges social marketing campaigns face is the sustainability of the campaigns in the long-run. Many campaigns are abandoned after a period of time or become ineffective. What can the BTS campaign do to keep the campaign fresh?
4. How is an advertisement for anti-littering different from a community-based social marketing campaign like Be the Street? An example of an anti-littering ad campaign is by Johannesburg Zoo by Y&R from 2011 with the slogan "Animals Can't Be Recycled. Please Don't Litter."
5. If you were given the task to design an anti-littering campaign in your region similar to the BTS program, how would you go about creating and implementing the campaign? Who would be the target audience? What strategies would you use?

6. Think of other social issues that can be addressed by community-based social marketing strategies. Create a strategy outline. Who would be the target audience? What strategies would you choose?
7. Think of other social issues that can use social media campaigns (e.g., video and meme contests) applied in the BTS program. Give suggestions for how they can be implemented.

Appendix 1: Review of Barriers, Motivators, and Marketing Tactics

Identifying and overcoming barriers	
Barrier	How to overcome
Social norms that encourage littering such as: *Context:* A littered/disorderly environment prompts others to litter *Peers:* Littering friends increase the likelihood of littering	Reframe the norm so that it is more aligned with the desired behavior utilize the norm of social disapproval, but do not vilify the offenders
FORGETFULNESS: Individuals may engage in passive littering as opposed to active littering; i.e., littering is not the intention; rather the individual forgets to dispose of an item	PROMPTS: Utilize visual cues near the trash receptacle to encourage individuals to remember to dispose of waste
Lack of proper repositories	Place additional repositories or utilize signs to clearly indicate repository locations
Lack of knowledge about litter: *Definition* (i.e., plastics are perceived as litter, but organics may not be) *Fate* (environmental/social consequences)	Identify the most prevalent misconceptions with regard to litter's definition or fate and target messages to address these specific information gaps
Emotional states: Bad mood, laziness, hurried. These emotional states can make people more prone to littering	Elevate motivators to demonstrate that litter prevention is more important than fleeting emotional states
The teenage brain is still under construction	Capitalize on the extremes of teenage behavior (i.e., idealism) to create social change
Age greatly influences littering behaviors, even within the small bracket of the target age group	Make littering unappealing by demonstrating that littering is something that "KIDS" do
Identifying and utilizing motivators	
Motivator	How to utilize
Social norms that encourage litter prevention	Align social norms with litter prevention behaviors (i.e., show responsible behavior as the norm and encourage others to follow suit)

(continued)

Concern for the environment among certain groups within the target audience	Demonstrate through messaging that litter prevention protects the environmental integrity
OWNERSHIP: desire to be involved and engaged among certain groups	Involve the target audience into program design and/or implementation
The desired behavior resonates with the underlying cultural values of the audience	Incorporate culture-specific messaging in the strategic direction of the campaign
The desired behavior is perceived as being "COOL"	Allow the campaign to be "owned" by the target audience and encourage the constant change and evolution of the message and/or brand
The desired behavior is perceived as being "FUN"	Include playful, interactive elements
How to get messages across	
Use ONLINE PLATFORMS as a central mechanism to message distribution	
SOCIAL NETWORKING, ON- AND OFF-LINE: Empower the audience to become a vehicle of communication through peer-to-peer messaging via social networking sites and word of mouth	
GET MOVING, GO MOBILE: Utilize text messaging and mobile advertising to reach the target audience	

Appendix 2: Promotional Tools Evaluation Outcomes

Promotional element	Evaluation outcomes
Facebook	More than 11,000 engagements including 5475 "likes" (July 2014). In two years since its creation, the BTS page has achieved 150% the "likes" of the similarly situated San Francisco Environment Facebook page. The Facebook engagement far exceeded the initial goals of the campaign, and this success was due in large part to using social media to reach the intended audience (https://www.facebook.com/BetheSt/)
Meme contest	The program initiated a meme contest in early 2014 that took place on Facebook. The meme contest asked the target audience to develop visual jokes or memes with pro-environmental messaging. A total of 104 user memes (from a goal of 100) were created and entered into a contest. More than 683 votes were cast and thousands of views and referrals were driven to the Facebook page as users promoted their memes to their friends and social networks
Instagram	This part of the campaign attracted more than 1626 interactions with fans and 113 followers across 185 posts. Of all of the outreach channels used, Instagram proved the most successful in encouraging peer-to-peer conversations. While many Facebook posts received comments, Instagram was the channel most likely to develop long, sustained conversations between fans

(continued)

(continued)

Promotional element	Evaluation outcomes
YouTube	As with the meme contest, the audience (and more importantly, the audience's friends) was asked to produce 15–20 s videos as entries. A total of 56 videos published on the BTS YouTube channel including 52 fan-submitted videos for the anti-litter video contest. This competition received more than 4800 votes cast and had 593 unique views of the 25-min awards show. At the conclusion of the video competition, the channel had received a total of nearly 16,000 views. Since then, total views on the channel have risen to more than 42,000, a 260% increase (July 2014). This element of the campaign suggests that the "participatory messaging" of the campaign will be operable long after the campaign organizers cease to design and initiate new activities. All 52 can be seen on the BTS YouTube page (https://www.youtube.com/user/BetheStreet/videos)
Mobile app	The app did not achieve the anticipated number of active players upon its launch. This shortfall is attributed to the development of the app taking longer than projected, leaving an insufficient amount of time for promotion. Here, too, the organizers of the campaign followed CBSM techniques: *be flexible in your approaches!*
Photo booths	The program developed a mobile photo booth that could be relocated across community events and allow fans to take pictures to be uploaded to varied social media outlets. For example, more than 750 photographs were taken and shared on Facebook. The photographs reinforced the social norm aspect of the campaign and literally "put a face to the campaign"
Website	The website has received more than 40,000 page views despite not being a key platform for communication with the target audience (i.e., traffic was driven predominantly to Facebook and Instagram) (website removed few years after the campaign due to lack of funds but Facebook page remains)

References

Astone. (2007). *BASMAA public opinion survey.*

Bator, R. J. (1997). *Effective public service announcements: Linking social norms to visual memory cues.* UMI.

Bates, C. (2010). Use of social marketing concepts to evaluate ocean sustainability campaigns. *Social Marketing Quarterly, 16,* 71–96.

Berkowitz, A. D. (2005). An overview of the social norms approach. In L. C. Lederman & L. P. Stewart (Eds.), *Changing the culture of college drinking: A socially situated health communication campaign* (pp. 193–215). Cresskill, NJ: Hampton Press.

Carins, J. E., Rundle-Thiele, S. R., & Fidock, J. J. T. (2016). Seeing through a Glass Onion: broadening and deepening formative research in social marketing through a mixed methods approach. *Journal of Marketing Management, 32*(11–12), 1083–1102.

Costanzo, M., Archer, D., Aronson, E., & Pettigrew, T. (1986). Energy conservation behavior: The difficult path from information to action. *American Psychologist, 41,* 521–528.

CWEA. (2014). *CASQA recognizes excellence in stormwater quality management.* Retrieved from http://cweawaternews.org/casqa-recognizes-excellence-in-stormwater-quality-management.

Furlow, N. E. (2011). Find us on Facebook: How cause marketing has embraced social media. *Journal of Marketing Development and Competitiveness, 5,* 61–64.

Keep America Beautiful. (2010). *Litter in America. Results from the nation's largest litter study.* Retrieved from http://www.kab.org/site/DocServer/LitterFactSheet_LITTER.pdf?docID=5184.

Keizer, K., Lindenberg, S., & Steg, L. (2008). The spreading of disorder. *Science, 322,* 1681–1685.

Lee, N. R., & Kotler, P. (2016). *Social marketing: Changing behaviors for good.* Thousand Oaks, CA: Sage.

Lynes, J., Whitney, S., & Murray, D. (2014). Developing benchmark criteria for assessing community-based social marketing programs: A look into Jack Johnson's "All at Once" campaign. *Journal of Social Marketing, 4,* 111–132.

McKenzie-Mohr, D. (1999). *Quick reference: Community-based social marketing.* Retrieved from http://www.rmportal.net/library/content/tools/biodiversity-conservation-tools/putting-conservation-in-context-cd/communication-and-education-approaches-resourses/Quick-Reference-Community-based-Social-Marketing/view.

McKenzie-Mohr, D. (2011). *Fostering sustainable behavior: An introduction to community-based social marketing.* Canada: New Society Publishers.

McKenzie-Mohr, D., & Smith, W. (1999). *Fostering sustainable behavior: An introduction to community-based social marketing.* Gabriola Island, British Columbia, Canada: New Society. Retrieved from http://www.cbsm.com/pages/guide/preface/.

Rogers, E. (2003). *Diffusion of innovations.* New York: Free Press.

Rogers, P. (2012). San Francisco Bay: A garbage can for 7 million people. *Mercury News.* San Jose. Retrieved from http://www.mercurynews.com/ci_19972044.

Schultz, P. W., & Stein, S. R. (2009). *Executive summary: Litter in America: National findings and recommendations.* Retrieved from http://www.kab.org/site/DocServer/Executive_Summary_-_FINAL.pdf?docID=4601.

Schuster, L., Kubacki, K., & Rundle-Thiele, S. (2016). Community-based social marketing: Effects on social norms. *Journal of Social Marketing, 6,* 193–210.

S. Groner Associates, Inc. (SGA). (2009). *Littering and the iGeneration.* Keep Los Angeles Beautiful.

The Coulee Clean-Up: A Social Marketing Program for Litter Pickup in Lethbridge, Canada

24

Katherine C. Lafreniere and Debra Z. Basil

Chapter Overview

This case from Lethbridge, Alberta, Canada, details a social marketing program called *The Coulee Clean-Up*, initiated by the Helen Schuler Nature Centre (HSNC) to encourage litter clean-up and an anti-littering orientation. The program encourages participation in an event-style litter clean-up whereby participants form groups with colleagues, friends, and/or family to clean an assigned section of the local coulees, which are ravines around the riverbed, and surrounding hillsides during the designated clean-up period. The program offers a fun, social experience to encourage participation. It has a secondary goal of instilling long-term anti-littering behavior change by sensitizing participants to the impact of litter, enhancing anti-littering social norms, and offering social proof against littering. Business employee groups, friend groups, and families are the key target markets for the program. The program provides volunteers with all necessary supplies, a month-long window of opportunity for flexible scheduling, and a fun barbecue at the end of the clean-up period to enhance program attractiveness. The program began in 2008 and has successfully grown over the past 10 years thanks to attention to volunteer needs and long-term corporate partnerships.

K. C. Lafreniere (✉)
Alberta School of Business, University of Alberta, Edmonton, Canada
e-mail: klafreni@ualberta.ca

D. Z. Basil
Dhillon School of Business, University of Lethbridge, Lethbridge, Canada
e-mail: debra.basil@uleth.ca

© Springer Nature Switzerland AG 2019
D. Z. Basil et al. (eds.), *Social Marketing in Action*,
Springer Texts in Business and Economics,
https://doi.org/10.1007/978-3-030-13020-6_24

Background

This case from Lethbridge, Alberta, Canada, details a social marketing program called *The Coulee Clean-Up*, initiated by the Helen Schuler Nature Centre (HSNC) to encourage litter clean-up and an anti-littering orientation. The program encourages participation in an event-style litter clean-up whereby participants form groups with colleagues, friends, and/or family to clean an assigned section of the local coulees, which are ravines around the riverbed, and surrounding hillsides during the designated clean-up period. The program offers a fun, social experience to encourage participation. It also has a secondary goal of instilling long-term anti-littering behavior change by sensitizing participants to the impact of litter, enhancing anti-littering social norms, and offering social proof against littering.

Motivation to Participate

Social norms are unwritten rules people infer about acceptable behavior. People often look to others' behavior to determine social norms or how they should behave (Lapinski & Rimal, 2005). Seeing that many others are involved with this, anti-trash effort should develop and reinforce social norms toward environmental protection, by making salient the idea that others find litter unacceptable. HSNC sought to underscore environmental protection social norms through their Coulee Clean-Up program, so that the immediate act of litter clean-up might also lead to long-term, pro-environmental attitudes and greater care for the environment. Additionally, the event is a volunteering opportunity. Volunteering allows participants to demonstrate social responsibility, which is becoming increasingly valued in Canada as well as worldwide (Cone/Ebiquity, 2015). Thus, volunteering and combatting litter are both important social norms that could motivate participation. Finally, this is a social event. People get together with others to participate and later celebrate their participation together at a barbecue. HSNC has positioned this as a fun and social way to spend time in nature.

The Theory of Planned Behavior (TPB; Ajzen, 1985) can be applied to explain behavior change in this situation. The TPB suggests that three primary factors determine an individual's decision to perform a behavior: their attitude toward the behavior, their perception of social norms regarding the behavior, and their perceived control or ability to make a difference by performing the behavior. If individuals have a positive attitude toward environmental protection, believe others do as well, and believe that picking up litter is an effective way of protecting the environment, these things together should increase their intention to participate in the Coulee Clean-Up, which should lead to participation.

Additionally, the social aspects of this event serve as an important motivator. HSNC positioned this event as a fun and social way to engage with nature from the beginning, and they continue to focus on this aspect of the program. People participate in groups. They either sign up with others or join in with a group to meet

Fig. 24.1 A Coulee Clean-Up volunteer group. *Source* Helen Schuler Nature Centre

others. Having a meaningful and environmentally friendly way to bond with friends, family, or colleagues, or to make new friends was and continues to be an effective motivator for participants (Fig. 24.1).

HSNC also sought to capitalize on corporate and organizational interest in team building, social responsibility, and volunteerism with the introduction of the Coulee Clean-Up. Cooperation among employees has long been recognized as an essential component of business success (Katz, 1964). Team-building efforts with a social responsibility component are a growing trend within businesses and organizations (Mullich, 2009), and companies increasingly are seeking to instill workplace cooperation through team building (Cain, 2011). Additionally, companies within Canada support or even encourage employee volunteering efforts (Basil, Runté, Easwaramoorthy, & Barr, 2009), companies view employee volunteering as part of their social responsibility commitment (Cook & Burchell, 2018), and companies wish to meet societal expectations that they demonstrate social responsibility (Cone/Ebiquity, 2015). The Coulee Clean-Up offers an event-style activity that can draw a team together and allow a company to demonstrate social responsibility by supporting employee volunteering.

Lethbridge Area

Residents of Lethbridge, Alberta, are very fortunate to have a vast river valley trailing right through the heart of the city. Eight urban parks in their river valley, a combined size of 16 km^2, form one of the largest urban park systems in North

Fig. 24.2 Coulees in Lethbridge, Alberta. *Source* http://www.lethbridge.ca/Things-To-Do/
Nature-Centre/Pages/Things-To-See.aspx

America and the third largest in Canada. Surrounded by coulees (which are gorges
or ravines carved out by rivers or streams; see Fig. 24.2), the river valley is home to
hundreds of species of birds and plants as well as a unique cottonwood forest
consisting of balsam poplar, narrowleaf cottonwood, and plains cottonwood.
Lethbridge River Valley is the only place in the world where these three species
interbreed to produce hybrids.

However, the size and topography of the river valley make it very difficult for the
small city of about ninety thousand residents to secure the resources required to
maintain it. By 2007, the city had received an unprecedented number of complaints
about the level of debris in the valley. Residents were not only submitting formal
complaints to City Hall but also publishing their grievances through letters to the
local newspaper. Something needed to be done about the trash littering this
otherwise beautiful reserve.

Around that time, HSNC, an urban nature center located between the river and
coulees near downtown Lethbridge, had just celebrated its 25th anniversary. The
center was awarded additional funding to grow their volunteer programs. The
funding allowed them to hire an employee who could focus exclusively on generating community involvement. The littered condition of the river valley and the
growing demand for project-based volunteer opportunities from local organizations
made a clean-up initiative an appealing option. This case study explores how HSNC

developed a sustainable, volunteer-driven clean-up program that offers fun, bonding, and team-building opportunities for organizations, families, and friends while cleaning the river valley and enhancing anti-littering norms within the community. The first Coulee Clean-Up took place in 2008 and attracted almost 250 volunteers. The program is still in place and successful in 2018.

Helen Schuler Nature Centre

Founded in 1982, the Helen Schuler Nature Centre (HSNC) is operated by the City of Lethbridge. Their mission is to deliver diverse and dynamic nature interpretive programs in the community through a team of volunteers, staff, and partners. Their vision is to be part of a community that appreciates and understands the local natural environment through experience and discovery. In order to fuel environmental stewardship in the community, the center offers nature exhibits, guided tours, nature reserve trails, teaching guides, and various conservation programs. They receive more than 52,000 visitors each year (2017).

SWOT (Strengths, Weaknesses, Opportunities, Threats) Analysis

The following assess the internal strengths and weaknesses, as well as the external opportunities and threats that faced HSNC when they developed the Coulee Clean-Up program in 2008.

Strengths

HSNC had about 40 volunteers who could help with organizing the Coulee Clean-Up.
HSNC had a great reputation in the community, which lent credibility to the Coulee Clean-Up effort.
During the 2007–2008 season, HSNC had about 25,000 visitors, providing an easily accessible target market for Coulee Clean-Up participants.
People within the Lethbridge area appreciate and value the beauty of the riverbed preserve.
There is generally a social norm toward environmental protection, volunteerism, and social responsibility. These social norms which support the goals of the program are an important part of the TPB model.
Participants have the opportunity to demonstrate to others their support of these social norms by participating.

The program offers a high level of control for participants. Anyone who is capable of walking around and picking up garbage can make a visible difference that they can see and appreciate, consistent with the TPB component of perceived control. The Coulee Clean-Up offers a fun activity to share with others that is free to all.

Weaknesses

HSNC did not have a dedicated volunteer coordinator or the resources to coordinate volunteers for the Coulee Clean-Up.

HSNC was not in charge of managing or maintaining the river valley, so in some ways, the Coulee Clean-Up was outside of the organization's purview.

Their focus had been primarily on education initiatives previously, so they did not have experience with creating and running behavior change programs.

The program was not well-suited to anyone with physical disabilities.

Opportunities

There was a growing demand for project-based volunteering; people wanted to get involved through one-time engagement efforts.

Local organizations were increasingly seeking team-building opportunities.

Canadian companies were increasingly supporting and encouraging employee volunteering.

Families were also looking for family bonding activities, as the community had a dearth of options to engage children.

Schools were looking for community engagement opportunities for their students.

Threats

Poor weather conditions could discourage participation.

The coulees are steep and cover a lot of areas—there may be physical isolation and safety risks.

The opportunity for other team-building or group/family activities, such as fun runs and river floats, was increasing in Lethbridge.

Various target audiences would require a different marketing strategy, which could be costly and time-consuming.

Coulees are very fragile when they are wet. People walking on wet coulees damage its ecosystem, which could limit HSNC's ability to offer the program at certain times.

Although the coulees are vast, clean-up spaces are still limited. There might not be enough area to assign to all interested volunteers.

Past and Similar Efforts

The task force formed for the purpose of carrying out the Coulee Clean-Up spent time researching past clean-up campaigns but could not find a campaign quite like the one they hoped to develop. The most similar initiatives were primarily national clean-up initiatives, such as Pitch-In and The Great Canadian Shoreline Cleanup. These national campaigns provided the task force with examples of advertising, checklists, and evaluation methods.

The task force was able to connect with representatives of Pitch-In Canada because of Pitch-In's partnership with the City of Lethbridge. Pitch-In Canada uses a marketing strategy that focuses primarily on the community and neighborhood, encouraging their target audiences to clean up and maintain urban areas, such as alleys and nearby parks. Their representatives indicated that the main barrier they found was participants' perception that they should not need to pick up other people's garbage. In general, prospective participants of Pitch-In thought that their yard was very clean and that they did a lot of work to keep it that way. They did not think that their neighbors were maintaining their property to the same standards and did not like the idea of having to clean up after them. For the Coulee Clean-Up, a similar barrier could affect recruitment of prospective volunteers. If prospective participants felt others were frequently littering, environmental protection might not be viewed as a social norm. Additionally, if they felt others would just keep littering, they may not have a sense of control with the behavior. They would not feel that they could actually make a difference. Without social norms and perceived control, the Theory of Planned Behavior suggests that behavior change, in this case participating in the event and subsequently littering less, is unlikely. The task force would have to address these potential barriers.

Target Audiences

While all Lethbridge residents were welcome to participate in the Coulee Clean-Up, the task force still needed to segment and target prospective groups for campaign effectiveness and efficiency. They identified four subsets of the Lethbridge population that were ready for action and easy to reach. These four subsets were business groups, new residents or unconnected individuals, family and friend groups, and middle schools. These groups were particularly efficient to target because they required unique but similar strategies for recruitment.

Business groups refer to local businesses or groups (e.g., churches, clubs) who have a community involvement mandate or interest. In 2008, local companies were developing volunteer policies and programs that supported employee volunteerism in a variety of ways. Sometimes, employees were allowed to volunteer during paid work hours. In other instances, companies would organize a group of employees for team-building exercises. As such, the Coulee Clean-Up offered local companies a team-building opportunity that also allowed them to demonstrate social responsibility to the community, both popular goals for businesses.

The task force also wanted to target individuals who were new to the community or who otherwise did not have social connections with whom they could participate. They recognized that there were people in the community who would want to participate but (1) were not comfortable coordinating a group, (2) were new to the community, or (3) did not feel like their friends and family would be interested in the program. For these individuals, the program could allow them to meet new people, and in the process, it could solidify perceived social norms regarding environmental protection. This target group was not differentiated by demographic variables, but rather by lack of social ties. In terms of psychographic and lifestyle segmentation, this group was interested in environmental and socially responsible behavior, as well as with making new social connections. For this group, then, an existing environmental attitude, a perception of social norms, and a sense of control (the ability to make a difference), would be key components for participation, consistent with the TPB.

The task force also targeted people who wanted to participate with family and friends. People in this group are characterized by being active and spending time outdoors. This target group includes friends who like to be active together and parents who want to provide their child with experiences that help them to become engaged, responsible citizens. Given their outdoor orientation, this group most likely had strong existing positive attitudes toward socially responsible behavior and environmental protection. The Coulee Clean-Up provided these groups with a new opportunity to be active in the community and spend time together. Similar to the previous target group, this group's attitudes and perceived norms fit well within the TPB framework. It also offered a fun bonding experience, which is particularly valued by family and friend groups.

Finally, the task force wanted to target middle schools in order to get that age group involved in the community. Based on the participation statistics from other HSNC programs, the task force recognized that there was a drop-in participation rates in community programs among kids ages 12 and up. Consequently, the task force wanted to give middle schools new opportunities to engage their students in nature and the community, reinforcing these social norms.

Objectives and Goals

HSNC's mandate for programs and services had always been to provide hands-on engagement with nature. The Coulee Clean-Up certainly met that requirement. Participants were able to spend one to two hours outside while having a positive impact on the environment. As they picked up litter, they were also noticing the different plants blooming and watching the bugs and animals that live in the area. In order to encourage participation in the program, HSNC had the goal to provide a comprehensive service that would appeal to all four target audiences.

Behavior Objectives

The program's overarching behavior goal was to engage individuals and groups in picking up trash throughout the Lethbridge River Valley. Longer term, the goal was to encourage these people to return to participate in the Coulee Clean-Up year after year. The task force determined that they needed about 550 volunteers each year for the program and hoped many of them would be recurring. Organizers initially feared that volunteer rates exceeding that number would invite new issues to the program, such as running out of clean-up sites. Volunteers who legitimately want to make a difference could begin to feel disappointed in their level of contribution if they did not have enough work to do. Volunteer numbers below this level would not be able to clean the entire river valley during the slated campaign period. Over time, the program expanded the number of clean-up areas and reduced the size of each area, thus allowing them to accommodate more volunteers.

Knowledge Objectives

Given the fragility of the coulee area landscape, it was important to educate volunteers about proper trash collection methods. It was critical that volunteers stay off the coulees after a rainfall in order to prevent permanent damage. The task force recognized that many people do not know how fragile the coulees are. Their knowledge objective was therefore to have participants know that walking on wet coulees causes unnecessary and irreversible damage to the environment, in addition to solidifying social norms toward environmental protection.

Belief Objectives

A general belief objective relevant to all target groups was that of solidifying social norms regarding anti-littering and environmental protection in general. Given that the program had four specific target groups, the task force had a specific belief objective for each target audience. They wanted business groups to believe that their business would benefit from the employee cooperation involved with this team effort and to believe they would benefit from this demonstration of corporate social responsibility. For unconnected individuals, the belief objective was that this program would allow them to get involved in their community and meet new people. The belief objective for family and friend groups was that this program was a fun and free opportunity to be active and spend time with loved ones, thereby reinforcing positive attitudes toward social responsibility, as well as a way to make a difference in the community, consistent with the control element of TPB. Finally, the task force wanted middle school teachers and administrators to believe that the Coulee Clean-Up would be an easy and fun way to engage their students in the community and nature, helping them to enhance students' environmental social norms.

Factors Influencing Adoption Behavior

A number of factors serve to encourage, and discourage, the desired behavior adoption.

Barriers

Participants are not all available to volunteer on the same day.

The coulees are very steep in some places, and some volunteers have limited mobility.

Cleaning a site for longer than two hours may become tedious or even physically difficult.

Volunteers may feel stigmatized when onlookers see them picking up garbage in public spaces.

Litter collection is weather dependent.

Touching litter can be dirty and unappealing.

Individuals new to the community or without social ties may feel too intimidated to reach out to the organization.

Benefits

Participation would evoke personal and community pride.

The event gives people an opportunity to spend time with family and friends.

Businesses can benefit from positive public relations through this show of social responsibility.

Businesses can enhance employee commitment through this cooperative effort.

Middle schools can solidify the social norms of social responsibility, volunteering, environmental protection, and anti-littering.

Competing Behaviors

Numerous other volunteering opportunities exist within the community. Individuals and companies can easily access other opportunities by contacting a local volunteering coordination organization, Volunteer Lethbridge.

Companies can facilitate team-building through many other means, such as kayaking the river, hiking in the beautiful nearby mountains, or even hosting a fundraiser.

Individuals seeking connections can join the Newcomers Association.

Families seeking opportunities to connect can take advantage of the many outdoor opportunities available in the area such as hiking and kayaking or they can enjoy various community events and festivals.

Those interested in enjoying nature can go to the many parks located throughout Lethbridge or the nature reserve in the river valley.

Simply not cleaning up and staying indoors are easier behaviors.

There are other outdoor activities and sports that may be more fun.

Positioning

The campaign was positioned as a fun group activity to help the environment. Both the social aspect and the socially responsible aspect were equally important. Communication to each target group differed somewhat, but the general positioning remained relatively consistent.

Marketing Strategies

Product Strategy

Litter pickup is the *product* for the Coulee Clean-Up. HSNC wants individuals, groups, and companies to sign up for a timeslot and location and agree to pick up litter for one-and-a-half to two hours at the assigned place and time during their campaign.

Augmented Products

Before a group cleans up a site, one of the group members has to pick up a clean-up kit. The group member signs out a kit and indicates when they will return it. Each kit includes a first-aid kit, sharps container, map, data sheet (to report how many bags were filled and any unusual items found), clean gloves, and garbage bags. It is designed to fit neatly inside any vehicle for easy access.

A more recent product augmentation is the use of road signs to reduce the stigma of picking up garbage. These signs give the Coulee Clean-Up legitimacy. They provide a positive image for the Coulee Clean-Up, making the activity look like a community rally (Fig. 24.3).

At the end of the Coulee Clean-Up each year, HSNC holds a windup party to thank all the volunteers. All participants are welcome to bring their family, even if their family did not participate in the clean-up themselves. About 150 guests typically attend the celebration. The party has games for the children, barbequed food, and draw prizes. The lead coordinator also uses this event to announce how much garbage was collected and some of the crazy items that were found. For example, once a volunteer found a student card from the 1950s. HSNC actually managed to find the card owner and return it to her. The windup is also an opportunity for

Fig. 24.3 A Web site image used to attract family volunteers. *Source* http://www.lethbridge.ca/Things-To-So/Nature-Centre/Pages/Get-Involved.aspx

businesses to promote their involvement. Businesses can sponsor the event or they can donate awards and prizes.

Price Strategy

The primary *price* faced by participants is that of devoting time to the event. Participants must sacrifice two hours' time, plus travel, and organization time, to pick up litter. There is no actual financial price to participants. All volunteers, including business groups, can participate in the Coulee Clean-Up at no charge. The only financial cost that volunteers may incur is related to transportation, depending on the location of the clean-up site. However, volunteer groups with limited transportation options can work with an event coordinator to find an area that meets their needs.

Place Strategy

A key *place* strategy has been to offer groups various options in terms of clean-up dates and sites. The "official" campaign starts on Earth Day and continues until the end of May. There is considerable flexibility for groups wanting to participate and Nature Centre staff message to the community that supplies are available at any time of year and that they will always support community conservation projects. Some clean-ups take place in the month of June.

At first, the campaign ran for a relatively short time period, but over the years, it was lengthened. By broadening the event dates, coordinators were able to accommodate volunteers with different schedules by letting volunteers pick their preferred clean-up date and time. It also ensured that groups would have time to reschedule their event in case of rainy weather. Due to the program's popularity, HSNC increased the number of sites by including other natural areas away from the coulees and river valley, such as the agricultural fields northeast of the city. This transition not only provided more options for groups with limited mobility but also made room for additional volunteers. Event coordinators were even able to attract groups willing to clean up construction and industrial areas.

Another place strategy was to make the clean-up sites more appealing to business groups. HSNC coordinators accomplished this task by strategically using the traffic count near each clean-up site. Coordinators use the traffic count map to provide educated estimates of the impact of sponsorship opportunities in terms of visibility. Business groups are then encouraged to display their own signs for promotional purposes.

Promotion Strategy

The *promotion* strategy had two stages. When the Coulee Clean-Up first started, the coordinators worked on recruiting new volunteers. They have since switched their strategy to focus more on keeping current volunteers, though new volunteers are still welcome. To initially attract volunteers from each target audience, the event coordinators relied primarily on direct marketing tactics and contacting potential volunteers at related events. They had a display set up in the nature center and trained their naturalists and tour guides to answer questions. They also attended expos and special events, such as the Home and Garden Show, which attracts event patrons characterized as active and outdoorsy. Event coordinators would promote the event by sharing stories and handing out information pamphlets. Directly marketing to potential participants allowed event coordinators to immediately address any concerns people had about participation as well as provide examples of how fun and engaging the event is for everyone.

Event coordinators attracted businesses by discussing ways of gaining public exposure for the company through event participation. They would encourage employees to wear matching t-shirts or display their corporate banner at the site. They would also recommend that businesses take a photograph of their team at their clean-up site for the center to use in their various forms of advertising. For instance, when the coordinators attend an expo, they would make sure to have a PowerPoint presentation rotating through the various pictures of volunteer groups. Event staff often found that once word got out that a particular business participated in the clean-up, other businesses in the same industry would follow suit. They also stressed the team-building aspects of participation.

Once the event coordinators hit their volunteer goal, they switched much of their promotional strategy to volunteer retention. When they first recruited volunteers, they made sure to collect contact information in order to create a distribution list. They spent less money on paid advertising and focused more on email and social media updates. Event coordinators also revised the advertising message. Since volunteers already had experience with the event, event coordinators did not have to focus on the benefits and barriers of participation, but rather the event details, such as important dates and reminders. Their updates would include images of volunteer groups from previous years and include a call to action, such as "please contact us if you would like to participate again this year" (see Fig. 24.4). Finally, event coordinators also did not have to spend so much time matching volunteer groups with appropriate clean-up sites. Many groups felt a lot of pride and ownership about their clean-up site and wanted to clean the same site each year. Due to natural attrition, some new volunteers would always be needed. Although a strong focus was placed on volunteer retention, the program continues to put forth the effort to recruit new volunteers as well.

People

HSNC had about 40 individuals who could help to develop and organize the program at its inception. Additionally, the center had about 30,000 visitors per year (in 2012) and 51,000 visitors per year (in 2017) who were potential contacts for program participation.

Process

HSNC employees carefully assign locations based on their knowledge of litter accumulation. Each year, event coordinators spend time matching volunteer groups to appropriate cleaning sites. They know which cleaning sites will have more garbage based on proximity to roads, parking lots, and access points (e.g., trails leading to the river or between coulees). Such information gives them an idea of the type of group that is needed to clean the site within two hours. Coordinators then collect information about the group in order to make a match. They ask questions related to group size, mobility, age range, and site preferences. Some groups prefer steep coulees in order to get a workout, while other groups prefer a more accessible site to accommodate young children. For unconnected individuals, HSNC coordinators organize a drop-in group. Drop-in groups have a designated place and time to

Fig. 24.4 Coulee Clean-Up recruiting flyer for 2018

meet each other and the designated coordinator. At that time, they receive all the information and tools they need to participate. This sort of planning and coordination allows HSNC to make appropriate assignments, so the product meets the expectations and abilities of the participants.

In order to minimize safety risks and confusion, coordinators offer an orientation meeting to all groups. At that time, volunteers are given a checklist that can be relayed to group members not in attendance. HSNC coordinators also work closely with the city's transportation department to minimize traffic safety risks. They look at a traffic count map to determine high- and low-risk clean-up sites. Large signs are then strategically placed on the side of the road near high-risk sites to make sure that motorists are aware of volunteers and parked vehicles in the area.

To reduce the burden of transporting garbage bags from a clean-up site to the appropriate waste facility, HSNC coordinators partnered with the city's parks department. Once volunteers are finished cleaning a site, they place the garbage bags at a centralized location alongside the road and leave the site. They do not have to worry about loading the garbage inside of their vehicles. Parks employees are scheduled to pick up all the bags after the clean-up. This means that the product can be limited to picking up garbage, rather than asking participants to also haul the garbage.

In order to minimize costs each year, event coordinators had to develop strong ties with other businesses and services in the community. HSNC partnered with the city's parks department, so volunteers would not have to transport garbage. They also partnered with other organizations to provide supplies for the clean-up kits. For example, the fire department has supplied first-aid kits and Home Depot supplied gloves. Similarly, Pitch-In Canada would provide extra garbage bags to the city's waste and recycling department that could then be donated to the Coulee Clean-Up. These bags had the additional benefit of promoting how much waste was actually found in a particular site. Their bright color made it easy for volunteers and onlookers to spot and point out from a distance. To encourage middle schools to participate in the event, they put aside some of the sponsorship funding to pay for school buses to transport students to and from the clean-up site. Corporate sponsorship and donations also enabled the event coordinators to grow their windup event. They attracted major prizes, such as RV rentals, canoes, barbeques, and kayaks. In particular, Pratt & Whitney Canada has been a dedicated, long-term supporter since program inception.

Evaluation Measures

Initially, HSNC's primary goal was to attract 550 volunteers to participate in the Coulee Clean-Up. This goal was met, and they continued to enjoy success with the program year over year. Each year HSNC tracks the number of participating volunteers, the number of designated areas cleaned, and the number of bags of trash collected to evaluate the program's success. Additional clean-up sites were added in

Table 24.1 Program measures

Year	Volunteers	Registered areas	Areas completed	Bags collected
2008	350	N/a	29	175
2009	400	N/a	60	565
2010	198	N/a	39	228
2011	454	N/a	54	506
2012	602	N/a	23	458
2013	228	N/a	22	296
2014	213	N/a	24	221
2015	517	46	46	306
2016	943	70	68	356
2017	1319	94	87	560
2018	1534	91	86	440

2018 statistics updated to actual as of June 30, 2018

2012, and the size of each plot was reduced to better suit volunteer interest and abilities as well as to provide enough opportunity for the growing number of volunteers. Approximately, a month was designated for clean-up, from late April through mid-May, in order to accommodate volunteer availability.

In 2008, 350 volunteers collected 175 bags of trash. In 2018, volunteer participation had expanded to 1437 participants, and 415 bags of trash were collected. Table 24.1 provides year by year statistics.

In addition to litter pickup, the secondary goal of Coulee Clean-Up was to instill a social norm of environmental protection. This seems to be succeeding as well. The number of bags of garbage collected per participant has continued to decrease since the program's inception in 2008. Since the size of each area was reduced somewhat, direct comparisons are not possible, but this trend is evident nonetheless.

Lessons Learned and Future Directions

The ease with which the Coulee Clean-Up attracts volunteers and sponsors each year demonstrates how wildly successful this program has been in Lethbridge. The task force researched successful clean-up models from similar programs and transformed it into a model that would work for them. Then, the event coordinators had a strategic marketing message and clear communication channels for target audiences. Finally, they were able to attract strategic partnerships in order to minimize costs and make the program sustainable each year.

HSNC has been sensitive to participant feedback, learning from volunteers how to improve the program. One key example of learning was evident when volunteers expressed some discomfort with how they might be viewed when collecting trash, as well as concern over the safety of collecting near roads. To address this, signs were developed to be placed on nearby roadways when volunteer crews are working. This contributes to safety, as well as informing motorists of the positive efforts of the volunteers. Due to this willingness to learn and adapt, the program continues to thrive.

The demand from the community to have more project-based volunteer opportunities in the river valley has inspired HSNC employees to develop new ways to get involved. One possible project is an annual weed pull wherein volunteers can foster biodiversity by removing invasive weeds and plants from the river valley. Such a program would require an educational component to ensure that volunteers are not removing native plants by accident. This educational component creates a new barrier because the program would no longer be a traditional project-based volunteering model that typically requires little to no training. However, the community interest certainly makes it potentially appealing.

Another project that may be of interest and perhaps a closer fit is the Shoreline Clean-Up, which is same concept as Coulee Clean-Up except every single piece of trash is tracked to produce reports indicating what was found where and in what quantity. This approach has allowed others to show with great certainty that cigarette butts are the number one item of trash affecting our shorelines (by items found and cataloged by volunteers). This project is a nice blend of conservation and citizen science.

Discussion Questions

1. Do you think the Theory of Planned Behavior is an appropriate way to frame this case? What are the strengths and weaknesses of applying that particular theory to this case?
2. What is another theory that could effectively be applied to this case? Please thoroughly explain the theory you select, as well as its application to this case.
3. "HSNC should have focused their attention on eliminating the behavior of littering before it occurs, rather than cleaning up after people litter." Elaborate on the pros and cons of this statement.
4. Identify and describe one way HSNC could increase company participation.
5. Identify an additional target audience the Coulee Clean-Up could seek. How would you suggest appealing to this audience?

References

Ajzen, I. (1985). From intentions to actions: A theory of planned behavior. In J. Kuhl & J. Beckmann (Eds.), *Action control. SSSP Springer Series in Social Psychology*. Berlin, Heidelberg: Springer. https://doi.org/10.1007/978-3-642-69746-3_2.

Basil, D. Z., Runté, M., Easwaramoorthy, M., & Barr, C. (2009). Company support for employee volunteering: A national survey of companies in Canada. *Journal of Business Ethics, 85*(2), 387–398.

Cain, S. (2011). Trends in teambuilding. *Meetings Today*. Retrieved from https://www.meetingstoday.com/magazines/article-details/articleid/16485/title/trends-in-team-building. Accessed June 11, 2018.

Cook, J., & Burchell, J. (2018). Bridging the gaps in employee volunteering: Why the third sector doesn't always win. *Nonprofit and Voluntary Sector Quarterly, 47*(1), 165–184.

Cone/Ebiquity. (2015). *2015 Cone Communications/Ebiquity Global CSR Study*. Boston, MA: Cone Communications LLC. Retrieved from http://www.conecomm.com/research-blog/2015-cone-communications-ebiquity-global-csr-study.

Katz, D. (1964). The motivational basis of organizational behavior. *Behavioral Science, 9*(2), 131–146. https://doi.org/10.1002/bs.3830090206.

Lapinski, M. K., & Rimal, R. M. (2005). An explication of social norms. *Communication Theory, 15*(2), 127–147.

Mullich, J. (2009). Team building trends: Socially responsible activities give meetings new dimension. *Wall Street Journal*. Retrieved from http://online.wsj.com/ad/article/globaltravel-team. Accessed June 11, 2018.

Applying Social Marketing to Koala Conservation: The *"Leave It"* Pilot Program

25

Patricia David, Bo Pang and Sharyn Rundle-Thiele

Chapter Overview
Koala populations are declining, and there are needs to reverse this trend. Using social marketing which aims to change behavior for social or environmental benefit, this case study demonstrates how social marketing was applied to achieve environmental change. A pilot program name "Leave It" was designed and developed with dog owners and experts including koala conservation officers and dog trainers in order to reduce dog and koala interactions. A four-week dog obedience training program was implemented, and a mixed method outcome evaluation was undertaken. Results indicate that five of seven dog behaviors measures were changed from baseline to follow-up, namely sit, stay, come back when called every time, wildlife aversion, and stay quiet on command. Findings of this pilot program provide evidence of the effectiveness and potential of social marketing to change behaviors in an environmental context.

Campaign Background

Koala (*Phascolarctos cinereus*) population levels are steadily decreasing in South East Queensland (Redlands Koala Conservation Strategy 2016). Primary koala threats include urban development, fragmentation of habitat, traffic, and predation

P. David (✉) · B. Pang · S. Rundle-Thiele
Social Marketing at Griffith, Griffith University, Nathan, Australia
e-mail: p.david@griffith.edu.au

B. Pang
e-mail: b.pang@griffith.edu.au

S. Rundle-Thiele
e-mail: s.rundle-thiele@griffith.edu.au

© Springer Nature Switzerland AG 2019
D. Z. Basil et al. (eds.), *Social Marketing in Action*,
Springer Texts in Business and Economics,
https://doi.org/10.1007/978-3-030-13020-6_25

by dogs (McAlpine et al., 2015; Law et al., 2017). In urban and semi-rural areas, mortality from domestic dogs poses a significant and often underestimated threat to koalas and other urban wildlife. According to the Queensland Department of Environment and Heritage Protection (2008), dog attacks and predation are the third most common cause of death in koalas after habitat loss and vehicle strikes. It is estimated that more than 600 koalas have been attacked by dogs over the past 15 years in the local council area that forms the basis of this study. Although various control measures that lower the likelihood of dog and koala interactions have been identified, including reducing pets' roaming periods, setting up buffer zones, provision of wildlife corridors, and placing a pole against a fence for koala egress, calls have been made for practitioners to be open to different ways of thinking to effectively engage the target community with the use of a social science approach to improve conservation policy, practice, and outcomes.

A social marketing pilot program named *Leave It* (see www.leaveit.com.au) was co-created with dog owners. The program drew on expert advice (e.g., koala conservation, environmental scientists, and dog training professionals) to deliver a program that engaged dog owners to participate in a training program, which had wildlife aversion training embedded as one of many skills. The overall aim of Leave It was to help residents change their dogs' behaviors through four training sessions. Leave It focused on the delivery of dog obedience training and was priced at $AUD150 for four sessions. These sessions were designed to decrease dog and koala interactions in the local council region over time. Leave It focused on helping dog owners to establish effective basic control of their dogs and training emphasized a series of behaviors including sit, stay, and koala aversion (Leave It). A community event *DogFest* was launched to raise awareness for the Leave It training program. The campaign was designed based on the Theory of Planned Behavior (TPB) (Ajzen, 1991). According to the TPB, three factors contribute to behavioral intentions and in turn behavior, namely subjective norms, attitudes toward the behavior, and perceived behavioral control. Data analysis indicated that the TPB model could explain the intentions of people to confine and restrain their dogs with 66% of variance explained, a level that is higher than most of other studies that have utilized the TPB to explain intention. Moreover, the provision of dog training for dog owners was designed to improve perceived behavioral control, which in turn was expected to change intentions to confine and restrain their dogs in addition to increasing the dog owners' control over their dog.

One canine expert was invited to partner with Leave It delivering positive dog management and wildlife aversion skills for the dog trainers leading the Leave It program. The canine expert demonstrated a range of positive dog training principles in addition to on koala aversion. The canine expert delivered one session to six dog trainers who indicated interest in partnering with Leave It. Leave It trainers were free to include koala aversion in their training programs where appropriate. The one-day canine expert led session covered a range of operant conditioning strategies, training plans, and canine problem-solving.

SWOT Analysis (Strengths, Weaknesses, Opportunities, Threats)

Strengths

Leave It was positively received by the majority of participants, and willingness to re-engage with the program was very strong.

DogFest was well attended (more than 1500 dog owners), positively received, and community intention to attend in future years was very high.

Australians are more inclined to accept pets as a potential conservation hazard than their overseas counterparts (Hall et al., 2016).

Weaknesses

There were confusions between Leave It and DogFest brands.

Program uptake for available Leave It group sessions was 31.25%. Uptake levels were impacted by limited promotion time and program availability (only one four-week period was available, which coincided with peak holiday season).

Pilot was reliant on volunteers leading to poor advice in some instances.

There was limited time to administer the pilot (10 weeks from approval to final Leave It session delivery, 3 weeks to promote Leave It).

Opportunities

Dog ability levels are low (sit, stay, Leave It, etc.).

Community is willing to partner in koala protection programs that are fun and dog-focused (not stigmatizing and victim blaming).

There is little competition in the region.

City council is willing to provide additional funding to support the program.

Threats

There existed a lack of interest in dog training from some members of the community.

Low dog abilities are sit, stay, come when called, and wildlife aversion.

Target Audience

The program targeted residents of the Redland area who are dog owners. The primary target audience of the program has a dog as a family pet. The audience believes that some dogs can pose a risk to koalas, but not small dogs. They also believe that dogs feel safe when they have their own space, such as a crate.

The secondary target audience consists of people that have a dog for security reasons. They believe a dog should roam freely in their backyard at night because they have a fenced area, they can go to the toilet, and they bark otherwise. Dogs of the target audience have received some type of training, such as puppy pre-school. However, despite having received training, dogs do not respond to basic obedience behaviors such as come back every time they are called, not chase things, and stay quiet on command.

Target Audience Barriers and Benefits

Research has shown that in order for people to control their dogs, they have to train their dogs. A series of questions about perceived benefits and barriers were asked in a community survey. On average, the target audience had a perception that by confining their dogs, they would be helping protect wildlife (benefit). On the other hand, the findings from the survey showed the target audience thought it would be cruel to confine their dogs, and that a barking nuisance could be created by engaging in this behavior (barrier).

Campaign Objectives

Following community based formative research identifying that 2 out of 3 people report that their dog does not respond to basic verbal commands, Leave It was designed as a program that focuses on basic dog obedience training; given that training basics must be in place before koala aversion can be taught. The overall aim of Leave It was to help local residents to improve their dogs' behavior and over time decrease dog and koala interactions. Leave It focused on helping dog owners to establish effective basic control of their dogs.

Specific objectives for the Leave It campaign were set according to the RE-AIM framework (Table 25.1).

Table 25.1 Leave It pilot program objectives

RE-AIM dimension	Objective
Reach	30% session uptake 1000 unique visits on Leave It website 10 registrations in the Leave It program 1000 DogFest attendees
Effectiveness	All dog obedience abilities will increase 10% through the training program Dog owners' perceived barriers to den the dog during the night will be significantly lower after the program
Adoption	High stakeholder satisfaction rating (6.5 out of 7) High stakeholder perceived benefit in pilot program participation (6.5 out of 7)
Implementation	Positive experience with DogFest (6.5 out 7) High Leave It registrant satisfaction (6.5 out of 7)
Maintenance	High intention to participate in Leave It again in the future (10% increase)

Positioning

In order to define a clear and potentially effective Leave It pilot program, six co-design workshops were held with residents of the local council area who gave their informed consent to participate and who owned one or more dogs. Co-design sessions started by eliciting dog owner opinions of ten campaigns that had previously been implemented to decrease koala and dog interactions. A group discussion followed to gain insights into program features, assisting the project team to understand what dog owners valued.

Participants were then split into groups of three or four. They were asked to design an effective campaign that they felt would engage community members in the local council area to decrease dog and koala interactions. Co-design workshops were audio recorded, and field notes were made. Workshop discussions were transcribed, and trends and patterns within and across groups were analyzed.

Taken together, co-design sessions highlighted that a positive, dog-focused program that delivered training, giving dog owners the skills needed to avoid wildlife, and was promoted through community events, could be offered within the project timeframe. The program actively avoided linking koala fatality to dogs and dog owners, so the target audience would engage with the program. Participants also indicated training should be convenient in terms of location and timing in order to increase commitment.

Competition

The competitors of the Leave It training program consisted of other training companies in the Redlands area. Companies such as Positive Dog Training competed directly with Leave It especially in location. Their competitive advantage was the fact they were established companies, while Leave It was a new program. However, Leave It was a city council endorsed program and was positioned as a program with a substantially lower cost, ensuring that more people in the community could afford the program. Another competition for the Leave It program to be considered is the opposite behavior: not engaging in a training program. There are benefits such as not spending time and money with registration. These are important factors to consider before creating the marketing strategy.

Marketing Strategy (Product, Price, Place, Promotion)

Product Strategies

Leave It was designed as a program that focuses on basic dog obedience training; given that training basics must be in place before koala aversion can be taught. The overall aim of Leave It was to help residents to improve their dogs' behavior and over time decrease dog and koala interactions in Redland City Council. In social marketing, product in its most direct form should be considered as a tangible product, or even a service that can be offered for purchase. Drawn upon the TPB framework, the core product for Leave It consisted of a four-week dog training program, which had koala aversion embedded as one of the skills in the program. Leave It focused on helping dog owners to establish effective basic control of their dogs, which was designed based on the perceived behavioral control construct in the TPB model. Steve Austin, Certified Professional Dog Trainer-Knowledge Assessed (CPTD-KA), partnered with Leave It delivering positive dog training and wildlife aversion training to Leave It dog trainers on June 2, 2017. Steve Austin demonstrated a range of positive dog training principles and provided training focused on koala aversion. Training was delivered to a total of 6 dog trainers who indicated interest in partnering with Leave It. Training offered by Steve Austin transferred skills allowing trainers to include koala aversion in training programs where appropriate. Leave It was designed as a multi-strategy, pilot social enterprise program and featured recruitment and awareness building activities which commenced at RSPCA Million Paws Walk, Indigi Day Out, and concluded with DogFest.

Pricing Strategies

Research was undertaken to understand the costs of a training package for dog owners in the Redland area. Leave It offered a package of four obedience training sessions charging a lower price that the average market price. The training package was advertised at AUD $150 per dog. In order to ensure an attractive offer, a discounted rate of AUD $120 was also promoted, as well as bundle discounts for dog owners that enrolled two dogs or more into the program.

In social marketing, price is the cost the consumer incurs, which in its most direct form is monetary cost. For Leave It, the fully listed price was AUD$150 for four training sessions. Moreover, the training sessions required the dog owner's time, energy, and consistent commitment, which also represented costs for participants in this social marketing pilot program. The program attempted to reduce costs by offering training sessions in convenient locations, limiting the length of each session to no longer than 90 min, and offering various training options to best suit dog owners' demands.

Place Strategies

The training sessions offered were within the Redland City Council area in Thornlands, Cleveland, and surrounding areas (Manly and Springwood). The trainers who provided Leave It training were experienced and qualified individuals who had completed training with Steve Austin on June 2, 2017. Ten dog training businesses in the Redland area were invited to partner with Leave It. Trainers were shortlisted from an initial list by interviews with experts. In addition, a Web search for local trainers in the Redland region was conducted. All potential trainers were contacted and screened for suitability according to Steve Austin's criteria. Given the short notice and training requirements for trainers to supply the location, the list was narrowed down to locals who had experience, were available within the project timeframe, could supply the venue, and were qualified according to Steve Austin's criteria. The dog training businesses that have delivered Leave It were Positive Response Dog Training (https://www.positiveresponse.net.au/) and ABC Dog Training (http://abcdogtraining.net.au/).

Promotion Strategies

To promote Leave It, a targeted integrated promotional strategy was implemented to reach dog owners residing in the Redland City Council area. The main promotional methods included: Web site (www.leaveit.com.au), Leave It flyers, email marketing, social media marketing (Facebook and Instagram), a promotional event (DogFest), and event exhibitions leading up to pilot program launch (RSPCA Million Paws Walk, Indigi Day Out). The Leave It promotion commenced on May 21, 2017, giving a total of 3 weeks to promote the pilot program. All the promotion materials were aiming to change residents' attitudes toward dog training, which was designed based on the TPB framework.

DogFest

DogFest was a free event held at Capalaba Regional Park two weeks before Leave It commenced. DogFest delivered a "mini-festival" feel, aiming to increase audience engagement, extend awareness, and to promote partnerships with retailers. Food trucks including a coffee van, a pizza stall, and a sausage sizzle were offered.

A wide variety of different retailers were present selling dog treats (puppicinos, dog beer, and dog tea), dog food, pet photography, dog washing, dog grooming, dog clothing, and more. Importantly, dog trainers and obedience clubs were present to deliver talks and obedience displays for interested dog owners. DogFest attracted over 1500 attendees.

Web site
All promotion strategies featured the Web site link, where detailed Leave It program information was made available. The Web site contained information on Leave It session types, the Leave It trainers, frequently asked questions, and program pricing. Further, the Web site provided information communicating the DogFest program of events.

Flyers and Emails

Both DogFest and Leave It were promoted through flyers and emails. Over 2500 flyers were distributed (Fig. 25.1). Over 450 emails were sent out to Redland residents.

Fig. 25.1 Flyer promoting DogFest

Social Media

A Facebook event was created for DogFest and promoted to Redland residents by Redland City Council. Over the course of the Facebook campaign, a total of 37,000 people were reached with 7200 people viewing the DogFest event page and 1000 people responding to the event, indicating interest in attending, sharing a post, and more. In addition, an Instagram account for Leave It was created in order to run a social media competition with the hashtag #leaveit2017. The aim of this strategy was to increase engagement with the brand and to raise awareness of both DogFest and Leave It.

Program Evaluation

The DogFest event attracted over 1500 attendees indicating that Leave It reached 5–10% of the 21,000 dog owners in the local council area. Specifically, the visitor survey sought to understand attendees' attitudes toward the event and their intention to attend the DogFest in the following year. Attitudes were measured with three seven-point bipolar scales, where respondents had to choose from opposite adjectives such as "Unpleasant–Pleasant" and intentions were measured using one unipolar scale from 1 to 7. The visitor survey was emailed to 319 people, with a response rate of 19.1%. Results show that attitudes toward DogFest were generally high. In addition, over 90% of all respondents reported a positive experience with DogFest, less than 5% a neutral reaction, and there was no negative experience reported. Next, visitors were asked how likely it would be for them to attend DogFest next year, if it was held again. 92.1% of respondents replied it was likely they would attend. When asked their opinions on the DogFest, the event visitors provided positive responses:

> Dogs got to socialize, and I saw vendors, vets, and groomers I may not have seen or been to before. Def needs to be back again next year. (Visitor's survey respondent)

> the training tip talks and the stalls and free gifts. (Visitor's survey respondent)

To evaluate the overall satisfaction with Leave It and to understand areas for improvement, four questions were included in the Leave It follow-up survey. Over 85% of respondents reported a positive experience and satisfaction with the training program. Participants were also asked whether they would participate in Leave It training program again next year if the program was run again and two-thirds indicated future participation in the program.

Field notes on 15 dogs that participated in the training sessions were collected over the four-week period. Trainers recorded the progress of each dog over the course of the training period and commented on the performance of both dogs and their owners during the training sessions. Successful koala aversion behaviors were noted for most of the dogs at the end of the Leave It program.

Discussion and Lessons Learned

This case study demonstrated that a program co-created with dog-owning residents that was fun, dog-focused, and helped owners to understand what they needed to do could effectively engage people. The pilot program, which was designed by dog owners and planned and implemented in partnership with stakeholders, was well received and positively evaluated. The process enabled effective engagement with dog owners and generated positive feedback and promising behavioral change outcomes. Additionally, having received instructions in koala aversion training, local dog trainers are now aware of conservation challenges and they are able and encouraged to integrate koala aversion elements into their regular training offerings, creating change that can last beyond the pilot program.

The program was valued by members of the local council community given they were willing to pay AUD $150 for four training sessions, which suggests that a program can be delivered in the longer term, and revenue can be generated to sustain programs. The results of this study provide pilot evidence that community members can voluntarily be engaged in activities that contribute to koala conservation and they are willing to pay for specialized dog obedience and koala aversion behavioral training. Upscaling this pilot program where two-thirds of participants are willing to continue to participate in the program can deliver a sustained revenue stream to support ongoing program administration that is not reliant on public funding. Results demonstrated that social marketing can effectively engage dog owners and can attract dog owners to enroll in a four-week paid training program that improves dogs' koala aversion skills. Participants who attended the project expressed high intention to rejoin DogFest and the Leave It project, which indicates potential for program sustainability and alterations of community norms in relation to dog training in the long term. This program is currently being developed into city-wide implementation with the support of the local city council. By scaling the program up to a city-wide implementation, an added benefit is raising awareness of the importance of dog training for wildlife conservation, and word of mouth can play an important role.

Leave It was designed and implemented in a short timeframe of 10 weeks, limiting the core dog training program offering to one four-week program that coincided with a peak holiday period. The program was limited to group dog training sessions, which limits the types of dogs that can participate (e.g., dogs must be socialized). A further limitation was the program which was only promoted via free channels such as social media. No paid broadcast media was used which limited broader community awareness. Delivery of sequenced alternatives is needed for enrolments in the advanced option given very few dogs are trained to this level.

Limited lead time was available in this pilot project to promote the community event and to secure dog trainers and training alternatives to advertise. Longer project time frames are needed to improve outcomes attained. Based on experience gained in this project, a 12-week time frame is needed to generate awareness for the program, word of mouth, and to promote the event within the community targeted.

Lead time ahead of promotion is needed to ensure a sufficient cross section of dog trainers, and training options can be secured. Further, broadcast media such as local radio is recommended to generate wider awareness for Leave It. Together, these changes would assist to increase the number of training registrations due to more available options and time to promote the program.

Discussion Questions

1. What is the core product Leave It provides to the target audience?
2. What "exchange" does Leave It offer to encourage dog owners to take their service? How could this be improved?
3. Do you have suggestions for improving their promotional efforts?
4. What can be offered to dog owners that do not feel confident to bring their dogs to training sessions due to dog behavioral issues?
5. How can Leave It improve the evaluation with a better response rate?

Practical Activity

Carins and Rundle-Thiele's (2014) paper identified that behavior change is more likely when more of social marketing's benchmarks are used. Find a benchmark framework and using information presented in the case identify the benchmarks that are present.

References

Ajzen, I. (1991). The theory of planned behavior. *Organizational Behavior and Human Decision Processes, 50*(2), 179–211.

Carins, J. E., & Rundle-Thiele, S. R. (2014). Eating for the better: A social marketing review (2000–2012). *Public Health Nutrition, 17*(7), 1628–1639.

Hall, C. M., Adams, N. A., Bradley, J. S., Bryant, K. A., Davis, A. A., Dickman, C. R., ... Calver, M. C. (2016). Community attitudes and practices of urban residents regarding predation by pet cats on wildlife: An international comparison. *PLoS One, 11*(4). https://doi.org/10.1371/journal.pone.0151962.

Law, B., Caccamo, G., Roe, P., Truskinger, A., Brassil, T., Gonsalves, L., et al. (2017). Development and field validation of a regional, management-scale habitat model: A koala *Phascolarctos cinereus* case study. *Ecology and Evolution, 7*(18), 7475–7489.

McAlpine, C., Lunney, D., Melzer, A., Menkhorst, P., Phillips, S., Phalen, D., et al. (2015). Conserving koalas: A review of the contrasting regional trends, outlooks and policy challenges. *Biological Conservation, 192*, 226–236.

Queensland Government, Department of Environment and Heritage Protection (2008). *Koalas and dogs. Queensland, Australia.* Retrieved from: https://www.ehp.qld.gov.au/wildlife/koalas/pdf/koalas-and-dogs.pdf (accessed May 2017).

Redlands City Council, Redlands Koala Conservation Strategy. (2016). Retrieved from: https://www.redland.qld.gov.au/download/downloads/id/2289/redland_koala_conservation_strategy_2016.pdf (accessed May 2017).

Co-creating a Sea Change Social Marketing Campaign for Ocean Literacy in Europe: A Digital Interactive Tool for Environmental Behavior Change

26

Christine Domegan, Patricia McHugh, Veronica McCauley and Kevin Davison

Chapter Overview

Sea Change was a European campaign (www.seachangeproject.eu) designed to bring about a fundamental transformation, a "Sea Change" in the way European citizens experience their relationship with the sea, by empowering them as "ocean-literate" citizens. With Sea Change using co-creation behavioral change theory principles across a number of campaigns, e.g., citizen science initiatives, youth camps, crab watching, marine litter with policy makers across Europe, and blue schools, this case study concentrates on one of the collaborative and cooperative campaign for a digital interactive tool in the educational sector.

Campaign Background and Context

European citizens are not fully aware of the true extent of the medical, economic, social, political, and environmental importance of the sea to Europe and indeed to the rest of the world (Hynes, Norton, & Corless, 2014; Tran, Payne, & Whitley,

C. Domegan (✉) · P. McHugh
Marketing Discipline, NUI Galway, Galway, Ireland
e-mail: christine.domegan@nuigalway.ie

P. McHugh
e-mail: patricia.mchugh@nuigalway.ie

V. McCauley · K. Davison
School of Education, NUI Galway, Galway, Ireland
e-mail: veronica.mccauley@nuigalway.ie

K. Davison
e-mail: kevin.davison@nuigalway.ie

© Springer Nature Switzerland AG 2019
D. Z. Basil et al. (eds.), *Social Marketing in Action*,
Springer Texts in Business and Economics,
https://doi.org/10.1007/978-3-030-13020-6_26

2010). Neither is there awareness of how our day-to-day actions can have a cumulative negative effect on the health of the ocean and seas (Strang, DeCharon, & Schoedinger, 2007)—a necessary resource that must be protected for all life on the planet earth to exist. In other words, European citizens lack a sense of "Ocean Literacy"—an understanding of the ocean's influence on us and our influence on the ocean. An ocean-literate person *understands* the importance of the ocean to humankind; can *communicate* about the ocean in a meaningful way; and is able to make informed and responsible *decisions* regarding the ocean and its resources (McHugh et al., 2016; National Oceanic and Atmospheric Administration, 2013; Schoedinger, Tran, & Whitley, 2010).

The Galway Statement on Atlantic Ocean Cooperation, 2013, reinforced this need for Ocean Literacy for Europe. Top marine scientists from EU, USA, and Canada identified convergences between their respective scientific agendas. They concluded that together we can build a capacity to understand and predict major Atlantic and Arctic processes, as well as the changes and risks they carry in relation to human activities and climate change. We can better understand the Arctic and North Atlantic Ocean to promote the sustainable management of its resources, particularly with regard to climate change.

Sea Change was a European campaign (www.seachangeproject.eu) designed to bring about a fundamental transformation, a "Sea Change" in the way European citizens experience their relationship with the sea, by empowering them as "ocean-literate" citizens—to make informed and responsible decisions regarding the ocean and its resources, and to take direct and sustainable action toward healthy seas and ocean, healthy communities, and ultimately, a healthy planet. Co-creating environmental behavior change was a central theory guiding the work of Sea Change. To create is to make something happen as a result of one's own actions. To co-create is to make something happen as a result of people working together. Co-creating a Sea Change was a collective process that connects and empowers people to become ocean literate. Co-creating a behavioral sea change was about people coming together and making Sea Change happen through their everyday choices, decisions, and behaviors.

With Sea Change using co-creation behavioral change theory principles across a number of campaigns, e.g., citizen science initiatives, youth camps, crab watching, marine litter with policy makers across Europe, and blue schools, this case study concentrates on one of the collaborative and cooperative campaigns for a digital interactive tool in the educational sector.

Strengths, Weaknesses, Opportunities, Threats (SWOT) Analysis

With the success of any environmental behavior change campaign first dependent on what is going on in the surrounding environment, a literature review was first conducted from a macro-Sea Change campaign perspective. This was followed by extensive formative research (Fauville et al., 2018) in the form of ocean literacy dialogue forums in eight European countries (Ireland, Sweden, Belgium, Denmark, Greece, Spain, Portugal, and UK) with stakeholder groups involved in teaching, education, outreach, curriculum, media, regulation, and policy. This market analysis uncovered 657 barriers and 316 benefits to teaching 12–19-year-olds across Europe about the ocean, which are summarized below.

Strengths

Each partner from the nine countries involved in the Sea Change campaign received environmental behavioral change training, learning how to co-create a transformative sea change in Europe (McHugh and Domegan, 2018).

Through Sea Change, ocean literacy can be brought into the classroom.

The process protocols developed for a digital interactive tool can be developed in a manner that acts as good practice and template for other environmental behavior change contexts. Sea Change's Massive Open Online Course "From ABC to ABSeas: Ocean Literacy for All" helps prepare teachers by informing them about ocean literacy and helping them incorporate marine education into educational practices (Fauville et al., 2018).

Sea Change project partners had extensive knowledge and experience of inquiry-based teaching.

Weaknesses

Culturally, the ocean is underappreciated, resulting in people having limited ability to understand the importance of the ocean in their everyday life.

There is no depository, database, or Web site where all ocean literacy resources can be accessed.

Sea Change resources such as the iBook, the Massive Open Online Course, the ocean edge directory, virtual laboratories, and ocean literacy games were all developed concurrently.

Many ocean literacy resources are only produced in English even though Europe is a continent of many different languages.

Opportunities

EU and national policies recognize ocean literacy as a priority.

The trend is towards innovative forms of Interactive engagement and collaboration—inquiry-based teaching—innovative teaching methods and hands on activities (McCauley, Gomes and Davison, 2018; Gomes and McCauley, 2016).

Wide-ranging, collaborative, and decentralized efforts are emerging to create a more ocean-literate society. For example, in America, formal and informal educators and curriculum and program developers have developed a "road map" that helps them build coherent and conceptually sound learning experiences for students from kindergarten through 12th grade (www.coexploration.org).

Ocean literacy has relevance (although not explicitly stated) within the existing formal curriculum and may provoke opportunities for thematic teaching/ cross-curricular interest within the traditional science subjects and across other subject areas (e.g., business studies and geography).

There is a shift toward online and tablet technology, reusable and open source, support mechanisms available to fuel motivation, and interest in the classroom (Comiskey, McCartan, & Nicholl, 2013; Maich and Hall 2015; Heemskerk, Volman, Admiraal, & ten Dam, 2012; Bingimlas 2009; Kim 2013).

Teachers are willing to participate in the design and evaluation of digital tools (McHugh and McCauley, in press), and therefore there is an opportunity to co-construct teaching methodologies that are best suited to their setting.

New partnerships across different networks could potentially integrate, share resources, and generate a "network of networks."

Threats

The ocean itself is a threat. Its inherent complexity challenges people's ability to get an overview of the ocean system. It can be difficult to access the ocean. The ocean is largely unseen and unexplored.

Current school structure and curriculum are land-based.

Many teachers, especially at the junior level, lack confidence in ocean knowledge; they may fear being asked questions that they do not know the answer to.

There are restrictions in terms of curricular demands, time constraints, and large classes. The primary goal for schools is to deliver the specified curriculum and *where time allows* an extension of further application and areas of interest.

Although some schools are close to the ocean, many are not. Therefore, many limitations arise in terms of getting to a sea location, e.g., insurance, distance, volunteers, and transport.

Health and safety issues surround visiting the ocean.

There is a lack of teacher training in the area of marine science/ocean literacy.

There is a lack of policy at EU and national levels to implement broader programs regarding ocean literacy.

Limitations across schools in terms of technology resource support for digital teaching and learning tools.

There is the perception that there are few marine careers beyond traditional marine jobs, e.g., tourism, fishing, and shipping.

Project partners learned how to overcome the weaknesses and threats detailed above through tailored, hands-on experiential training in environmental behavior change. Co-creation theory and five fundamental co-creation concepts for environmental behavior change underpinned the work in Sea Change (McHugh and Domegan, 2018):

- *People's behavior*—understand why people do what they do at present, their thoughts, and motivations.
- *Choices*—understand people have lots of choices, and this represents competition.
- *System thinking*—recognize the importance of the system people are living in with all its political, cultural, social, technological, and economic characteristics.
- *Creativity*—there must be elements of imagination, creativity, and innovation to make behavior change as attractive and motivating as possible.
- *Values*—it is important to understand what people value and do not value.

Target Audience

Many complex problems, including the challenge of creating an ocean literate society, "encompasses or affects numerous people, groups and organizations ... where no one is fully in charge ... and many individuals, groups and organizations are involved or affected or have some partial responsibility to act" (Bryson, 2004, 23–24). Setting boundaries and engaging with stakeholders ensure that all potential groups and individuals who can affect or be affected by creating an ocean-literate society were considered. Thus, the market was defined as the formal and informal education sectors across Europe, spanning landlocked and coastal regions. The primary target audience was secondary school teachers of 12–15-year-olds in formal education. The secondary target audience consisted of the students that are being taught, while the tertiary target audience focused on informal educators, organizations/institutions engaged in informal education such as marine institutes, museums, and aquariums. The targeted audiences spanned both iPad and non-iPad schools where intended users had the ability and capacity to access and use digital technology.

For co-creation, collaborating and empowering each of these target audiences together (Fig. 26.1) were foundational to Sea Change and its approach to its target markets.

Active versus passive participation is more empowering because it reflects values important to the target audiences for community participation. It enables target groups to become dynamic and equal in developing a deep understanding of experiences. It builds relationships with the target audiences to provide for mutual learning. Importantly, the coordinating systems (formal and informal education) around the behavioral change come into operation, which means public policy and media are relevant too (Bunn, Savage, & Holloway, 2002). The target audience's systems have to facilitate the manifestation of the new Sea Change ocean literacy, or it cannot come into being.

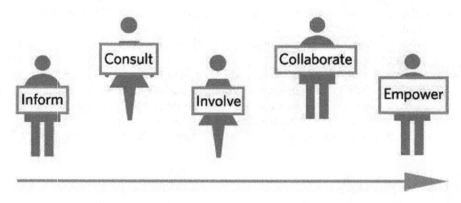

Fig. 26.1 Levels of participation. *Source* Davies and Simon (2013)

Campaign Objectives

Sea Change had two overarching goals. The first goal was to empower educators, students, and educational communities across Europe to integrate and promote ocean literacy principles. The second goal was to measure if change was happening and to ensure that efforts to sustain an ocean-literate society in Europe continued beyond the life of Sea Change.

Behavioral Objectives

Sea Change's empowerment goal was translated into three behavioral objectives. The first was to strengthen the capacity and self-efficacy of teachers to introduce ocean literacy into their curriculum (science and nonscience subjects). The second was for teachers to anchor an increase in students' ocean literacy in a curriculum that lacks marine science within the secondary classroom. Thirdly, to transform instructional content so that students could engage with a more digitally interactive experience. The aim was for the campaign not only to introduce marine science into the regular curriculum, but to act as a tool to engage teachers and students in behavioral change because of the multiple possibilities to connect to their real-life experiences.

Co-creation Objectives

Legacy goals for Sea Change were captured in its co-creation objectives for the campaign. These were to (a) continually sense and learn with all the formal and informal educational stakeholders and adapt the campaign accordingly and (b) design and implement an approach for sustainable social change incorporating the five fundamental co-creation concepts.

Competition

In Sea Change, it was important to identify the competition (Kotler and Lee, 2010; McHugh and Domegan, 2018). There were three competing factors that could interrupt or delay the desired behavior change: "choices target audiences would prefer over the ones Sea Change are promoting" (e.g., digital games); "choices target audiences have been doing 'forever,' such as a habit that they would have to give up" (e.g., using green, land-based examples as opposed to ocean examples); and "organizations and individuals who send messages that counter or oppose the desired behavior change" (e.g., textbooks are easier to use, accessible to all, and more economical than iBooks).

Positioning

Building on current trends in social marketing toward interactive games technology for behavioral change (Russell-Bennett et al, 2018; Mulcahy, Russell-Bennett and Rundle-Thiele, 2015), Sea Change positioned this campaign as a digital interactive tool (McHugh, McCauley, Davison, Raine, & Grehan, in press) to support curriculum teaching and learning as opposed to a mandatory course book. Importantly, the campaign was not simply the digitized content of a book originating from a print format. The various interactive functionalities had the potential to create a connected seamless transition from awareness to knowledge acquisition and assessment to behavioral change, through empowered edutainment *with* students. It is this seamless transition that was the key benefit for the teacher in using this product.

The campaign also had to factor in two further positioning possibilities—the primary target audience (teachers) and secondary target audience (students), in particular, could be either "digital residents" or "digital visitors" (McHugh and McCauley, in press). This positioning recognizes that digital visitors (non-iPad schools) are enamored with the technology and other product features, whereas digital residents (iPad schools) may have other technology demands of the offering; for example, they may expect it to be quicker and more capable. The tertiary target audience (outreach officers, marine museums, etc.) were more likely to be "digital residents" themselves but could be dealing with either "digital residents" or "digital visitors."

Marketing Strategy

Product Strategy

The core behavior change sought was to strengthen the capacity and self-efficacy of teachers to introduce ocean literacy into their curriculum. The digital interactive iBooks would strengthen the confidence, belief, and abilities of teachers in teaching and incorporating ocean literacy into their curriculums, and as a consequence of their new knowledge, attitude and beliefs would then increase students' awareness and knowledge of ocean literacy. Supporting the desired behavioral change was the tangible product; a digital interactive iBook for Harmful Algal Blooms (HABs) (Fig. 26.2—https://itunes.apple.com/us/book/harmful-algal-blooms/id1214392876?mt=11). The tangible product offering captured two benefits of engagement and interactivity with fun for the target audiences supporting the edutainment positioning. The augmented product offering included technology features such as images, videos, experiments, games, interactive quizzes, and interactive design widgets embedded in the book, enabling students to take notes. Other product features for transformative instructional content for teachers included keynote presentations, interactive images, interactive galleries, scrolling sidebars, pop-up functionality, videos, study cards, scientific glossary, access to dictionary, curiosity facts, and quizzes. The HABs iBook has five topical chapters that linked with Sustainable Development Goals suitable for non-science subjects such as English and art (Fig. 26.3) with each chapter ending in multiple-modal choice questionnaire consisting of seven questions, and a final subsection that collates content for student project development.

Price Strategy

While no monetary price was charged for the HABs product, costs are incurred by the target audiences: Time had to be spent familiarizing themselves with the HABs materials. For some target audiences, there was the unfamiliarity and discomfort of working digitally, while others had to overcome school norms toward land-based lessons.

Place Strategy

The iBook store provided free accessible download of the iBook in 51 countries worldwide. See https://itunes.apple.com/us/book/harmful-algal-blooms/id1214392876?mt=11. The iBook is not available on Android. Other online resource depositories also provided digital access such as Scientix.eu and EMSEA. Physical access was possible in locations such as aquariums and marine centers that featured the offering as part of an exhibit.

Promotion Strategy

Sea Change pursued an integrated marketing communication campaign using an online and off-line promotional mix. Traditional advertisements appeared in

Fig. 26.2 Digitally interactive HABs iBook

local newspapers and on local radio, supported with complimentary social media activities such as tweets and Facebook postings (see https://www.facebook. com/SeaChangeProjectEU) (Figs. 26.4 and 26.5).

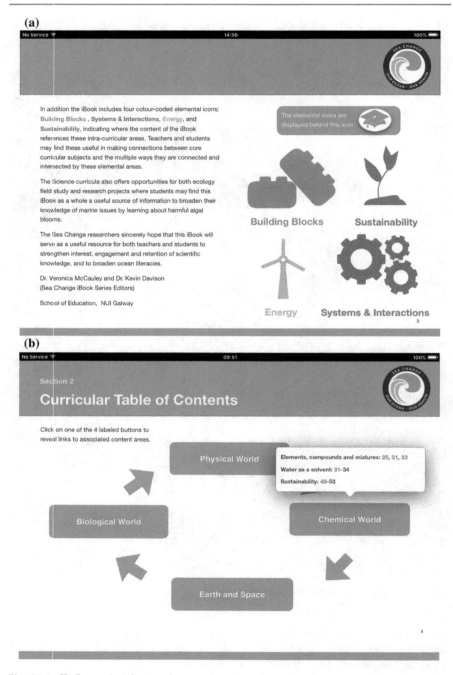

Fig. 26.3 HABs product features for nonscience target audiences

INVITATION

seachangeproject.eu

You are cordially invited to the launch of

Harmful Algal Blooms

Harmful Algal
Blooms
Robin Raine

An iBook by:

Dr. Robin Raine
(Marine Scientist, School of Natural
Sciences, NUI Galway)

This iBook will be launched by Prof. Colin Brown, Director of
the Ryan Institute, Earth and Ocean Sciences

Monday 13 March 2017, 16.00

Moore Institute Seminar Room, G010
Hardiman Research Building
National University of Ireland, Galway

Refreshments will be served. All welcome!

To confirm your attendance, register online:
www.eventbrite.ie/e/launch-of-harmful-algal-blooms-ibook-tickets-32407091483

Opportunities to increase ocean literacy are limited in the
Junior Cycle Science Curriculum across Europe. This iBook is
designed to infuse the diverse and engaging story of Harmful
Algal Blooms into teaching across the sciences. The author
will speak about his research at the heart of the book and the
audience will be introduced to the pedagogical design aimed
to ensure the content can be taken up by science teachers
and students to advance a sea change in Irish and European
ocean literacy.

TWITTER
@SeaChange_EU

FACEBOOK
SeaChangeProjectEU

WEBSITE
http://seachangeproject.eu/

This project has received funding from the European Union's Horizon 2020
research and innovation programme under grant agreement No. 652644.
This output reflects the views only of the author, and the European Union
cannot be held responsible for any use which may be made of the information
contained therein.

Designed & developed by AquaTT

Fig. 26.4 Sample promotional materials

Fig. 26.5 Sample promotional materials

People Strategy

The co-creation nature of Sea Change resulted in a highly participatory people–process steeped in collaboration, empowerment, and direct active engagement with the target groups. This meant speaking, listening, and working *with* target audiences on their own terms throughout all of the campaign and not *on* or *for* the target groups.

Process Strategy

The key outcome of this Sea Change campaign is co-creating change. This process started with the co-discovery of lived experiences, values, attitudes, beliefs, knowledge, motivations, and current behaviors among the three target audiences. For example, over 100 people were involved in scoping out the initial design of the HABs tool including teachers, students, marine educators, scientists, teacher educators, and Sea Change European partners. It also embraced system actors such as media and policy stakeholders through the ocean literacy dialogue forums discussed in the SWOT analysis above. This was followed by a co-design phase to capture new meanings through the digitally interactive HABs iBook ending (see evaluation below) with co-delivery through the existing channels of distribution in schools, marine centers, and aquariums that either blocks or empowers individuals to alter their behaviors.

Research and Program Evaluation

To measure if change was happening, the first phase of evaluation focused on feedback from scientists, teachers, students, and other informal education stakeholders across European countries to help with the pedagogical design of the tool. This evaluation consisted of semi-structured interviews, teacher journal reflections, and post-lesson student exit cards (McHugh, Domegan, & Duane, 2018). Pilot data revealed a number of ways that students were making connections to their everyday lives and past experiences, which in turn strengthened their personal interest in the ocean. Fifty-three percent of student exit cards noted that the interactive elements in the iBook were fundamental to their learning about the ocean. The three aspects students mentioned on a continual basis were pictures, videos, and the review questions. For example:

> The pictures, it was interesting, the test at the end of the chapters, the resources within the book, the videos, the variety of chapters and topics. I loved the 'did you know' tabs, pictures, videos, fun facts. (Clare, Exit Cards, Lesson 3)

> Images, review questions and 'did you know' sections helped me learn about the oceans. (Jake, Exit Cards, Lesson 1)

A second form of evaluation to measure if change was happening comes in the form of download metrics. With the campaign just launched, initial metrics show 128 downloads within first few months across multiple countries (Figs. 26.6 and 26.7).

However, the official metrics for the iBook downloads can be deceptive as they only measure when an individual user downloads the iBook once. If that same user then transfers the iBook to a class set of 35 iPads, the official iTunes metrics considers this as only one download and therefore is not reflective of the actual iBooks in use or the potential reach of the information and ocean literacy.

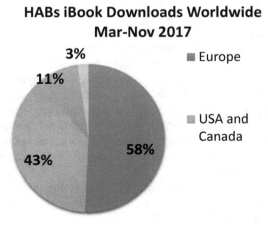

HABs iBook Downloads Worldwide Mar-Nov 2017

Fig. 26.6 HABs iBook downloads worldwide, March–December 2017

HABs iBook Downloads Europe Mar-Nov 2017

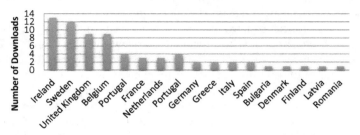

Fig. 26.7 HABs iBook downloads across Europe, March–December 2017

Discussion and Lessons Learned

From the outset, Sea Change fundamentally recognized that complex environmental and sustainable societal problems do not occur in a vacuum. Such problems incorporate multiple stakeholder groups at multiple levels of influence (McLeroy, Bibeau, Steckler, & Glanz, 1988; Dibb, 2014; Hastings and Domegan, 2018). Without co-discovering the issues and without debating and discussing complex engagement issues, we run the risk of multiple and uncoordinated attempts at addressing the issue, without all parties at the table. The evidence shows this can result in many false starts if behavioral change deliberations do not engage a multiplicity of macro-micro-stakeholders that can contribute different insights and expertise toward meaningful strategies for change. Co-creating change through a highly participatory design approach is one of many valuable inclusivity strategies for social marketing. Co-creation, its five fundamental concepts (McHugh and Domegan, 2018), and the processes of co-discovery, co-design, and co-delivery (Hastings and Domegan, 2018; McHugh and Domegan, 2018) in this case provide theoretical and practical contributions for social marketing. The integrative and people-powered approach of co-creation theory facilitates top-down and bottom-up thinking. It also considers pathways and priorities for future actions, allowing groups to come together to co-design and co-create change.

The multiplicity of stakeholders, from co-discovery to co-design and co-delivery of the campaign, not only was useful to fine-tune the social marketing strategy but can potentially have a catalytic effect on the ongoing and growing conversations on oceans and waterways; e.g., the iBook is currently being translated for use in Europe and South America.

Lesson Learnt: Co-creation is a framework for seeing interrelationships rather than things, for seeing "patterns of change" rather than static "snapshots" (Senge, 2006; McHugh and Domegan, 2013; Biroscak et al., 2014). The most universal and powerful influences on a person's behavior are those closest to them—the ones they take for granted and ones they do not even realize are there and cannot discuss or describe. Their immediate environment and the system around them have a powerful impact on their lives whether they realize it or not.

However, deep one digs in a bid to understand a person's behavior, and the social marketer will not get a full picture unless the importance of the system the target audiences are living in, with all its political, cultural, social, technological, and economic characteristics, is recognized. Every person is influenced by the circumstances in which they find themselves. For sustainability, it is important to think about wider-scale change and transformation as well as individual behaviors.

Lesson Learnt: *Co-creating behavioral change means a large portion of the knowledge is acquired through the participatory process. Relationship marketing is critical to success.*

Interactivity as a behavioral change force in a campaign appeals to personal relevance and experience. Digital interactive tools and games offer multiple opportunities to engage audiences for behavioral change. Interactivity creates inherent interest leading to attention and engagement in real-world scenarios that facilitate behavioral change. It also presents a novel domain where the target audience are, as digital residents, experts.

Within this campaign, major aspects of the co-creation "defenestrated" and did not act as predicated (Dede, 2005, p. 6). This allows for a self-corrective and adaptive process, enabling modification and assurance of a closer line between theory and technological innovation (Hoadley, 2004; Wang and Hannafin, 2005). The lesson learnt was of the bottom-up, grassroots route to self-organization for behavioral change. With this in mind, this campaign can be lifted from the immediate context of ocean literacy and adapted to other interactive technology contexts such as energy efficiency and Sustainable Development Goals.

Lesson Learnt: *No matter how complex or removed the problem, connecting the problem to personal experiences and personal relevance is central to digital interactivity and its success. A bottom-up and grassroots approach compliments top-down and policy initiatives.*

Evaluation and measuring impact are not always easy, as shown by the download metrics, but it should not be treated as an after-thought or a last line of defense (Bayliss-Brown, McHugh, Buckley, & Domegan, 2015).

Lesson Learnt: *For the possibility of legacy, scaling out, and replicating its success more widely, it is important to reflect on what is being worked on, together, and determine if change is actually happening.*

Discussion Questions

1. What has co-creation theory to do with environmental behavioral change?
2. What competitive analysis could be conducted to further inform the positioning decisions?
3. What other social marketing theories could inform the co-creation participatory process?
4. What engagement strategy would you recommend as part of the people strategy?
5. What partnership strategy would be the most appropriate to the campaign?

References

Bayliss-Brown, G. A., McHugh, P., Buckley, P., & Domegan, C. (2015). *D8.1-The sea change collective impact assessment framework.* EU Sea Change Project, Cefas, United Kingdom.

Bingimlas, K. A. (2009). Barriers to the successful integration of ICT in teaching and learning environments: A review of the literature. *Eurasia Journal of Mathematics, Science & Technology Education, 5*(3), 235–245.

Biroscak, B., Schneider, T., Panzera, A. D., Bryant, C.,A., McDermott, R. J., Mayer, A. B., ... Hovmand, P. S. (2014). Applying systems science to evaluate a community-based social marketing innovation: A case study. *Social Marketing Quarterly, 20*(4), 247–267.

Bryson, J. M. (2004). What to do when stakeholders matter? *Public Management Review, 6,* 21–53.

Bunn, M., Savage, G., & Holloway, B. (2002). Stakeholder analysis for multi-section innovation. *Journal of Business and Industrial Marketing, 17*(2/3), 181–203.

Comiskey, D., McCartan, K., & Nicholl, P. (2013). *iBuilding for Success? iBooks as Open Educational Resources in Built Environment Education,* translated by Academic Conferences Limited, 86.

Davies, A., & Simon, J. (2013). Engaging citizens in social innovation: A short guide to the research for policy makers and practitioners. A deliverable of the project: "The theoretical, empirical and policy foundations for building social innovation in Europe" (TEPSIE), European Commission —7th Framework Programme, Brussels: European Commission, DG Research.

Dede, C. (2005). Why design-based research is both important and difficult. *Educational Technology, 45*(1), 5–8.

Dibb, S. (2014). Up, up and away: Social marketing breaks free. *Journal of Marketing Management, 30*(11–12), 1159–1185.

Fauville, G., McHugh, P., Domegan, C., Mäkitalo, Å., Friis Møller, L., Papathanassiou, M., Chicote, C., ... Gotensparre, S. (2018). Using collective intelligence to Identify barriers to teaching 12–19 year olds about the ocean in Europe. *Marine Policy, 91,* 85–96, Retrieved from: https://doi.org/10.1016/j.marpol.2018.01.034

Gomes, D. M., & McCauley, V. (2016). Dialectical dividends: Fostering hybridity of new pedagogical practices and partnerships in science education and outreach. *International Journal of Science Education, 38*(13–14), 2259–2283. Retrieved from: http://dx.doi.org/10.1080/09500693.2016.1234729.

Hastings, G., & Domegan, C. (2018). *Social marketing rebels with a cause* (3rd ed.). Routledge UK.

Heemskerk, I., Volman, M., Admiraal, W., & ten Dam, G. (2012). Inclusiveness of ICT in secondary education: Students' appreciation of ICT tools. *International Journal of Inclusive Education, 16*(2), 155–170.

Hoadley, C. M. (2004). Methodological alignment in design-based research. *Educational Psychologist, 39*(4), 203–212.

Hynes, S., Norton, D., & Corless, R. (2014). Investigating societal attitudes towards the marine environment of Ireland. *Marine policy, 47,* 57–65.

Kim, J. H. (2013). Apple's iBooks author: Potential, pedagogical meanings. In *Transforming K-12 classrooms with digital technology* (119).

Kotler, P., & Lee, N. R. (2010). *Social marketing: Influencing behaviors for good.* Newbury Park, CA: Sage Publications.

Maich, K., & Hall, C. (2015). Implementing iPads in the inclusive classroom setting. *Intervention in School and Clinic.* https://doi.org/10.1177/1053451215585793.

McCauley, V., Gomes, D. M., & Davison, K. (2018). Constructivism in the third space: Challenging pedagogical perceptions of science outreach and science education. *International Journal of Science Education.* https://doi.org/10.1080/21548455.2017.1409444.

McHugh, M., & McCauley, V. (in press) By Hook or by crook: Designing physics video hooks with a modified ADDIE framework. *The Journal of Applied Instructional Design.*

McHugh, M., McCauley, V., Davison, K., Raine, R., & Grehan, A. (in press). Anchoring ocean literacy: participatory iBook design within secondary science classrooms. *Technology, Pedagogy and Education.*

McHugh, P., & Domegan, C. (2013). From reductionism to holism: How social marketing captures the bigger picture through system indicators. In K. Kubacki & S. Rundle-Thiele (Eds.), *Contemporary issues in social marketing.* UK: Cambridge Scholars Publishing Ltd.

McHugh, P., Domegan, C., McCauley, V., Davison, K., Burke, N., & Dromgool-Regan, C. (2016) *Ireland's national report on the consultation protocol—Sea change: Our Irish Ocean Conversations Report.* EU Sea Change Project, Whitaker Institute, NUI Galway, Ireland.

McHugh, P., & Domegan, C. (2018). *D6.3—Revised ocean literacy co-creation (principles) toolkit.* EU Sea Change Project, Whitaker Institute, NUI Galway, Ireland.

McHugh, P., Domegan, C., & Duane, S. (2018). Protocols for stakeholder participation in social marketing systems. *Social Marketing Quarterly, 24*(3), 164–193.

McLeroy, K. R., Bibeau, D., Steckler, A., & Glanz, K. (1988). An ecological perspective on health promotion programs. *Health Education & Behavior, 15*(4), 351–377.

Mulcahy, R., Russell-Bennett, R., & Rundle-Thiele, S. (2015). Electronic games: Can they create value for the moderate drinking brand? *Journal of Social Marketing, 5*(3), 258–278.

National Oceanic and Atmospheric Administration. (2013). Ocean literacy: The essential principles and fundamental concepts of ocean sciences for learners of all ages. Retrieved from: http://www.coexploration.org/oceanliteracy/documents/OceanLitChart.pdf. Accessed January 2018.

Russell-Bennett, R., Mulcahy, R., McAndrew, R., Swinton, T., Little J.A., & Horrocks, N. (2018). Case study 4 reduce your juice: A digital social marketing programme for reducing residential electricity use. In G. Hastings & C. Domegan (Eds.), *Social marketing rebels with a cause* (3rd ed.). Routledge UK.

Schoedinger, S., Tran, L. U., & Whitley, L. (2010). *From the principles to the scope and sequence: A brief history of the ocean literacy campaign. NMEA Special Report, 3,* 3–7. Retrieved from: http://coexploration.org/oceanliteracy/NMEA_Report_3/NMEA_2010-2-History.pdf.

Senge, P. M. (2006). *The fifth discipline: The art and practice of the learning organization* (1st ed.). Century business): Random House. Kindle Edition.

Strang, C., DeCharon, A., & Schoedinger, S. (2007). Can you be science literate without being ocean literate? *The Journal of Marine Education, 23*(1), 7–9.

Tran, L. U., Payne, D. L., & Whitley, L. (2010). Research on learning and teaching ocean and aquatic sciences. *NMEA Special Report, 3,* 22–26.

Wang, F., & Hannafin, M. J. (2005). Design-based research and technology-enhanced learning environments. *Educational Technology Research and Development, 53*(4), 5–23.

Enhancing Health by Means of Massive Open Online Courses

27

Gonzalo Diaz-Meneses

Chapter Overview

The current case study refers to a project that attempted to develop a social marketing plan to enhance engagement in co-creation of a series of massive open online courses (MOOCs). The purpose of the social marketing plan was to encourage several target groups (people with diabetes, pregnant women and breastfeeding mothers, the elderly, children, and teenagers), in select countries (Belgium, Denmark, Germany, Holland, Ireland, Italy, Spain, and Sweden) to co-create massive open online courses (MOOCs) for public benefit. With the aim of implementing suitable promotional strategies for each target group in every country, a survey was carried out, and so, the structure of the social marketing problem was described as a planning process whose antecedents were three key variables: digital literacy, health literacy, and digital health literacy. The most successful recruitment methods were implemented by the national coordinators, who played a crucial role in promoting engagement in the co-creation activities. In the end, this social marketing plan was useful in helping to promote and improve e-health literacy for the sake of the "European dream."

G. Diaz-Meneses (✉)
Faculty of Economy, Management, and Tourism,
University of Las Palmas de Gran Canaria, The Canary Islands, Spain
e-mail: Gonzalo.diazmeneses@ulpgc.es

© Springer Nature Switzerland AG 2019
D. Z. Basil et al. (eds.), *Social Marketing in Action*,
Springer Texts in Business and Economics,
https://doi.org/10.1007/978-3-030-13020-6_27

411

Campaign Background

The current case study refers to a project[1] that attempted to develop a social marketing plan to enhance engagement in co-creation of a series of massive open online courses (MOOCs). Co-creation is a user-centered design approach, the process of which consists of the active participation of people in the development of the MOOCs' content alongside researchers, healthcare professionals, and web designers. In this case, the MOOCs were courses tailored to the needs of specific target audiences and dedicated to several health-related issues, such as diseases like diabetes, and vulnerable groups such as pregnant women and breastfeeding mothers, the elderly, children, and teenagers, as well as addressing social trends. These co-creation activities were organized through communities of practices, or a group of people engaged in a shared process of learning, working, and contributing (Perello & Avagnina, 2017).

The reasons for and aims of the MOOCs are multifold. First, these MOOCs aim to increase digital health literacy in Europe, especially as regards specific topics such as the vulnerable groups mentioned above. This is not only because diabetes, pregnancy, breastfeeding, aging, childhood, and adolescence are connected to vulnerable groups, but also because the MOOCs represent an opportunity to develop social participation in the context of new technologies. Second, these MOOCs attempt to enhance peer learning techniques whose co-creation methodology will be used to advise and legitimize the European Union policies on health. Third, as far as the MOOCs diffusion and engagement are concerned, the sustainability and efficiency of the European welfare state will benefit from fostering citizen and stakeholder involvement with this openly accessible and massive initiative.

The purpose of the social marketing plan was to encourage several target groups in select countries to co-create massive open online courses (MOOCs) for public benefit. The MOOCs were developed by making good use of the Course Builder tool provided by Google Open Online Education and are accessible on mobile devices as well. So, the present project brought into focus a social marketing plan whose objective was to bring about the desired conduct of co-creation from individuals belonging to five different target groups (children, teenagers, pregnant women and breastfeeding mothers, the elderly, and patients with diabetes) from eight European Union countries (Belgium, Denmark, Germany, Holland, Ireland, Italy, Spain, and Sweden). The co-creation response consisted of taking part in offline and online meetings over a six-month period in order to contribute to the MOOCs content and design. In this way, representatives of the target groups were recruited in the eight countries and organized into communities of practice formed by health professionals, educators, academics, and other practitioners. To be

---

[1]This case study is inspired by a project that has received funding from the European Union's Horizon 2020 research and innovation program under grant agreement No. 727474. The content of this case study reflects only the IC-Health social marketing subproject author's views. The European Union is not liable for any use that may be made of the information contained herein.

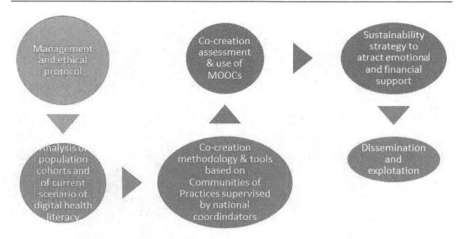

Fig. 27.1 Flowchart of the MOOC's project steps and milestones

specific, the activities of these co-creators consisted of co-designing the MOOCs, contributing the content to the courses, and even testing the courses.

The MOOCs project comprises six work packages (Fig. 27.1).

This social marketing plan was embedded in the European Union IC-Health project organization, which itself was comprised of fourteen different organizations under the management and coordination of Gobierno de Canarias (The Government of the Canary Islands) and four other entities with strategic responsibilities (University of Ulster, Consulta Europa Projects and Innovation, Associazione Comitato Collaborazione Medica, and the European Health Management Association), each organization played a different function and was in charge of a different area of responsibility as shown in Fig. 27.2.

The remaining organizations performed supporting activities related to their specializations. First, five universities are: Université Catholique de Louvain (Institute of Psychological Sciences), Universita Degli Studi di Udine (Department of Medical and Biological Sciences), Universidad de La Laguna (Department of Didactic and Educational Research), Tallinn University (Center for Educational Technology), and Universidad de Las Palmas de Gran Canaria (Faculty of Economics); second, one research center: Consiglio Nazionale delle Ricerche (Social Informatics and Computing); two non-profit organizations: Scanbalt Forening (Health and Bio-economy) and Funka (e-Technology for disabled people); and one hospital: Azienda Ospedaliero Universitaria Anna Meyer (children's hospital).

The University of Las Palmas de Gran Canaria (ULPGC) was appointed as the head organization to draw up the social marketing plan for engaging the co-creators.

The structure of the social marketing problem might be described as a planning process whose antecedents were three key variables: digital literacy, health literacy, and digital health literacy (EC, 2010, 2012, 2014, 2016; Giudice et al., 2017; Giudice & Poletto, 2016; HLS-EU, 2012; Montanari, Perello, Avagnina, &

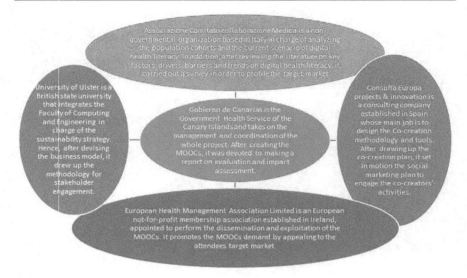

Fig. 27.2 Social marketing plan

Giudice, 2017; WHO, 2013). These variables also represented the criteria for assessing how likely each target group from each country was to take part in co-creation processes (see Fig. 27.4). We understand digital literacy as the degree to which individuals have the ability to access, understand, and use electronic devices and the Internet. Similarly, health literacy regards the capacity to search, process, and comprehend health information. Finally, digital health literacy is the level to which a person can make informed decisions about health care, disease prevention, and health promotion thanks to their ability to use new information technologies related to electronic devices and the Internet (EC, 2014). This social problem structure was further interpreted by considering the model for health behavior change (Chang, Choi, Kim, & Song, 2014) and the technology acceptance model (Liu, Chen, Sun, Wible, & Kno, 2010). While the former allowed a specific application of its key variables, such as health behavior information, health behavior motivation, health behavior skills, and health behavior itself, the latter considered other dimensions such as perceived usefulness, ease of use, perceived interaction, and intention to use (Fig. 27.4).

Therefore, the mission of this social marketing plan was to take on the responsibility for enhancing digital health literacy across specific vulnerable target groups in Europe by means of the co-creation of a series of online courses designed to improve citizens' well-being. To this end, the social marketing project comprises three different phases (diagnosis, formulation, and implementation) including thirteen steps (Fig. 27.4), and so, the output of the social marketing plan was the engagement of the co-creators.

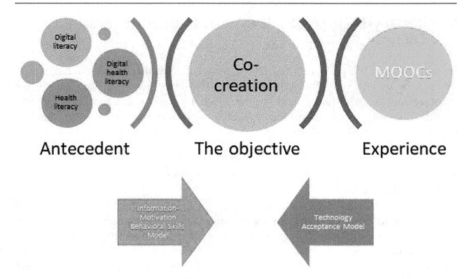

Fig. 27.3 Structure of the social marketing problem as regards co-creation on the 35 MOOCs on health

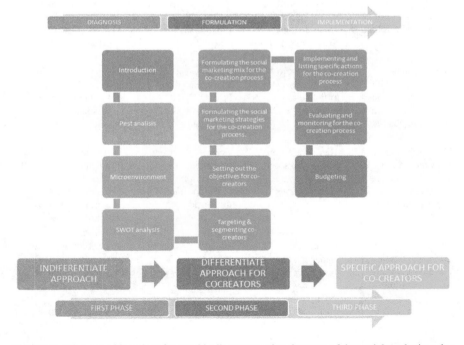

Fig. 27.4 Diagram of flowchart for graphically representing the steps of the social marketing plan

SWOT Analysis (Strengths, Weaknesses, Opportunities, and Threats)

In order to identify the internal and the external variables that can either enhance or impede the social marketing performance and influence how well it accomplishes its objectives, a SWOT analysis was carried out. To achieve this aim, four different analytical sections were considered: strengths, weakness, opportunities, and threats (Table 27.1).

Target Audience

While targeting consists of identifying the main audience, segmentation is a matter of distinguishing different homogeneous groups in order to apply specific policies, thus optimizing the responses of the market. Therefore, identifying market segments and targets is essential in order to connect with customers and co-creators (Kotler & Keller, 2012) in public health (Lefebvre & Flora, 1988).

Table 27.1 SWOT analysis

Strengths	Weakness	Opportunities	Threats
Highly qualified, intrinsically motivated, and multidisciplinary human resources	There was a lack of an exclusive organizational structure to perform this plan	The subject matter was highly innovative in an emerging e-health market	The existence of significant segments of digitally illiterate target audiences
International organization with representatives in every country where this project is working	There was no budget specifically designed to financially support this social marketing plan	There was a strong trend related to health, digital literacy, well-being, and quality of life in Europe	There was a rise in concern about privacy and commercialization of personal data on the Internet in Europe
The social marketing plan fell within the framework of the European Union project with its own fund	There were few formal links with the industry or any business organization	There were strong international networks for e-health in Europe and all over the world	There was a relatively significant institutional and legal discoordination stemming from a very fast and volatile technology
The project showed good reputation due to social responsibility and non-profit values	The executive manager of the social marketing project did not belong to the main partner organization, and thus, coordination was time-consuming	e-health was an EU priority	Austerity might affect the quality and long-term output of the project

In order to target effectively, it was necessary to ask three different questions (Vázquez & TresPalacios, 1994). Firstly, who were they? What do they look like? The answer pertained to the sociodemographic and situational characteristics of people who might become a co-creator. Secondly, what were they like? In this case, the answer related to their psychographic characteristics in terms of personality and values. Thirdly, how could the co-creators' needs be satisfied?

The segmentation task entailed dealing with the main audience, not as if it were a mass market, but rather as if it were comprised of different groups or segments.

Be that as it may, co-creators were recruited by selecting individuals who showed the highest level of involvement with each specific course. In other words, they were experienced citizens, preferably with knowledge of the course subject matter, along with enough digital literacy to contribute to the course content. Hence, they were interested in the courses due to the fact they were either children, teenagers, pregnant women and breastfeeding mothers, elderly, or diabetics, or simply that they belonged to the personal or professional social circle of the potential attendee. In any case, despite the selection process being described by another plan of the project, the social marketing plan focused on designing effective and efficient methods for catching the attention of these target audiences. On this basis, they were people who were involved in the course topic due to their job, cohort, or social circle; they were proactive, open, creative, reflective, and sociable, and what they strive for is to live up to their self-fulfillment needs.

Consistently, they were divided into different homogeneous groups in order to encourage involvement by considering the specific course subject matter that was promoted. In addition, given that for the co-creation sustainability process, sustained collaboration was a key point, they were recruited, trained, and offered a course of action in accordance with their convenience and sense of meaning. In terms of the diffusion of innovation theory (Greenhalgh, Robert, Macfarlane, Bate, & Kyriakidou, 2004), it might be pointed out that the social marketing plan targeted the innovators in order to guarantee quick and easy recruitment, rather than the early adopters, whose engagement it was aimed at securing later on when the courses' attendees were considered.

Therefore, the co-creator population was broken down into eight different nationalities belonging to the five cohorts considered by the project. So, while the criteria for segmenting were nationality and cohort, the criteria for targeting were involvement, experience, and self-fulfillment needs, as well as digital and health literacies.

Campaign Objectives

Social marketing for enhancing e-health across the European Union was the mission of this plan by means of promoting a co-creation process for 35 MOOCs. It drew up a course of action divided into three parts—*upstream, midstream, and downstream*—for the sake of efficacy and efficiency. First, the upstream and midstream levels consisted of mega-marketing and alliance strategies, respectively. Second, the downstream level entailed a set of promotional techniques, such as *block leader*, *commitment*, *objective setting*, and *prompt*, whose success depended on the match between the thoroughly experienced, highly involved, and self-seeking potential co-creator and the antecedent nature of the incentive. Also, some consequent techniques were devised for less-involved co-creators. On this basis, the present social marketing plan showed not only concrete and pragmatic courses of action to recruit co-creators for the MOOCs, but also innovative and ground-breaking theoretical approaches designed to deal with any deficiency in regard to digital literacy, health literacy, and e-health literacy across five specific cohorts in eight European countries.

As the co-creation process considered the design of 35 MOOCs, the number of co-creators was fixed in accordance with the co-creation management requirements. In fact, it was expected to comprise of 780 participants allocated to six target groups, after separating patients with diabetes type 1 and diabetes type 2, along with the four remaining cohorts, and only six "country" groups by putting together Denmark, Germany, and The Netherlands, besides the remaining project countries (see Table 27.2). The number and distribution of the co-creators were fixed after taking account of the recommendations of the IT, health, and social workers participating in the project. Children and the elderly were contacted through their schools and elderly associations, respectively, and co-creation was offered as after-school and social activities (Perello & Avagnina, 2017).

The criteria for recruiting the co-creators were different depending on the participant profile. For children and teenagers, the age was between 10 and 13 and 14 and 18 years old, respectively, with gender balance and with a small quota of the immigrant minority. For the elderly, age was considered to be over 60 years old, and for adults, in general, diverse backgrounds in terms of education and social class, a minimum digital and health literacy, and level of fluency in the national language were considered, as well as a small quota of certain minorities such as the disabled and other vulnerable groups.

Table 27.2 Co-creation objectives in terms of participants

Cohort/country	Spain	Italy	Belgium	UK	Sweden	Denmark Germany Netherlands
Children	40	80	20		20	20
Teenagers	20	60	20		20	20
Pregnant women and breastfeeding mothers	40	20	20		20	20
The elderly	40	20	20	40		20
Patients with diabetes 1	20	40	20		20	20
Patients with diabetes 2	20		20		20	20
Total	180	220	120	40	100	120
Overall total	780					

Barriers and Benefits

Insofar as the engagement of the community of co-creators took place both offline and online, the barriers and advantages were different. The offline activities consisted of 95 meetings divided into two different phases. First, the objective was to generate trust and a positive predisposition toward the project. Second, it aimed at building and testing the MOOCs. Therefore, the main barrier stemmed from the fact that although all partners were European, they were far away from each other and, therefore, collaboration needed to be planned quite some time in advance. In addition, despite the team members being willing to develop a good rapport, they did not have any experience working together in the field of social marketing. Finally, this social marketing plan had no history or tradition and thus was not well-known either by the potential contributors or the moderators.

In respect to the online activities, the participants in the communities of practice were induced to register on the digital platform and, once they became members, were assigned three different user roles whose organization represented a key advantage. The administrators were two partners of the project (Consulta Europa and EHMA), the moderators were the national coordinators, and the participants were users, the vast majority of whom had been former members of the community of practice (651). However, the social marketing manager neither took part in the communities of practice nor had direct access to the Internet resources that had been built as the direct result of these virtual meetings.

In addition, the online platform provided some advantages that could increase productivity and efficiency in a moment when these benefits were highly appreciated at the EU. These perceived advantages, along with the shared belief that e-health was in high demand because of its ability to improve patient satisfaction, made the online users and administrators feel really committed. Particularly fruitful was the fact that the administrators, predominantly, were convinced that e-health represented a new trend, and social marketing for health was quite well-consolidated: experience and creativity together.

In addition, the specific profiles of these co-creators and their personal circumstances determined certain disparities of responses. For example, pregnant women and breastfeeding mothers were more inclined to take part online, while seniors preferred to attend face-to-face meetings. Children and teenagers were easily recruited in schools thanks to the generous collaboration of teachers and parents. Theoretically speaking, one might point out that co-creation in health services is more effective if the consumer's circumstances are potentially value affected by the output and outcome of the co-creation activities (Nambisan & Nambisan, 2009). For example, it seems clear that partnership development is more convenient, the existence of robust structures such as healthcare centers and schools results in efficient organizational efforts, and the possibility of direct meaningful experience based on dialog, access, and risk-benefit perceptions increase the potential co-creators will and self-realization.

Furthermore, inhibitors and advantages might be analyzed from the perspective of the social learning theory and the health belief model by taking into account perceived benefits and hindrances stemming for the co-creation participation. In fact, it stands to reason that potentially affected profiles would be more responsive, given that they would feel a higher level of susceptibility, severity, and threat from the MOOCs' subject matter (Rosenstock, Strecher, Becker, 1988). For example, pregnant women and people suffering from diabetes would be more willing to take part in co-creation activities than non-pregnant women and people free of diabetes. Similarly, in accordance with the trans-theoretical stages of change model (Prochaska & DiClemente, 1982), it seems logical to think that the people most likely to be engaged in the co-creation activities would be those in the contemplation and preparation stage. For instance, the elderly and the young were expected to show a more positive predisposition toward the communities of practices than middle-aged people. This favorability might be attributed to their higher level of awareness and preparation, whose positive valence represents a clear advantage in adopting the conduct advocated.

Finally, the application of social marketing was quite innovative and represented the most advanced approach to promoting social benefits. In fact, by applying commercial marketing doctrines to social marketing (Grier & Bryant, 2005; Wood, 2008), it was possible to distinguish three levels of product as follows: the core benefits (the sense of self-realization felt by co-creators), the actual creation responses (the contributing behavior), and the augmented co-creation features (the promotional resources and techniques to induce co-creation).

On the basis of these barriers and benefits, some alliances were formulated. The strategy of alliances assumed that the most preferable contributors to the MOOCs were the manager and the key specialized or highly skilled professionals in any potentially allied organization. These alliance strategies took account of the midstream approach laid out in Table 27.3 and so were systematized by considering the following threefold taxonomic criteria: sector, geographical scope, and cohort population. We understand by "midstream" an approach consisting of influencing groups and organizations (Russell-Bennett, Wood, & Previte, 2013). In this way, a crosstab was designed with three different dimensions. Firstly, profit, non-profit, public, non-formal organizations, lobbies, and miscellaneous fell into the sector criterion of classification. Secondly, international, the European Union, national, regional, and local items fell into the geographical scope criterion. Thirdly, the criterion as regards children, teenagers, pregnant women and breastfeeding mothers, the elderly, and diabetics.

Being that the course subject matter was the key criterion (35 MOOCs with different subject matters), besides the particular target audience (children, teenagers, pregnant women and breastfeeding mothers, the elderly, diabetics), the identified allies, and the role to be played by each of them was researched differently in each country.

Table 27.3 Detecting potential problematic levels of development and consequently positioning predispositions

		DL	HL	eHL
Belgian	Children	30% insufficient	70 insufficient	Worse than others
	Teenagers	Worse than others	55% insufficient	Worse than others
	Mothers	Better than others	19% limited	The lowest
	The elderly	The lowest	25.5% limited	Worse than others
	Diabetics	Divide	15.3% Inadequate	The lowest
Danish	Children	Better than others	52.3% limited	Medium
	Teenagers	Better than others	27.4% limited	Better than others
	Mothers	Better than others	22.2% limited	Medium
	The elderly	Better than others	40.9% limited	Better than others
	Diabetics	Divide	Worse than others	Better than others
Dutch	Children	Negative score	Better than others	The best
	Teenagers	Better than others	Better than others	Better than others
	Mothers	Better than others	15.1% limited	The best
	The elderly	The best	15% limited	The best
	Diabetics	The best and divide	The best	The best
German	Children	Worse than others	89.3% limited	Worse than others
	Teenagers	Better than others	40% limited	Better than others
	Mothers	Better than others	40.6% limited	Worse than others
	The elderly	29% limited	63.1% limited	Worse than others
	Diabetics	Medium	41.5% limited	Medium
Italian	Children	Worse than others	Worse than others	The lowest
	Teenagers	The lowest	Worse than others	Worse than others
	Mothers	Better than others	The lowest	The lowest
	The elderly	Better than others	12.4% inadequate	The lowest
	Diabetics	Worse than others	38.9% limited	Worse than others
Spanish	Children	Medium	61% limited	Better than others
	Teenagers	Better than others	48% limited	Better than others
	Mothers	Better than others	The lowest	Worse than others
	The elderly	Better than others	34.6% limited	Divide
	Diabetics	Divide	The best	Divide
Swedish	Children	Worse than others	Worse than others	Worse than others
	Teenagers	Better than others	Better than others	The best
	Mothers	Better than others	Worse than others	Better than others
	The elderly	Better than others	Worse than others	Worse than others
	Diabetics	Better than others	Medium	Medium
UK	The elderly	Better than others	35.3% limited	Better than others

Positioning and Competition

To understand the positioning of the MOOCs from the perspective of the target audience, the plan brought into focus the three variables that described the social marketing problem structure: health literacy, digital literacy, and digital health literacy. It was assumed that the target audience was going to interpret the opportunity to take part in the co-creation process depending on their capacities, skills, appraisal, and on how they were able to use and apply digital health information. For example, it was thought that people showing a low level of digital skill and health literacy would be apprehensive and maybe more likely to consider negatively their predisposition toward adopting the co-creator behavior.

On the basis of the social marketing literature (Kotler, Roberto, & Lee, 2002; Andreasen, 2006; French, Blair-Stevens, Mcvey, & Merritt, 2010), competition was not represented by other organizations, but rather the alternative processing and moderating psychographic variables that might work as replacements for the desired conduct of this plan. As the co-creation responses to generate the content of the MOOCs were the product of this social marketing campaign, the competitors were any other alternative response the target audience might perform instead of contributing to the courses.

In addition, it seemed logical to think that there were various competitors for every course and that this *competition* needed to be defined by considering the subject matter of every course for each cohort in each country. Therefore, it was important to indicate the related benefits that every target audience was accustomed to and preferred over the desired conducts of co-creation and enrollment on the courses.

However, the generic competition was listed by cohorts as follows:

Children: It was assumed that they would prefer playing in the traditional sense over contributing to the courses. For this reason, the MOOCs integrated "gamification" so that a sense of fun was generated in order to compete against traditional free-time activities. For example, an app with games was designed for children.

Teenagers: It was assumed that they would prefer meeting with their peers over contributing to the courses. Hence, for instance, it seemed logical to recommend the construction of a forum where they could chat, share, and grow with their peers within the MOOC platform.

Pregnant women and breastfeeding mothers: It was assumed that they would prefer consuming media elsewhere than contributing to the online courses. Therefore, it was suggested that video/audio clips and other streaming resources were offered, for example, by making good use of some free recording software, such as screencast.

The elderly: It was assumed that they would prefer books, brochures, catalogs, and other kinds of traditional paper-based resources over online contributing resources. Consequently, the MOOCs were offered with some traditional resources associated, such as books and so on, for example, by contacting some publishers in order to encourage them to solicit book and catalog donations.

Patients with diabetes: It was assumed that they might find other sources of information more helpful in encouraging them to exercise and eat well than the courses. Hence, the courses set some offline activities so that they felt they were doing something real to combat their disease, for example, by recruiting some volunteers to organize sporting activities.

Research

A survey with self-administered questionnaires was carried out in order to gather information about digital health literacy from the MOOCs' target populations (Giudice et al., 2017; Montanari et al., 2017). These questionnaires were designed after reviewing the literature on e-health and developing eight focus groups conducted in Spain and Italy, the results of which were useful for adapting and improving the measuring instruments. The sampling procedure of the survey followed a non-probabilistic system with quota assignment to each cohort and country, and the final sample reached 1704 units. The results of this survey led us to diagnose the level of development of these variables across the potential target co-creation population. The results of the survey are laid out in Table 27.3, whose evidence inspired the implementation of the social marketing formulations and practices for engaging the co-creators.

Marketing Mix Strategy (Product, Price, Place, Promotion)

Consistently with the social marketing approach (Kotler & Zaltman, 1971; Lefrebvre & Flora, 1988), the *product* of this project was not the MOOCs themselves, since this would be a mere commercial approach. In fact, the product was the co-creation response developed by the target audience. In this sense, we understood the co-creation response to be not only the desired behavior of contributing with contents to the digital platform but also taking part in the meetings that can be scheduled within the whole participation process, for example, the communities of practice.

Furthermore, the literature on experiential marketing was addressed as an interesting theoretical resource that could yield the co-created value and deep engagement (Ranjan & Read, 2016). Experiential marketing and co-creation are necessarily linked (Prahalad & Ramaswami, 2004) as they share the paradigm that allows value to be created by considering the consumer more as a "prosumer" rather than as a mere passive user (Galvagno & Dalli, 2014). Thus, the social marketing plan made good use of the five modules of experience: cognitions, emotions, activities, social interactivity, and sensory elements. On this basis, the co-creation process entailed intensive reflections, amusing and surprising affections, vivid activities, empathic and fruitful relationships, and all-encompassing *five senses* atmospheres (Schmitt, 1999).

The co-creation *place* was mainly offline.

The offline policy with the aim of inducing contributions by the potential co-creator audience took place at the following locations:

- the MOOCs office,
- the co-creator organization,
- the co-creator's home, and
- in outdoor contexts such as at events and festivals.

For the MOOCs and for the social marketing campaign, monetary costs were not the point so much as the emotional costs and inhibitors to perform the desired conduct. On this basis, the main barriers to adopt the co-creation response on the part of the authorities' target audiences were not only related to their personal background in IT literacy, health literacy, and IC-Health literacy, but also to how busy they were in their day-to-day lives. No doubt, the co-creation process was quite time-consuming, and henceforward, the co-creation plan was concerned about any delay, time wasting, and dispersal sequence of demanded commitments. These subjective costs were what we consider as *price*.

The formulation of *promotional strategies* for stimulating the number of co-creators was divided into *pull* and *push* initiatives. On the one hand, and within the pull strategies, one pointed to *mega-marketing* initiatives. A pull promotional strategy was defined as a general and long-term policy whose the objective consisted of motivating the main audiences to adopt the desired conduct of co-creating and contributing content to the MOOCs and involved the social marketing project as a whole. On the other hand, the push promotional strategy entailed direct contact with the co-creators in terms of straight tactics and actions. In this case, there was a downstream approach that focuses and places all the change responsibility on the final consumer (Russell-Bennett et al., 2013). So, a wide range of promotional techniques was employed in order to bring about the desired conduct of contributing to the courses.

The mega-marketing initiatives were legitimized due to the fact that this social marketing campaign, in particular, and the e-health project as a whole were conducive to a non-profit and public cause. These initiatives were categorized in accordance with the taxonomy of geographical levels (international, European, national, regional, and local) and issues (health, new technologies, education, children, teenager, women, the elderly, and welfare).

This mega-marketing initiative was assumed to be able to engage the authority, politicians, and the manager—who represented the power—in the contributing process of co-creation so that they became co-creators. In fact, mega-marketing can be considered an upstream approach, given that it includes politicians and institutional leaders (Russell-Bennett et al, 2013). It was achieved in different ways based on direct marketing techniques and public relations tactics, for example, as follows:

- visits to the target organization so that a personal and direct meeting were possible with leaders, potential co-creators, and possible promoter of co-creation;
- phone calls, emailing, and traditional correspondence to provide physical marketing materials;
- events for VIPs in external places organized by the social marketing organizations or, alternatively, by any other external agency, for instance, a health conference;
- receptions and meetings in the social marketing organizer place.

Following the principles of the applied behavior analysis and social marketing (Geller, 1989), it was considered that any promotional downstream activity matched with the profile of someone who showed a high level of interest, involvement, and gratification with their own contributing behavior, the kind of promotional techniques to be employed appropriately was more antecedent than consequent. Specifically, the techniques of antecedent constraints or incentives for the promotion of co-creation proposed for this project were as follows: *prompts, explicit commitment*, the *goal setting* approach, and the *block leader*. The definitions of these techniques are given in Table 27.4 and inspired in Mckenzie-Mohr & Smith (1999). Insofar as this approach is loosely based on the theory ascribed to Petty, Cacioppo, and Schumann (1983), the highly analytical and motivated people should be induced by employing central routes of persuasion, invoking endured commitment, and demanding a high level of effort toward reaching an agreement. In contrast, it is advisable to use peripheral routes of persuasion if the target audience is lesser motivated.

Nevertheless, in some cases, consequent techniques were applied in order to stimulate the collaboration of co-creation if the target audience was not intrinsically motivated (Petty et al., 1983). The definitions of these techniques are inspired in Mckenzie-Mohr & Smith (1999) and gathered below (Table 27.5).

On the basis of the positioning analysis, the implementation plan was divided into the following sections: the promotion of co-creation and, in the case of difficulties, the promotion of co-creation when the co-creator market is not highly involved.

Table 27.4 General characteristics or the main antecedent promotional techniques

Techniques	Definition
Prompts	The individual was exposed to written or oral information
Commitment	An application or declaration was made by the subject in which he/she promised his/her intention to comply with the requirements of the program
Objectives	The individual was asked to achieve levels of participation and a volume of material or content to contribute
Block leader	Individuals who had already participated in other contribution programs were used to persuade their peers

Table 27.5 General characteristics of consequent techniques

Techniques	Definition
Reward	Consistent stimulation or reinforcing technique, which consisted of providing rewards to participants in a co-creation program through a "chip" or token-saving system
Feedback	Consistent stimulation or reinforcing technique, which consisted of providing information about the performance of the contribution behavior to the interested party or target audience
Punishment	Consistent stimulation technique consisting of applying an aversive stimulus to the subject or in the withdrawal of a satisfactory stimulus

Program Evaluation

The recruitment of co-creators reached 749 participants quite rapidly and thus might be considered successful from the beginning. Nevertheless, it represents fewer contributors (31) than was initially planned. To be specific, while Spain, Italy, and Sweden were the most effective countries at calling for co-creators, Germany, Denmark, Netherland, and Belgium engaged fewer than planned. Nonetheless, once the first communities of practice were organized, the number of co-creators easily surpassed the planned number not only in all the countries but also for all the vulnerable groups considered (Fig. 27.5).

Once the exhaustive and extensive social marketing plan was handed in with punctuality to the project manager, it could be seen that evaluating and monitoring were also key tasks to correct any outcome. We knew that more than mere vague

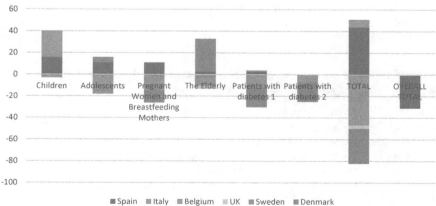

Fig. 27.5 Calculating the recruitment gap between the defined and real number of co-creators

comments were necessary if rigorous evaluation and monitoring work were to be carried out. For this reason, the evaluation and monitoring tasks were broken down into two different sections, and specific indicators—qualitative and quantitative— were put forward to make possible the assessment and the logically consequent measures that were adopted in order to correct and optimize the continuous outcome.

So, the assessment of the co-creation managerial performance was done by distinguishing quantitative and qualitative indicators. The quantitative indicators could, in turn, be broken down into *instrumental* (for example, number of receptions) and *final* (for example, number of co-creators). Consistently, the qualitative indicators for assessing the performance was also divided into *instrumental* (satisfaction of advocates) and *final* (quality of contents).

On this basis, and considering a user-centered approach, the assessment of the MOOCs usage was designed to allocate a perceived quality questionnaire before and after attendees took any course. In this way, not only was the satisfaction level of participants measured, but also suggestions were strongly generated, and a continuous improvement endeavor was embraced.

Discussion and Lessons Learned

Ultimately, the whole social marketing plan to enhance and get people engaged in the co-creation process, and the reality of what actually transpired did not find the best match, given that not only was the set number of co-creators not too high but also because recruiting co-creators across Europe was much easier than we expected. In fact, the engagement of the co-creators was achieved in less than four weeks by simply contacting the potential target market of co-creators. It is true that in Germany, Belgium, and some Scandinavian countries, the selection of co-creators took place a little bit later, but in the rest of the countries, it was easy— mainly in Spain and in Italy where they were recruited just in a few days.

The most successful recruitment methods were implemented by the national coordinators, who played a crucial role in promoting engagement in the co-creation activities. First, they launched a marketing campaign by including a call for co-creators in the partners' newsletters, institutional websites, and social media, and it made a big impact. As a side note, pregnant women and breastfeeding mothers were quite sensitive to this type of online technique. In addition, the national coordinators contacted people that had been involved in the previous survey and focus groups. For instance, elderly people were quite receptive to further collaboration. Similarly, they were also responsible for translating all the promotional materials into their national languages and handed in these resources in the multiple meetings that they held during the recruitment period. Finally, the national coordinators learned how to employ specific recruitment methods by considering the particular circumstances of each target group. For example, for recruiting children and teenagers, they learned that contacting the schools was the easiest way, and for pregnant women and breastfeeding mothers, the most convenient channel was through healthcare professionals, such as midwives, medical doctors (gynecologists and pediatricians), and other health workers. Similarly, centers for health and leisure for the elderly represented the most effective way of contacting senior citizens. Lastly, diabetics were found thanks to medical specialists and specialized associations (IC-Health, 2018).

On this basis, we wonder if a social marketing plan for engaging the co-creators was really necessary. We even wondered if this essential task could have been carried out in a quite spontaneous fashion and without drawing up a specific social marketing plan. Did we use a sledgehammer to crack nuts, so to speak?

Possibly the answer is yes, we did, but we did not "die of success" due to the fact we were able to come up with extra benefits and because we achieved the objectives effectively. The goal was to promote co-creation so that selected people contributed some content to the MOOCs. On this basis, it might be stated that the degree to which this goal was successful indicated how effective the whole project was and, in addition, the social marketing plan has been positive and advantageous for different reasons as outlined below.

It provided more inspiration regarding how to launch the campaign to the final users and attendees rather than to the co-creation participant. Therefore, as enhancing health literacy in Europe was the tacit mission of the current social marketing project, the degree to which this kind of knowledge about health, wellness, and quality of life exists in the population might also be considered a key variable in evaluating and monitoring how well this planning effort worked.

Social marketing and social media marketing were put together, but they were neither misunderstood, nor confused. We were able to distinguish between the non-profit marketing devoted to bringing about the desired conduct of co-creating and the marketing dedicated to handling social media, electronic devices, and the Internet. It is not only a stubborn mistake to confuse both terms and types of marketing, but it also works against the good practice of marketing. On this basis, this project might represent one of the few cases of application in which social marketing and social media marketing set a good example for the project practitioners and the course attendees/target audience, and even for teaching purposes related to university students.

Some additional benefits were generated, such as the high level of satisfaction of the co-creator and the originality of their contributions. The effort of the co-creators was self-gratifying, given that they had resources and skills to share, they wanted to be helpful, and their generous contributions made them feel happy. In fact, the social marketing plan was useful in that it lived up to the co-creators' expectations and enhanced the quality of their work. This positive output of the social marketing plan might be explained in accordance with Lefebvre and Flora (1988) since there is an exchange principal infusing some health interventions whose success consists of putting together the organization's and the volunteers' needs and motivations.

This social marketing plan was useful in helping to promote and improve e-health literacy for the sake of the "European dream," an endeavor that is both greatly needed and entirely possible. After this plan for enhancing the engagement of co-creators and inspiring the promotion of the courses amid the potential attendees, a new door is open within the EU through which to introduce social marketing.

Discussion Questions

1. As you know, social marketing and social media marketing are not exactly the same. Please, could you detail the similarities and differences between social marketing and social media marketing?
2. What are the three key variables to explain the structure of the social marketing problem posed by the co-creation planning process related to e-health literacy?
3. After reading the case study, can you define the concept of co-creation?
4. There are some other digital healthcare platforms such as: *CarePages*,[2] *PatientsLikeMe*,[3] *Health unlocked*,[4] *CureTogether*,[5] *Smart patients*,[6] *Treato*,[7] *Patient opinion*,[8] *The HealthTap*,[9] *The Ginger Iio Platform*,[10] among many others, but they are not targeted as competitors. Why are they not considered competitors of the MOOCs from a social marketing perspective? Please, look up one of the above websites and explain why it was not listed as a competitor.
5. This project will employ the block leader, commitment, prompt and objectives techniques. Why does the downstream promotional approach of this project prefer antecedent techniques over consequent techniques such as rewards, feedbacks, and sanctions?

References

Andreasen, A. (2006). *Social marketing in the 21st century.* Sage Publications.
Chang, S. J., Choi, S., Kim, S. A., & Song, M. (2014). Intervention strategies based on information-motivation-behavioral skill model for health behavior change: A systematic review. *Asian Nursing Research, 8*(3), 172–181.
European Commission. (2010). *Communication from the Commission to the European Parliament, the Council, the European Economic and Social Committee and the Committee of the Regions.* A Digital Agenda for Europe.

[2]http://www.carepages.com/maintenance.html.
[3]https://www.patientslikeme.com/.
[4]https://healthunlocked.com/.
[5]https://curetogether.com/.
[6]https://www.smartpatients.com/.
[7]https://treato.com/compare.
[8]https://www.patientopinion.org.au/.
[9]https://www.healthtap.com/.
[10]https://ginger.io/.

European Commission. (2014). *European citizens' digital health literacy* (p. 404). Flash Eurobarometer: Report.

European Commission. (2016). *Second draft of guidelines: EU guidelines on assessment of the reliability of mobile health applications*. Consard.

European Commission. (2012). *E-health action plan 2012–2020*. Innovative Healthcare for the 21st Century. EN.

French, J., Blair-Stevens, C., Mcvey, D., & Merritt, R. (2010). *Social marketing and public health. Theory and practice*. Oxford: Oxford University Press.

Galvano, M., & Dalli, D. (2014). Theory of value co-creation: A systematic literature review. *Managing Service Quality, 24*(6), 643–683.

Geller, S. (1989). Applied behavior analysis and social marketing: An integration for environmental preservation. *Journal of Social Issues, 45*(1), 17–36.

Giudice, P., Poletto, M., Bravo, G., Montanari, A., Vandenbosh, J., López-Valcárcel, B. B., … Avagnina, B. (2017). *D1.2 results of the survey on digital health literacy, IC-Health*. Improving Digital Health Literacy in Europe.

Giudice, P., & Poletto, M. (2016). *D1.1 report on key factors, drivers, barriers and trends on digital health literacy. IC-Health*: Improving Digital Health Literacy in Europe.

Greenhalgh, T., Robert, G., Macfarlane, F., Bate, P., & Kyriakidou, (2004). Diffusion of innovations in service organizations: Systematic review and recommendations. *The Milbank Quarterly, 82*(4), 581–629.

Grier, & Bryant, C. (2005). Social marketing in public health. *Annual Reviews of Public Health, 26*, 319–339.

HLS-EU Consortium. (2012). *Comparative report on health literacy in eight EU members States*. The European Health Literacy Survey HLS-EU.

IC-Health. (2018). *Second report on ethics*. IC-Health Ethical Committee.

Kotler, P., & Keller, K. (2012). *Marketing management*. Boston: Pearson Education.

Kotler, P., Roberto, N., & Lee, N. (2002). *Social marketing: Improving the quality of life*. Sage.

Kotler, P., & Zaltman, G. (1971). Social marketing: An approach to planned social change. *Journal of Marketing, 35*(3), 3–12.

Lefrebvre, C., & Flora, J. (1988). Social marketing and public health intervention. *Health Education and Behavior, 15*(3), 299–315.

Liu, I.-F., Chen, M. C., Sun, Y. S., Wible, D., & Kno, C. H. (2010). Extending the TAM model to explore the factors that affect intention to use an online learning community. *Computers and Education, 54*, 600–610.

Mckenzie-Mohr, D., & Smith, W. (1999). *Fostering sustainable behavior*. New Society Publishers.

Montanari, A., Perello, M., Avagnina, B., & Giudice, P. (2017). *D1.3 report on profile of target groups. IC-Health*. Project: Improving Digital Health Literacy in Europe.

Nambisan, P., & Nambisan, S. (2009). Models of consumer value co-creation in health case. *Health Care Management Review, 34*(4), 344–354.

Perello, M., & Avagnina, B. (2017). D1.5 methodology for co-creation of MOOCs. Project: Improving Digital Health Literacy in Europe.

Petty, R. E., Cacioppo, J. T., & Schumann, D. (1983). Central and peripheral routes to advertising effectiveness: The moderating role of involvement. *Journal of Consumer Research, 10*(2), 135–146.

Prahalad, C., & Ramaswamy, V. (2004). Co-creation experiences: The next practice in value creation. *Journal of Interactive Marketing, 18*(3), 4–14.

Prochaska, J., & DiClemente, C. (1982). Transtheoretical therapy: Toward a more integrative model of change. *Psychotherapy: Theory, research & Practice, 19*(3), 276–288.

Ranjan, K., & Read, S. (2016). Value co-creation: Concept and measurement. *Journal of the Academy of Marketing Science, 44*, 290–315.

Rosenstock, I., Strecher, I., & Becker, M. (1988). Social learning theory and the health belief model. *Health Education Quarterly, 15*(2), 175–183.

Russell-Bennett, R., Wood, M., & Previte, J. (2013). Fresh ideas: Services thinking for social marketing. *Journal of Social Marketing, 3*(3), 223–238.

Schmitt, B. (1999). Experiential marketing. *Journal of Marketing Management, 15,* 53–67.

Vázquez, R., & Trespalacios, J. (1994). *Marketing: estrategias y aplicaciones sectoriales.* Madrid: Editorial Cívitas, SA.

Wood, M. (2008). Applying commercial marketing theory to social marketing: A tale of 4Ps (and A B). *Social Marketing Quarterly, 14*(1), 76–85.

World Health Organization. (2013). *Health literacy: The solid facts.* World Health Organization for Europe.

Use of Social Marketing to Improve Science Teaching in Maharashtra, India: 2014–18

28

Sameer Deshpande

This case study is based on personal communication and reports [Lagvankar, (n.d.) (a); (b); (c)] shared by the principal investigator of this project, Mr. Hemant Lagvankar.

Chapter Overview

This case study narrates a story of an India-based educator, Mr. Hemant Lagvankar, whose team trained teachers of grades nine and ten in the public schools of the western state of Maharashtra to improve their science teaching skills and improve the learning levels of students. The social marketing planning process proposed by Lee and Kotler (2015) was employed to elaborate on the steps taken by Mr. Lagvankar's team to design and implement the behavior change initiative. Science teachers were trained in the constructivist education approach (Gruender, 1996) through workshops. The emphasis of the training workshops was to teach how to prepare and use science kits as an aid to better deliver the science curriculum.

Campaign Background

In early 2014, as Mumbai-based educator and science communicator, Mr. Hemant Lagvankar was browsing through the government reports, he lamented the continued education-related challenges that India faced among students enrolled in secondary school grades (grades six through ten, in Maharashtra schools). According to the Indian census reports, the literacy rate in 2011 remained low at 73% (Office of the Registrar General and Census Commissioner, India, n.d.) although it had increased from 64.8% in 2001. Similarly, the dropout rate was

S. Deshpande (✉)
Griffith University, Nathan, Australia
e-mail: s.deshpande@griffith.edu.au

© Springer Nature Switzerland AG 2019
D. Z. Basil et al. (eds.), *Social Marketing in Action*,
Springer Texts in Business and Economics,
https://doi.org/10.1007/978-3-030-13020-6_28

433

3.13% in 2012–13 among those enrolled in grades six to eight (National University of Educational Planning and Administration, n.d.) and 14.54% in grades nine and ten. The situation was worse among female students and those belonging to the lower caste. Hemant knew that this dropout rate reflected many socioeconomic factors as well as the difficulties that students faced in science, mathematics, and English subjects. But dropout was not the only consequence of the subject difficulty.

While these statistics painted a grim picture, his experience informed him that the problem ran deep even among those who were currently enrolled in schools. The system failed to deliver the content well, with the result that students continued to show poor understanding in math and science. While several organizations were active in improving literacy among children in India, very few dealt with improving the quality of curriculum delivery, especially in science content in the western state of Maharashtra.

Deep in his thoughts, he pondered.

Rather than just remembering definitions and theories, understanding of concepts by practically witnessing them, and thereby applying those concepts, is an effective way to learn science. Similarly, observations, analysis, validation, and arriving at correct conclusions are the right steps to embrace scientific method. Unfortunately, in our schools, science is taught just by "chalk-and-talk" method. What difficulties do teachers face in carrying out activity-based science instruction in classrooms? How can we deliver better science education to our children? What is the solution to this problem?

Hemant decided to do something about it.

He embarked upon on a systematic, extensive, and grassroots-led teacher-training project to change the landscape of science education and positively influence teaching standards and student experience. He launched this project after working for four years, assembling the team of a nonprofit organization (NYASS Trust), support of school principals and senior teachers, cooperation of the Department of School Education of the Government of Maharashtra, and utilizing resources (such as kits, experiments, and activities that help teachers in the teaching-learning process) developed by several government organizations like the National Council of Educational Research and Training (NCERT), and individual activists like himself, as well as non-governmental organizations.

Hemant implemented the solution proposed by India's India's National Curriculum Framework (NCF) by NCERT (2005) and Maharashtra State Curriculum Framework (SCF) by MSCERT (2010). This approach, popularly called "Activity-Based Science Learning" (ABSL), adopted a constructivist approach of demonstrating science concepts and experiments with science kits in the classroom. Hemant called this project, "Mission NCF 2005 for Science Learning in Classroom" and promoted the use of science kits to equip teachers to be effective educators. Thanks to the vision of Mrs. Ashwini Bhide, then the Principal Secretary of the Department of School Education of Government of Maharashtra, Hemant profusely documented every aspect of his project, a rare practice among social change managers in India.

Target Audience

At the pilot stage, Hemant focused on improving teaching skills among science teachers of grades eight and nine. In the main studies, he shifted his focus to grades nine and ten due to the requirements of Government of Maharashtra's Education Department.

SWOT Analysis (Strengths, Weaknesses, Opportunities, Threats)

Hemant was confident about his success in this intervention because he perceived the strengths and opportunities would overcome the challenges posed by weaknesses and threats.

Hemant had immense prior experience working on improving education standards in Maharashtra, including the capacity to conduct workshops for science teachers. Thanks to this experience and participation in science education movements, he was in close touch with several science teachers in the state. Additionally, by the time he launched this project, Hemant had served as a member of the Curriculum Committee of Primary and Secondary Education of Maharashtra.

Hemant and NYASS also had the advantage of learning from others' experience. Many organizations and even government bodies had in recent past organized teachers training workshops to demonstrate how science teaching aids can be effectively used in the classroom. Previous workshops in other parts of India had revealed that teachers respond well to these workshops and commit to using this method in the classroom. However, teachers do not necessarily follow up on their intentions. To overcome this challenge, Hemant organized meetings with various teachers, organizations, and government bodies and created appropriate teaching material.

Interactions with various stakeholders created one more advantage. Hemant secured their financial and moral support. Schools, school principals, nonprofit organizations, and the state education ministry agreed to partner. The education ministry offered an official endorsement and complete support to the initiative. Similar institutional linkages were established with key organizations working in the field of school education and teacher training such as the District Institute of Education and Continuous Professional Development (DIECPD) and the State Council for Educational Research and Training (SCERT).

However, the biggest challenge was potentially posed by teachers who were reluctant to attend the workshops and to implement the teaching aids in the classroom. Previous experience taught Hemant that teachers found the teaching aids a burden on the already overwhelming syllabus that they had to deliver in a brief period of time and ensure students do well in exams, a key metric for student success as put forth by school principals and parents. Teachers of the older generation were especially reluctant to change their well-established habits. Teachers were also confused between *teaching aids*, *experiments*, and *scientific toys*.[1] Hemant was aware of these challenges and took steps to overcome these hurdles.

Campaign Objectives

The primary objective of the social marketing intervention was to create and utilize science kits in the classrooms (*actual product* (Lee & Kotler, 2015)) and thus adopt a constructivist approach to science education (*desired behavior*). Teachers were invited to attend workshops organized by Hemant (*augmented product*) to become aware of and get convinced of the superiority of the constructivist approach in science education over the "chalk-and-talk method" (*current behavior*).

Target Audience Analysis

Hemant carefully analyzed the perceptions of his audience group. He knew he had to exploit the benefits teachers perceived from the desired behavior, retain benefits of their current behavior, and reduce barriers from the desired behavior.

Benefits to Desired Behavior (Delivering Science Curriculum Using a Constructivist Approach)

Workshops were expected to improve teacher skills, and use of science kits in the classroom would enable them to teach the concepts more effectively. The ABSL method was a way to enhance student learning, increase involvement in the learning process, and improve grasp of the material that students were likely to remember beyond exam time and the academic year. Students would potentially take ownership of the learning process and come up with creative ways to learn the material. They would thus develop an interest in the science curriculum, which is otherwise considered boring, and appreciate teachers for imparting science lessons in an innovative manner.

Benefits to Current Behavior (Delivering Science Curriculum via Chalk-and-Talk Method)

Teachers, especially of the older generation, were used to teaching in the traditional way, which is well-suited to deliver the syllabus on time and achieve positive test results. This was consistent with the metrics of teacher performance, which did not

---

[1] Additional threats are discussed in the "Target audience analysis" section.

include increased understanding of science concepts. Teachers felt, "why unnecessarily change the system that is not broken?"

Barriers to Desired Behavior

Teachers perceived the act to create, familiarize with, and use the kit, and modify the curriculum delivery as extra work and time investment, disrupting the habit of teaching science the old way. Combined with the discomfort of embracing the new teaching style, teachers were anxious about the errors and awkwardness they will face in front of students. Teachers were also uncertain whether students will like the science kits and whether they will learn more. In addition to these non-monetary entry costs, teachers perceived incurring the monetary cost of either purchasing the kit or purchasing materials to prepare the kit. Finally, teachers perceived incurring the non-monetary costs (time and travel) of attending the workshop.

Positioning and Marketing Strategy

Factors described in the audience analysis strongly shaped the marketing strategy of Hemant's behavior change initiative. He positioned the NCF 2005 initiative as a mechanism superior to the traditional chalk-and-talk method to empower and transform teachers into excellent educators and positively shape the student learning experience. To deliver this positioning, Hemant crafted the following 4-P marketing strategy.

Product Management

The *core product* (core benefit to the audience) was to enjoy the teaching process and produce better educational outcomes. This benefit and the desired behavior were tangibilized in the form of the *actual product*, a 2-foot by 1-foot science kit packed in a transparent plastic box that weighed less than a kilo (Fig. 28.1). The contents of the kit in the pilot stage highlighted 43 concepts from the science syllabi of grades eight and nine explained through 50 experiments, which were expanded in the main studies to 200 concepts of grades nine and ten syllabi explained via 215 activities. These contents were arranged concept-wise in small plastic bags so that teachers could conveniently carry relevant bags to the class. Support resource materials, in print and digital format, contained PowerPoint presentations, aids to conduct in-class experiments, teaching methods, manuals, and photographs and videos of activities.

The *augmented product* was the workshop that teachers attended and learned how to create and use kits and related resources in their classroom (Fig. 28.2). The training program displayed the following features:

Fig. 28.1 Science kit

Fig. 28.2 Hemant Lagvankar conducting a training workshop with teachers

The interactive program was conducted over five days split into two parts: a two-day workshop on pedagogy and teaching aid development outside his/her school and a three-day support mechanism within the classroom. Each teacher learned how to deliver the constructivist approach by taking an actual lesson followed by receiving feedback from senior teachers regarding his/her on-the-job performance.

The creation and use of kits and support resources were taught by highlighting three broad topics related to grade eight (reflection of light, electric current, and metals and non-metals) and three related to grade nine (why bodies float, energy, and music of sound).

The training took place before the end of August so that teachers could execute the new teaching method in their classrooms on time.

Before, during, and after the training program, digital communication between science teachers, organizing team, government officers, and resource persons was set up to facilitate continuous dialog and support.

Price Management

The barriers to desired behavior were reduced by:

- delivering the training program free of cost to the teachers;
- seeking approval for quality (of content and of the trainers) from the state education ministry, thus giving assurance of high standards;
- ensuring that the workshops were delivered and attended by peers that were known to teachers to reduce stranger anxiety and facilitate improved learning;
- patiently responding to teacher queries, improving their skills and confidence, and encouraging them to embrace the new teaching style; and
- ensuring that the materials used to prepare the kit were something teachers had easy access to and the cost was affordable at INR 1500 (US$23).

Place Management

Organizers ensured convenience by organizing workshops at easy-to-reach locations as well as at the place where they work (their classroom). Convenience was also ensured by restricting kit creation with easy-to-access materials and easy-to-carry concept-wise plastic bags.

Promotion Management

The attractiveness of the training program was communicated with the promise of improvement in teaching skills, empowerment, and enhancement of the student experience. The message was delivered to teachers by school principals on behalf of DIECPDs.

Implementation

Mr. Hemant implemented the project in three parts: the pilot study in 2014, followed by the first main study in 2015–16, and ending with a larger, second main study in 2017–18.

Pilot Study

The pilot study was undertaken in 15 selected schools of two cities of Kalyan and Dombivli in Thane district. The schools represented distinct categories such as municipal schools, government-aided private schools, and non-aided private schools. Each workshop was attended by 25–30 science teachers. The pilot study was funded by the NYASS Trust.

Experts in innovative science teaching were invited to serve as master resource persons (MRPs). The pilot study was implemented in three phases. In the first phase, the kit of teaching aids was prepared, followed by organizing meetings with MRPs and school principals. In the second phase, an action plan was finalized in terms of dates when MRPs will visit the schools. In the third phase, teachers were trained, and observers (representing senior teachers, educationists, parents, and NGOs) were sent to schools to observe teachers perform with and without teaching aids.

Observations of 30 teachers delivering 48 lectures revealed that:

- Teachers liked the kit and its concept-wise categorization, making it easier to carry (Fig. 28.3);
- Few teachers had already used the kit prior to observers visiting them;
- Several teachers actively involved students while using the teaching aids in the classrooms (Fig. 28.4);
- Before the workshop, among a small sample of 25 teachers, 80% envisioned difficulty in implementing the constructivist approach in the classroom. Teachers found the actual experience to be contrary. With teaching aids,

Fig. 28.3 Positive experience of teachers under training

Fig. 28.4 Teacher delivering science curriculum using the science kit

teachers found it easier to explain the abstract concepts of physics and to "show" the chemical reactions;

- Teaching aids allowed teachers to cover the same topic in lesser time;
- Teaching aids benefitted teachers with comparatively weak communication skills as the learning depended less on the communication skills of a teacher;
- Many teachers added their own ideas to the teaching aid kit to teach other lessons as well as other grades;
- Teachers and schools realized that the constructivist approach can be implemented without disturbing their regular school timetable and schedule and that they did not require any extra time to deliver the contents; and
- With teaching aids, students could drive the instructional process. This resulted in an overall increase in student learning and excitement in their participation (Fig. 28.5).

Two representative quotes reflect positive feedback from the participant teachers:

It was very interesting to teach using activity kits. In this method, students understand the concept clearly. The kit is not only useful for 8th and 9th standard but also for 6th, 7th, and 10th standard. It is also useful for teachers to understand lessons. Students pay more attention in the class when learning takes place through activities. They were very eager, curious and happy to handle the kits.

Fig. 28.5 Positive experience of students with the constructivist approach to science learning

Mrs. Jayashree Walimbe, Mrs. Jayalakshmi Sreeram, and Mrs. Dipti Pore, Greens English High School, Dombivli

Students gets real satisfaction of learning when the concepts get cleared. I experienced this when I prepared Leclanche Cell and showed it in the class. Students enjoy learning through activities and experiments. Though students watch their image in the mirror every day, they enjoyed the class when I took mirror in the classroom to explain reflection of light. The teaching-learning process became enjoyable due to this approach.

Mrs. Rutuja Patankar, Gajanan Vidyalaya, Kalyan

Main Study

Thanks to the positive results of the pilot study, the state education ministry invited Mr. Hemant and NYASS to scale up the study to reach teachers in all 36 districts of the state. The project was coordinated and implemented by SCERT, Pune, and the State Institute for Science Education (SISE), Nagpur, in coordination with NYASS Trust for grades nine and ten. The main study was undertaken into two parts. The first study was conducted in 2015–16 and the second one in 2017–18.

Main Study 1

In phase one, science kits, a teachers' manual, and a CD consisting of presentations, manuals, video, and photograph links were designed by Hemant's team and produced by the supplier selected by the state education ministry. WhatsApp groups, as well as online networks, were formed at district and regional levels with key stakeholders. In phase two, representatives of each district were trained in a two-day workshop on the content of the audience workshop and the creation and use of the science kit. In phase three, four key resource persons (KRPs) from each district were trained in two-day workshops held in eight regions of the state. In phase four, teachers were trained in 36 two-day workshops at the district level. In each district, 25 schools were selected. In phase five, five MRPs conducted two-day workshops in their district for 25 teachers (one from each district) and took demonstration lessons on the constructivist approach to learning. In phase six, reports from all activities were documented and submitted to the government.

A total of 1,060 teachers were trained through 44 workshops, approximately 30 from each district, out of which five, with state-level training, were capable to serve as resource persons to train their peers for the next level of the project. The training workshops received a positive response from journalists. Several Marathi language newspapers highlighted this effort (e.g., Fig. 28.6).

Main Study 2

The 2015–16 training program was scaled up in 2017–18. In phase one, approximately five MRPs (along with two representatives from DIECPD) from each district were invited back to receive a state-level orientation in a two-day workshop. In total, four workshops were conducted with a total of 175 MRPs and DIECPD attendees from across the state. Later, 315 workshops were conducted August 2017 onward that trained more than 13,000 science teachers in 36 districts of the state. Of these, more than 80% (approximately 10,400 teachers) had changed their teaching style and adopted ABSL (*behavioral outcomes*).

Observations by MRPs and KRPs, monitoring of the effectiveness of the training program with the help of SISE and DIECPD, and a written survey among select participants revealed similar results as the pilot project. Teachers were largely pleased with the training program and reported positive experience delivering the concepts with teaching aids.

Budget

The total budget for the two main studies was INR 290 million (US$4.46 million) funded by the state ministry of education. Funds for the state-level and regional workshops were channelized through SISE, and funds for the district-level workshops were channelized through DIECPD.

Fig. 28.6 Media coverage in a prominent Marathi newspaper, *Lokmat*, on March 13, 2016

रविवार विशेष

एक अभिनव विज्ञान प्रशिक्षण!

The NCF 2005 project has empowered teachers; they were thus expected to spread the good word among their peers. Along with teachers, their school principals, MRPs and KRPs, and the government officials were satisfied with the outcomes of the project. Only time—and subsequent third-party monitoring reports—will tell whether students have enhanced their understanding of science (*intervention impact*). But so far Mr. Hemant Lagvankar feels satisfied with his accomplishments of influencing 10,400 science teachers to adopt a constructivist teaching style. While he and his team have achieved remarkable milestones, he knows he has miles to go in the future.

Discussion and Lessons Learned

Mr. Hemant learned from his experience the value of tangibilizing the desired behavior (i.e., delivering the science curriculum by using science kits). If he had directly asked teachers to adopt the ABSL approach in their teaching, they would have been confused and uncertain on what to do and how to implement this approach. Tangibilizing the behavior facilitated the adoption of the desired behavior and made it easier and joyful.

Involvement of key stakeholders such as school principals and government officials improved the brand recognition and perception of quality and authority, and thus the adoption of the desired behavior.

Delivery of the training program with the help of peers improved the relevance and believability of the content and thus the involvement and adoption of the behavior.

Finally, the proof was in the pudding. Better response from students increased confidence in the constructivist approach and the efficacy of the science kit, thus enhancing the motivation levels of teachers.

Discussion Questions

1. Referring to Andreasen (2002), which social marketing benchmarks seem to play a prominent role in the success of the initiative?
2. How did the marketing strategy overcome audience perceptions regarding barriers to the desired behavior?
3. How did the organizers implement the stakeholder management approach?
4. What underlying theory explains the success of the intervention?
5. Was social marketing appropriate for improving teaching standards in Maharashtra schools?

References

Andreasen, A. (2002). Marketing social marketing in the social change marketplace. *Journal of Public Policy & Marketing, 21*(1), 3–13.

Bandura, A. (1977). *Social learning theory.* New York: General Learning Press.

Bandura, A. (1997). *Self-efficacy: The exercise of control.* New York: W. H. Freeman.

Gruender, C. D. (1996, May–June). Constructivism and learning: A philosophical appraisal. *Educational Technology, 36*(3), 21–29.

Lagvankar, H. (n.d.) (a). *Activity-based science learning pilot project: Project report.* Dombivli, India: NYASS Trust.

Lagvankar, H. (n.d.) (b). *Report of "mission NCF—2005 for science learning in classroom"an innovative training project under RMSA Maharashtra in the academic year 2015–16.* Rashtriya Madhyamik Shiksha Abhiyan & NYASS Trust.

Lagvankar, H. (n.d.) (c). *Activity based science learning in classroom: An innovative training project for secondary science teachers under RMSA for 2017–18—Project report.* Rashtriya Madhyamik Shiksha Abhiyan.

Lee, N., & Kotler, P. (2015). *Social marketing.* Thousand Oaks, CA: Sage.

Maharastra State Council of Educational Research and Training (MSCERT). (2010). *State Curriculum Framework 2010.* Pune.

National Council of Educational Research and Training (NCERT). (2005). *National Curriculum Framework 2005.* New Delhi.

National University of Educational Planning and Administration. (n.d.). *U-DISE: United District Information System for Education.* Retrieved February 19, 2018 from http://dise.in/.

Office of the Registrar General & Census Commissioner, India, Ministry of Home Affairs. (n.d.). CensusInfo. Retrieved February 19, 2018 from http://censusindia.gov.in/.

A Case of Co-created Social Marketing Campaign: The Spanish Ana Bella Social School for Women's Empowerment

29

Yolanda Díaz-Perdomo, Luis I. Álvarez-González and M. José Sanzo-Pérez

Chapter Overview

This case study addresses, from a social marketing perspective, the start-up of the Ana Bella Social School for Women's Empowerment, a project jointly co-created by Danone (through the Danone Ecosystem Fund), Momentum Task Force, and Ana Bella Foundation, with the objective of empowering female victims of gender violence, through professional training and labor integration as brand ambassadors at Danone's points of sale. In addition, the benefits of the implementation of the Ana Bella Social School for Women's Empowerment have been analyzed from a triple point of view, i.e., women involved in the project (micro-level), participating organizations (meso-level), and society (macro-level). Thus, this study shows how the link between social marketing and co-creation of value can lead to the desired social impact, in this case, the improvement of economic, personal, and social–relational conditions of female survivors of gender violence. In this context, we define the marketing strategy (product, price, place, promotion, people, and process) carried out to empower women and assess the results and possible improvements to be made in the future.

Y. Díaz-Perdomo (✉) · L. I. Álvarez-González · M. J. Sanzo-Pérez
Facultad de Economía y Empresa, University of Oviedo, Oviedo, Spain
e-mail: yolandadiazperdomo@gmail.com

L. I. Álvarez-González
e-mail: alvarezg@uniovi.es

M. J. Sanzo-Pérez
e-mail: mjsanzo@uniovi.es

© Springer Nature Switzerland AG 2019
D. Z. Basil et al. (eds.), *Social Marketing in Action*,
Springer Texts in Business and Economics,
https://doi.org/10.1007/978-3-030-13020-6_29

Campaign Background

Social Marketing, the Service-Dominant Logic, and Co-creation of Value

Social marketing is usually conceptualized as the use of marketing theory and practices to "sell" ideas, attitudes, and behaviors and promote social change. This discipline has evolved in parallel to the "marketing" or "value" concept itself, in such a way that "the importance of co-creation of value, relational thinking and longevity in social marketing is well recognised" (Gordon, 2012, p. 126), and "the concept of value and co-creation of value is an interesting proposition, as literature has proposed that the customer relationship management techniques rooted in service logic can be applied to social marketing" (Domegan, 2008; cited in Gordon, 2012, p. 124).

Thus, recent studies in marketing have focused on the role of co-creation of value, particularly in the context of the Service-Dominant Logic (SDL) (Vargo & Lusch, 2004; Vargo, Maglio, & Akaka, 2008). This approach provides an understanding of how firms, customers, and other market participants co-create value through their interactions (Vargo & Lusch, 2004).

Co-creation of value can be defined as "joint activities by parties involved in dyadic direct interactions aimed at contributing to the value that emerges for one or both parties, or all parties in a larger network" (Grönroos & Ravald, 2011). Therefore, a process of co-creation of value can involve different stakeholders (Lee, Olson, & Trimi, 2012). Furthermore, "SDL, with its core notions that (1) service is the fundamental basis of exchange, (2) service is exchanged for service, and (3) the customer is always a co-creator of value, is especially compatible with social and non-profit marketing" (Vargo & Lusch, 2008, p. 6). So, "by understanding and addressing consumption as an active process of exchange and co-creation, social change can be aimed at the appropriate phase in the process such as changing an attitude or producing substitute behavior to facilitate the co-creation of social marketing offerings of value" (Dann, 2008, p. 98).

Particularly, "collaboration between nonprofit and business sectors is widely regarded as a value creation process that benefits society, business, and nonprofit organizations (NPOs)" (Omar, Leach, & March, 2014, p. 657). Such partnerships allow firms and NPOs to share complementary skills, infrastructure, and knowledge, and to work together and co-create in different social fields, through the development of social innovations (Brugmann & Prahalad, 2007).

A social innovation is characterized by showing a "social" nature in both its aims and its means. That is, a social innovation attempts to satisfy social and/or environmental needs, and at the same time, has a collaborative nature, since it requires that citizens, employees, customers, and NPOs play a proactive role during the innovation process (Sanzo-Pérez, Álvarez-González, & Rey-García, 2015). Consequently, a social innovation can be considered as a process of co-creation of value (Voorberg, Bekkers, & Tummers, 2015).

The current case study shows an example of co-creation of value by means of a business-nonprofit partnership, i.e., the Ana Bella Social School for Women's Empowerment, describing a novel type of social marketing campaign based on collaboration and co-creation.

Actors Involved in the Campaign

Three main actors co-created this campaign: Ana Bella Foundation, Danone (through the Danone Ecosystem Fund), and Momentum Task Force.

The Ana Bella Foundation, an NPO located in Sevilla (Spain) and created by Ana Bella (a survivor of gender violence), is an NPO whose mission is to stop gender violence and promote a more positive social perception of women who suffer from this type of violence, in such a way that they can be seen as "survivors" with highly valued capabilities and not only as "victims" or "problems."

For its part, Danone, a global company born in 1972 and present, currently, in about 130 countries, focuses its efforts on four categories of healthy products (fresh milk products, water, infant nutrition, and medical nutrition), going beyond simply marketing food and drink to actively promote healthier eating habits. Supported by the Danone Ecosystem Fund, 47 local branches of the company around the world collaborate with up to 57 NPOs in the search for solutions to specific and local social, environmental, and economic challenges. Through the co-creation of value, they combine their respective fields of specialization, to jointly find economic, social, and environmental solutions, from project design to collaborative management.

Finally, Momentum Task Force is a Spanish consultant company focused on providing qualified human resources in order to implement marketing, advertising, and/or commercial activities. This firm performs intense social work incorporating the most disadvantaged groups of people to business' teams.

In 2011, these actors co-created in Spain the "Ana Bella Social School for Women's Empowerment," an innovative social project that attempts to find, through training and employment of women who have suffered from gender violence as Danone's ambassadors, new ways of satisfying economic and social needs, empowering the beneficiaries, and changing the perceived image of these women in society.

Ashoka, an NPO that supports social entrepreneurship, and which had selected Ana Bella as a social entrepreneur in Spain, promoted the collaboration among them.

SWOT Analysis (Strengths, Weaknesses, Opportunities, Threats)

Mellen and Murillo (2015) evaluated the social impact of the Ana Bella Social School, through a qualitative analysis methodology, with data from interviews with female victims of gender violence, participants in the project, and other agents directly involved. The SWOT analysis of the project based on these opinions is as follows.

Strengths

Combination of social (empowerment of women, change in society's perception about gender violence) and economic objectives (improved performance of firms involved).
Economic remuneration.
Positive view of life (women are not seen as "victims" but as "survivors").
Labor insertion.
Positive testimony before society.
Commitment and professionalism of the ambassadors.
Economic value of the ambassadors.
Combination of resources and strengths of different types of organizations.

Weaknesses

Lack of commercial orientation of the School.
Lack of systematization of accumulated know-how.
Scarce standardization of information.
Organizational structure not very standardized.

Opportunities

Replication of the School's success model/high potential scalability of the project.
Possibility of incorporating other ambassador profiles.
Change in society's perception and awareness about gender violence.
Expansion of points of sale and number of ambassadors.
Management improvements that increase the demand for services.

Threats

Questions about the economic sustainability of the project.
Loss of capacity for empowerment due to lack of economic and employment progression of the ambassadors.
Overdependence of the project on personal leadership.
Lack of capacity to maintain the structure of management and attention to women.

Target Audience

In Spain, "gender violence is, unfortunately, a widespread problem. One of the most common factors among cases of women victims of abuse is the economic or financial dependence on their partners" (Abenoza, Carreras, & Sureda, 2015, p. 103). Under this scenario, there are three main targets of the program. First, women who have suffered from gender violence. Second, for-profit companies, for whom one relevant objective of the project is to make companies aware about the economic value of these women as highly motivated and professional employees. Third, the whole society, for whom the project aims that people do not perceive these women as "victims" but as part of the solution.

Campaign Objectives

The global aim of the Ana Bella Social School is to carry out processes of integral empowerment of women who have suffered from gender violence, which affect three dimensions: economic, personal, and social–relational (Abenoza et al., 2015).

Economic. One of the factors that favor the empowerment of women is the availability of social and economic resources. Having a job makes women more economically independent and, therefore, their freedom also reaches other spheres of their lives.

Personal. Having a job makes women feel useful, self-confident, and optimistic about life. A paid job not only gives them income, but also increases their confidence and self-esteem, which, in turn, reinforces the process of empowerment.

Social and relational. Once economic independence has been achieved, women gain a more positive view of themselves and experience changes in their relationships with others. They begin to interact with improved trust and can participate in the mobilization of self-help groups.

Through this project both social and business goals are achieved at the same time. On the one hand, women who have been mistreated need job opportunities that empower them. Danone, through this initiative attempts to materialize its Corporate Social Responsibility Objectives, to demonstrate that it is a committed organization, with social values and concerned about its environment, which will result in a better positioning in the market. Furthermore, the company also needs qualified personnel to act as brand ambassadors at its points of sale. The project provides a solution to this business need and obtains an effective labor insertion of surviving women. Such types of initiatives serve to counteract a highly relevant social problem that conditions the personal development of women at risk of socio-labor exclusion.

This integral process will help companies and the entire society change their perceptions about the value of these women, generating a virtuous cycle that reduces active discrimination. Women, "through their participation in the project, do not only empower themselves and get ready to lead their own lives, but they also become agents of changeable to empower other people. And companies, in addition to having effective and committed employees that are an asset prepared to achieve their objectives, change their perception of surviving women, thus contributing to its own economic and social development" (Mellen & Murillo, 2015, p. 11).

Barriers, Benefits, and Competition

The barriers faced by women "are those of an introverted, fearful personality or, sometimes even, annulled, terrified and without opinion, built as a result of years of abuse" (Mellen & Murillo, 2015, p. 27). The project competes against these traits and attempts to overcome the situation of isolation (and related behaviors) in which these women live. The consequence of the overcoming process and labor integration in Danone is that women can develop their full potential by performing useful jobs as brand ambassadors, feeling that they are not being employed because they are survivors but because of their strength and personal qualities, which can be highly positive for their self-esteem (Abenoza et al., 2015).

Women who survive have a series of positive capabilities, which makes them a fundamental value to carrying out the job of brand ambassadors, as well as to achieve their empowerment and desired social impact (Mellen & Murillo, 2015). Among them,

- Strength,
- High tolerance to failure,
- Recover quickly from frustration,
- Great ability to reinvent themselves to move forward,
- Perseverance,
- Commitment,
- Optimization of resources,
- Experience in body language,
- Ability to work alone under pressure.

Moreover, the situation in which most abused women live, characterized by a host of disadvantageous circumstances which make these women be at risk of social exclusion, highlights their difficulty to easily access this type of program (little family support, difficulty in accessing the labor market, etc.) (Mellen & Murillo, 2015). The exclusion suffered by abused women can be avoided by providing valuable labor opportunities that create social and economic value for companies (https://www.changemakers.com/), through:

Showing the success of the Danone ambassadors so that there are more companies that carry out the same policy.
Standardizing the commercial and social model of the program through collaboration with business schools.
Investing in scalability abroad thanks to the Ecosystem Fund of Danone.
Detecting NPOs that generate change in the countries where Danone operates.

Positioning

The Ana Bella Social School provides value to beneficiaries (micro-level), organizations (meso-level), and society (macro-level), by generating changes in their behaviors and therefore a social change.

More specifically, the project attempts to promote a different image of women who have suffered from gender violence in these women themselves, firms, and society; moving from viewing them as "victims" to "survivors" (a more positive perception associated with people whose past experiences have given them high-value capabilities that make them valuable for firms and society).

Research

This initiative started with a pilot test aimed at assessing whether those female survivors of gender violence trained at the School were prepared to work as brand ambassadors (Abenoza et al., 2015, pp. 101–102). The results were the following:

The pilot test showed that the survivors of gender violence trained at the School were a profile of suitable employees to lead promotional campaigns due to their high commitment and responsibility.
The results exceeded the expectations of all project partners, being much better than those they had with other people with less personal difficulties.

Marketing Strategy

Introduction

In this section, the basic tools of social marketing (i.e., product, price, place, promotion, people, and process) are described. Moreover, as the case details an example of co-creation of value, the dimensions of what co-creation means are also highlighted. These dimensions comprise (Bharti, Agrawal, & Sharma, 2015): (1) The effective *participation* of those partners involved in the process (e.g., the partners share relevant information to the collaboration, provide suggestions and/or participate in the making of real decisions); (2) the *involvement* of partners (e.g., through cash contributions, in-kind contributions, infrastructural and/or equipment contributions, and/or corporate volunteering); (3) the *collaboration and commitment* between the company and the NPO to foster loyalty among the partners and a long-term relationship; and (4) *mutuality* (receptivity and active initiative toward the other).

Product

The Ana Bella Social School for Women's Empowerment offers active empowerment to women who have suffered from gender violence, through individual coaching, professional training (the training is carried out by Momentum Task Force), and a job opportunity as brand ambassadors at Danone's sale points (a two-year contract). The new Danone ambassadors promote health and nutrition at the sales points.

The empowerment of women who have suffered from gender violence is a complex and multifactorial process (Mellen & Murillo, 2015, p. 13).

It affects diverse areas such as the workplace, the social network of family relationships or friendship, and self-esteem.

The loss of links to friends or other relatives and the deprivation of participating in the labor market are factors that relegate women to the domestic sphere, and this fact means to lose confidence in themselves and their ability to face the labor market and occupy a job.

Thus, "the majority of women survivors of gender violence tend to suffer multiple risks of social and labor exclusion, so to speak of true empowerment, it is necessary to foresee the creation of a means by which women have access to resources that they need to be able to make informed decisions and take control of their lives" (Abenoza et al., 2015, p. 103). Consequently, these women need job opportunities that empower them. This project offers a new way of reintegrating victims of gender violence in the community and changing the perceptions of society.

Specifically, the global service provided by the Ana Bella Social School includes the following activities (https://www.fundacionanabella.org/), generating economic and social value:

- Visibility. Through positive testimonies of female survivors of gender violence, it identifies female victims who do not dare to denounce.
- Training. Based on personal abilities and individual professional concerns, to ensure that women access on equal terms to the selection processes.
- Empowerment. To overcome gender violence and become survivors capable of acting as agents of social change.
- Sensitization. In firms, to achieve job opportunities based on the contribution of commitment and social value of the survivors trained in the School.
- Labor insertion. 150 women a year join the Danone company as brand's ambassadors, contributing to the sustainable growth of the firm.
- Accompaniment. Process of personal coaching to the employees to reinforce their effectiveness and their personal empowerment.

Price

There are several types of costs associated with the service. With regard to women, they probably have to devote a high psychological effort to commit to the project after (in many cases) years of emotional and physical abuse. They have to face emotions such as fear, low self-esteem, mistrust, and so on. Furthermore, as Mellen and Murillo (2015, p. 17) note, for women there are two major risks associated with the School, "The first one is the risk to become accustomed to the current situation, with what the aspiration of a positive rotation would stop being effective. The second one is the possible creation of dependency of women on the School or Danone" (Mellen & Murillo, 2015, p. 17).

Regarding the companies and the NPO, costs involve time, funding, and other resources provided by each of them.

Place

Since the project consists in a service offer, production, distribution, and consumption occur simultaneously. Two moments of truth are particularly outstanding. The first one is the Ana Bella Social School, where women are trained and motivated. The second moment is the Danone points of sale, where women carry out their jobs as brand's ambassadors.

Promotion

Several means are used to promote the campaign.

The Web site of the project: http://escuela.fundacionanabella.org/.

Each partner employs its own communication channels with this objective. For example, their Web sites include information about the School and the partnerships: www.fundacionanabella.org/la-escuela-ana-bella/ http://corporate.danone.es/es/descubre/sostenibilidad/un-enfoque-empresarial-unico/ www.momentumtf.es/responsabilidad-social.

The Ana Bella Social School is also promoted by "looking for more companies that need empowered and committed employees to carry out commercial actions" (Mellen & Murillo, 2015, p. 11). In this sense, Ana Bella Social School is promoted by offering its potential clients: (1) high profile and highly trained ambassadors (more hours of professional and personal training), (2) increased credibility through a profile closer to the buyer (women of the same age, concerns, and experience), and (3) increased commitment and decreased turnover and absenteeism, which is usually very high in this type of program, thanks to having committed ambassadors who value the job opportunity.

Women are recruited through the "positive rotation," understood as the process by which a woman who has had a job opportunity in Ana Bella Social School passes her position as ambassador to another woman who has also suffered gender violence, so that the latter can also be empowered.

Awards: the project has been recognized as the Best Co-Creation European Project with economic and social impact for Changemaker Ashoka, Zermatt Summit 2014 (http://www.inmujer.gob.es).

Diffusion of case studies elaborated by different well-known institutions such as ESADE (see http://www.esade.edu/en/news/social-entrepreneur-ana-bella-esade-women-who-have-been-abused-are-not-problem-were-part-solution/2475-318046).

Other activities: participation in European Projects (such as *Horizon 2020: Boosting the Impact of Social Innovation in Europe through Economic Underpinnings*, or SELAB: Social Entrepreneurship Laboratory), collaboration with Spanish universities, attendance to (and organization of) conferences (see https://www.fundacionanabella.org/wp-content/uploads/MEMORIA-ECONOMICA-Y-DE-ACTIVIDADES-FUNDACION-ANA-BELLA-2015.pdf).

People

People involved in the program, in addition to the beneficiaries (women who have suffered from gender violence), are the personnel and volunteers from the three partners who have co-created the Ana Bella Social School.

Table 29.1   Resources provided by each partner

Ana Bella Foundation	Access to victims of gender violence Knowledge about the social problem Image and reputation Facilities Other services provided to women (refuge, legal advisory services, ...)
Danone	Funding Visibility Job opportunities
Momentum Task Force	Professional training.

Source Own elaboration

Process

In this case, the "product" is a service that results from a process of co-creation of value. The activities are carried out by for-profit firms (Danone and Momentum Task Force) and a nonprofit (Ana Bella Foundation), supporting the creation of value by the other party through various mechanisms, such as:

- Co-design: The companies participate in the development processes of design projects carried out by the NPO (e.g., design of the social project) through direct interaction with the design team.
- Co-production: The resources of the companies are dedicated to the social projects of the nonprofit entity.
- Co-management: The management and supervision tools are established collectively.
- Each of the partners provides complementary resources to the alliance (Table 29.1).

Program Evaluation

The project has contributed to improving the three areas of empowerment that the Ana Bella Foundation wants to work with: personal, social–relational, and economic (Abenoza et al., 2015). In fact, 97% of those employed as ambassadors of the Danone brand make a positive assessment of the work they carry out and have felt that they are not being employed because they are survivors but because of their strength and personal qualities. In contrast to the disdain they had previously received from their partners, the job recognition helped them and gave them confidence to prove their worth, both in their jobs and in their environment.

Table 29.2 Benefits of the co-creation of the Ana Bella Social School

Firms	Can obtain economic benefits
	Improve their image and reputation
NPO	Fulfill their missions more effectively
	Increase their resources
	Acquire new skills and practices
	Improve the quality and quantity of their network of contacts
Women	Are inserted in the labor market, trained
	Are empowered
	Act as agents of social change, also producing a benefit at the macro-level, by serving as an example to other women victims of gender violence.

Source Own elaboration

The results of the start-up of the Ana Bella Social School have exceeded the most optimistic expectations, so far reaching about 1000 women who have built their own stories of success and improvement, reducing absenteeism by more than 90% in those sale points that have these women as Danone ambassadors, increasing sales, and improving the quality of service (http://www.danone.com/es). Furthermore, this project has been recognized as the Best Co-Creation European Project with economic and social impact for Changemaker Ashoka, Zermatt Summit 2014 (http://www.inmujer.gob.es), and other companies have progressively joined the program (e.g., Fontvella, Campofrío, Bonduelle), fostering the scaling of the project.

Danone was one of the first companies that believed in the potential of survivors as a sales force. This project led to organizational benefits for the company (such as the increase in Danone sales). Also, results, such as a decrease in the rotation from 63 to 2% in 2013, a decrease in market absenteeism from 40 to 2%, and 97% positive feedback from the sales force, are factors that explain why the Ana Bella School together with Momentum Task Force have been awarded by Danone as Best Service Provider 2012, thanks to the excellent results of the campaign (https://www.fundacionanabella.org/).

Table 29.2 shows the benefits derived from the project and obtained by each of the three organizations involved.

Discussion and Lessons Learned

This case is a clear example of how co-creation of value contributes to provide benefits at the micro (individuals), meso (organizations), and macro (society) levels. Co-creation between firms and NPOs allows the creation of true synergies by the combination of resources of both partners, generating greater economic and social value than if the projects or campaigns were carried out unilaterally.

To assess the social impact of the Ana Bella Social School, Mellen and Murillo (2015) carried out a qualitative analysis, with data from interviews that took place throughout the months of June, July, and September 2014. Particularly, 46 interviews were conducted, 25 of them with female victims of gender violence, participants in the project as brand ambassadors, and 21 with other agents directly involved in the project (*stakeholders*). This analysis sought to understand the impact of the project on the process of empowerment (economic, personal, and relational–social) of the participating women, concluding that economic empowerment has a positive impact on the improvement of women's self-confidence (personal dimension) and in social relations with their environment and their community (relational–social dimension).

According to Mellen and Murillo (2015, p. 71), some of the elements of this program were partially achieved. In this sense:

Economic empowerment is the objective that has been achieved to a lesser extent, that is, the objectives related to the remuneration or training of the ambassadors have been achieved relatively.
The objectives of helping other women or contributing to the social awareness of the problem of gender violence have been achieved partially, since its scope has been moderate and there are still things to be done.

Likewise, Mellen and Murillo (2015, p. 72) propose a series of explicit objectives to carry out:

- To guarantee the sustainability of the project as a way to guarantee the permanence of the effort made over time.
- To accompany the School toward its economic viability, by means of empowering, training, and acting as a relationship agent between Ana Bella and other organizations.
- To strengthen the positive rotation of the ambassadors. To focus work profiles toward a non-finalist orientation.
- To expand the client portfolio to favor the scalability of the project. To disseminate the project to share the relevance and role of Danone in this initiative with other organizations that may be also involved.

The start-up of the Ana Bella Social School for Women's Empowerment is a clear example of how cooperation can improve the lives of many women and the performance of the organizations participating in the project, changing simultaneously society's vision of gender violence. Thus, from social marketing, "the idea is that social marketers and their customers can become active relationship partners and can engage to co-create various aspects of the marketing offering" (Gordon, 2012, p. 124).

This is a vital fact, because if this paradigm, with a clear and central objective of combining economic and social progress, is generalized to the greatest number of possible organizations, it can lead to a real improvement in the quality of life of many people.

Discussion Questions
In this section, five questions are presented to stimulate the critical thinking of those interested in the study of co-creation of value through cross-sector partnerships.

1. Explain the objectives that the Ana Bella Social School for Women's Empowerment has and the benefits for surviving women that are part of the program.
2. In your opinion, what are the main challenges and problems involved in partnerships between business and NPOs?
3. Based on the four critical dimensions of co-creation, please provide recommendations to make this collaboration as effective as possible.
4. What type of resources can be provided by firms and nonprofits to the alliance?
5. Do you think this is a truly social marketing campaign or it is merely a nonprofit effort? Support your position.

References

Abenoza, S., Carreras, I., & Sureda, M. (2015). *Colaboraciones ONG y empresa que transforman la sociedad*. Programa ESADE-PwC de Liderazgo Social 2014–2015.
Bharti, K., Agrawal, R., & Sharma, V. (2015). Literature review and proposed conceptual framework. *International Journal of Market Research, 57*(4), 571–604.
Brugmann, J., & Prahalad, C. K. (2007). Co-creating business's new social compact. *Harvard Business Review, 85*(2).
Dann, S. (2008). Adaptation and adoption of the American Marketing Association (2007) definition for social marketing. *Social Marketing Quarterly, 14*(2), 92–100.
Gordon, R. (2012). Re-thinking and re-tooling the social marketing mix. *Australasian Marketing Journal (AMJ), 20*(2), 122–126.
Grönroos, C., & Ravald, A. (2011). Service as business logic: Implications for value creation and marketing. *Journal of Service Management, 22*(1), 5–22.
Lee, S. M., Olson, D. L., & Trimi, S. (2012). Co-innovation: Convergenomics, collaboration, and co-creation for organizational values. *Management Decision, 50*(5), 817–831.
Mellen, T., & Murillo, D. (2015). *Proyecto Danone y Fondo Ecosystem—Fundación Ana Bella: Balance y perspectivas (2011–2014). Análisis del impacto social de la Escuela Social Ana Bella para el Empoderamiento de la Mujer*. Barcelona: Instituto de Innovación Social de ESADE.
Omar, A. T., Leach, D., & March, J. (2014). Collaboration between nonprofit and business sectors: A framework to guide strategy development for nonprofit organizations. *VOLUNTAS: International Journal of Voluntary and Nonprofit Organizations, 25*(3), 657–678.
Sanzo-Pérez, M. J., Álvarez-González, L. I., & Rey-García, M. (2015). How to encourage social innovations: A resource-based approach. *The Service Industries Journal, 35*(7–8), 430–447.
Vargo, S. L., & Lusch, R. F. (2004). Evolving to a new dominant logic for marketing. *Journal of marketing, 68*(1), 1–17.

Vargo, S. L., & Lusch, R. F. (2008). Service-dominant logic: Continuing the evolution. *Journal of the Academy of Marketing Science, 36*(1), 1–10.

Vargo, S. L., Maglio, P. P., & Akaka, M. A. (2008). On value and value co-creation: A service systems and service logic perspective. *European Management Journal, 26*(3), 145–152.

Voorberg, W. H., Bekkers, V. J., & Tummers, L. G. (2015). A systematic review of co-creation and co-production: Embarking on the social innovation journey. *Public Management Review, 17*(9), 1333–1357.

Webliography

Andreasen, A. R. (1994). Social marketing: Its definition and domain. *Journal of Public Policy and Marketing,* 108–114.

APAC Effie Awards, & Tenasia Group Pvt. Ltd. (2015). *2015 APAC Effie Awards Gold.* Retrieved from http://www.apaceffie.com/docs/default-source/resource-library/ae2015-gold–help-a-child-reach-5.pdf?sfvrsn=2. Accessed February 24, 2018.

Claessen, J.-P., Bates, S., Sherlock, K., Seeparsand, F., & Wright, R. (2017). Designing interventions to improve tooth brushing. *International Dental Journal, 58,* 307–320.

CSR Vision. (n.d.). SAVLON Swasth India embarks on a unique initiative this world hand hygiene day. *CSR India.* Retrieved from http://www.csrvision.in/savlon-swasth-india-embarks-on-a-unique-initiative-this-world-hand-hygiene-day/.

Dettol. (n.d.). *About banega swach India.* Retrieved from http://www.dettol.co.in/en/banega-swachh-india/about-banega-swachh-india/.

ET Brand Equity. (2016, November 14). Savlon flags off new brand activation campaign. *Swasth India Mission.* Retrieved from https://brandequity.economictimes.indiatimes.com/news/advertising/savlon-flags-off-new-brand-activation-campaign-swasth-india-mission/55413246.

Fishbein, M., & Ajzen, I. (2011). *Predicting and changing behavior: The reasoned action approach.* New York: Taylor & Francis.

HUL. (2012, October 15). *Lifebuoy leads pledge to help children reach their fifth birthday.* Retrieved from https://www.hul.co.in/Images/lifebuoy-leads-pledge-to-help-children-reach-their-fifth-birthday_tcm1255-463910_en.pdf.

HUL Brand Lifebuoy. (n.d.). Retrieved from https://www.hul.co.in/brands/our-brands/lifebuoy.html.

Law, A. (2017, July 1). ITC campaign for Savlon mission bags Cannes award. *Hindu Business Line.* Retrieved from http://www.thehindubusinessline.com/companies/itc-campaign-for-savlon-mission-bags-cannes-award/article9744777.ece.

Nicholson, J. A., Naeeni, M., Hoptroff, M., Matheson, J. R., Roberts, A. J., Taylor, D., et al. (2015). An investigation of the effects of a hand washing intervention on health outcomes and school absence using a randomized trial in Indian urban communities. *Tropical Medicine & International Health, 19*(3), 284–292.

Official Ana Bella Foundation website. https://www.fundacionanabella.org/. Consulted to date 26/12/2017.

Official Ashoka Changemakers website. https://www.changemakers.com/. Consulted to date 25/05/2018.

Official Danone website. http://www.danone.com/es. Consulted to date 26/12/2017.

Official Institute for Women and for Equal Opportunities website. http://www.inmujer.gob.es. Consulted to date 27/12/2017.

Official Momentum Task Force website. http://www.momentumtf.es/. Consulted to date 27/12/2017.

Social Samosa. (2013, March 29). *Social media campaign review: Help a child reach 5 by lifebuoy.* Retrieved from https://www.socialsamosa.com/2013/03/social-media-campaign-review-lifebuoy/.

The Economic Times. (2016, December 23). Creating sanitation change leaders at community level. *CSR compendium touching lives 2016*. Retrieved from https://economictimes.indiatimes.com/csr-compendium-touching-lives-2016/initiative/creating-sanitation-change-leaders-at-communitylevel/articleshow/56137361.cms.

The Economic Times. (2016, December 23). Driving change through dettol school modules. *CSR compendium touching lives 2016*. Retrieved from https://economictimes.indiatimes.com/csr-compendium-touching-lives-2016/initiative/driving-change-through-dettol-school-modules/articleshow/56136613.cms.

The Economic Times (2016, December 23).Improved sanitation facility. *CSR compendium touching lives 2016*. Retrieved from https://economictimes.indiatimes.com/csr-compendium-touching-lives-2016/initiative/improved-sanitation-facility/articleshow/56137465.cms.

Unilever. (2014, September 24). Unilever appeals to first ladies to help a child reach 5. *Unilever News*. Retrieved from https://www.unilever.com/news/Press-releases/2014/14-09-24-Unilever-appeals-to-First-Ladies-to-Help-A-Child-Reach-5.html.

Unilever. (n.d.). *Towards universal hand washing with soap—Social mission report 2015*. Retrieved from https://www.unilever.com/Images/lifebuoy-way-of-life-2015_tcm244-418692_en.pdf. Accessed February 24, 2018.

Unilever. (n.d.). *Unilever sustainable living plan: India progress 2015*. Retrieved from https://www.hul.co.in/Images/unilever-sustainable-living-plan-india-2015-progress-report_tcm1255-483536_en.pdf. Accessed February 24, 2018.

Unilever. (n.d.). Retrieved from https://www.unilever.com/brands/our-brands/lifebuoy.html.

WAGGGS. (2017, October 13). *WAGGGS partners with lifebuoy to drive handwashing with soap in India*. Retrieved from https://www.wagggs.org/es/news/wagggs-partners-lifebuoy-drive-handwashing-soap-india/.

WHO. (2017). *Newborns: Reducing mortality factsheet*. Retrieved from http://www.who.int/mediacentre/factsheets/fs333/en/. Accessed February 24, 2018.

CPSIA information can be obtained
at www.ICGtesting.com
Printed in the USA
LVHW051625290519
619458LV00001B/3/P